SKATE SAILING

RICHARD FRIARY, PH.D.

𝓶𝓹
MASTERS PRESS

A Division of Howard W. Sams & Company

Published by Masters Press
A Division of Howard W. Sams & Company
2647 Waterfront Pkwy E. Dr, Suite 100, Indianapolis, IN 46214

96 97 98 99 00 01   10 9 8 7 6 5 4 3 2 1

Library of Congress Cataloging-in-Publication Data
Friary, Richard, 1942 -
      Skate sailing / Richard Friary.
          p. cm.
      Includes bibliographical references (p.).
      ISBN 1-57028-098-3
      1. Skate sailing. I. Title. II. Series.
   GV852.5.F75 1996   96-32308
                                       CIP

TABLE OF CONTENTS

Credits:

Cover design by Kelli Ternet

Edited by Steve Slosarek

Proofread by Pat Brady

Front cover photo by Steve Magditch

Back cover photos (from the upper left hand corner clockwise) by Wolf Beringer, Windskate, Inc., Dr. David Wiencke, Ken Hoffman, Wolf Beringer, Windskate, Inc., Wolf Beringer, Windskate, Inc., and Richard Myers

ACKNOWLEDGMENTS

This book represents many people's labors, not only its writer's work, and, like any other author, I incurred numerous debts of gratitude in composing it. So it is a pleasure to acknowledge the contributions made by sailing companions, and by strangers and friends in six countries on two continents. For useful comments, I am grateful to J. Fred Gerecht, Basil Kamener, Bob Montgomery, Jim Oakes, John Palubniak, and Christian Voight. I thank my editor, Steve Slosarek, whose suggestions brought improvements; Kelli Ternet, whose art graces the cover; photographer Steve Magditch, who found the cover illustration at the end of a damaged roll; novelist Barry Nazarian and skate sailor Bill White, whose continued encouragement always blew from the right quarter; and photographer and chemist Alan Mallams, who followed me onto river ice.

For illustrations in the book, I am grateful to the individuals and institutions named. One who deserves special thanks is Beth Davis, curator of the World Figure Skating Museum and Hall of Fame in Colorado Springs. Another is Marvin Resnick, Commodore of the Skate Sailing Association of America. I thank the Amateur Yacht Research Society and the International Glaciological Society. Contributors whose illustrations we ultimately did not use are no less deserving of my gratitude, which they have.

In gathering other material, I was fortunate to receive help from Richard Pace, former commodore of the Skate Sailing Association of America, who taught me where and when to look for sailable ice, and how to read any ice I found. I learned much about skate sailing from correspondence or conversations with sail makers Erik Ansteensen of Sport Sail, Inc., Jamie Budge of Windskate, Inc., and David Wiencke of Blizzard Sails. Skate sailors in Sweden kindly told me interesting and delightful tales that were always informative: my thanks go to Anders Ansar, Rolf Clifford, Tomas Forsman and Alexander Sahlin. Also, I am indebted to William Tuthill of the World Ice and Snow Sailing Association, George Theriault of the North American Parawing, Co., and Wolf Berringer, the European developer of parawing sailing. Soon after receiving it as a gift, Charlie Wilson let me try his parawing, so I thank him for the ride.

Sidney Broadbent, Richard W. Draper, Eleanor Shargorodskya, Marty Hill, and James J. Kaminski also helped, so I thank them. For close readings and detailed criticisms I am especially grateful to Art Hammond, John Hartshorne, Ann Markusen, John B. Newkirk and Sara Shaw Rhoades.

Pride of place in this acknowledgment goes to my friend Al Goldberg. He inspired this book in 1987, invited me to join writing it during 1988, and his contributions pervade the finished work. For example, Al provided much of the material that informs Chapters Five and Seven, marked up drafts of these and other chapters with good advice, and drew many of the illustrations. When other demands on his time stilled his pen, Al generously passed his rights in the book to me. Any reader who takes pleasure or knowledge from *Skate Sailing* must pay thanks to Al, as I do.

PREFACE

There were many reasons to write this book, foremost among them a desire to bring a joyous sport before a larger public. Along with the Skate Sailing Association of America, I wanted "to develop, encourage, and stimulate the sport" and to prolong it through the 21st century. New participants would rejuvenate the old sport by improving equipment and refining techniques. A comprehensive guidebook, as this is, might draw these sportsmen and sportswomen from the vast numbers of sailors, skiers, and skaters in the United States and Canada where skate sailing is feasible. Their sports, as this book shows, are allied with ice skate sailing. In this way, the ranks of happy skate sailors might be augmented by design, not merely filled by luck.

Filling a gap in sports literature also induced me to write about ice skate sailing. In English there exists no book dealing exclusively with this sport, although several books published between 1890 and 1995 treat skate sailing cursorily. Articles from contemporary American periodicals describe the thrills of skate sailing, but say little about getting started in the sport. Surprisingly, no prior work teaches how to make a Hopcatcong skate sail, which has represented the standard American design since 1917. Nor does any published source other than this one discuss the principles relating sail size to a sailor's body size and posture. The periodical literature contains no article detailing the pros and cons of modern sailing skates, which this work sets down.

Skate Sailing seeks to be comprehensive, modern, and provident above all. It furnishes the essential, indispensable, practical details that make skate sailing feasible, safe, and affordable. Here you will learn the elements of the sport in six chapters: Modern Skate Sails, Technique, Ice Lore, Sailmaking, Sailing Skates, and Safety.

The book includes a history to captivate the general reader; to lure skaters, skiers, and sailors; and to satisfy the accomplished skate sailor's curiosity about the origins of his sport. It presents pictures and tales drawn from a 200-year period, and notes important events and developments. In compiling these tales I depended largely upon materials published in English and found through public libraries in the United States. Consequently, the history could not offer a coherent, continuous account of skate sailing in any country where the sport is practiced. Too few data are available in indexed English-language books, magazines, or newspapers to permit such a treatment. Hence, the stories presented here are necessarily anecdotal, but captivating despite inescapable discontinuities. Specific published sources for them are cited in the bibliography.

The historical chapter and the other chapters contain information gathered from several private sources, which comprised the Skate Sailing Association of America, the Skate Sailing Section of the Swedish Ice Sailing Association; correspondence with North American and Swedish skate sailors; and personal experience. Members of the Skate Sailing Association lent many personal photographs and provided photocopied drawings. As a skate sailor myself, I drew heavily on my own observations and upon conversations with sailing companions, ice boaters, and ice fishermen.

Mathematically adept readers may be interested in the sources of the equations and tabulated numerical values that Chapters Three and Seven contain. If so, they may write to me in care of my publisher to obtain the appendices deriving and evaluating the equations.

My prowess as a skate sailor and my authority as a chronicler bear mentioning. Agreeing with Frederic M. Gardiner, who wrote *Wings on Ice*, I quote from his 1938 iceboating book:

I want no misunderstanding of my position in connection with preparing the book. I do not pretend to be the greatest expert on [skate sailing], there are plenty of builders, sailors and racers whose technical knowledge far exceeds mine. My job as author has been primarily to form a pattern, to collect the facts and sort them out, and to put them together in logical, readable form; together with such designs and illustrations as appear to be of value to those interested in the sport.

Finally, to practicing and prospective skate sailors everywhere, I wish black ice, sharp skates, and steady winds!

Richard Friary
Bridgewater, New Jersey 1996

SKATE SAILING

To my wife, Diane

CHAPTER ONE: AN INVITATION

"Each Skater His Own Ice Boat"
— headline, *The New York Times*, Feb. 26, 1881

Not even in dreams does she feel this free, as she sails into the darkening afternoon, her silent skates skimming yet scoring the flawless ice. Exhilaration envelops her. She seems to escape gravity as she outruns the wind, a feat beyond the reach of gliding birds. Within her grasp, this exalting freedom comes as her sail thrusts her upwind and her skates set her course over a vast, black, transparent plane. So invisible is the ice, so effortless the steering, so smooth and swift the passage that she feels a sense of flight through dimensions reserved to her.

She could sail forever if the bronze descending sun did not stay the wind and steal the light. It signals closure to the day and to her expansive feeling, so she reluctantly lifts the sail to relinquish the waning wind. The ice skate sailor smiles as momentum carries her safely to the beach. Victorious in her race against the fading light and failing wind, she knows another winter's day will soon summon her to the ice.

Indeed, shortly before the next dawn's first glow, she leaves home carrying a rolled sail and skates sharpened the previous night. New black ice, sighted after a 45-minute journey, makes her stop to inspect the surface of a thickly frozen lake. A wind steady at 10 mph promises smooth, fast runs, so the ice skate sailor rigs her sail, laces on her skates, then picks up her 10-foot-high, 65-square-foot craft. A two-handed grip lets her easily raise the kite-like sail overhead and face into the wind. She stands momentarily still to choose a course. Then the sailor lowers the boom onto her left shoulder, turns almost 90° to her right, and seizes the mast with her windward, left hand near her knee. These nearly simultaneous gestures are hailed by a crack of air on cloth, sounding like a shot from a starter's pistol.

The force of wind acts on the sail, passes through the sailor's body to her blades, and overcomes the slight resistance of ice. It thrusts her instantly and noisily forward as if she were a fighter plane catapulted from a carrier deck. To absorb shocks, she stands with her knees bent and feet apart, her windward blade leading. The sail boom lies on her upwind shoulder and, like a skater, she holds one arm behind her back. Her sailing speed soon doubles the wind velocity, and she is content because her early departure lets her sail over ice unsoftened by the midmorning February sun.

Next, the ice skate sailor's leeward hand seeks the sail boom, as a preliminary to shifting her weight. Without checking her speed or releasing the mast, she reaches backward to grasp the boom with her arm fully extended. This motion turns her trunk until her upwind shoulder faces forward and her back touches the sail. A transfer of body weight to her downwind blade then frees her upwind foot. She raises it entirely off the ice sheet, and, at the same time, fluidly crosses it over the downwind boot. Equal forces acting in opposite directions quickly secure her balance, and she sails on one 19-inch blade alone.

She hurtles across the black ice sheet, as her blade alternately chatters and hisses on a constantly changing surface. All the while, the lake bottom passes darkly underfoot, in sight through the transparent ice and water. She feels elated, by her speed and more by the harmony of sailor, sail, and skates.

The wind freshens, and her nearer hip and shoulder lean onto the

WHAT SKATE SAILORS SAY

Harmony

"Skate sailing gives you a feeling of absolute freedom. You become your own iceboat; you control your own path (with a little help from the wind, of course)."

A. Darling, *American Way*, Dec., 1983.

"Skate sailing...is the most bird-like of winter sports. The personal element..., the unique sensation of being a human sailing craft unto yourself, is the reason for this. Your body is the mast, your feet the hull and the skates are the keel and steering gear."

E. H. Jessup, 1923.

"...a skate sailor sustains the parts of boat, sail, keel, rudder, ballast, captain, and crew..."

J. M. Heathcote, C. G. Tebbitt, and T. M. Whitham, 1894.

1

sail. Still balanced on only one skate, she angles her body until, seemingly aloft, it inclines more than 25° from the vertical. Now lying on the wind, the ice skate sailor begins a mile-long, two-minute run toward an upwind mark, borne by the air yet warmed by the sail.

The pleasure of ice skate sailing isn't a new sensation. Thousands of people from nine countries spanning two continents have sailed on skates for a century and a half. The simple requirements of this recreation include only a few prerequisites. Because its appeals are many and its demands are few, the sport is joyful, invigorating, and affordable. It invites you to take part.

THE APPEALS OF ICE SKATE SAILING

Unique Attractions

Harmony in Motion

Ice skate sailing brings an exhilarating sense of harmony in motion that rewards a fast, controlled run over a smooth course. The notes of this chord are wind and ice, and sail and skates. Like a musical staff, the sailor relates these notes to one another.

Indeed, ice skate sailors and their gear actually are their sailing crafts. This identification makes skate sailing an often re-invented sport, distinguishing it from most other kinds of sailing. The low ice friction and the high sailing speed make skate sailors the ultimate sailing vessels.

Their bodies physi-cally transmit force from their shouldered sails to their skate blades moving along a chosen course. They connect aerodynamic forces acting on the sail to hydrodynamic ones acting on the skates. Hence, the sailors act as the masts of boats, not as mere travelers conveyed as passively as freight. Other sailing crafts — ice boats and boards, land yachts, windsurfing rigs, and softwater boats — all require inanimate masts to transmit wind force.

A sailor's skates behave like the keel of a boat, the wheels of a land yacht, or the runners beneath an iceboat. They oppose the side force of the wind, creating thrust in the desired direction. Skates are as essential as keels, centerboards, wheels, or runners, but, unlike all of these, are lashed to the sailor's feet. As a result, she is exquisitely sensitive to the surface over which she moves. Moreover, the lashings enforce sensitivity because the sailor cannot ignore a rough passage signaled by chattering blades.

A skate sailor's body serves as her own ballast when she opposes the heeling force of wind to retain her balance. The force of wind on a shouldered skate sail pushes the sailor to the side, threatening a collapse to leeward. To counter this heeling force, a skate sailor leans her windward hip and shoulder on the sail, so bringing her own body weight to bear in a righting movement.

An ice skate sailor then lies on the wind, in a position more comfortable than precarious, despite her angle of 45° or more from the vertical. Lying on the wind lifts much of the sailor's weight from her feet, dispersing it over her sail. It also reduces the sideforce on her sail so much that she no longer needs to fight her sail to keep her balance.

If the ice is smooth and the wind is high, weightlessness, effortlessness, and speed cooperate to bring an extraordinary sense of harmony in motion. Black ice that is almost invisible augments this sense because the sailor seems suspended in air, not bound

WHAT SKATE SAILORS SAY

Harmony

"To be one's self the mast and the tiller and the boat, this is the sport of skate sailing. The man himself is the live ballast. Every tremor of the sail passes through him, and he adapts himself momentarily to the variations of an off-shore breeze. The old world dream was of a centaur — man-horse — two natures in one body. In this twentieth century, we have realized a man-boat."

A. H. Goodwin, *Country Life in America*, Dec., 1904.

"One feels the wind much better; than in the best balanced boat, and is much more sensitive to, and can take better advantage of, the puffs and flaws. The speed is much more like that of an ice boat, which a skate sailor can beat on smooth ice in light winds."

A. Vallé, *Country Life*, Dec., 1914.

to earth. A similar feeling arises on a clear night when one views a lamp-lit town from a low-flying plane.

In contrast, the same heeling force that lets skate sailing resemble flying can cause a sail boat to tilt ominously and an ice boat to hike spectacularly but no less dangerously. To stay balanced, many softwater sailboats must carry weights in addition to the crew, passengers, and gear; and must also deploy the people to counteract the heeling force. When an iceboat runner, plank, and fuselage abruptly rise several feet in the air, the supine skipper lacks time to deploy ballast, so she carries none. Her salvation lies in falling off the wind, riding out the maneuver, and perhaps in avoiding occasions for hiking in the future.

As for the skate sailor, her arms move the skate sail forward or aft on her windward shoulder. This motion increases the sail area ahead or behind the sailor, who pivots in response to the changed balance of fore and aft forces on the sail. The sail turns like a rudder.

A skate sailor not only plays the roles of her own vessel and rigging but acts as her own captain and crew. She sets the course, commanding the helmsman to correct it as needed, and she rigs the sail and raises it overhead to turn or slow. Other rigged sailing crafts can (and sometimes inadvertently do) depart and travel without any crew or captain at all. The crews and captains of sail- and iceboats, although they are needed to control their boats, are therefore inessential to sailing motion itself. By contrast, skate sailors are indispensable not only to controlling their own sailing motion, but to starting and prolonging it as well.

Cost

Affordability is an advantage of skate sailing over certain other sports. For example, a newly built DN iceboat, which is the smallest commercially available, was recently offered for sale at $10,000. Capital expenses for a complete set of new skate sailing gear would have cost 15-25 times less. Maintenance expenditures for skate sails are also small, often amounting to no more than a few dollars a year for small parts and other materials. An ice boater, however, can expect to spend several thousand dollars to replace a broken mast, which, on a skate sail, would cost $50 at most.

With icy lakes closer and perhaps more plentiful than snowy mountains, a skate sailor's traveling expenses are likely to be slight compared with a skier's. An hour's journey by automobile will often suffice to find sailable ice, so air fares as well as board and lodging costs can be saved.

Many lakes and estuaries are freely accessible to the public, unlike ski slopes. Hence, shore dwellers do not sell lake passes to sailors, as slope owners sell lift tickets to skiers. Skate sailors keep the money that would otherwise pay admission fees.

Skate sailors pay no licensing fees to practice their sport, either. Most winter sports that take place on frozen lakes are unregulated, with one exception. Ice fishing requires a license in many states, which charge a fee to issue one.

Convenience

Even a large skate sail is low in weight and small in bulk, so transporting it is easy. The weight of a rolled skate sail plus spars normally ranges from nine to 12 pounds, while the sail and spars make a package

WHAT SKATE SAILORS SAY

Speed

"You can accelerate like a rocket. You're squashed between your skates, which are holding the ice, and the wind, which is pushing on the sail. Like a melon seed [squeezed between two fingers], you shoot forward."

Ralph Albrecht, *Outside,* Jan., 1987.

"Skate sailing has speed and the kind of sailing which is a challenge. When I am really moving I just lean against the sail and let the wind carry me along."

Ray Whittaker, *The Christian Science Monitor,* March, 1967.

"I like being able to maneuver that sail at high speeds. There's something mysterious about using the wind. It's a challenge to harness something as thin as air to make you go."

J.B. Mc Clure, *American Way,* Dec., 1983.

that is three to four feet long and five to six inches in diameter. Rolled skate sails will fit in an automobile, and no roof rack is needed to carry the spars, which are usually jointed. The interior of an automobile will accommodate disassembled spars. All these features make it easy to travel from lake to lake in search of good, better, and the best sailable ice.

Looking for the best ice is a luxury not available to iceboaters. Their boats are large and complex enough to require trailers or roof racks for transport, as well as vast tool kits for assembly. As the result, leviathan iceboats often stand sadly moored at the same lake all winter, because of poor ice conditions there and despite better ones elsewhere. Skate sailors, however, migrate as winter advances, forsaking snowy lake ice that formed before any snow fell but was obstructed afterward. These sailors, contrasted to those who sail iceboats, travel easily to distant, salty estuaries that froze only because of the same storms and therefore remained free of snow.

What Skate Sailors Say

Flying

"The sensation when going at full speed is peculiar. At first, you feel that you have lost your hold on the earth, and your whole attention is drawn downward toward your skates; you wish they were heavier, so as to afford more ballast. But soon you gain confidence, a feeling of security takes possession of you, and if the ice is favorable and the road clear, you will attain what must be very similar to the sensation of flying. You seem scarcely to touch the ice, which appears streaked."

T. F. Hanmer, *Century Magazine*, Feb., 1882.

"[skate sailing] offers a very peculiar charm, and, when a swift wind causes [the sailor] to glide over the surface of the ice, he feels himself lifted and experiences a sensation analogous to that of flight."

La Nature, *Scientific American*, Nov. 14, 1885

"Without a doubt, skate sailing is as near to flying as any outdoor exercise known to the world of sport."

W. F. Ollie, *Outing*, Jan., 1905.

"If you try [skate sailing] you will have the nearest approach to the feeling of flying that anything short of an airplane can give you."

C. H. Claudy, *Woman's Home Companion*, Jan., 1912.

"Feels like I'm flying with my landing gear still on the runway!"

Excelsior (Minnesota) High School senior, *Hi Way*, Dec., 1961.

Shared Appeals

How many of us move indoors, responding to the low temperatures, short days, and cold winds that herald winter. They push us to postpone or abandon outdoor pursuits, while we are pulled inside by comfortable surroundings. Sedate indoor comforts, however, invite the boredom that so soon attends confinement. Moreover, shut-in coziness starkly contrasts exhilarating outdoor exploits. An adventuresome sailor beneath a brilliant winter sky can feel the irresistible acceleration and sustained speed that fulfill the promise of skate and ski sailing. When the wind blows steadily and strongly, even the sight of metallic ice below a pewter sky breaks a cabin fever instantly. Ice and snow sailing help dispel the frustrations that winter creates.

Get out of the house to win rewards finer or more diverse than adventure and speed. Opportunities for camaraderie abound, whether in developing old friendships or in creating new ones with an astonishing variety of other participants. The skate- and ski-sailing sports also offer physical exercise, round trips, and racing. If your sailing velocity nears your speed limit, these controlled sports give you the chance to brake.

Returning to a Starting Point

Unlike hot-air balloonists, skate sailors are not confined to drifting downwind at a velocity that is less than the windspeed. As in all other kinds of sailing, round trips are always possible. Better still, they can be extraordinarily fast if they are sailed on ice skates.

Round trips require no change in wind direction, but call for sailing upwind instead. Advancing to an upwind mark is feasible because a skate sailor can travel as close to the wind as an estimated 35° before her sail luffs uncontrollably (Figure 1-1). Because she can sail no closer than this, it is often necessary to break the journey into two or more stages, which is tacking. Even though sailing directly into the wind is impossible, skating or walking tediously back to a starting point is unnecessary, as are the chase vehicles that balloonists need.

Going Fast

Enjoyment in sailing is directly proportional to speed; and sailing on ice skates provides this pleasure to all who seek it. Thanks to the low friction of ice, the speed attained can amount to an estimated 2.5 times the wind velocity. This factor, about half that in iceboating, nearly doubles the greatest one observed in softwater sailing, namely 1.4 for a fast catamaran. Because sailing on ice skates in winds of about 30 miles per hour is possible (but inadvisable to all but experts), thrilling speeds of over 70 miles per hour have been recorded.

Racing

Skate sail races, organized for the first time almost 100 years ago, balance the thrill of speed against the satisfaction of judgment. Most races are sailed back and forth along a fast, straight course perpendicular to the true wind, or around a slower, triangular course. Back-and-forth races call for the fewest judgments and bring the greatest speed, because the course itself holds the sailor's angle to the wind at 90°. This restriction means that racers have only to time their turns properly and to avoid collisions with one another and the course markers. Turns must begin as soon as needed to prevent sailing beyond the course marker, which wastes time. A competitor must curve around the outside of the marker, not the inside, so turns must also start late enough to accomplish this. A premature turn made short of the mark must be sailed again, and such a mis-timing usually means a missed chance to win.

Sailors must round the mark without touching or moving it. Race rules penalize such collisions, and oblige a racer who displaces a marker to return it to its original position. Paying this penalty for inaccuracy can severely handicap a racer.

A triangular race course calls for judgment not only in rounding the marks but also in choosing course angles. This is true partly because of the usual relation of a triangular course to the wind direction, which requires the racers to sail one leg upwind and another downwind. Sailing too close to the wind on the upwind leg, the racers will slow while their sails luff uncontrollably. Traveling too far from the wind on this leg, they will make inadequate progress toward the next mark or the finish line.

On the downwind leg, sailors will travel at less than the wind speed if they sail with the wind at their backs. Faster progress and a more exciting contest will result if racers sail the downwind leg at an angle to the wind. Sailed across the wind, the third leg resembles a back-and-forth race taking place

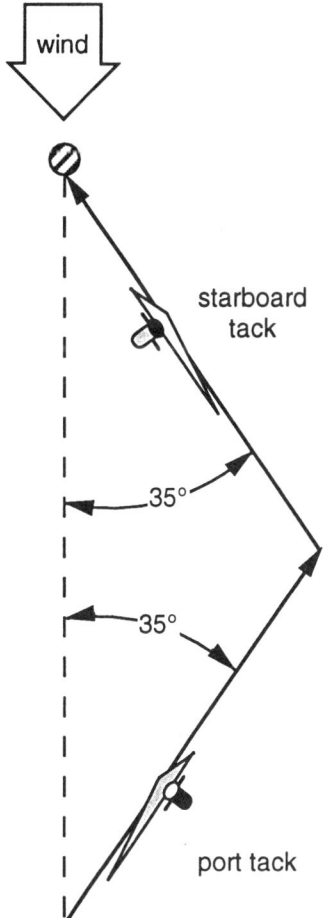

Figure 1-1. Skate Sailors Advancing to an Upwind Mark

perpendicular to the true wind. This cross-wind leg is often the last one and, because of its relation to the wind direction, encourages all participants to finish fast.

On the second lap of a triangular course, each choice of sailing angle must be independent of what the corresponding angle was during the first lap. Choices made for the first lap should not necessarily dictate selections made in the second lap. The wind may have shifted after the first circuit, and almost any shift in the wind direction gives each competitor a new chance to gain or lose time. Having to consider again what the best directions are for each of the three legs adds complexity and demands judgment.

Braking

Nothing beats a fast finish, but prospective skate sailors should understand that speed is not a necessity of the sport. Skate sailors govern their speed by making proper choices of sail area and course angle. Sailors already underway can slow themselves by heeling or spilling the wind. Having spilled the wind, they can brake as skaters or skiers do, using both feet.

To slow or stop by braking without veering sideways is an appealing and distinctive safety feature of skate and ski sailing. In no other kind of sailing is it possible to stop so fast. Like an experienced skater, an expert skate sailor can brake hard enough to shave the ice with her blades and spray the shavings ahead of her stopping point. Other sailing crafts lack braking devices altogether or, like a certain few ice boats, possess only a rudimentary brake.†

Camaraderie

Companionship, often of newly made but soon cherished friends, contributes both to sailing pleasures and memories. Among my favorite companions is an elderly, retired engineer, more than 50 years a skate sailor

yet still a racer. When the races end, he sails from cove to cove like an 18th-century voyageur or a 20th-century tramp steamer, calling on ice fishermen as scattered as ports.

Exercise

Skate sailing is valuable because it exercises sailors of ordinary strength. They may be as old as 80 or as young as 6. For the most part, the sport uses muscles of the upper body, arms, and hands. These muscles are especially needed in raising the sail to turn or stop. Other muscles see use in different techniques. Sailing cross-legged on one foot, for example, requires strength and stamina in the large muscles of the thighs. This technique, however, is not an obligatory one, even for the expert sailors who practice it. Consequently, the amounts of exercise sailors take during a day's sailing are largely under their own control, as is their speed.

A skate sailor controls three of the principal factors that determine exertion: her sail area, sailing time, and course angle. Exertion, which increases with area and time, can be reduced in several obvious ways. A sailor's choices are to shoulder a smaller sail in a wind of constant strength, to lay a sail down to rest, or to fall off the wind. Making any of these choices requires that she be a good judge of her physical condition, her available strength, and the wind speed.

Two factors that contribute to exercise and fatigue admittedly lie outside a sailor's control: the wind speed and the surrounding air temperature. Exercise increases as wind velocity does because maneuvering the sail is more difficult in higher winds than in lower ones. For example, a stronger wind presses the sail harder against the sailor, so that raising the sail to turn, slow, or stop

---

† The brake on a Yankee-class iceboat consists of a manually worked lever tipped with a steel spike. Pulling on the lever drags the spike along the ice and stops the boat. Only when the iceboat has spilled the wind and is slowly coasting does the sailor use the brake, which is not powerful enough to stop the boat moving at full speed.

requires a greater effort.

For a given exertion, fatigue increases as air temperature decreases. In temperatures of 20° F or less, a sailor expends more food energy merely in keeping warm than she would on a warmer day. Then, she draws on a diminishing energy reserve unless she eats constantly. At the end of a cold day's sailing, sailors leave the ice more tired than they would in higher temperatures, other factors like wind speed and sail area having been equal. But ice skate sailors come home more exhilarated than mindful of fatigue.

"Sail More: Skate Sail!"

In an appeal to ice, softwater, and dryland sailors, the Swedish skate sailors distribute bumper stickers exuberantly reading, "Sail more: skate sail!" During any given season, converts to skate sailing can expect to sail more often than they can hope to do if they were to keep their allegiance to ice boating, for example. Sailing on skates requires less wind than ice boating, is safe on ice too thin to support an ice boat, and needs a smaller area. Skate sailors benefit from all three factors, which tend to increase the number of opportunities to sail in a given season.

Acceleration from a standstill demands less wind in skate sailing than in ice boating. Consequently, a skate sailor's companions need not push her forward to start her sailing. An ice boater and her fellow sportswomen, by contrast, must often begin her voyage by shoving her craft until it catches the wind. Ice boats are many times heavier than skate sails, and their runners frequently freeze to the ice. Indeed, 19th-century, stern-steering ice boats are massive crafts made from almost intact tree trunks, and even the small modern DN ice boats of fiberglass weigh hundreds of pounds. The weight difference between an ice boat and a skate sail also means that some ice thick

enough to bear a skate sailor is thin enough to break beneath an ice boater.

Large turning radii exclude ice boats from frozen ponds smaller than about half a square mile. On such a pond, a heavy, speeding ice boat cannot turn fast enough to avoid striking shore disastrously. But half a square mile of ice is vast and inviting to a skate sailor who needs less room to turn than an ice boat. Skate sailing needs only about 10 acres of ice, 32 times less than an ice boater's minimum area. So, small icy ponds — which are not uncommon — welcome skate sailors.

A lack of brightwork and an extension of the sailing season are the special offers that skate sailing makes to certain softwater and dryland sailors. Brightwork, often a deterrent to softwater sailing, refers to the partly ornamental wood and metal components of a sailboat that require all-too-frequent refinishing and polishing. None of them decorates purely functional skate sails, so none of them must be laboriously re-worked before each sailing season, or repaired during it. Maintaining several skate sails requires no more than one hour annually, which is often spent merely in examining rather than arduously in mending them.

Softwater sailing in southern Canada and the northern United States takes place nearly exclusively from spring to fall and most of it occurs in the summer. This makes for a sailing season that is three to nine months long, so taking up skate sailing would add three months (at most) to the sailing season, a substantial increase. In a favorable year, such an increase would extend the available sailing time by one third or would double it.

Some softwater sailors carry on despite the winter months, but skate sailing nevertheless beckons to them. Those resolute winter sailors known as frostbiters crouch to race dinghies amid ice floes, for example in the freezing Piscataqua River between Portsmouth, N. H., and Kittery, Maine. Other adamant sailors use shallow-hulled, amphibious boats indigenous to the Great South Bay of Long Island, N. Y.

Such an amphibious boat, called a Scooter, bears two pairs of long iron runners beneath its hull. The runners and hull respectively allow the wooden boat to travel over ice and in water. In a smashing transition from one medium to another, the skipper aims her Scooter at a likely looking floe, then slams into it. The momentum of the boat drives it forward, while its buoyancy and stout, curved bowsprit push and pull it upward. Escaping the fate of the Titanic, the Scooter mounts the ice sheet.

Once atop the ice, an unsplintered Scooter can double the windspeed before running out of ice. Scooters on the Great South Bay, which rarely freezes completely, do run out of ice, and they soar from its edge like 16th-century ships sailing off a flat earth. However, like 20th-century nose cones having plummeted through the terrestrial atmosphere, these iceboats splash into open water at 70 to 80 miles an hour.

To hardy frost- biters and Scooter sailors, ice-skate sailing holds out another chance: sailing dry, unshaken, and erect.

THE REQUIREMENTS OF ICE SKATE SAILING

Prerequisites

Skating

Sailing erect requires only enough skill to stand on ice skates: skate sailing demands no advanced skating techniques, nor any knowledge of special skating styles. Prospective sailors may be skate dancers, barrel jumpers, or slap shooters; but even the least experienced skater can sail on figure, racing, or hockey skates. The merest ability to skate is the only prerequisite skill that skate sailing demands.

Fitness

The only other prerequisites for the sport are not skills but physical fitness, mental alertness, and proper equipment. Skate sailing is not exclusively a strong or young person's sport, so great, long-lasting strength is unnecessary. On a long straight run, for example, the sailor lies relaxed and balanced upon the sail while the wind itself bears much of her body weight. Skate sailing does presuppose sufficient physical fitness to carry, rig, and maneuver the sail. Yet, the sport does not force its adherents to sail under strenuous conditions of rough ice or high winds. Fitness and alertness, consequently, are more important than strength or stamina.

Alertness

Crossing rough ice in a high wind may cause a fall, so sailors must be alert to the condition of ice that lies ahead. A safe passage also demands an awareness of any stationary obstructions like ice fishermen or approaching hazards like iceboats. Safe sailing requires eternal vigilance, and therefore mental alertness is an indispensable prerequisite to practicing the sport.

Equipment

Children wearing ice skates who open their coats to be blown downwind re-invent skate sailing every winter, and need scant equipment to take part in the sport. Adult skate sailors, however, will need certain items of equipment, among them a sail, not an open coat; a pair of sailing skates; safety gear; and suitable winter clothing. Sailing a round trip requires a proper sail, and getting one is among the subjects of Chapters Three, Seven, and Ten. Which ice skates are most suitable and safe for sailing is covered in Chapter Eight. For safety, skate sailors should carry ice awls and wear helmets as well as flotation gear, all of which Chapter Nine describes.

Skate sailors need certain items of clothing that skaters do not require. Warm mittens are indispensable because practitioners of the sport must hold their sails in one or both hands. No one can sail long with cold, bare hands, nor can anyone sail while warming both hands in her pockets as a skater can.

Unlike skating, skate sailing hardly exercises a sailor's feet, which may become uncomfortably or dangerously cold. Properly fitting leather skate boots are notorious for allowing feet to become cold. These boots must fit tightly to furnish control, and wearing more than one pair of socks beneath loosely fitting boots foolishly relinquishes control without solving the problem of cold feet. Consequently, sailors who wear proper skate shoes wisely provide overboots for warmth on the coldest days. Overboots,

however, are only one of several solutions, all of which Chapter Eight presents.

Necessities

To satisfy a developing passion for skate sailing, a novice must repeatedly meet the needs and experience the pleasures of the sport. Among the necessities are willingness to seek sailable ice and diligence to keep safe. Learning advanced sailing techniques and applying them under circumstances that change daily are among the recurring pleasures of ice skate sailing.

Willingness

Finding sailable ice requires a volition to look for it. Looking is a perennial need for an avid sailor who is not content merely to await good ice conditions on a favorite lake, simply because it lies close to home. Television and radio do not broadcast the locations and conditions of safe, sailable ice sheets, nor do newspapers report them. Skate sailors differ from skiers, who can read daily reports or listen to hourly updates on snow conditions. They must rely on themselves to discover ice.

A knowledge of prevailing ice conditions, which quickly becomes obsolete, must be actively and repeatedly sought. A skate sailor must know how to search rationally for this information. Where and when to look for sailable ice, how to recognize it, and what to do when she finds it are among the subjects of Chapter Six, which presents ice lore.

Diligence

Sailing safely on ice skates is a simple compound of two elements: sound principles bonded to faithful practice. Chapter Nine offers these principles, which concern avoiding danger and escaping harm. Those principles in the first category are probably the more important ones; yet whatever their relative importance, unpracticed principles are ineffectual and futile.

Knowledge

Chapter Four sets forth the relatively few techniques of skate sailing, which are conceptually simple and easy to learn. Applying them under constantly changing conditions is more challenging than learning them. Consequently, the task of improving skate sailing techniques will be engrossing even after decades of experience, and the improvements will be intensely satisfying even to the most ancient of mariners.

Two centuries' improvements in sailing techniques and skate sails are related in Chapter Two.

CHAPTER TWO: A HISTORY

"It is an exhilarating sport, this skate sailing, almost like flying. So swift the motion, so bird like and so effortless, the body seems without weight. [The] excitement of the possibility of a spill and of the motion and the necessity for alertness of guiding is so great that, purely as a sport, skate sailing has few equals."

C. H. Claudy, Skate Sailing for Life, 1910.

Henry Ford said "History is bunk," perhaps referring to stories of hooked game fish that escaped with the bait. Leaving no permanent trace of their sizes, the creatures vanish, compelling the empty-handed fishermen to return home with unverifiable tales of prowess. Similarly, physical evidence of prehistoric or historic skate sailing has disappeared, if the practice existed before the 14th to 18th centuries. The only extant traces that might be cited are ancient bone skates, which represent prerequisites as much as artifacts specific to the custom. Although prehistoric peoples crossed frozen Northern European lakes wearing skates carved from animal bones, they left scant evidence or testimony that they sailed.

Time therefore shrouds the origin of ice skate sailing, a practice probably begun by the sailors and skaters of prehistoric Northern Europe. The lack of any archeological record of ice skate sailing is a likely consequence of the perishability of the materials available for sails. Early ice skate sails would have used only comparatively short-lived organic substances like rawhide, wood, and leather or wool. Indeed, without identification and radioisotope dating of any preserved sails, the time when skaters first sailed may never be known with certainty. But an age limit can be placed on this custom.

Even though people have sailed in boats for more than 5,000 years, the practice of sailing on ice skates must be younger than five millennia. It requires equipment that was invented relatively recently, namely skates. Made from comparatively durable inorganic matter, primitive skates date to 3,000 years before the present era, which started two millennia ago. They made use of thick, metacarpal bones taken from horses, deer, oxen or cows. Recovered from a Swiss lake, the earliest example of such bone skates now resides in the Stadtsbibliothek of Berne, Switzerland. Thongs held these skates to the wearer's feet, and the bottoms of the bone blades were ground flat. Unlike their modern counterparts, the skates bore relatively broad running surfaces. The other surfaces of the bones were intact except for drilled holes to admit the thongs.

Bone skates had dull edges that made conventional skating motions impossible. Instead, a skater equipped with bone skates held a pole between his legs to move over an ice sheet. To thrust himself forward, he used both hands to jab the pole into the surface — somewhat as cross-country skiers do on snow — and pushed backward. This method of propulsion, supplanted by modern skating only in the 17th century, persisted through the 12th century. In his "Description of London," published in 1180, Fitz Stephen wrote:

> When the great fenn or moore (which watereth the walls of the citie on the North side) is frozen, many young men play on the yce...some striding as wide as they may doe slide swiftlie; asome tye bones to their feet and under their heels, and shoving themselves with a little picked staffe do slide as swiftlie as a birde flyeth in the aire or an arrow out of a cross-bow.

Although bone skates made ice skate sailing possible, only downwind sailing was

Table 2-1: Advent of Ice Skate Sailing	
Britain	1880
Canada	1880
Denmark	1857
Germany	1892
Holland	1880
Norway	1880
Sweden	1880
Switzerland	1893
United States of America	1881

feasible upon them. The skates would have offered no opposition to the sideforce of the wind. This force thrusts a sailor in the true-wind direction, and compels him to withstand the thrust if he is to travel crosswind or upwind. Without sharp edges to grip the ice, little or no resistance to the sideforce would have been possible. Heeling a skate sail — which means inclining it from the vertical — would also have been unworkable regardless of whether it lay to windward or leeward of the sailor. Contemporary skate sailing techniques awaited modern skates.

Modern ice skates feature metal blades. An account of such skates with iron blades appeared as early as the year 200 in the manuscript *Historia de Gentium Septentrionalium*. This Latin work, written by the Swedish bishop Olaus Magnus, was not published until 1567. Perhaps because of the delay, these skates lacked popularity until the century after publication — 1,400 years after Magnus first illustrated them.

Iron finally replaced bone in 17th-century Holland. The widespread change to iron blades lent strength to the resulting skates, which comprised blades set into wooden foot-boards bound to wooden shoes. Iron blades held an edge, could be sharpened, and bore running surfaces less wide than high. Sharp edges gripped the ice to make poling obsolete. They allowed skaters' legs to regulate their speeds, determine their directions, and halt their motions, freeing their arms to serve purposes other than propulsion. Dutch skaters fashioned clubs to play Kolf, an ice game that inspired hockey and golf.

By the 14th century, the hard edges of iron blades had inspired the fundamental and now familiar skating technique known as the Dutch roll. The practice became popular among Dutch skaters in the 1600s. The skater first transferred his body weight from the inside edge of his left blade, for example, to the outside edge of his right, pushing with the left leg as he advanced the right. Then he rolled from the outside edge of his right skate to the inside edge, before beginning another weight transfer, this time to his left foot. The Dutch roll imparted the characteristic grace of all modern skating, and permitted hockey, figure, and speed skating styles to evolve.

Modern ice skate sailors also benefited from the development of sharp blades. The grip on the ice offered by iron and steel — the latter an alloy of iron and carbon first made 1,200 years before the present era — made it practicable to sail on or across the wind. Holding such courses had previously been impossible because of side slipping. With sharp blades and a large sail, however, a sailor could travel at an acute or right angle to the true wind. The sailor could outrun the wind with, for example, a sailing speed of almost 40 mph arising from a true-wind velocity of only 15 mph.

An increased speed ratio was not the only legacy from 17th-century Dutch society. Sailing to an upwind destination became feasible, thanks to iron blades that prevented downwind drifting. A skate sailor could complete a round trip with them, yet needed no chase vehicle or long skating journey to return to a starting point. With sharp blades, furthermore, he could heel as much as 60° from the vertical, if his blade height adequately exceeded his boot width. Heeling gave the sailor a means to slow himself and made sailing effortless, as long as his sail lay to windward. Finally, the development of sharp edges brought a safety feature that few other sailing sports possess. It let fast-moving skate sailors brake sharply once their sails had spilled the wind.

Metal skate blades represent a prerequisite to modern ice skate sailing. Although they prevailed in 17th-century Holland, nearly 100 years would pass before any account of the practice appeared. The earliest report of ice skate sailing dates the sport to the 18th century. The renowned Swedish botanist and explorer Carolus Linnaeus (1707-1778) supposedly saw skaters bearing sails that resembled wings. After Linnaeus' sighting, however, 100 years or more elapsed before ice skate sailing became commonplace. By the late 19th century, skate sailing was popular all over the northern hemisphere (Table 2-1). The sport then attracted skaters and sailors from at least seven Northern European countries, as well as from Canada and the United States.

To relate its history of skate sailing, this chapter divides it into sections dealing with Northern Europe, Sweden, and North America and Canada. The rich history of the sport in Sweden merits a section separate from that accorded the European story.

In Northern Europe

Variety in sail design stands out as the most conspicuous aspect of Northern European skate sailing history. Illustrated below, the designs include the Danish square-rigged sail, the English lateen sail, and the ubiquitous parallel trapezium sail. Each of these designs called for a single sailor. But in Norway and Germany, two- and three-person sails were commonplace during the last two decades of the 19th century. Other noteworthy pieces of equipment were the long skate blades

Figure 2-1: A Danish Skate Sail on a Starboard Tack

favored in Germany and Norway a century ago. They spanned more than two feet and prevented sideslipping. At high sailing speeds, the long blades also averted foot and leg vibrations as well as back and forth rocking in the sailing plane.

In Britain and Norway, 19th-century skate sailors practiced touring, making round trips as long as 30 miles under sail. During excursions in Denmark, skate sails served as utilitarian conveyances rather than as mere implements of sport.

Denmark

As early as 1857, Danish skaters strapped square-rigged skate sails to their backs (Figure 2-1). Sailing on skates transported hunters on the Sound between Denmark and Sweden, and they rapidly reached places where ducks and geese flocked. Transport of fowlers is the first recorded example of useful work done by a skate sail. That these sails can do such work may explain the origin of sailing on skates, a practice which arose when few people could devote much time purely to recreations.

The square-rigged sail, known as *The Dane*, bore spruce spars and sailcloth made from stout cotton duck. It could be rolled into a package only a little more bulky than

Figure 2-2: Top Hat Set and Topsail Lowered

Figure 2-3: Lateen Skate Sail with Mast Strapped to Sailor's Leg

Figure 2-4: Skate Sailing in Britain: W. F. Adams, with the Wind Right Aft about 1890

an umbrella, weighing about seven pounds. The Dane occupied 35 square feet, 12 of them allotted to the topsail, which the sailor lowered to shorten sail in a stiff breeze. A proficient sailor could sail The Dane to within five points (56°) of the wind, and did so from the leeward side (Figure 2-1). Headgear for a sailor underway included a top hat (Figure 2-2).

Raising the topsail called for the sailor to stand with his back to the wind, and to bend at the waist. The wind then hoisted the sail, sometimes with a blow to the sailor's head. Sailors were advised to wear thick woolen caps to lessen the impact of the blow.

With the square rigged Danish sails, wrote an anonymous *Scientific American* correspondent, "falls [were] not to be dreaded, because they almost always [occurred] backward." Nonetheless, skate sailors may have feared falling, especially with the sail lashed to their bodies. Such an arrangement must have made it difficult to extricate themselves after a tumble into open water. Condemning all such fixed sails in 1904, one American skate sailor commented:

> *The gravest error of the foreign skate sails is that most of them must be lashed fast to the body of the skater; that this is a serious fault will never be doubted by a beginner when he finds himself traveling at a breath-taking speed with the wind at his back and an air-hole dead ahead of him.*

Britain

Some lateen (triangular) skate sails, known as English rigs, did bear a vertical mast bound by two straps to the sailor's windward calf (Figure 2-3). To return to his starting point, the sailor stopped to remove the straps. Only when he had bound them to the other leg did he sail off on the new course. Other English rigs lacked both straps and the mast.

In 1879, an Englishman writing under the pseudonym Glacianaut recommended a two-man sail:

Two people can manage a sail together with great comfort. The 9 ft. by 6 ft. sail is none too large. When two go together, the sail is under perfect control. The front skater steers, and the hinder one, who is in command, trims the canvas correctly by the wind. It is equally easy to gybe or tack, and one can always stop immediately by coming head to wind. I have found this a most exciting sport, and it might be utilized for racing to any extent.

A drawing published in 1892 shows W. F. Adams, Honorary Secretary of the London Skating Club, scudding before the wind and propelled by a 42-square-foot sail (Figure 2-4). He wore a topcoat over striped trousers, dangling a monocle fixed to a lapel. Adams said he could "sail within three points [34°] of a steady breeze, and that with a fresh wind from the most favorable quarter slightly before the beam he [could] attain a speed of thirty miles an hour." Bastman of the Sportsmagasin in Stockholm made Adams' sail, which comprised white duck sailcloth and bamboo spars. Adams' kindness led to a demonstration of skate sail maneuvers, executed with dexterity on the Club Rink located in Regent's Park, London.

The year 1896 saw a British skate sailor, also named Adams, travel 30 miles in 60 minutes on Whittlesea Mere in the Lake District of England. Whether this Adams was the aforementioned Honorary Secretary went unrecorded, however.

Norway

Nineteenth-century Norwegian skate sailors sailed on skate blades 1 meter (39.4 inches) long! For braking, the bamboo masts of their sails bore spurs at either end. Skate-sail touring on the fjords of Norway began in the last century, when sailors on the Sognefjord north of Bergen crossed distances as great as 60 miles.

Figure 2-5: The Norwegian Skate Sail

Figure 2-6: Muggelsee Skate Sails Combined

A two-man sail called the Norwegian may reflect an early Scandinavian influence on the sport (Figure 2-5). Cane fishing poles, spruce, or bamboo were suitable for the spars and mast, and making the sail was simple. To sail this rig, the person at the bow used his leeward arm to hold the boom just aft of the forward mast. With his outstretched windward hand, he also grasped the boom behind him. Steering was the duty of the sailor at the stern of the craft. "The man in front must trust to Providence and the steersman."

Germany

Named after a lake near Berlin, Germany, three Muggelsee skate sails united to propel three sailors before World War I (Figure 2-6). Devotees of the sport formed the Berlin Sail Skating Club in 1892, about two years after skate sailing gained favor in Germany. At the turn of the century, seven sailing companions were drawn in a French magazine, *L'Illustration* (Figure 2-7). Sometime before 1911, German skate sailors had adopted especially long, clamp-on skates for sailing. These skates spanned 25.5 inches (Figure 2-8).

Figure 2-8: 25.5-Inch German Sailing Skate

Switzerland

Before the turn of the century, skate sailing enjoyed popularity on Lake Silvaplana, in the Swiss Alpine resort of St. Moritz (Figure 2-9). The illustrated sailors used a rectangular sail and a trapezium sail.

Sweden

For a more than a century, Swedish skate sailors have been numerous, active in the sport, and inventive above all. Their extraordinary contributions include skates on stilts, 95-square-foot sails, a technique for sailing cross-legged on one foot, and the aerodynamically efficient ice wing. Illustrations and descriptions of these skates and sails appear in this section, which defines the cross-legged sailing technique. Chapter Four gives detailed instruction in this technique, and Chapter Ten describes the icewing. This craft, unlike any traditional skate sail, combines outstanding

Figure 2-9: Skate Sailing in Switzerland about 1893

aerodynamic efficiency with radical design. It deserves a section of its own, even though it is sailed by a skater — whom it encloses.

Swedish skate sailors, like their counterparts in North America and elsewhere in Northern Europe, practiced skate sail touring. They invented and improved sail designs. Parallel trapezium sails, which were maneuvered from their leeward sides, found use in Sweden as they did in much of the rest of the northern hemisphere. The modern Swedish Dragon sails were among the first to incorporate jibs for balance, and to solve the problem of a

Figure 2-7: Skate Sailors on the Muggelsee, Berlin, Germany

luffing leading edge. Like skate sailors elsewhere, the Swedes favored long blades for the sport and nowadays combine them with rigid ski boots. Another development common to Sweden and North America was the founding of associations to promote the sport and to foster organized racing.

The severity of Swedish winters is sometimes exaggerated, so this history of skate sailing in Sweden opens with a description of the prevailing weather during the sailing season.

Climate

Thanks to the warm Gulf Stream, much of Sweden enjoys the brisk winds and mild winters that permit skate sailing and make it a pleasure. Wind speeds near Stockholm commonly reach 12 to 17 miles per hour. Anti-cyclones moving to shore from the Atlantic Ocean strengthen the winds which then attain speeds of 23 to 34 miles per hour. In February, mean temperatures range from 27° F in Stockholm to 30° F in Lund. These temperatures, although cold enough to freeze the many lakes in southern Sweden, do not preclude the rains needed to smooth the surfaces without destroying the ice sheets. Southern Sweden is blessed by desirable freeze-thaw cycles like much of the northern United States and southern Canada. The cycles persist long enough to give Sweden a four-month sailing season, beginning in mid-November and lasting through mid-March. To some extent, its length compensates for the shortness of the winter days there.

Winter temperatures in Sweden also provide sailable ice over the Baltic Sea, which freezes regularly. It is shallower and less saline than the Atlantic Ocean, for example. But sea ice brings its own perils. Here is what the Swedish Skate Sailing Association cautions: "Large areas of ice can lose contact with the mainland when the wind is blowing from land. This happens especially when the ice breaks up at the beginning of spring."

Touring

Despite the danger of being stranded, skate sail touring began at the end of the 19th century. It was popular for the views of the rocky Baltic coast that it afforded. In recent years, however, the practice has declined. Today, ice-breaking ships open channels among inhabited islands in the Stockholm archipelago. Wide enough to admit ferries serving the islands, the channels cannot be crossed by skaters or skate sailors, except with the creativeness born of determination. For example, writes Anders Ansar from Stockholm,

> Four kite-sail sailors were sailing in the Stockholm archipelago some years ago. To reach good ice, they had crossed a shipping lane where the ice floes had frozen together after the last ship passed. While they were sailing, another ship came and broke the ice in the lane. One sailor opted to re-cross the lane before this boat arrived, but the other people carried on sailing over the good ice. When it was time to return home, the remaining sailors tied their sails together and pushed them across the lane, mast side upward, at a place where the ice floes were densely packed. The thickness of the floes was only about four inches! The brave sailors then crept onto the spars, balancing with their hands on the sailcloth, all arriving safe and dry on the other side of the shipping lane.

Origins

As an organized sport, skate sailing in Sweden dates to 1880-1907. This period saw fleets of early sails, founding of the Stockholm Skate Sailing Club in 1901, and organized races as well as national championships.

In 1887, the first skate sailing race in Sweden took place on Lilla Värtan Lake near Stockholm. In 1903 Oscar II, then King of Sweden, awarded a cup to the winner of a Swedish skate sailing race. The recipient, a banker named Zethraeus, later gave the race-winning sail to the U.S. Amateur Speed

Skating Union Hall of Fame in Newburgh, N. Y. Individual Swedish championship races followed in 1907, as did team races in 1921.

Early Trapezium Sails

Early Swedish sails took the form of a parallel trapezium, ranging in size from 38 to 48 square feet (Figure 2-10). Like their German counterparts, these Swedish sails may have had a weather helm, tending to turn the sailor upwind. A line fixed to the lower corner of the bow evidently controlled this turning motion.

Here is what a contemporary observer, W. W. Thomas, the United States Envoy Extraordinary and Minister Plenipotentiary to Sweden and Norway, noted about the use and performance of these early Swedish sails.†

One afternoon, as I came in sight of the frozen vik [strait], I stopped to gaze upon a lively winter picture. Among the dark masses of the skaters, twenty or thirty white sails were swiftly skimming over the ice; some bearing away before the wind, others tacking to and fro from shore to shore; all gleaming brilliantly white in the level rays of the low December sun.

Here were the sails, to be sure; but where was the boat and the mast? There were neither; or, rather, a boy in his own proper person was both. Every sail was in the form of a truncated capital

Figure 2-10: Early Swedish Trapezium Skate Sail

A thus, A*; and a skater taking the cross-bar over his shoulder and leaning against the breeze, shot away with the speed of the wind.*

The sail extended upward a foot and a half above the head, and the sailor was always in the lee of his sail. When beating to windward, the sail is not turned around in coming about; only the boy turns, and, taking the cross-bar over his other shoulder, speeds gaily away on the other tack.

The light canvas is stretched flat as a board, and the skater can sail very near the wind, leaning well to windward if the breeze be strong. The greatest speed, however, is gained with the wind over the quarter. In this position a mile has been sailed in Sweden in less than two minutes. Swiftly blown over the ice without exertion, you experience the sensation of flying more nearly, perhaps, than in any other mode of locomotion.

I believe the form of this skating-sail is peculiar to Sweden. It is simple and practical, and so light that at the end of an afternoon's sport the Swedish lad rolls up his canvas on the poles, and carries the roll home as easily as his skates.

Modern Dragon Sails

Kite-shaped sails of a type still popular first appeared in 1915 (Figure 2-11). These sails, known as Dragon sails (Drakseglen), resemble part of a dragon's mythical anatomy. A piece of flesh supposedly shaped like the sail appears between the creature's forelegs and body.

Dragon sails, which include a steel cable in a jib pocket, solved the problem of a luffing leading edge. Stretching the sail along the boom transmits tension to the cable and thus to the leading edge, flattening it. Without a flat leading edge, a sail can vibrate uncontrollably, especially when the sailor points high into the wind. The master of one of these crafts sails it from its leeward side.

One-man Dragon sails reached the astonishingly large areas of 110-118 square feet in experiments carried out from the

†Appointed by Abraham Lincoln, Thomas served in Sweden from 1863 to about 1891, and saw skate sailing in the Stockholm archipelago. He recorded his observations in *Sweden and the Swedes*, Rand Mc Nally & Co., New York, 1893, pp. 177-178.

Figure 2-11: Dragon Sail, with a 5-Foot Vertical Rule Giving the Scale

1960s to the early 1980s. These sails exceeded the sizes of those found on many small boats and of skate sails used in the United States. For example, they were more than one-third larger than the sails (75 square feet) of Skeeter- and Yankee-class ice boats. Skate sails of about 65-70 square feet are the largest commonly seen in races of the Skate Sailing Association of America. The much larger Swedish sails satisfied desire for speed and allowed sailing in winds that would otherwise be too light.

Alexander Sahlin, a fluid mechanician and a wind-tunnel researcher employed at the Royal Institute of Technology in Stockholm, carried out another design experiment in 1979. To reduce the aerodynamic drag of the crossed skate sail masts, he covered them with a second piece of sailcloth (Figure 2-12). The extra cloth extended from the jib to a point aft of the sailor, and from top

Figure 2-12: Sahlin's Experimental Dragon Sail

to bottom. The extra cloth contained a circular hole through which the sailor grasped the masts. Sahlin wrote, "That sail was up to 15% faster than the others, especially in light wind."

Partly as a result of large-sail experiments, the Skate Sailing Section of the Swedish Ice-Sailing Association now restricts sail areas to 95 square feet in sponsored Dragon-sail races. A 95-square-foot Dragon sail stands 11 feet, 7 inches high and is 11 feet, 6 inches long. The boom of such a sail extends several inches beyond the leading edge, making the whole rig longer still.

Skates on Stilts

In what may seem like an odd practice to the uninitiated, Swedish skate sailors wear skates on stilts spanning eight inches from the blade edge to the boot sole.

An understanding of this practice calls for an appreciation of the design problems associated with large skate sails. Mast height is ordinarily proportional to sail area, so a larger sail might seem merely to require a higher mast with no accompanying changes in design. The sailor's body height, however, limits his mast height, because the boom, which lies halfway along the mast, must ride the sailor's shoulder. Without making other changes to the sail, lengthening the mast above a certain limit causes the mast to strike ice, toppling the sailor. Obviously such a sail would be useless.

A second problem is that the designer must not merely lengthen the sail, keeping the mast height constant. This effort would lead to a large sail, but one with much more area behind the sailor who would turn strongly into the wind. Controlling such a sail would call for a greater physical effort than steering a sail having its center of effort near the mast. Indeed, a long unbalanced sail would represent a throwback to an earlier age: nearly a century ago designers first recognized the need to balance skate sails.

The Swedish solution to these problems was to raise the sailor's shoulder, and thus his sail boom. Exploiting the commercial availability of rigid ski boots, sailors in Sweden adopted high skates to raise their shoulders. This experiment effectively increased their heights and allowed longer masts, yet demanded no changes in sail shape. Such skates allowed mast heights to increase in proportion to sail area, but required no disproportionate increase in the sail area aft of the sailor. High skates also increase the ratio of blade height to boot width. Increases allow heeling at a greater angle than would otherwise be possible.

The first sailor to use skates on stilts was Agge Sahlberg of Stockholm, who in 1974 made skates that were five and one-half inches high. In 1980, Alexander Sahlin of Hägersten, Sweden, took full advantage of high ski-boot skates. He built and sailed a 115-square-foot sail with a moderate ratio of height to length. His sail proved to be stable and he handled it easily, wearing 8-inch-high skates. Referring to his gargantuan sail, Sahlin wrote, "it was inevitably faster than other sails in winds below 12 knots [13.8 miles per hour]." His 8-inch skates soon set the Swedish standard.

Nowadays another restriction besides sail size governs Dragon-sail races in which skates on stilts are popular (Figures 2-13 through 2-18). Skate heights are limited to 8 inches from blade edge to boot sole. Contrast this distance with the usual 2 inches separating edge and sole of ordinary racing skates. Merely donning these extraordinary skates, which can be done from a kneeling position on the ice, requires a special balancing technique.

Modern Swedish sailing skates are often homemade, having blade lengths of 18-20

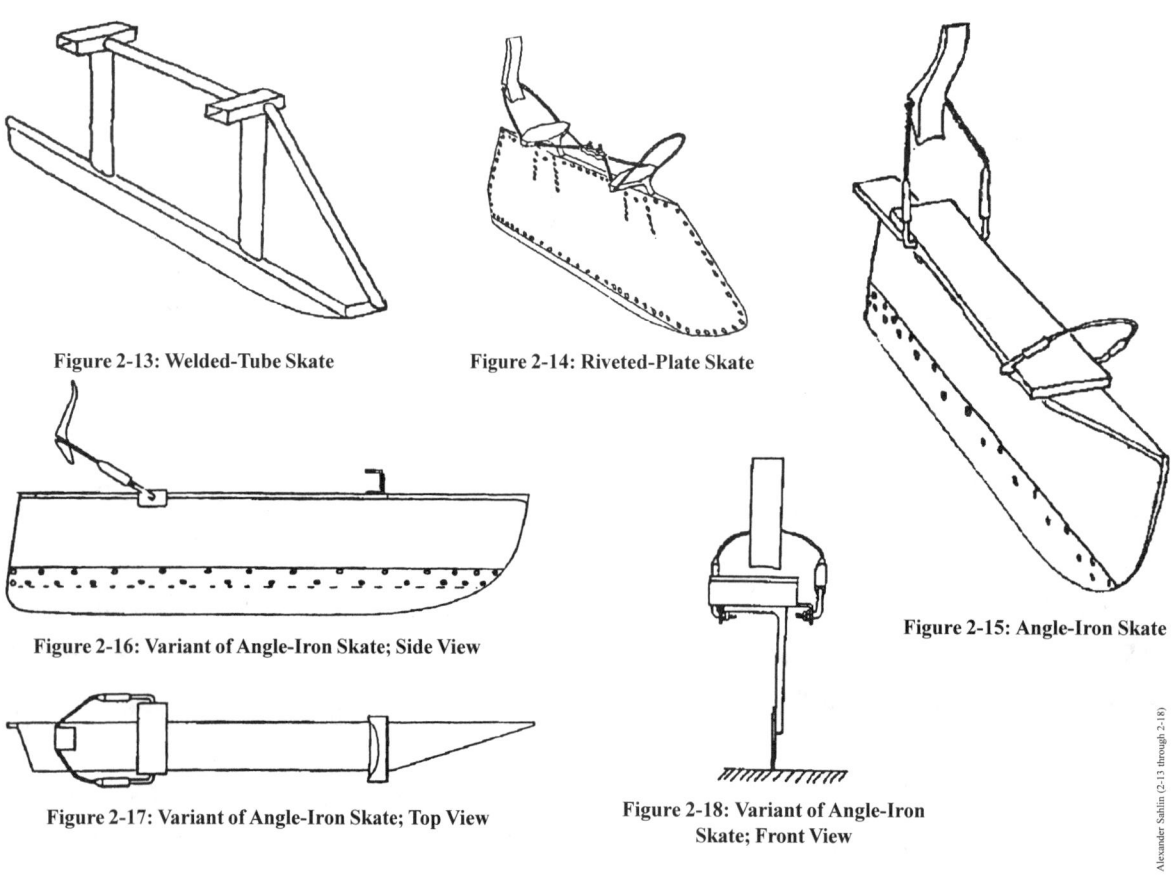

Figure 2-13: Welded-Tube Skate

Figure 2-14: Riveted-Plate Skate

Figure 2-16: Variant of Angle-Iron Skate; Side View

Figure 2-15: Angle-Iron Skate

Figure 2-17: Variant of Angle-Iron Skate; Top View

Figure 2-18: Variant of Angle-Iron Skate; Front View

Alexander Sahlin (2-13 through 2-18)

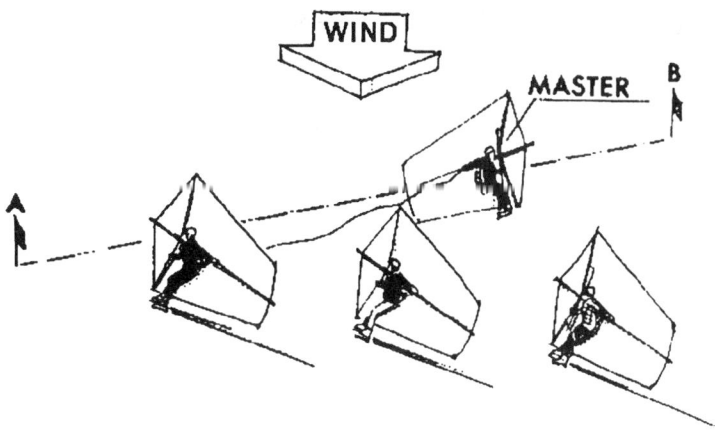

Skate Sailing Section of the Swedish Ice Sailing Association

Figure 2-19: Racing Start by a Master Skate Sailor

inches. Blade lengths should not be shorter than 22-24 inches, according to one Swedish authority. Such long skates permit safe passage over rough ice. The minimum recommended height for sailing skates is four inches, which allows heeling at an angle as great as 45°.

Sailing on One Foot

For more than 30 years, skate sailing cross-legged on one foot alone has been a common practice in Sweden. It's not done to show off, but does challenge sailors. The technique, used only on a straight course by proficient sailors, reportedly (but arguably) minimizes resistance and optimizes balance. It requires smooth, unobstructed ice and a steady wind. Rough ice or wind gusts make it hazardous either to raise the windward skate to adopt the cross-legged position or to lower that skate to steady one's self. (Chapter Four discusses the technique of one-legged sailing in detail.)

Races

The Skate Sailing Section sponsors annual races in two classes, in which sailors of experimental and kite-shaped sails compete separately. Icewings, discussed in Chapter Ten, dominate races in the experimental class. Races of kite-shaped sails take place on a triangular course that the racers sail twice. A typical course is equilateral, with one leg parallel to the wind

direction; the racing distance is six miles. Races are often sailed near Stockholm, where the Baltic Sea sometimes affords black ice.

The Swedes commonly use a master-start method to begin races of kite-shaped sails (Figure 2-19). A master skate sailor, chosen from among the contestants, takes a position 27 to 33 yards beyond flag A. At a signal from the race manager, the master departs along the line AB. He drags behind him an 11-yard-long strip of plastic, sailing close-hauled on a port tack leeward of flag A. Every other racer begins when the strip passes him. At flag B, the master joins the race, dropping the strip and going round to a starboard tack.

Ice Skate Sailing Described on the Internet

In keeping with a national spirit of innovation, one Swedish ice skate sailor created an Internet home page. Accessible by modem-linked computer, its address is the following:

http://130.240.16.18/~tomasfskridske.html

The home page answers more than a dozen frequently asked questions concerning ice skate sailing. It illustrates the sport, including an action photograph of its author. Plans and instructions for sewing sails and for making spars and dedicated sailing skates can be downloaded. Racing results are posted on the Net, as are the addresses and telephone numbers of 38 ice skate sailing clubs.

IN NORTH AMERICA

Improvements in sail designs and, to a lesser extent, ice skates, play prominent roles in North American skate sailing history.

The most distinctive North American skate sailing inventions surely include Norton's double diamond sail (Figure 2-21), Pearson's sport vehicle (Figure 2-26), and Martin's Windhawk (Figure 2-38). The double diamond craft was the earliest to allot two sails to one sailor. Of all hand-held skate sails, only the sport vehicle allows the skater to travel seated. Dating from late in the 20th century, the Windhawk embodies aerodynamic principles developed early in the century. It features a rigid sail with an airfoil shape and cross-section, and a high ratio of height to width. It is sailed from its windward side, so no contact between the sailor's body and the craft distorts it.

Many developments in North American skate sailing find parallels in Northern European practices. Common innovations include skate sails balanced by jibs, which are small, forward sail panels. To prevent luffing in the leading sail edges, the jibs contain mechanical devices lying in forward pockets. These devices are taut cables in Swedish Dragon sails and flexed rods or tubes in American Hopatcong sails. Both the Dragon and the Hopatcong sails are sailed from the leeward sides. They attach jibs to mainsails shaped like parallel trapezia held sideways. (In such an arrangement, the parallel sides of the geometric figure lie vertically.) Such sails may have a common ancestor of unknown but probably European identity. This predecessor may have been the upright parallel trapezium sail familiar in Sweden during the 19th century (Figure 2-10).

The Dragon and Hopatcong sails have survived from an age when aerodynamic principles were undeveloped or little known. Because they are sailed from the leeward sides, their sailors' bodies contact the sailcloth and deform the lower sail halves. European and American inventors streamlined these sails by reducing drag from the mast, boom, and sailor. Sahlin in Sweden and Van Claussen in the United States respectively widened the leading edges of the Dragon and Hopatcong sails to deflect the airflow around the sailors' bodies and spars. Although these improvements never became widespread, they effectively culminated in Ansar's icewing. This Swedish craft encloses its sailor completely and was invented independently. Described in Chapter Ten, it resembles the upturned tip of an airplane wing.

Sailors in at least four countries on two continents adopted skates with relatively long and flat blades. Many in Sweden and the United States now favor rigid boots for skate sailing. The passage devoted to New Jersey describes modern sailing skates. Other examples of parallel development include organized races, skate sail touring, and associations of skate sailors.

Enlivened by tales of sailors, most of this account is organized by geographical regions. It opens describing the bat wing and the country rig, turn-of-the-century sails not assignable to any of the States or Provinces.

The Bat Wing

The simplest American skate sail was the bat wing, which consisted only of a five-sided piece of cloth and six straps. The straps held the finished sail to the sailor's wrists, ankles, head and waist. To make the sail, the builder tacked sailcloth to a floor. Then he lay atop the cloth with his feet spread and his arms stretched at right angles to his body. The crown of his head, and his ankles and wrists defined five points, which a helper marked on the cloth with chalk. Cutting the cloth, hemming the sides and attaching the straps completed the sail. It

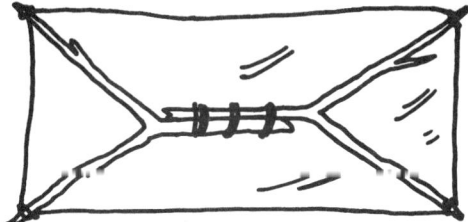

Figure 2-20: The Country Rig

worked like this:

> By spreading the arms, the sail is set; when the arms are folded the sail is furled. The man-bat steers with his feet, using his legs and arms for sheet-lines. Skaters rigged up in this novel style present a most grotesque appearance as they flap their wings about in going through various evolutions.

The Country Rig

Another simple sail was the so-called country rig, which bore two sailors (Figure 2-20). Here is a contemporary procedure for making it:

> The two forked sticks from which the framework of this sail is made must necessarily be nearly of the same dimensions. After their ends have been firmly lashed together as shown, a sail made of an old piece of carpet, awning, hay-cover, or any cloth that is strong enough or can be made strong enough by doubling, may be lashed on at the four prongs of the forks. This rig will convey a crew of two over the ice with as much speed as the more elaborate Norwegian sail [Figure 2-5]. The country sail may not be handsome, but it possesses the advantage of being easily constructed and costing little or nothing, except the work of cutting and trimming the spars and sail.

Figure 2-21: Norton's Double Diamond Skate Sail

Figure 2-22: A Schenectady Skate Sail; on Ballston Lake, N. Y.

THE UNITED STATES AND CANADA

New York State

In 1881, police in Brooklyn forbade a skate sailor to embark on either of two frozen ponds in Prospect Park. As a sailor, he was denied a skating pond and, as a skater, he was denied a sailing pond reserved for ice boats.

The anonymous sailor did eventually sail on skates, propelled by the extraordinary double diamond sail designed by C. Ledyard Norton (Figure 2-21).

In 1900, skate sailing runs of one to 10 miles were common on Lake Erie, which gave its name to an isosceles sail design (Figure 2-23). By 1904, the sport had taken hold among members of the Buffalo Yacht Club. A turn-of-the-century photograph shows 11 skaters drawn behind a single sail.

On Long Island, skate sailors from Patchogue made two-and-a-half-mile runs to

Figure 2-23: W. F. Ollie's Lake Erie Skate Sail (left)   Figure 2-24: J. S. Apperson with His Schenectady Skate Sail about 1910 (right)

a schooner frozen into the ice of Great South Bay in January 1904, or before. During short intervals the sailors reached speeds of 60 miles per hour, like scooter boats. In the 1903-1904 winter, five-mile runs were commonly made by skate sailors from Water Mill and Southhampton, also on Long Island.

The year 1895 marked the coming of skate sailing to Schenectady and Albany. Credit goes to Eskill Berg, a Swedish engineer employed by the General Electric Co., who introduced the sport to residents. They sailed on Lake George, where winds often clear enough of the ice surface to permit skate sailing throughout the season. It was the scene of a burst of skate sailing activity in the years immediately before and after World War I. Shortly after 1904 the outdoorsman and conservationist John S. Apperson demanded and got useful work from a skate sail. Apperson, fearing continued erosion of Dome Island in Lake George, placed rip-rap to shore up the shore. He used a large skate sail to haul the rocks on a sled built from bicycle tubing, drawing the sled behind him with a long towline.

Skate sailing became so popular that, in 1909, enthusiasts sought permission from the Schenectady Railway Co. to carry disassembled sails on two railway lines, the Schenectady and the Amsterdam. Apperson opened his home to fellow engineers in 1916

and, aided by a foot-powered sewing machine, they made an estimated 50 sails. Fifty-eight skate sailors from the Schenectady area competed in a race held in the 1924-1925 season, and the city lent its name to a sail design.

The Schenectady skate sail, designed by Apperson soon after 1904, was among the first balanced sails (Figures 2-22 and 2-24). It was sometimes sailed with a detachable jib, which balanced it. Then its center of effort, which fell on the boom because of symmetry, lay close to the point where the mast and boom crossed. The sail was trapezoidal and featured jumper stays to pull the sailcloth taut. Placed fore and aft, the four stays required that the boom overshoot the sail by a foot or more. The cotton sail, which was lashed to the mast and tail spars, lacked windows. Its area varied from 60 to 65 square feet. Like Swedish Dragon sails of the same era, the Schenectady sail bore a stretching harness at the bow; it had spruce spars and was durable. One made by Apperson in the 1930s saw hard use in the 1990-1991 sailing season on Ballston Lake (Figure 2-22).

A third example of skate sails as useful vehicles also comes from New York State. In 1904, A. H. Goodwin wrote, "a skate sail is an excellent way for a boy to get to school, if the lake or river, or bay, lies nigh the school-building. It will allow him to sleep a

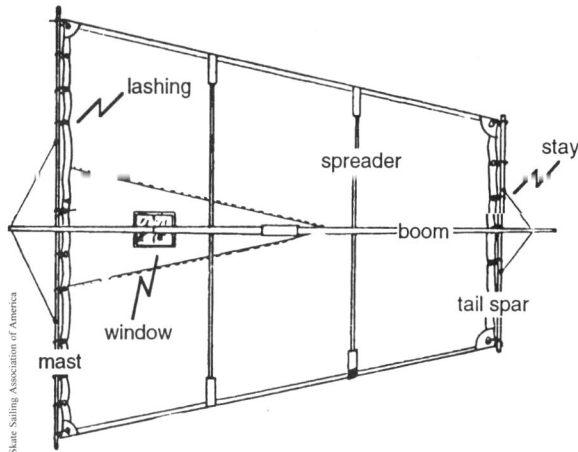

Figure 2-25: R. M. Mann's Nyack Skate Sail

little later in the mornings. Such a use is made of skate sails by the practical boys and girls of the south coast of Long Island."

The City of Nyack on the Hudson River also lent its name to a trapezoidal skate sail, which was light in weight and fast in low winds (Figure 2-25). Noticeable tail pressure made this sail tiring in long distance races, however. The Nyack sail, designed by Randolph M. Mann in 1908, is little seen these days. This sail resembles the Schenectady: both were lashed along the lengths of the mast and tail spar, and both used jumper stays to keep the sail taut.

The stays of the Nyack sail, leading from the boom to points midway along the mast and tail spar, were shorter than the stays in the Schenectady. The Nyack sail bore windows and two spreader spars in addition to its boom and tail spar. By contrast, the Schenectady sail lacked windows and spreaders, and could be sailed with a detachable jib. Sailors of either craft stood on its leeward side, bearing the booms on their windward shoulders, and gripping the masts.

Although Apperson's design for the Schenectady sail predates Mann's for the Nyack, the earlier designer did not influence the later one. On the contrary, several sail designers — Apperson, Mann, Herreshoff, W. C. Biddle, and Claussen — developed

their sail plans independently. For the greatest range of wind speeds and sailing skills, all remarkably chose 50- to 54-square-foot sail areas.

Interestingly, the Schenectady and Nyack sails take the shapes of parallel trapezia. These sails, if rotated 90° to stand on their forward ends, would resemble the early Swedish and German crafts. The modern Hopatcong and Dragon skate sails also include parallel trapezia to which jibs have been added.

In another contribution to skate sailing, New York State and, in particular, New York City, were home to the founding of the Skate Sailing Association of America (S. S. A. A.). This association owes its existence to a reader and a magazine article. Illustrating skate sails, the article interested a Manhattan sportsman, Wally Van B. Claussen, who began the S. S. A. A. in 1922. Claussen (1888-1966), designer of the Hopatcong skate sail, was the first national secretary of the association, its second commodore, and its 1923 U. S. champion. For more than 40 years, Claussen's enthusiasm made him a tireless sailor, organizer, correspondent, and writer on behalf of the association. Indeed, a memoir that he wrote at 75 partly forms the basis of this account.

An ingenious sailing craft is the unique and versatile Sport Vehicle, so named by its inventor, Martin Pearson of Rockville Centre, N. Y. (Figure 2-26). This craft was designed to bring ease, comfort, and enjoyment to diverse sailing sports. It lets the sailor travel seated, although it makes him use skis or skates. Pearson's sport vehicle is the only hand-held sailing craft to seat a sailor wearing special footgear.

Wearing skis or skates, he mounts the long, hollow shaft, and takes a seat astride like a horseman. The sailor supports the vehicle on the transverse knee rest, which

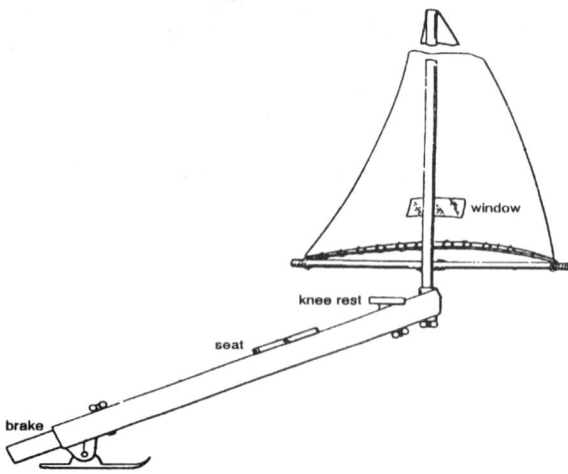

Figure 2-26: The Pearson Sport Vehicle Outfitted for Sailing on Snow

resembles a plank and projects at right angles from either side of the long shaft. The knee rest may lie above the shaft, as shown, or below it. With this rest beneath the shaft, the craft fits a shorter sailor. He controls the sport vehicle by gripping the ends of the horizontal boom that bears the sail and vertical mast. For safety, the long shaft includes a telescoping brake, which retracts for ski sailing and extends for roller and ice skate sailing. To brake on pavement or ice, the sailor lifts the forward part of the sport vehicle. This action forces the shaft to move downward until the block contacts the sailing surface, which slows the craft.

Pearson's craft is versatile because, with modifications, it sails on a variety of surfaces. Its inventor wrote, "the short snow ski "[enables] even an inexperienced skier to negotiate difficult slopes and jump a considerable distance." To use the craft on ice, the sailor substitutes a skate blade with one or two runners for the illustrated snow ski. Rollers replace the ski for skate sailing over pavement. Finally, when a buoyant material like Styrofoam fills the long, hollow shaft, the sport vehicle sails on water. It conveys a seated sailor wearing water skis.

Pennsylvania

Introduced to skate sailing by a friend, W. C. Biddle Jr. (1878-1953) bought his first sail from a Boston manufacturer in 1910. The sail, which was triangular and measured seven feet by seven feet, proved too small. During the next year Biddle began making sails, becoming a tireless and prolific skate sail designer and builder. In a six-year span, he made five skate sails. He designed the reefable sail in 1916, which H. R. Summerhayes adapted to the Hopatcong model (Figure 2-35). Concerned to reduce the weight of skate sails, Biddle introduced the use of lightweight aluminum spars during the 1931-1932 season.

In 1913 or 1914, Biddle conceived a two-person, two-masted skate sail. His craft was to bear its own weight, perhaps because its tubular steel spars were so heavy. Biddle's notion was that both the sail and its sailors would stand on skates. The resulting self-supporting sail bore four blades, one at each end of its two masts. His design, re-drawn from a 1926 sketch, yielded the crystal-shaped contraption shown (Figure 2-27). The self-supporting skate sail evolved from a predecessor Biddle made in 1912, which also bore a wired crosspiece stemming from the intersection of mast and boom (Figure 2-29).

The self-supporting sail not only sported two masts but also bore two horizontal crosspieces that lay perpendicular to the masts and boom. Seamless, drawn-steel tubing formed the five spars, which 14 airplane wires linked. The assemblies that ended in the four skate blades included ball-bearing swivels and hinges (not shown). The finished sail weighed 24 pounds and occupied 60 square feet. Taken apart for convenient transport, its longest piece spanned no more than three feet. Biddle made the sail symmetrical about the boom to permit coming about and jibing. He did not explain how the sailors, who stood between the airplane wires and the sail, managed this last maneuver. Jibing is tricky

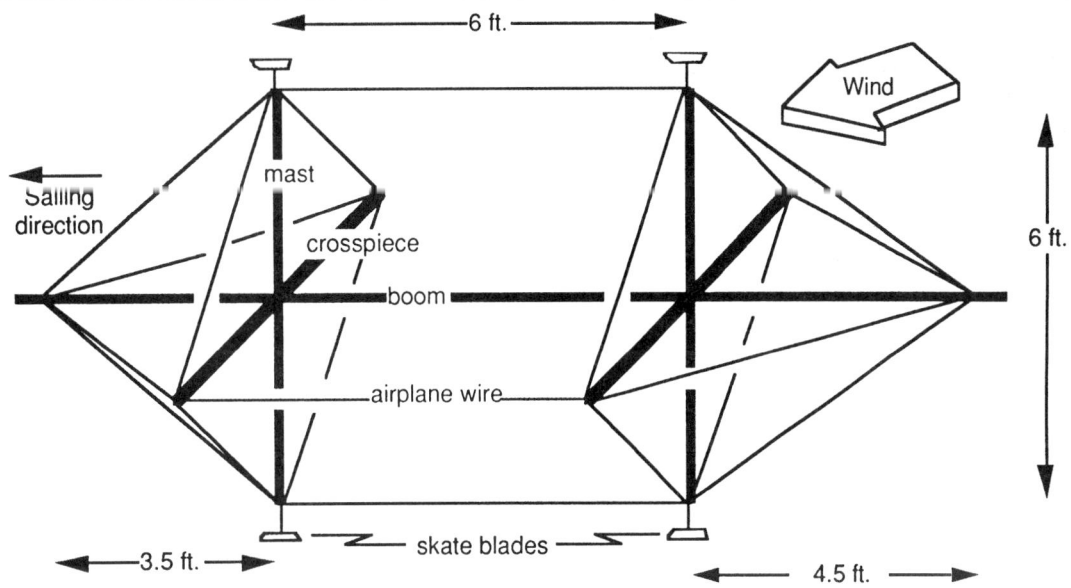

Figure 2-27: Self-Supporting, Two-Man Skate Sail

Skate Sailing Association of America and James W. Spring

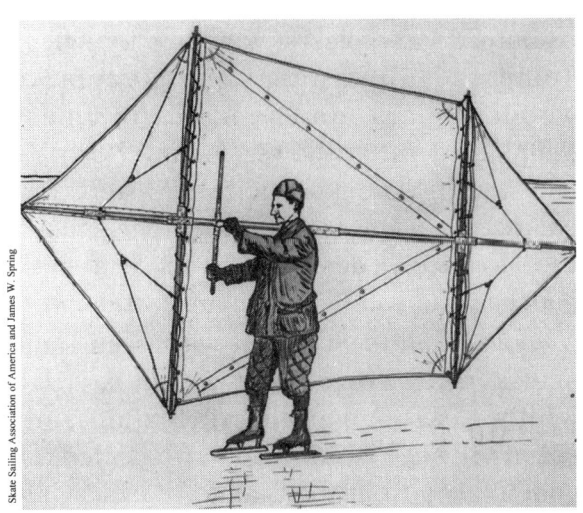

Figure 2-28: W. C. Biddle, Jr.

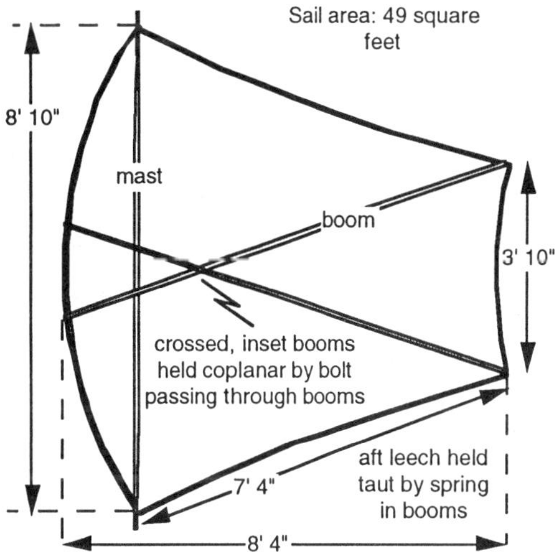

Figure 2-29: The Crossed-Boom Skate Sail Re-drawn from a February, 1928, Sketch

enough with a wire-free sail, which brings no risk of garroting the sailor. On the ice, Biddle's sail propelled two sailors who leaned against the boom, traveling satisfactorily over smooth ice. Rough ice was the downfall of the sail, if not of the sailors. Alack, it vibrated too much, and Biddle scrapped it the next year. Undaunted, he recycled its parts in building a new sail.

The jib and tail bows of the Hopatcong design are one of its successes. They flatten the sail when they bend during assembly, usually keeping the mainsail and jib coplanar in the rigged craft. In other designs, however, the tail can twist downwind while the jib and forward part of the mainsail can twist upwind. In use, the components of such a sail lacked coplanarity, a flaw noted by Biddle in 1928. In that year he designed the crossed-boom skate sail to eliminate the fault (Figure 2-29). His sail was to occupy 49 square feet, and a spring was to pull the boom ends apart and keep the tailing edge taut.

By 1936 Biddle's reefable sail had become a source of dissatisfaction. It

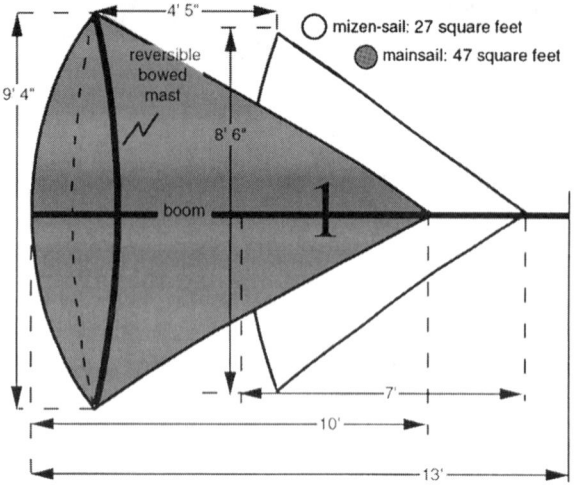

Figure 2-30: The Ketch-Rigged Skate Sail
Re-drawn from a January, 1936, Sketch

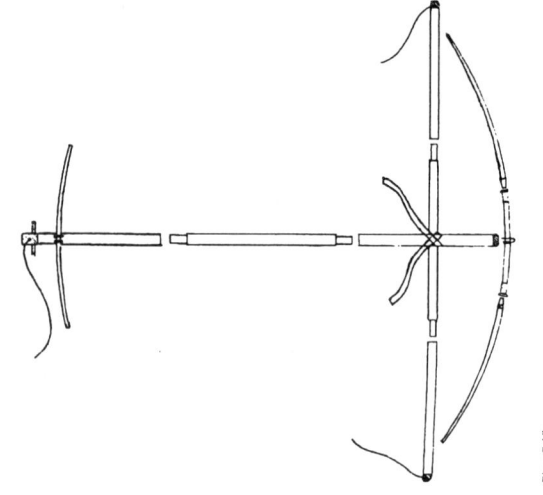

Figure 2-31: Spars and Bows of an Icicle Skate Sail

weighed more than he cared to carry when he had reduced sail, and the cloth of the reefed sail bunched. To solve these problems, he designed and built the unique ketch-rigged skate sail from the sailcloth of a registered, numbered predecessor (Figure 2-30). Its 47-square-foot mainsail lay forward of the 27-square-foot mizen-sail. With both sails aloft, the craft provided 65 square feet of effective sail area, weighing only 16 pounds. Two minute's work detached the mizen-sail. When only the mainsail was in service, the bowed mast occupied the position shown by the dashed line. A horizontal forward motion of the mast vertically aligned the centers of effort and lateral resistance, and let the ketch rig sail straight.

Connecticut

Skate sailing has a long history in Connecticut, stretching to the early years of this century. In the 1970s, A. Albert Goldberg founded Waterfun, Inc. to manufacture Icicle skate sails in Stamford. U. S. Patent 3,768,823, granted for its claims of certain unique components, was assigned to Waterfun. Its durable, colorful skate sails came in 32-, 48-, and 54-square-foot areas, indicated by large blue, yellow, and red wedges of sailcloth. The wedges made the sails easy for onlookers and race

judges to identify. Woven white polyester formed the sailcloth, and the finished sails contained large plastic windows for safety. Tempered aluminum tubing replaced wooden spars, and tapered fiberglass supplanted rattan bows (Figure 2-31). In use, the lightweight Icicle sails were flat, balanced, and durable. Like other sails of the Hoptacong design, they made a small package and were convenient to transport.

Cove Pond in Stamford witnessed skate sailing races every Saturday in the 1915 winter season. Parallel trapezium sails occupying 45 square feet propelled 15 competitors from the Stamford Yacht Club around a two-mile-long triangular course. Recording these events for The New York Times, an awed reporter wrote, "the speed attained has reached forty-five miles an hour. And it could be faster than that except that there is a limit to human endurance." Called Yachting Without the Aid of a Yacht, the article began the sports section on Sunday, Feb. 14, 1915. Eight photographs and a diagram instructed readers in skate sailing techniques.

In an example of American skate sail touring, an unaccompanied skate sailor rashly but safely crossed almost 30 miles of unknown ice, making his first voyage. At 2:15 p.m. on January 4, 1884, L. Z. Jones left Hartford, Conn., by the frozen Connecticut River. In 25 minutes, he sailed the first eight miles to Windsor, then entered the Farmington River where he rested 20 minutes. After walking around a break in the ice, he had a fine run to the Windsor Locks. Having sailed 2 miles on the nearby canal, he spent one hour walking 3 miles of a snow-covered tow-path, where he passed another stretch of open water. Taking to ice again, he sailed through sunset and darkness to Springfield, Mass. In the office of a Springfield friend, Jones inquired the time, then 5:15 p.m. "Just three hours," wrote Jones, "thirty miles, all stops and troubles included, and not a bad record for a first attempt, after all."

Massachusetts

Novel in 1910, a skate sailing technique called for its one-man crew to stand on the colder, windward side. The sailor counterbalanced the wind force by leaning backwards. He gripped his craft by encircling the horizontal main spar with one arm, using the hand on that arm to grasp his own clothing. With his other hand holding the vertical mast, he trimmed and steadied the sail. Seen rarely on ice nowadays, the technique is credited to Nat Herreshoff, Jr., of Bristol, Mass. Sailing from the windward side is popular among roller skate sailors, especially with Roller Sails and Windskate sails (Chapter Ten).

Minnesota

Among the longest-lasting stimulations to the sport of skate sailing was the 1957 publication of Skate Sailing. Written by Rufus C. Jefferson of Wayzata, Minn., this booklet represented the first attempt to describe the sport extensively. In eight short chapters selling for $1, Jefferson discussed skate sailing theory, sail plans, technique, safety, ice lore, and skates. His pleasant sense of ironic humor pervaded the work, and his acknowledgment spoke eloquently for skate sailors everywhere. Jefferson

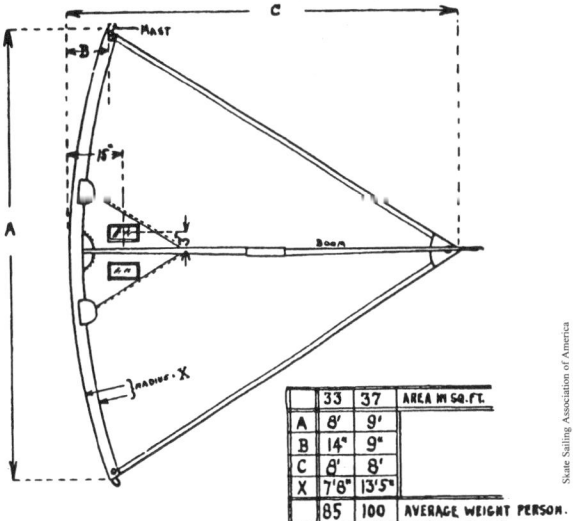

Figure 2-32: The Cape Vincent Sail

wrote, "Infinite is the debt for limbs that work, lakes that freeze, and winds that blow."

New Jersey

The Skating Club of Orange saw its first skate sail in 1902; the sail was the Cape Vincent model (Figure 2-32). Such sails were evident on the Shrewsbury River in 1914, and the Skate Sailing Association of America still distributes plans for these sails. They are remarkable because, to use these crafts, their sailors stood to windward of them. Before 1904, a rectangular sail with bamboo spars crossing on the diagonals was popular on lakes near Newfoundland.

Jersey City was home to the inventor B. M. Lupton Jr., who received a 1916 U. S. Patent for a skating appliance. His device, also to serve as a buoyant life preserver, comprised two right triangular panels strapped to a skater's body in five places (Figure 2-33). The panels bore tassels, which the skater grasped to extend the sails and catch the wind. When he released the tassels to spill the wind, rubber bands along the diagonals snapped the panels to his body. Lupton wrote, "The primary object of my invention is to provide a skating appliance that permits free use of the skaters

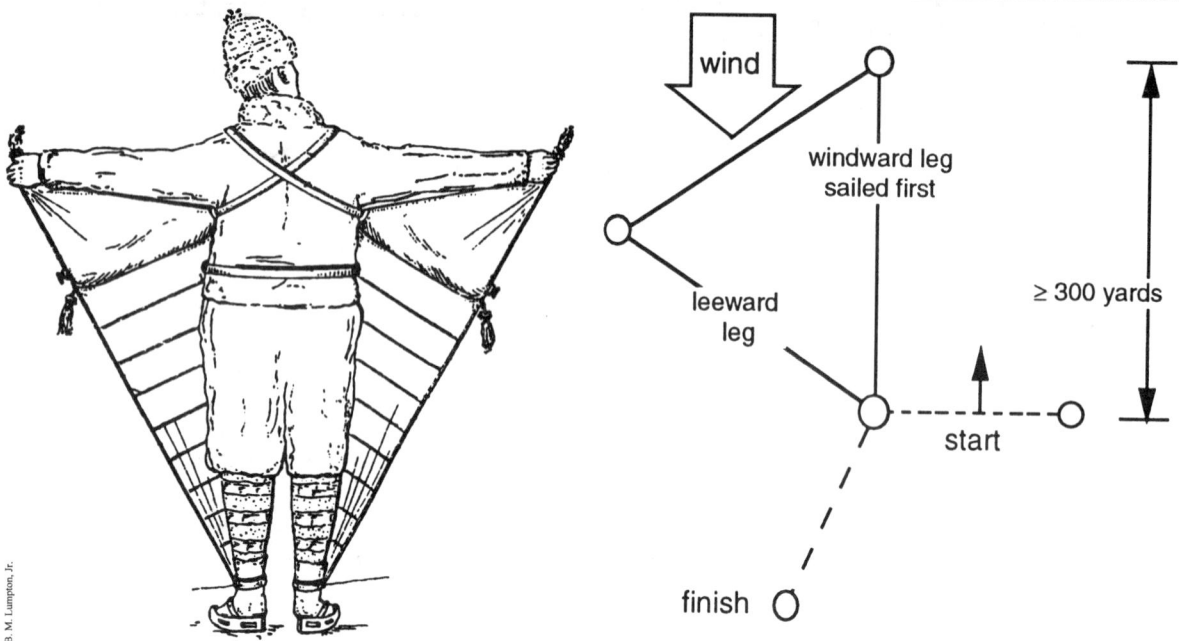

B. M. Lumpton, Jr.

**Figure 2-33: Patented Retractable Skating
Appliance and Life Preserver**

Figure 2-34: Race Course

hands and arms when the sail is not extended."

In 1917, a Swedish skate sailing technique impressed W. Van B. Claussen, S. S. A. A. founder. He wrote,

> ...two husky Swedes were there [probably at Oceanport] with their imported sails, and the way they drove at full speed down the length of the Shrewsbury [River] was enough to stir the blood of a Viking! Lightning-like speed and rough ice held no terrors for them. At one place a crack had opened in the ice and during high tide a quantity of seaweed and oyster shells had been forced up and frozen on the surface in a broad band across the width of the river and about ten to fifteen feet wide; on approaching this, instead of stopping and picking their way across it as did everyone else, they drove right at it, full speed ahead, and cleared it with a hop that took them not more than five or six inches clear of the ice!

Races sponsored by the Skate Sailing Association of America have taken place in New Jersey ever since the 1922-23 ice-sailing season. They became so popular that the association adopted its Racing Regulations and Sailing Rules in 1936. This still-used pamphlet was the first to set out association standards for closed-race

courses. Courses were triangular, with leg lengths depending on the available sailing area (Figure 2-34). Each leg was to be at least 300 yards long, and contestants sailed the course in a counterclockwise direction. One leg lay dead to windward, as a test of sailing tactics. Competitors sailed the windward leg first, and a leeward run on the last leg made for a driving finish.

In or before the 1931-1932 sailing season, varied kinds of formal races gained popularity among association members. A cruising race took place over a four- to five-mile distance on Lake Hopatcong, N. J. The course, laid out for the challenge of sailing in broken winds, led the racers between islands, or among islands and the mainland. In a relay race, competing teams passed a single sail among participants. The sails received rough handling in the transfers. Pursuit races, in which passed sailors dropped out of competition, were sailed: the last two contestants had hard going. National champions received a silver cup donated by Commodore Marcus Goodbody in 1933, and still awarded annually.

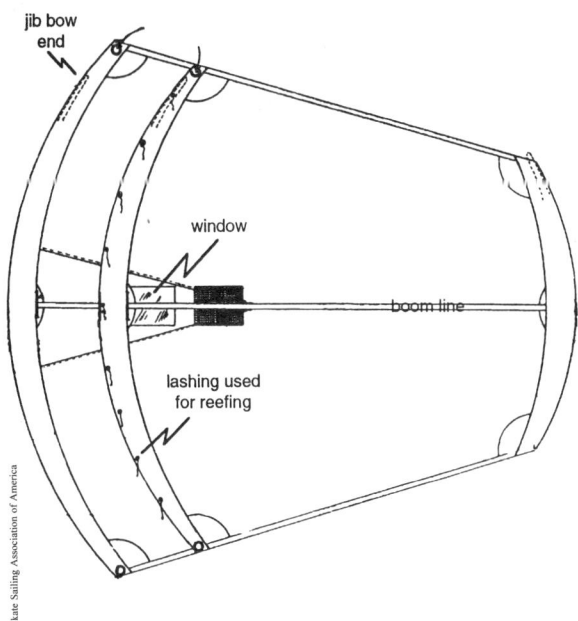

Figure 2-35: H. R. Summerhayes' Reefable Hopatcong Sail

Skate sailing is fun, and to keep it that way, the association recently introduced new kinds of formal races and varied the courses of established races. Contestants now race over an obstacle course, sail a straight out-and-back race for speed, and compete from prone positions in an ice pick race. Each racer holds ice picks and, in alternating hand-over-hand motions, drives them into the ice and uses the set pick to pull himself forward. In an après-skate sailing glüg contest, competitors submit samples of hot, spiced wine to judges. A tasty recipe if not a high proof determines the winners, thought to be the judges as much as the contestants.

On two occasions, association members agreed to sail for the sake of newsreels photographed by Fox Movietone. A description of one such event, which took place between 1935 and 1944, appears in a 1971 letter written by Jim Cawley of Kingston.

During one day's filming, there was practically no breeze. When we did sail, it was at about six miles an hour. Clearly shown trotting beside us was a little dog. The accompanying sound track,

Figure 2-36. W. V. D. Claussen with His Hopatcong Skate Sail

which described the sport, went something like this. "These intrepid sportsmen, members of the Skate Sailing Association of America, regularly race on Lake Hopatcong. They are shown thundering down the course at speeds exceeding a mile a minute."

The Hopatcong sail (Figure 2-35) represents the most successful American skate sail design. Claussen designed the Hopatcong skate sail, naming it after the New Jersey lake that remains a favorite among skate sailors (Figure 2-36). He committed the essential idea to paper in 1917, stating decades later that he conceived it in 1913. Claussen's idea, which he did not patent, solved the problem of flattening the leading edge of a skate sail with a jib. Flexible bows, borne in sail pockets and initially made from rattan, ran the full lengths of the jib and tail in the Hopatcong model. Stretching the sail along the boom forced the bows to curve and transmitted and tail bows reduced vibrations associated with earlier sail designs. The Hopatcong design admittedly did not abolish vibrations if such a sail pointed high into the wind, and the angle of attack remained limited.

In the 1920s and 1930s, Claussen planned Hopatcong sails for other sailors. His customized designs included values for the distance between the sail center of effort and the mast. These values, referred to planar, stationary sails (and excluding rigging and sailor), are important elements of skate sail design. Suitable values ensure that the sail has proper balance, whereas incorrect values create unwieldy weather or lee helms.

Claussen obtained the center-of-effort values by making measurements with cardboard scale models, which survived him. For example, in September 1923, he planned a 66.4-square-foot Hopatcong sail for C. M. Capes. The center of effort, which lay on the boom because of symmetry, fell 31 inches from the mast. Recent calculations with the old sail dimensions yielded a value close to Claussen's: 31.7 inches.

The development of aviation during the 1920s and 1930s emphasized the importance of wing design. Knowledge of wings and experience of sails led Claussen to modify the Hopatcong sail he designed. He experimented with a sail having a five- to six-inch-wide jib bow. Such a bow would decrease or abolish the detrimental effect of the sailor's body on sail efficiency, Claussen thought. The jib-bow width was to place the sailor in a partial vacuum, sheltering him from the leeward slipstream.

Like ordinary bows, this one curved along its length and tapered to a one-half- to one-inch-diameter. Claussen made the broad bow from split bamboo and brass joints. According to his written recollections and the memories of another Skate Sailing Association member, Claussen occasionally

New Jersey News Photos

Figure 2-37: John Palubniak's Eighty-Nine-Square-Foot Hopatcong Skate Sail with Double Boom

the resulting tensile force to the sailcloth. The force made the cloth flat. This was especially important in the jib that balanced the sail because it projected forward of the sailor. Sail balance made it possible to travel effortlessly along a straight course.

Making a skate sail leading edge lie flat was problematic. Certain early sails had floppy jibs, even though taut lanyards stretched the jibs along the masts. Floppiness was undesirable because a luffing sail spilled wind, slowing the sailor. Pointing a sail with a floppy jib high into the wind caused vibrations which, if severe, resulted in loss of control if not a fall. Claussen's jib used a sail incorporating this bow in the years 1935-1944. The wide jib bow never became popular among other sailors, despite Claussen's success with it. He attributed the lack of popularity to the difficulty of making the wide bow. No instructions for making the bow nor any photograph of it survived him, alas. In a performance test, Claussen rigged a sail with the broad bow, attaching tiny flags to the windward sail side. With a mirror, he watched the flags when he had gotten underway. Watching let him determine if the wind pressure were uniform on the windward sail side.

The broad jib bow satisfied Claussen's expectations on four counts. At high speeds it brought steadiness, so the sail did not flutter when pointed high into the wind. The new bow abolished the tendency of the sail to jump off the sailor's shoulder when he sailed close to the wind. A sail with it pointed higher than sails with narrower jib bows. Despite the complicated construction, a sail with the broad bow proved as easy to transport, rig, and handle as sails with narrower bows.

In a recent series of successful experiments, John Palubniak of Garfield, N. J., devised means to raise a large skate sail off the ice. Raising the sail allowed a sailor of a given height to carry a larger sail. Palubniak, an industrial arts teacher, used laminated ash to create a symmetrical, curving, double boom (Figure 2-37). The lower part of the double boom dropped below the center line of the unfenced sail, and the upper part of the boom rose above the center line. An 89-square-foot Hopatcong behemoth equipped with this boom carried Palubniak to victory in the 1989-1990 season, bringing the Marcus Goodbody Trophy of the Skate Sailing Association of America.

Members of the Skate Sailing Association of America used Donahue skates in the early 1920s. These skates, however, proved unsuitable for sailing because their wooden soles struck ice during sharply banked turns. The impact lifted the low-placed blades from the ice, causing falls. Club and clamp skates, which were also current then, were too short. Short blades made it difficult to hold a course. They also caused vibrations, which constantly increased in amplitude until it became necessary to fall off the wind to avert a fall onto the ice. Tubular racing skates with longer 18-inch blades, which prevented vibrations, soon became the still popular standard.

Fallen sailors often slide feet first on their backs traveling 100 feet or more. Unlike an erect skater, a sliding sailor cannot brake with his skates. Slides risk striking bystanders, ice boats, or docks; and the risk increases as the slide length does. A cold bath can also end a long slide.

To avoid these risks, Skate Sailing Association members designed a braking spur for their skates. The device was a short metal spike attached to the heel of each blade. The long axes of the spike and blade ran parallel. To use the spur, a fallen, sliding sailor first dragged an arm. This tactic changed a foot-first slide to a head-first one. Then he dragged the spurs over the ice, which halted the slide. For a time, the Canadian Cycle and Manufacturing Co. furnished sailing skates with braking spurs attached.

By about 1956, skate sailors began to mount racing skate blades onto the stiff, high, leather boots favored by hockey players. Mark Otterbein, a former S. S. A. A. secretary, replaced racing skate blades on these boots with industrial hacksaw blades. Other modern sailing skates exploit the hard plastic boots and soft inserts used by in-line roller skaters. The lightweight plastic boots surmount outdoor racing blades that are 19 inches long. Such skates are now available from the Dutch manufacturer Zandstra. Skates homemade

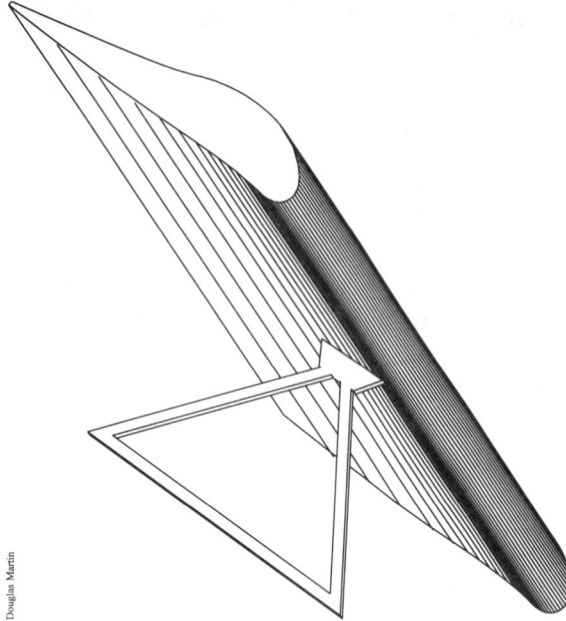

Douglas Martin

Figure 2-38: Rigid, 28-Square-Foot Windhawk, with a Liebeck Section

from solid plastic Alpine ski boots and industrial hacksaw blades are also popular nowadays. (Chapter Eight details these skates.)

In the early 1970s, Walter Miller, a former association commodore, also modified industrial hacksaw blades for use in skate sailing. Their teeth laboriously ground off, the hacksaws served as ice skate blades. The hard titanium edges needed only infrequent sharpening. A decade or more later, Ken Miller of North Plainfield, N. J., the former commodore's son, persuaded a Massachusetts manufacturer to supply the Association with small quantities of toothless blades. The commercial availability of such blanks then made them popular as ice skate blades. They were much more readily adapted than those with teeth.

Maine

In the 1960s, Douglas Martin, a Maine oar maker, began to build different kinds of skate sails, among them a rigid airfoil. Martin's wing-like craft, which did not enclose its crew of one, stood eight feet high and two and a half feet wide. In practice it

was unstable, a fault traced to its design, which Martin corrected in another model.

He designed, built, and sailed his first successful wing-shaped skate sail in 1976. Like its predecessor, this model was rectangular and eight feet tall; Martin sailed it from the windward side. The new skate sail, which had Mylar sailcloth, resembled a section of an airplane wing standing on end. Success with this model led Martin to design a series of wings intended for sale.

Called Windhawks, the wings ranged from 24 to 32 square feet, and spanned seven to nine feet (Figure 2-38). The chord length of the wings was 3½ feet. A pine and plywood frame, two struts, and an aluminum tubing spar brought the needed airfoil shape to a covering of 3.8-ounce Dacron sailcloth. One minute's work sufficed to assemble a wing from a 10-pound package that was 12 inches by five inches by nine feet. Disassembly required only removing the struts and certain handles.

A grip on these handles, located at waist and head height, held the one-person crew to the Windhawk sail. No harness or lashing fixed him to his craft, nor did it enclose him, except in an early model (Figure 2-39). Standing upwind of the wing, its sailor held it perpendicular to the sailing surface, which could be ice, snow, pavement, or water. The wing could also sail aslant, when its top tilted toward the sailor. "This mode is useful in all winds on snow and water, but only in light winds on ice," said Martin.

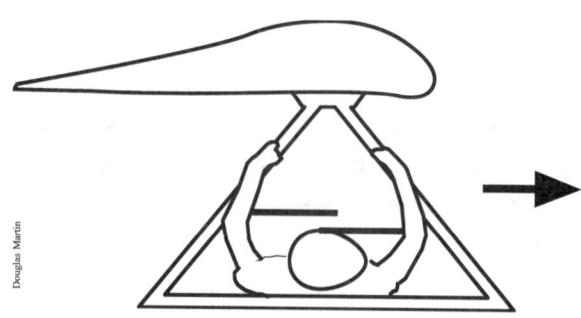

Douglas Martin

Figure 2-39: Sailing a Windhawk; top view

Windhawk wing sails were aero-dynamically stable and efficient. Controlling them reportedly required less effort than needed to maneuver a standard Hopatcong skate sail. The semi-rigid wing construction made them resilient, so the wings lacked any tendency to luff. Because the wing lay to leeward of its sailor, even a strong wind could not overpower the skipper before he had time to release his craft. The wind advantageously carried the released sail away from the sailor. A smaller wing area sufficed to move the Windhawk sailor than the area required for a traditionally flat skate sail.

Mississippi

In 1884, the U. S. Patent Office granted Patent No. 302,517 to Cornelius Holte Nelson for what he called a Skating Sail. Remarkably, he was a resident of Sheppardstown, Mississippi, a warm state not usually associated with skate sailing. Nelson substantially claimed to have invented the Danish sail.

California

Quackery ensued when knowledge of skate sailing reached Hollywood in or before 1935, where Disney included the sport in a cartoon titled *On Ice*. The cartoon, available nowadays in a 1982 collection called *A Walt Disney Christmas*, opens showing dozens of skaters and two skate sailors on a frozen river bay, all gliding in time to a Viennese waltz. One of the skate sailors was the antic Donald Duck, who strapped himself to his craft. Blown harrowingly downwind to the lip of a waterfall, he was miraculously rescued from an ice floe by Mickey Mouse. Donald Duck's skate sail was kite shaped and bore two spars that lay at right angles to one another (Figure 2-40). The sail, which left the drawing board only in the cartoonist's imagination, stood erect on its tail. Its horizontal spar carried two straps that fixed the sailor's wrists to his craft, making it impossible to steer, come about, or stop.

Canada

In the early part of this century, Canadian sailors designed a two-man sail; some of them sailed on the St. Laurence River. Another sail design, the segment-shaped Cape Vincent (Figure 2-32) reflects the popularity of the sport in Canada, especially on Lake Ontario.

Nearly a century after the Cape Vincent sail first saw use, a Canadian inventor received U. S. Patent 4,269,133 for a variant on this design (Figure 2-41). Richard L. E. Brown of Kingston, Ontario, modified the older design in three ways. (1) He added a flexible U-shaped section to the middle of the otherwise rigid aluminum boom. The flexibility of this piece helped give the proper airfoil configuration to the sail. It also provided a convenient handle, and helped assemble the craft. (2) Brown omitted the

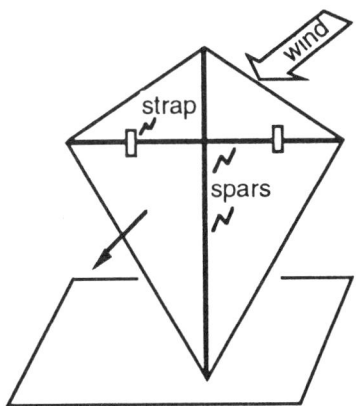

Figure 2-40: Donald Duck's Rudimentary Skate Sail

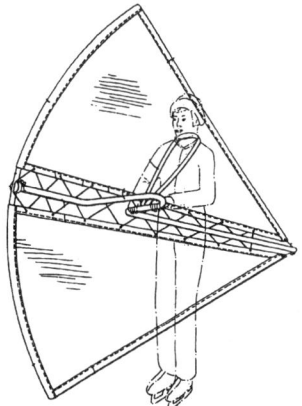

Figure 2-41: R. L. E. Brown's Hand-held Skate Sail

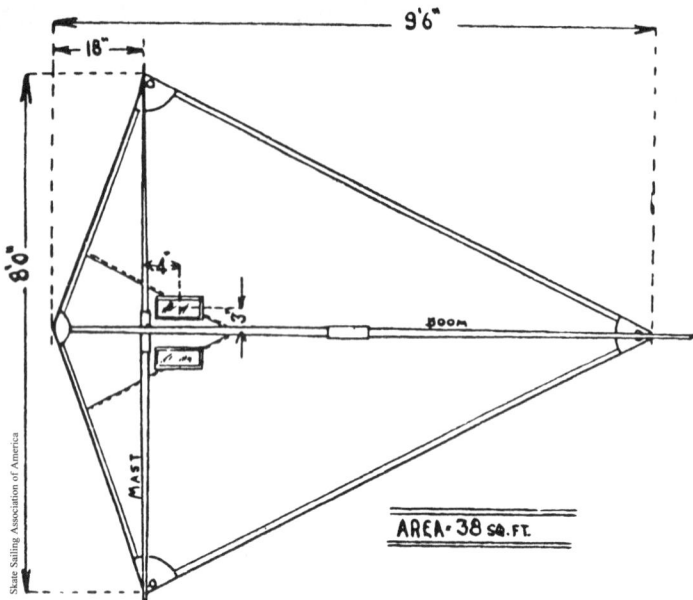

Figure 2-42: Kite-Shaped Sail

windows found in the earlier version, and divided his hand-held sail into halves laced together near the boom and shaped like pie wedges. The resulting broad opening between the circle sectors gave the sailor a forward view that inclined downward. This divided Cape Vincent sail resembled in its conception the Norton double diamond craft (Figure 2-21) of the previous century. These sails, and Biddle's ketch-rigged craft (Figure 2-30) distributed their areas over two separate panels, and were the only ones to do so. (3) The divided Cape Vincent bore a harness that helped support the sail and left the sailor's hands free to control the craft. This flexible harness encircled his neck (somewhat like a noose). It served the same purposes as the rigid, triangular device adopted by Douglas Martin's Windhawk, which enclosed the sailor's entire body (Figure 2-38).

The Cape Vincent and the Windhawk were similar in two respects. Both sail designs required the sailor to stand apart from his craft and to windward of it. As a result, the sailor's body did not distort the sail shape. Another desirable consequence of sailing to windward took effect if the sailor freed the

sail: the wind carried it away from him. The triangle and the harness, however, made it impossible to escape trouble merely by releasing one's grip upon the sail. By contrast, in contacting the Hopatcong sail, for example, the sailor's body deformed the would-be aerodynamic shape. With the sail boom resting on the sailor's leeward shoulder, and with no harness, the sail could be released instantly. However, it was driven by the wind toward the sailor.

An unnecessary modification to the kite-shaped sail (Figure 2-42) lay among the claims of the 1979 U. S. Patent 4,136,631. The modification (not illustrated here) provided for a mechanical coupling device to join the two halves of the mast to the boom. In the assembled sail, the coupling allowed the halves to fold parallel to the boom..."when for example the skater wishes to retrace his path quickly against the wind. [Folding]...will effectively reduce the area of sail susceptible to wind forces and thus make the [skate sail] readily transportable." The inventor misunderstood that both kite-shaped and Hopatcong models sail upwind, and that they return their sailors to their starting points. Referring to the Hopatcong sail, he wrote ... "[it] suffers the disadvantage that [it] has to be completely taken to pieces for ease of transportation against the prevailing wind."

In an article entitled "The Girl and the Skate Sail," C. H. Claudy illustrated the kite-shaped sail (Figure 2-42). The jibs of these sails provided balance by applying force ahead of the sailor. Dated to 1912, such sails remain current. Modifications to a kite-shaped sail were the subject of a 1980 U. S. patent issued to George B. Harpole of Middletown, Wis.

"Skate Sailing for Life," a short story by C. H. Claudy, appears in the February 1910, issue of *St. Nicholas Magazine*. It is the only serious English-language work of fiction that skate sailing inspired. In short, howling Canadian wolves hunt a 16-year-old heroine skate sailing at minus 25 °F to summon a physician to her injured brother's aid. Ends well for the siblings.

CONCLUSION

This history concludes by summarizing the remaining problems and enduring solutions of ice skate sailing. Both arose from efforts to design and use ice skate sails. Such efforts were more recreation than occupation to those skaters who attempted to invent or improve skate sails. Advances made in the late 19th or early 20th century owed much to their enthusiasm and trial-and-error methods. Their obligation to wealthy patrons was non-existent, and in some cases their debt to the new science and technology of aerodynamics was scant. Wind tunnels and, decades later, computers gave little help to skate sail designers. Despite their successes, however, design improvements inspired by performance deficiencies were perhaps fewer than they might otherwise have been. Short sailing seasons restricted the opportunities to experiment and observe, as did variable weather during the winter months.

Remaining Problems of Skate Sail Design

Three fundamental problems confront designers of any new skate sail. An ever-present issue is the sailor's position relative to the sail and true wind. Another is the danger posed by any harness or lashing linking the sailor to his craft. Finally, there is the drag caused by his body in the airstream.

The designer of a traditional, hand-held skate sail often decides the sailor's windward or leeward position relative to his craft. If the sailor stands on the windward side and apart from the craft, his body causes no sail deformation. His position allows the sail to maintain the airfoil shape introduced by the designer. If a novice sails with no other link to the craft than his grip, he can release the sail to escape difficulties on the ice. Because the sail lies downwind of the sailor, the wind carries the freed sail harmlessly away.

However, several skate sails maneuvered from windward use harnesses, lashings, or solid frames to link or enclose the sailor. These devices avert constant strain on the sailor's arms and improve his control of the craft. In addition, a solid frame can permit the sailor to heel his skate sail, which reduces his sail area effectively and decreases his speed usefully. But linking mechanisms all pose some danger to an immersed ice skate sailor. The sail can hamper his effort to extricate himself, while the task of removing his harness, lashing, or frame can delay rescue.

Hand-held skate sails like the Dragon and Hopatcong models are usually sailed from their leeward sides. From this position, their sailors can heel them easily, lying upon them comfortably. They can sail with less physical exertion. Such a traditional sail does not fasten to the sailor, who can release it quickly if trouble looms. A loosed sail of this type, however, travels downwind toward its sailor, and a collision between them can hurt. Furthermore, when the skate sailor inclines his craft, his hip and shoulder distort the lower sail half. Distortion sacrifices aerodynamic efficiency and forward thrust to comfortable sailing.

Thrust is also lost to the drag resulting from interaction of the sailor's body with the surrounding airstream. His body creates drag regardless of his leeward or windward position relative to the sail. A similar interaction of an inefficient sail also creates drag and reduces thrust. This last situation is what inventors strive to prevent or remedy. Good aerodynamic design can minimize drag due to the sail. However, drag caused by the sailor may vastly exceed that caused by the sail. Aerodynamic improvements to conventional sails may be insignificant in this case. A lasting problem of traditional skate sail design is the unknown relative contributions that these two drag components make to the total.

Characterizing skate sail designs on the ice is problematic because opportunities to sail on ice skates are comparatively few. So it remains to measure three properties of each popular skate sail design. The first is the greatest upwind speed attained under defined conditions. They include a measured course, a known angle to the true wind, and a timed run in a wind of certain velocity. Other important conditions are the area of the sail and the weight of the sailor. Seventy mph for Hopatcong skate sailors represents the best present estimate, despite the ill-defined circumstances of this record run.

The second characteristic comprises the maximum ratio of sailing speed to wind velocity. The ratio varies with sail design and course angle, as it does in softwater sailing crafts. The third property is the smallest angle from the true wind at which the skate sail can travel upwind. Crude estimates of the smallest angle and the maximum ratio are 30° and 2.5 for the Hopatcong design.

Comparing and contrasting skate sails would help find the best design and variant. Favorable circumstances would allow definitive races among expert sailors using different sails, like the Windhawk and Hopatcong models. Sails of similar designs, for example a Dragon versus a Hopatcong, might also race. To date, however, no national skate sail races have taken place in the U. S. Its sailors have never competed in any international matches. On several occasions, the weather failed to cooperate during attempts to stage national or international competitions. Finding and demonstrating the best skate sail design remains a problem in search of a solution.

Regardless of the problems specific to designing skate sails, two essential requirements face all inventors. They must define the problem they seek to solve and establish that no solution already exists. Without a thoughtful definition and some historical knowledge, a skate sail designer may take on an impossible or needless task. Skate sail designers unacquainted with the history of their sport risk re-inventing it.

Enduring Solutions of Skate Sail Design

To sail on ice skates is not only possible but thrilling. Established solutions to old problems prevail, and include sail stability and balance, and sail durability and visibility. Stable sails occupying or exceeding 55 square feet result from stiff leading edges. Stiffening prevents luffing when the sail points high into the wind. It allows sailing closer to the wind than was possible previously. Cables or bows within forward pockets stiffen the leading edges of many modern sails. Rigid spars at the leading edges of the Erie and Schenectady sails served the same purpose. The Dane, with which this chapter began (Figure 2-1), sailed no closer to the wind than 56° in the 19th century. Its modern counterparts, the Hopatcong or Dragon sails, can travel at about 30°.

In North America, balanced sails arose from the addition of jibs to the mainsails of transitional models like an early version of the Schenectady. Jibs increased the forward sail area and abolished the tendency of jibless sails to turn strongly upwind. The Nyack sail, unlike the Schenectady, accepted no jib, turned upwind, and was tiring to control. Because of its tendency to turn upwind, the Nyack model resembled the Erie. These sails made it difficult to carry out two necessary tasks. Acting simultaneously, their sailors had to seize the masts and align the centers of lateral resistance and effort.†

The jibless, triangular shape of a 60-square-foot Erie sail brought the center of effort far aft. In this model as in others, vertical alignment of the centers of effort and lateral resistance allowed sailing a straight course. But to sail the Erie straight, the center-of-effort position forced the sailor aft to align the centers. To grasp the mast, he reached as far forward as he moved aft. Seizing the mast then made him extend his controlling arm almost completely (Figure 2-23). With an unmodified Erie sail somewhat larger than 60 square feet, his reach would have exceeded his grasp. By contrast, a Dragon sailor's center of lateral resistance lies (horizontally) close to the center of effort. He need not reach forward to grasp the mast nor move aft to align the centers. Sailing the Dragon is comfortable, despite its 95-square-foot area. It balances the forward sail area with the aft one, so its sailor's reach lies within his grasp.

No longer do damp skate sails decay as did the drab, canvas sailcloth of the last century. Nor must miniature skate sail windows balance safety with economy any more. Plastics available today are not only transparent but inexpensive. Affordable, safe sails can incorporate the equivalents of picture windows instead of peepholes, or be entirely transparent. Colorful, innovative fabrics bring the durability and visibility that modern skate sails offer. These and other modern materials inform Chapter Three.

---

†The center of lateral resistance lies on the ice between the skate sailor's feet. The position of the center of effort falls within the sail plane and, to a first approximation, is determined by the shape of the stationary sail.

CHAPTER THREE: MODERN HOPATCONG SKATE SAILS

"The perfect [skate] sail for a high average of speed, portability, and responsive steering is the triangular. It will inevitably become the dominant type." — A. H. Goodwin, "The Joyous Sport of Skate Sailing," 1904.

To sail on skates, you'll need a sail but not a private fortune. About $100-$500 will equip you, depending on whether you make or buy a new sail. Either way, expect a cared-for sail to last two lifetimes; a skate sail is a long-term investment. In the short term, skiers who become skate sailors can look forward to saving cash and patience as lift tickets and lines vanish into memory. Après skate sailing, falling asleep at one's own dinner table costs nothing.

Whether you are building a skate sail for the first time, or buying a new or used one, questions abound. This chapter answers them. It offers information bearing on the design and construction of Hopatcong skate sails. The purposes served by various sail parts appear here, as do the traditional and modern materials that go into them. The chapter presents alternative methods for making certain mechanical parts, especially those that fasten the sail to the mast, the mast to the boom, and the boom to the sail. To facilitate choosing among the many available kinds of sailcloth, it sets forth some sailcloth properties and how they can influence the choice.

Proving that math does more than schoolwork, a discussion of sail geometry ends the chapter. It introduces the ideas of sail fencing and aspect ratio, factors that bear upon sail performance as sail area does. Also included are numerical values for 13 sail dimensions that characterize skate sails (Table 3-4). Fifteen sets of values, applying to sails of as many different areas, extend the scope of previous compilations. Using these numbers, you can build standard sails without having to make your own calculations. Table 3-4 also provides values of two important but often neglected parameters Q_{uf} and H. Respectively, Q_{uf} and H represent the horizontal distance from the mast along the boom to the sail center-of-effort and the perpendicular distance from the mast-boom crossing to the sail edge (Figure 3-25). These parameters respectively set upper limits to the sail sizes that a sailor of a given reach and height can handle, and so sailmakers and sail buyers must take them into account.

JIB, TAIL, AND MAINSAIL

The jib, which lies forward of the mast and sailor, balances the sail and makes traveling a straight course easy (Figure 3-1). The jib occupies 19% of the total sail

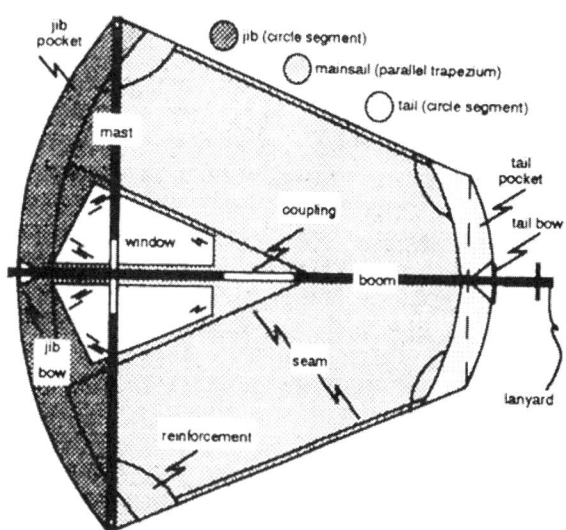

Figure 3-1: Components of a Hopatcong Sail Seen from Leeward

area, so it contributes substantially to the sailor's speed. Sail area is not the only determinant of sailing speed, but is a major contributor because speed does increase with area. Of the three sail components, however, the mainsail makes the greatest relative contribution to sailing speed. The mainsail occupies the largest part of the total sail area, amounting to 79%. The tail, occupying only 2% of the area, makes a proportionately smaller contribution to speed. However, because the jib and tail contain tensioned bows, they serve another purpose, tautening the sail. A smooth run requires a taut sail.

The size and presence of the jib influence the direction taken and the sailing ease. With too large a jib, a skate sail shows a lee helm and tends to turn downwind. In this situation, the sailor must physically force her craft to sail a straight course. Without a jib, a greater proportion of the sail area falls aft of the sailor, giving the craft a heavy weather helm. Last popular at the turn of the century, such a jibless sail required its sailor to counter its inherent tendency to turn upwind. This made sailing tiring, turning a relatively undemanding pastime into a challenge of strength and stamina. Although contemporary North American skate sailors favor sails with jibs, the importance of jibs has been controversial for almost 100 years. Two latter-day sailors who are father and son disfavor the standard jib proportions, building sails with small jibs and sailing them superbly.

Jib and Tail Components

The jib of a Hopatcong skate sail features a cloth pocket with a curved bow lying in it, and grommets as well as reinforcements at the corners where the mainsail meets the jib at the mast. The tail resembles the jib, except that it is smaller, not fixed at its corners to any spar, and therefore lacks grommets.

Jib and Tail Pockets

The cloth pocket spans the whole jib and bears openings at either end that admit the bow. The pocket also opens in its center to accept the boom, which fastens to the jib bow. Sailmakers sometimes make this center opening by cutting through only the leeward layer of sailcloth in the pocket. In Figure 3-1, however, the center opening passes completely through the jib pocket. Either kind of opening allows for fastening the bows to the boom. The tail pocket is similar to the jib pocket.

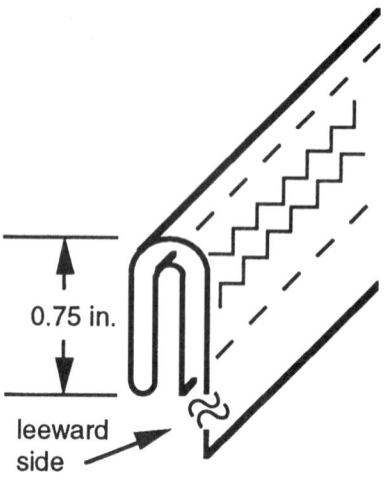

Figure 3-2: Rolled Pocket Seam

Pocket Seams

The jib and tail bear pocket seams made by overlapping as many as four layers of sailcloth for strength (Figure 3-2). Such finished seams span about three-quarters of an inch, and each pocket seam requires a cloth allowance of $2^3/_4$ inches. Narrower seams made from as few as two layers of sailcloth are also workable. These seams can span only one-half to five-eighths of an inch, yet be durable enough to have lasted more than 20 years.

One or three seams are needed to make a pocket, depending on sail design. Different designs require varying numbers of sail cloth panels to complete the sails, and these numbers determine how many pocket (and other) seams are needed. One design calls for making the entire sail from only two panels, whereas the sail plan presented in Chapter Seven requires five panels. In the former case, one seam per pocket suffices. In the latter case, three seams per pocket are necessary; and four of the five panels form the jib, mainsail, and tail. The fifth sailcloth panel yields two curved strips that must be sewn to the assembled sail to give the pockets. Strips of Dacron™ reinforcing tape connect the sail to the pocket material at the leading edge of the jib pocket and at the trailing edge of the tail pocket.

Grommets

In the corners where the jib meets the mainsail, the sail contains holes made by setting four brass grommets into the fabric. The grommets pass through the pocket and through reinforcing patches to admit fastenings that fix the sail to the mast. Each end of the pocket contains two aligned grommets, one in the leeward layer of sailcloth and the other in the windward layer. The inside diameter of the grommets ranges from $3/8$ to $1/2$ of an inch. Grommets and the special tool needed to install them are available in kits sold by hardware stores and marine suppliers.

Reinforcements

Four patches shaped like pie wedges reinforce the sail at the corners where the jib and the tail join the mainsail. Spanning the jib and the mainsail, and the tail and mainsail, these patches ordinarily lie on the leeward side. Some skate sailors, however, ornament the windward sail sides with reinforcements of contrasting colors. In any case, sailcloth scraps provide the reinforcing patches and, in a 55-square-foot sail, have a radius of four to five inches. Sew them in before turning or sewing the pockets, and make them from the scraps of sailcloth that arise from cutting the panels needed for the jib, mainsail, and tail. Two reinforcements

per corner are desirable.

Sailmakers occasionally reinforce the interior seam that runs parallel to the boom from the jib to the tail by using sail tape or a narrow strip of sewn-on sailcloth. The small section of the sail beneath the mast-boom crossing also needs reinforcing if hose clamps connect these two spars. The advantages of connecting the spars with hose clamps, which do tend to abrade the cloth, appear in this chapter's section entitled Boom-Bow and Boom-Mast Fastenings.

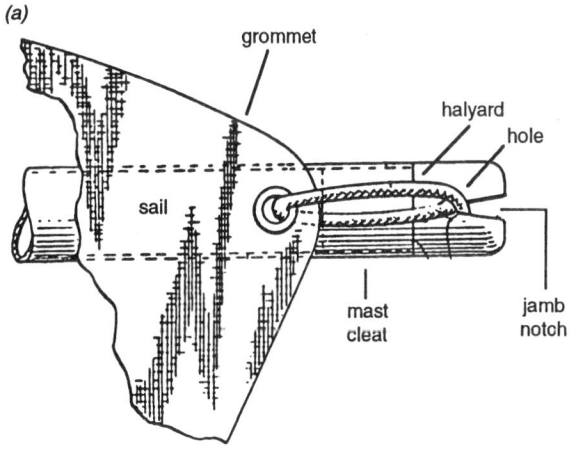

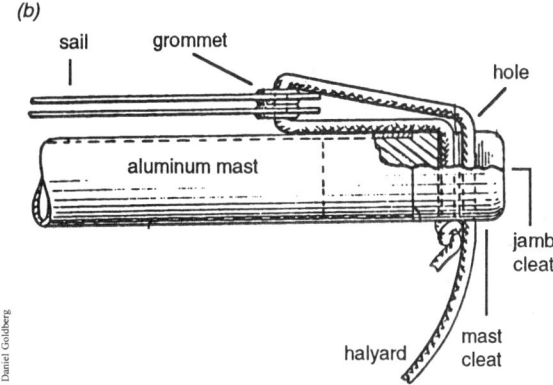

Figure 3-3: Mast Halyards: (a) Top View and (b) Side View

Fastening the Sail to the Mast

Three methods serve to fasten the sail to the mast, all using the grommets at the corners where the jib and mainsail meet. Lashing is among the oldest methods

(Figure 3-3). The illustrated method requires wooden plugs fitting inside the aluminum tubing that forms the mast. Alternatively, the sailmaker can shape the ends of a wooden mast as shown.

Lashing the sail to the mast is advantageous if the cloth stretches when wet, as nylon does. Tightening the lashings restores sail tautness, which other fastenings do not accomplish. However, untying the knots of lashings is difficult when they are wet or icy. The sharp point of an ice pick will help. Even so, untying the knots often requires the sailor to remove her gloves, and wets her hands on the cords.

The second method for fastening the sail to the mast requires either of two kinds of metal hooks (Figure 3-4). Hooks do not permit crosswise tightening of a loose, wet sail, but make detaching the sail from the mast easy. Gloved hands do the job. The skate sailor, however, must make the hooks, which are not commercially available. This requires metal working skill and may entail riveting or soldering, depending on the kind of hooks.

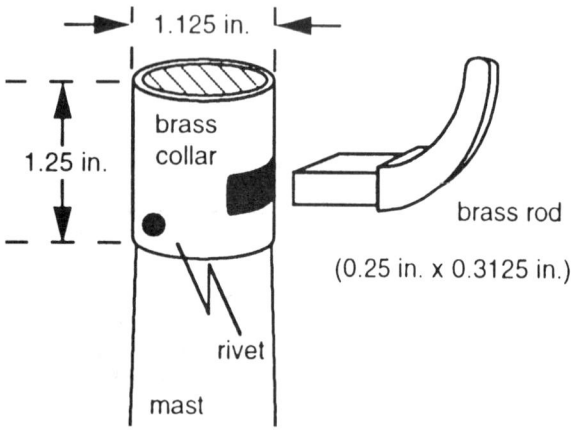

Figure 3-4: Hook Fastening Jib to Mast

In the third fastening method, a combination of machine screws, washers, and wing nuts acts like the hooks. The machine screws pass through grommets and holes drilled in the mast ends. Wing nuts on the leeward sail side secure the screws.

The parts are readily available, and you can easily attach or detach the sail when your hands are gloved. The wing nuts will wear away your gloves, however. Another disadvantage is that the sets of fasteners tend to fall into deep snow or disappear amid the jumbled contents of a duffel bag. Taking several sets is advisable.

Mainsail Components

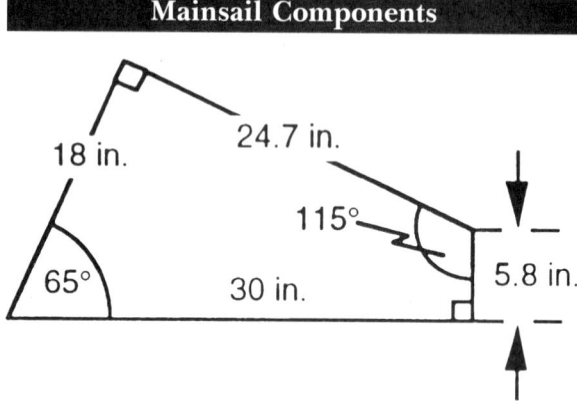

Figure 3-5: Dimensions of a
Three-Square-Foot Quadrilateral Sail Window

Perhaps the most important features of the mainsail are the windows. Serviceable windows, which should be symmetrical about the boom, can comprise pairs of triangles and quadrilaterals, or even single circles. In any case, the window area should total at least three square feet regardless of sail area. In 1917, when the only available plastic was expensive celluloid, sail plans called for a total window area of little more than one square foot. The plans recommended two rectangular windows, each covering only 8 x 10 inches in a 67 square-foot sail. Nowadays, sailors attribute poor visibility to the small size of such windows.

Placement of Windows

Window placement is also important, especially when the windows are small. If the sailor stands with her back to the sail, her sideways visibility through 8 x 10 windows is almost nil. With her leeward arm stretched backward on the boom, she must turn her head through 90° just to see forward. Her position then compels her to shift only her eyes to see sideways, yet the upper window lies well forward of her head. The forward placement of small windows in older sails and in many old but still current sail plans drastically restricts needed visibility.

Length of Windows

Window length (measured horizontally along the boom) is critical to good visibility. A skate sailor's angle of vision changes as she slides the boom forward, so her sail windows must be long enough to give good side visibility when she pushes the boom forward as far as her windward arm reaches. Thus, the horizontal distance between the jib bow and the window should increase as the sail area does. The window placement should provide adequate forward visibility when your windward shoulder lies at the mast-boom crossing.

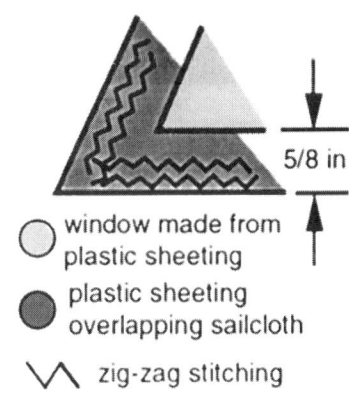

5/8 in.

○ window made from plastic sheeting
● plastic sheeting overlapping sailcloth
⋁⋀ zig-zag stitching

Figure 3-6: Detail Showing Window Stitching

Design of Windows

A workable design for modern skate sail windows calls for two quadrilaterals (Figure 3-5). Each window comprises two opposing right angles, an acute angle of 65°, and an obtuse one of 115°. At $1^{1}/_{2}$ square feet each, these windows are large enough for a 65 square-foot sail, as a result of their length and placement (Figure 3-1).

The lengths given in Figure 3-5 represent distances in the plastic sheet from which

the sailmaker cuts the window. Lengths in the finished window are smaller because it contains a standard $^{5}/_{8}$-inch seam (Figure 3-6).

Window Material

The most common material used in skate sail windows is polyvinyl chloride (PVC). Useful thicknesses range from 3 to 20 mils (one mil equals one thousandth of an inch). Loosely rolling a sail for summer storage does not crack or crease such windows. They do stiffen in cold weather but don't crack then, either. Scratching PVC windows is possible, however, and they can become cloudy if stored wet. Extruded polyester film, which is available as Monofilm™, also makes serviceable skate sail windows. It finds use in the windows of surfboard sails.

Polished vinyl plastic 20 mils thick is preferable for sail windows. Such windows can last over 20 years. The Herbert Lushan Plastics Corp. of Newton, Mass., originally manufactured the sheeting, intending it for use as tops and side curtains in convertible automobiles. The plastic contains ultraviolet light absorbers, which inhibit degradation, and also contains plasticizers as well as stabilizing agents. The plasticizers keep the windows flexible. The stabilizers and plasticizers extend the life and clarity of the windows. A special press-polishing, which ordinary vinyl sheeting lacks, clarifies the plastic.

Finally, when you are looking for plastic to make windows, inspect it before buying it, ensuring that the plastic has no optical distortions.

Window and Sail Repairs

Transparent, adhesive-backed sail tape, available in rolls from sailmakers, repairs a cut in a window. The plastic tape should more than cover the tear length on both sides of the window. Four pieces of sail tape that is about two inches wide will distribute the wind force over a large area, preventing further damage. Carrying a roll of tape on every voyage is a good precaution because it temporarily repairs the sail itself.

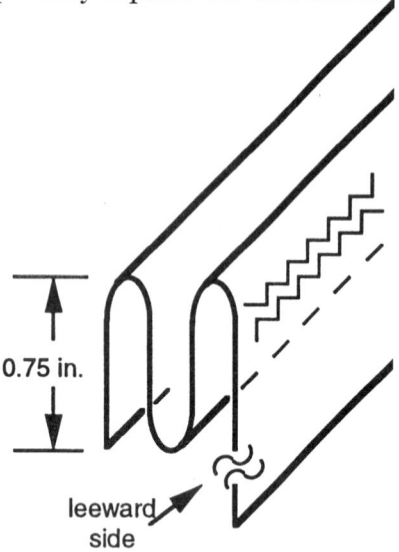

Figure 3-7: Four-Layer Rolled Tabling

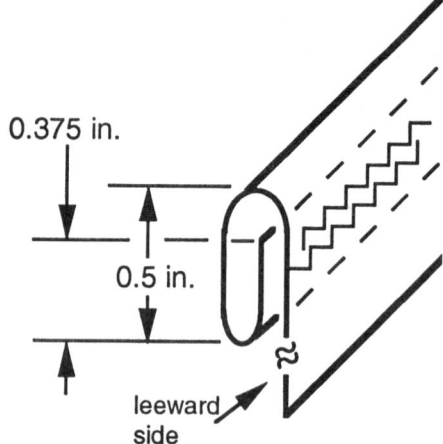

Figure 3-8: Three-Layer Rolled Tabling

Edge and Interior Seams

The edge (Figure 3-7) and interior seams are held together with zigzag stitching. (Edge seams are known as tablings.) The selvedge on some sailcloths is probably too flimsy to hold a stiff edge when the sailor tightens the sail, so tablings are advisable. For a stiff edge, some skate sailors make the tabling concave rather than straight and, for strength, recommend rolling the edge (Figs. 3-7 and -8). In Figure 3-7, the tabling is formed from four layers of sailcloth and uses a $2^1/_4$ -inch-wide (3 x 0.75 inch) strip. Three layers go into the other kind of rolled tabling (Figure 3-8), which uses a piece of sailcloth that is only $^7/_8$ of an inch wide (0.5 + 0.375 inch).

If the sailcloth is cut as Chapter Seven describes†, then the three-layer, three-quarter-inch tablings detract almost three square feet from the area of a sail that would nominally occupy 60 square feet, a decrease of about five percent. The lost area is directly proportional to the nominal one, increasing

with sail size. If the three-layer, one-half-inch-wide seams are adopted, then the area lost amounts to less than one square foot. These three-layer seams are preferable because they are strong enough to give many years' use. They reduce the finished sail area less than the other rolled seams.

A skate sail has one or more interior seams, depending on the method used to cut the sailcloth. One ever-present seam runs the length of the sail and lies behind the boom when the sail is rigged. It arises from overlapped sailcloth panels that are stitched together. Doubly overlapping the panels makes lap-felled interior seams and zigzag stitching finishes them (Figure 3-9). They span about three quarters of an inch and require a cloth allowance of about one and a half inches. Narrower, one-half-inch wide seams made by simple overlapping are also serviceable, and detract less area from the finished sail than the doubly overlapped ones.

To obtain the best thread, it is wise to heed the advice of the sailmaker who provides the sailcloth.

SAILCLOTH

The history of sailcloth development resembles a footrace in which one runner

---

† The cutting method given in Chapter Seven does not call for extra cloth to allow for making seams. The edge and interior seams use cloth that would otherwise maintain the planned area in the finished sail. Finished sails made by this method are always smaller than those planned according to the dimensions of Table 3-4.

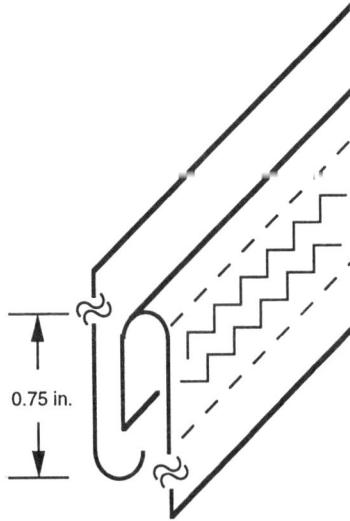

Figure 3-9: Lap-Felled Interior Seam

leads but is soon overtaken by another. The second leader yields to a third, who succumbs to a fourth, etc., with the winner unknown as yet. Cloth made from European flax dominated sails before the 1820s, but was supplanted in the U.S. by less stretchy cloth made from American cotton fibers. Cotton-fiber sails led from the 1850s to the 1920s when sailmakers introduced long-staple Egyptian cotton. Long-staple cotton sails were even less stretchy than cotton-fiber ones. Stretch resistance aside, however, cotton suffers from several other flaws. It absorbs water and gains weight, and it rots and mildews. Because of flaws associated with cotton, synthetic sailcloths eclipse natural ones. New chemical reactions and physical processes produce modern synthetic sailcloths.

Modern Woven Sailcloths

The race for an ideal sailcloth gained speed shortly before and after World War II, with the advent and development of modern polymer chemistry. Chemists devised new polymers from which they could prepare novel fibers. For the first time, these innovations allowed manufacturers to control the chemical and mechanical properties of sailcloth. Merely accepting sailcloth properties had been the only choice

with natural-fiber cloth. Advances in chemistry enabled various fibers made from pure, synthetic polymers to dominate the sailcloth market, displacing cotton fibers made from the impure, natural polymer polysaccharide (Table 3-1).

Dacron

One of the first synthetic fibers to gain wide acceptance was Dacron, a polyester that resists rotting. The threads of Dacron sailcloth are tightly woven as well as heat set under pressure. They give a smooth, impervious, stable fabric. Made available in the 1950s, Dacron has retained its popularity in sails of all kinds.

Table 3-1: Sailcloth Composition

Fibers		Film
Dacron™:	polyester	
nylon:	polyamide	
Kevlar™:	aromatic polyamide	Mylar™: polyester
Spectra™:	polyethylene	
cotton:	polysaccharide	

Many sailors prefer Dacron for skate sails. It is comparatively inexpensive, lasts for decades, resists stretching when wet, and lies flat. Unlike nylon, polyester resists sagging when the wind rises, making a flatter sail. Sag causes the draft (fullness) of the sail to increase just when many sailors would prefer the draft to decrease, so the flatness imparted by Dacron makes for a good racing sail. Not all Dacron works, however, so the choice of sailcloth demands care. A marine supply house or a sailmaker will provide the genuine article.

Nylon

Sailcloth made from a forerunner of modern nylon, a polyamide synthesized in the late 1930s, tended to rip, a major setback. Manufacturers have solved the ripping problem, and modern nylon sailcloth goes into the spinnakers used for sailing boats downwind. Such sailing entails heavy, initial shock loading, so sailors value nylon because it withstands these forces.

Popular in skate sails, modern nylon sailcloths are readily available in colors, and are inexpensive and durable. However, they are stretchy, unlike Dacron sails. Some skate sailors swear by the stretchiness of nylon, claiming that it aids recovery from gusts especially when the sailor is lying on the wind. In light winds, nylon sails can sag under their own weight, which is detrimental to their aerodynamic shapes.

Sailcloths from Extrusion and Lamination

Mid-20th-century innovations in chemical engineering made it possible to form novel sailcloths by new physical processes. Supplementing and perhaps surpassing the ancient weaver's art, these processes are extruding and laminating. Extrusion of molten plastics, prepared from synthetic polymers, produces useful thin films. Lamination of these films to synthetic fabrics yields other modern sailcloths.

To prepare laminated sailcloths, manufacturers usually combine polyester film with woven polyester, aromatic polyamide, or polyethylene fibers. Somewhat confusingly, these sailcloth laminates bear the same names as the film (Mylar) and the fibers (Kevlar and Spectra).

Lamination maximizes the number of opportunities to control sailcloth properties. Thus, sailcloth manufacturers choose among the number and relative orientations of layers, the fiber and film compositions, the fiber diameter, and the film thickness. Any of the layers can be film or woven fabric, and the films and woven fibers can differ in chemical composition. Weaving, which determines sailcloth geometry, brings more choices. The amount of crimping and the directions in which fibers or bundles of fibers

run can vary. Changes in any of these characteristics influence the mechanical and chemical properties of the finished cloth.

Mylar

One such laminated film, a Mylar Monofilm, can be used alone as sailcloth. Some windsurfers favor transparent Monofilm sails for lightness in weight, for resistance to stretching, and for all-around visibility. Such sails reportedly have little tear resistance, however.

Kevlar

Another modern synthetic fiber used in sailcloths is Kevlar, valued for its stretch resistance. It is expensive, however, and appears only as a component of laminated cloths. In this respect, Kevlar resembles Spectra, a fiber that combines low stretch with lightness in weight. These laminates have seen little use in skate sails.

An Introduction to Sailcloth Properties

This section briefly discusses some of the important sailcloth properties (Table 3-2), beginning by contrasting the tasks that skate sail and sailboat cloth should accomplish. Skate sail cloth must pass between the horns of a dilemma: it should be suitable for sailing on and off the wind. Sailing to windward requires relatively flat, well shaped sails to form an effective airfoil, and although strength is still an important consideration, maintaining this airfoil shape without stretching is more critical, according to T. Whidden and M. Levitt, authors of a book on sail materials.†

In long races, sailboat skippers can change sails to suit their course and wind. Hence, concerns in sailboat races are choosing a strong sail (nylon) for downwind travel and selecting one that resists stretching (Kevlar) when the boat sails into the wind. By contrast, skate sail racers

---

†A detailed account of the complex chemical and mechanical properties of various modern sailcloths lies beyond the scope of this book. Interested readers might consult *The Art and Science of Sails: A Guide to Modern Materials, Construction, Aerodynamics, Upkeep, and Use*, by Tom Whidden and Michael Levitt (St. Martin's Press, New York, 1990; ISBN 0-312-04417-8).

confront Hobson's Choice: they must choose a single sailcloth for the entire course.

Hopatcong skate sails, moreover, comprise only two to five panels of cloth according to different interpretations of a single 1913 design. The panels keep the direction of greatest stretch nearly parallel to the force imposed by the outhaul lanyard, not by the wind pressure. Skate sails, because they contain so few panels, do not take advantage of the stretch control that modern sailcloths offer. Little, if anything, is known of pressure distributions in a moving skate sail.

In contrast, many more panels make up the mainsails and spinnakers of modern boats. Sailmakers orient each panel so that its direction of least stretch parallels its direction of greatest wind load. Experienced sailmakers know much about panel loading,†† and some use powerful computers to reckon the loads. Computer calculations help to design the panel shape and placement, and can even model the sail aloft.

Stretch Resistance

Sailcloth geometry and fiber composition largely determine the stretch resistance of woven sailcloth. Resistance is least in the bias direction, but woven sailcloth also stretches in the warp and fill directions that

Table 3-2: Important Chemical and Mechanical Properties of Sailcloth

geometry	flexibility
stretch resistance	porosity
tear resistance	density
strength	water absorption
ultraviolet light absorption	

parallel the lines of the corresponding fibers (Figure 3-10). Elongation in the fiber direction is a property of the fiber composition and, consequently, different fibers stretch to varying extents. The rank order of increasing stretch resistance (and cost) is cotton < nylon < Dacron < Kevlar. The last of these fabrics costs the most and stretches the least.

Crimping, which refers to the curved path followed by the fibers as they travel over and under one another, also contributes to stretchiness (Figure 3-11). Running the crimp only in one direction minimizes crimping stretch. Laminating reduces both crimping and bias stretch.

Density

Nylon and Dacron cloths suitable for skate sails respectively weigh 1.5 to 3, and 1.5 to 7.5, ounces per square yard (1,296 square inches). These densities can contribute a little or a lot to the weight of a

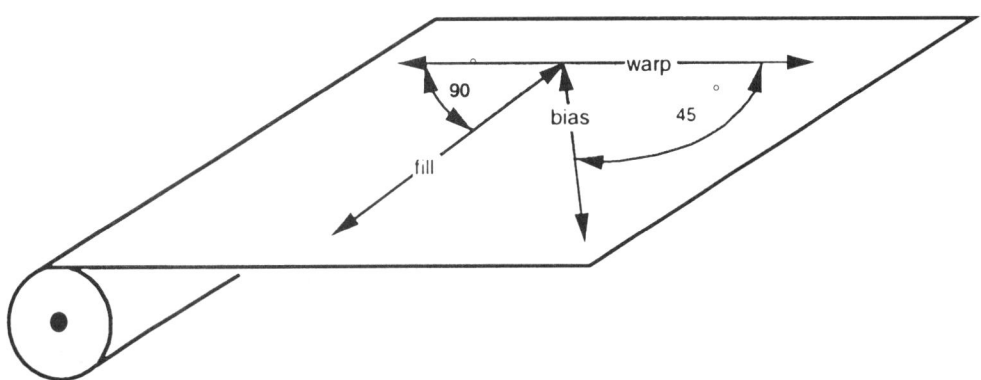

Figure 3-10: Orientation of Warp and Fill Fibers

††For an opposing view, see *Aero-Hydrodynamics of Sailing* by C. A. Marchaj (International Marine Publishing Co., Camden, Maine, 1988; ISBN 0-87742-993-6), pp. 501-503.

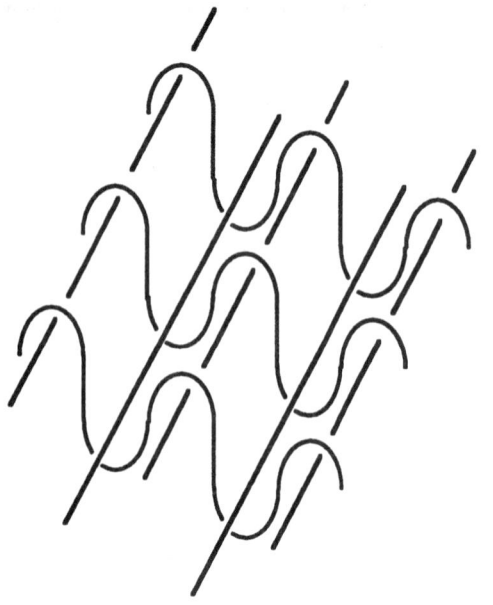

Figure 3-11: Highly Oriented Plain Weave, with Crimping in One Direction

skate sail, which varies with spar and bow materials and with sail area. Pieces of sailcloth respectively occupying 25 and 95 square feet and having densities of 1.5 and 7.5 ounces per square yard would weigh 0.3 and 5 pounds.

The density of sailcloth partly determines sailcloth strength. Each fabric must attain a certain minimum density to prevent the fibers from breaking and the cloth from losing elasticity. Loss of elasticity, a phenomenon known as yielding, limits the useful sail lifetime, especially in racing yachts. The tear resistance of sailcloth also limits the minimum useful cloth density.

Densities exceeding the minimum influence the ease and speed with which sailors handle sails. Heavy sails also increase the weight aloft and tend to make a boat heel. In light airs, dense sailcloth makes boat sails sag under their own weight, which degrades their aerodynamic shapes. Handling characteristics and other effects of density, however, are more influential in boat sails than skate sails.

Water Absorption

Cotton and nylon sailcloths absorb water, with nylon suffering a reversible 3% increase of stretchiness. Also, water absorption decreases the strength of nylon fibers by 15%. Finishing nylon sailcloth with a water repellent, however, minimizes the loss of stretch resistance. Untreated nylon stretches when it becomes wet, so the sail-to-mast fastenings should be lashings because they allow cross-tightening.

Porosity

Skate sailors are sometimes overly concerned with porosity, which refers to the tendency of sailcloth to leak air from the high-pressure to the low-pressure side. In most sailcloths, however, porosity lacks importance, except perhaps in the lightest nylon, which weighs 1.5 ounces per square yard. This cloth ordinarily forms spinnakers and occasionally skate sails. Tight weaving of other modern cloths and resin coating of nylon reduce porosity and make leakage negligible.

Light Absorption

Ultraviolet radiation from the sun degrades some synthetic materials, but hardly affects skate sailing. Light degradation of sailcloth is significant only near the equator, where favorable weather affords much sailing but not on ice skates.

Dacron sailcloth shows a self-protecting effect. Ultraviolet light absorption superficially degrades Dacron, but the products of the accompanying photochemical reaction coat the cloth surface to prevent light from reaching the remaining Dacron and stop further decay.

Buying Sailcloth

Sailcloth is specified by weight, for which the unit is usually ounces per yard of length.* To purchase a suitable sailcloth, the buyer must know the differences between

American and British fabric weights. American fabric is based on a 28.5-inch width per yard, while British fabric is based on a 36-inch width. This is so because American sailcloth fabrics are approximately 20% heavier. For example, a 2.4-ounce American cloth is equivalent to a 3.0-ounce British cloth. Either is right for a 54-square foot skate sail, but a larger one should use 3.2-ounce (American) or 4.0-ounce (British) sailcloth.

SPARS

The spars of a Hopatcong sail comprise the mast and boom, which are 1¼ to 2 inches in diameter. If the mast diameter greatly exceeds this range, then an adult will experience difficulty getting the needed firm grip on the mast. Both spars usually have a round cross section. It allows the boom to slide easily over the sailor's shoulder, and makes steering easy. The purposes of the mast comprise steering, coming about, jibing, placing the sail in stays, and fencing. A round or oval cross section makes the mast comfortable to grip, which is especially desirable in a strong wind when the sailor pulls hard on the mast. The boom is longer than mast by six to 12 inches, to accommodate a cleat or a stretching harness (read on).

The mast and boom, which are fixed together where they cross, help to hold and flatten the sail by providing a rigid framework on which the sail can be tightly stretched. Both spars should be strong enough not to break. Nor should they bend, for a sail with bending spars is impossible to control. They should also be cut to the proper length lest an overlong mast strike ice and trip the sailor. Cutting the spars to length is usually carried out only after a successful first trial of a newly made sail.

The job should be done only when the finished sail can be compared to the uncut spars, lest the sailmaker cut them short.

The practical requirements of skate sail spars are a round cross section, strength, inflexibility, low cost, and availability. Also, the material that goes into them should be easily and quickly worked with common hand tools, or with simple power tools.

Padding the Boom

A day's sailing in a strong wind sometimes causes morning-after soreness from the boom pressing on the sailor's shoulders. Consequently, some skate sailors pad their booms for comfort. Polyurethane foam sold in sheets makes effective padding. Furnished by camping goods stores, these sheets ordinarily find use on rough ground beneath sleeping bags. Foam sheeting a quarter- to three-eighths-inch thick is suitable, depending on compressibility. If you do cushion your boom, take care not to make the pad more than an inch or two thick. A thick pad raises the boom farther from the ice, and so it also raises the sail center of effort. Raising this center too far will make controlling the sail difficult.

To prepare a boom cushion, cut the foam into long strips about 2 inches wide. Wrap the strips around the boom in a spiral, letting the end of one strip abut the beginning of the next. A small piece of electrical tape holds each strip temporarily in place. Add strips until they form a cushion that is about 18 inches long and one inch thick above and below the boom itself. When you have added enough strips, trim them with a utility knife and cover their surface with overlapping lengths of black electrical tape or brightly colored, plastic adhesive tape. Either kind of tape makes a durable covering that will slide easily over your shoulder as you shift the boom to steer. A

* Sailcloth density is sometimes expressed with a special phrase, ounces per sailmakers yard. The phrase refers to a piece of cloth measuring 28.5 by 36 inches.

cushion with two inches of padding between shoulder and boom will not adversely affect the maneuverability of a 65-square-foot sail.

Traditional Wooden Spars

Fir

The most popular spar material is fir. It is inexpensive, sufficiently strong, and readily available from lumber yards as round closet poles 12 feet long and $1^1/_4$ to $1^3/_8$ inches in diameter. This diameter suffices to prevent breaking or bending unless the sail is exceptionally large or the wind uncommonly strong. As the result, fir spars last for decades.

Other Woods

Several other woods can be used to make the mast and boom. They are Sitka spruce, traditionally used for spars in softwater sailing craft, as well as ash, elm, hickory, maple, and white oak. Lumber yards sell these woods as planks, unlike fir that is available as round poles. The milling charges for turning planks into poles with round cross sections add substantially to the cost of spars. The charges can exceed the cost of the wood needed for a single set of spars.

Beware of Bamboo

Bamboo spars are too flexible for large, modern sails. Often found in small 19th century sails, nowadays they see little use. First-time skate sail builders, who show a faultless tendency to re-invent the use of unsuitable bamboo, should remark this point. Otherwise, a first voyage with a sail bearing bamboo spars may bring disappointment rather than exhilaration.

Modern Spar Materials

Aluminum

Untempered aluminum tubing makes suitable spars. Such tubing has an outside diameter of $1^1/_2$ to 2 inches and a wall thickness of 0.03 inches. The greater diameter serves sails larger than about 60 square feet. Tempered aluminum is stronger

but more expensive, especially when the sailmaker needs only enough for one sail.

Some skate sailors prefer aluminum spars because the metal tubing weighs less than a wooden rod of the same length and diameter. Other sailors prefer the more solid feel of the wood, especially in the shouldered boom. Yet other differences lie in the much greater heat conductivity and slipperiness of the metal. An aluminum mast can feel uncomfortably if not painfully cold, even through two pairs of gloves or mittens. Such a mast, if it is large (about two inches) in diameter, can be impossible to grip firmly with unfaced woolen gloves. Gripping firmly may require gloves or mittens made from rubber, or faced with it on the palms and fingers.

Insulating an aluminum mast makes it comfortable as well as easy to hold. The adhesive-backed tape used on racing bicycle handlebars is a good choice of insulation. A layer of water-pipe tape beneath a layer of electrical tape also insulates the mast, but bicycle tape is preferable for its greater durability and its non-slip surface.

Plastics

Fiberglass and carbon-fiber tubing offer other possibilities for spars, if the tubing is purchased in quantity. Both are commercially available. Fiberglass tubing composes the masts of windsurfers, while carbon-fiber tubing forms the frames of certain high-technology racing bicycles. Like the cost of tempered aluminum tubing, however, the costs of fiberglass and carbon-fiber tubing are high enough to be prohibitive for a single sail. Neither kind of tubing is readily available, for example in hardware, home-center, or plumbing stores.

JIB AND TAIL BOWS

Jib and tail bows tighten the skate sail and force the forward and aft parts to lie flat. A flat sail reduces luffing and is more

Table 3-3: Bow Materials

Traditional

rattan	white oak
hickory	ash
lemonwood	maple
	elm

Modern

fiberglass
  rod
    rod and tubing
carbon-fiber
    tubing combined with
      fiberglass rod

controllable than a luffing one. Luffing was a pre-World War I problem that the invention of these bows solved, so they represent the greatest advantage of the Hopatcong sail design. The design calls for the bows to curve like circle arcs, which implies that the bows must taper.

Jib and tail bows are made from flexible or permanently curved materials. Flexible bows curve when the sail stretches during rigging, and they straighten when it relaxes during disassembly. Comparatively easy to make or buy, flexible bows are more common than permanently curved bows. However, laminating and shaping strips of ash yields strong, rigid jib and tail bows bearing permanent curves. Such bows are comparatively heavy, and making them requires woodworking skills; they are not items of commerce.

In the Hopatcong design, the ends of the tail bow project an inch beyond the tensioned sail on either side. The two projections ensure that the more durable bow rather than the abradable sailcloth contacts the ice if the sail drags. To avoid damaging the tail bow, sailors sometimes cover its ends with cane or crutch tips made from rubber. The tips prevent splintering.

The jib bow should not project beyond the pocket of the stretched sail. If the jib drags, then the stout ends of the mast, but not the fragile sailcloth, strike the ice. The jib bow should fall about two inches short of the pocket ends when the sail is stretched.

Traditional Wooden Bows

Rattan Bows

Materials for flexible jib and tail bows include the traditional rattan, as well as other woods (Table 3-3). The source of rattan is the springy stem of an East Indian plant imported for use in furniture. Rattan is preferable to hickory, but a ⅝-inch-thick piece of the latter is useful if it is very pliable. Straight and fairly green stock is a good choice, but kiln-dried lumber is not. Rattan jib and tail bows last for decades.

Made with a one-inch diameter, a rattan jib bow tapers at either end. A bow having a 1¼-inch diameter is recommended. It narrows along an 18-inch distance and ends in a ¾-inch diameter. A tail bow also tapers, reaching half an inch at its ends. If rattan forms the tail bow, a piece with a one inch diameter is serviceable.

Tapered Wooden Bows

Tapering ensures that the ends of the bow curve more than the midsection when the sail is stretched. The bow then adopts the circular curve of the jib or tail. Without tapering, the bow tends to form a parabola.

One procedure for tapering a wooden bow requires you to use a plane and some talcum or chalk powder. For a distance of a few inches, powder the end of the bow where its diameter is to be reduced the most. Then shave that end with the plane until you have removed all the powder. Beginning at the same point, powder the end again, but this time for a distance twice as long. Again shave off the powder with the plane. Repeat the shaving and powdering, each time over a greater length, until the bow has the desired taper.

Bows from Synthetic Materials

Fiberglass

Fiberglass bows can be made from rod, or from a short piece of rod and two long ones of tubing. Plastics houses, fishing goods stores, and certain suppliers of chemical laboratory equipment provide fiberglass rod in varying lengths and diameters. Chemists use frameworks of fiberglass rod to hold laboratory glassware and other equipment.

For a solid fiberglass jib bow, a $^5/_8$-inch diameter is suitable. This material has proved itself in skate sails, some of which have seen 20 seasons sailing. Even the inexpensive fiberglass bow from a child's bow-and-arrow set makes a durable tail bow.

Fiberglass tubing, adapted from inexpensive cross-country ski poles and combined with fiberglass rod, makes a serviceable, three-section jib bow. Such bows need no tapering because the tubing flexes more than the rod that forms the mid-section. The tubing has approximate outside and inside diameters of $^9/_{16}$ and $^{15}/_{32}$ of an inch, respectively.

Where the jib bow meets the boom, the bow carries an insert of fiberglass rod for strength. Glue holds the insert in place, so that the tail forms a single piece. Without the insert, a bow made only from tubing will snap in a high wind. Similarly, fiberglass tubing from ski poles is not suitable for a tail bow without such an insert. The tubing alone is not strong enough for a tail bow, which can break at its midpoint during sail assembly.

Carbon-fiber

Carbon-fiber tubing, also combined with a short piece of fiberglass rod, serves as a jib bow. Sporting goods stores sell this tubing as tapered, telescoping smelt poles. The fishing poles are affordable, flexible, strong, and durable. Sawing, filing, and measuring are the only skills needed to make carbon-fiber bows from smelt poles. A disadvantage of a jib bow made from a carbon-fiber smelt pole is its fragility, and the larger ends of the bow can splinter after several season's use.

Buy two complete smelt poles to make one jib bow, but use only the thinnest section from each pole. The thickest section flexes too little to be useful. At the smaller end, the thinnest section has an outside diameter of three eighths of an inch; the outside diameter at the larger end spans half an inch. A piece of half-inch fiberglass rod joins the jib bow halves, as described in the section on Boom-Bows and Boom Mast Fastenings.

PVC

Several sailors have used PVC (polyvinyl chloride) tubing to make jib bows, with varying success. Sold in plumbing supply houses, the heavier of two grades of PVC tubing does not crack in the cold, but does form bows with parabolic rather than circular arcs. This useful, heavy grade of PVC tubing bears identifying codes, namely PVC 1120 and ASTM-D1785. It has a $^3/_4$-inch inside diameter and a $1 ^1/_{16}$-inch outside diameter, and forms one-piece bows. Bows made from the lighter PVC tubing reportedly crack in cold weather.

BOOM-BOW AND BOOM-MAST FASTENINGS

Fastening the Boom to the Jib Bow

In Hopatcong sails, the forward end of the boom must be fastened to the jib bow, which helps transmit physical tension throughout the sailcloth. This tension, a result of stretching the sail with the outhaul lanyard, flattens the cloth and creates the airfoil shape needed for sailing. Boom-to-bow fastenings include a traditional hole-and-pin device and a recently invented S-hook assembly. With modification, each of these mechanisms can be used on a tubular or rod-like boom.

Hole-and-Pin Devices

Traditionally, a simple hole-and-pin device connects the bow either to a wooden plug fitting into an aluminum boom, or to a wooden boom (Figure 3-12). A piece of wood makes the pin. Alternatively, the sailmaker can drive a two-inch, number 10 brass or galvanized wood screw into the plug or boom end, and cut off the slotted head of the screw. The resulting pin fits into a hole drilled into a tubular brass coupling, which connects the jib bow segments.

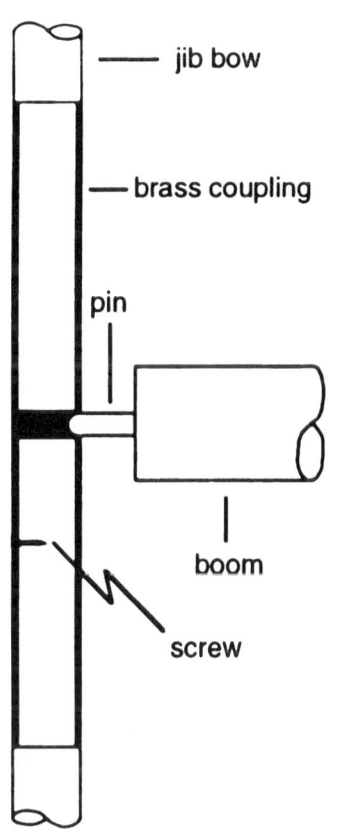

Figure 3-12: Hole-and-Pin Device Linking Jib Bow to Boom

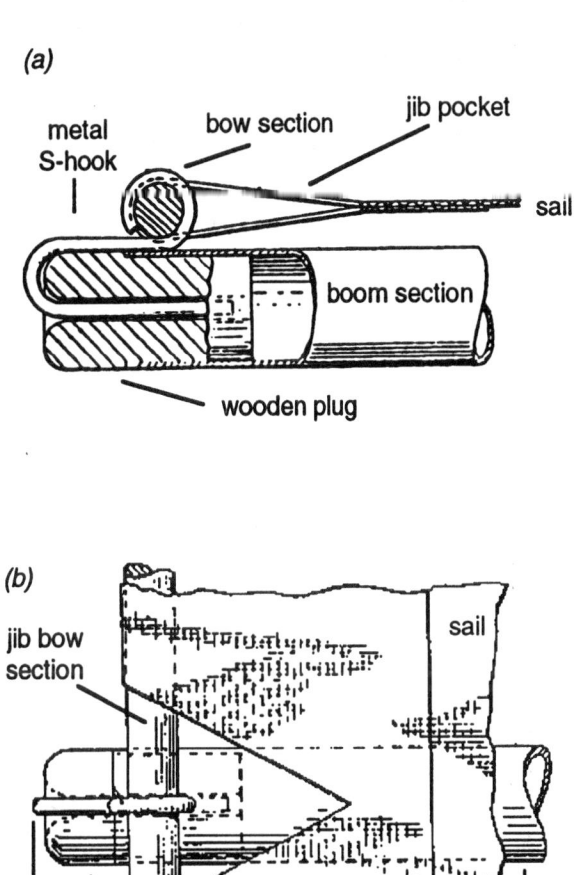

Figure 3-13: S-Hook Assembly: (a) Side View, and (b) Top View

The hole-and-pin assembly of Figure 3-12 will serve a boom made of aluminum tubing. In this case, the sailmaker prepares a round wooden plug that fits inside the tubing. The plug should be six to seven inches long, and its forward end should be grooved to accept the bow. (However, several seasons sailing suggests that the traditional pin is unnecessary. Held in place by sail tension, the boom did not slide along a jib bow lacking the pin. As a result, the absence of a pin did not hamper sail handling, but facilitated sail rigging.)

S-Hook Assembly

Another device that fixes the jib bow to the boom comprises a doubly curved piece of heavy-gauge wire and a wooden plug (Figure 3-13). The wire resembles a distorted letter S. The smaller curve of the wire crimps tightly around the bow; and the end of the larger curve fits into a conical hole drilled into the wooden plug. The plug lies inside the forward end of an aluminum boom, and a screw fastens the plug to the boom. Boring a conical hole in the end of a wooden boom would adapt the boom to use with an S-hook assembly. Individual examples of these devices must be homemade.

Joining Jib Bow Sections

The jib bow of a 60-square-foot Hopatcong skate sail spans 119 inches when the sail is taut. To transport such a long jib bow inside an automobile would be awkward if it were a single piece. Hence, two or three sections joined by couplings usually make up such a bow. Tubular metal couplings link the bow sections that are made from wood or solid fiberglass rod (Figure 3-12). Ferrules sold by fishing goods stores and meant to link sections of fishing poles can be useful for this purpose. Conversely, rod-shaped couplings join sections made from tubing (Figure 3-14).

Tubular Couplings

If a traditional wood like rattan forms the jib bow, then 18-gauge aluminum tubing makes a suitable coupling (Figure 3-12). The coupling joins the inner ends of a two-piece bow. A screw fastens a nine-inch-long piece of tubing to one bow section. With squared ends, the wooden sections fit snugly inside the tube. Square brass tubing will serve

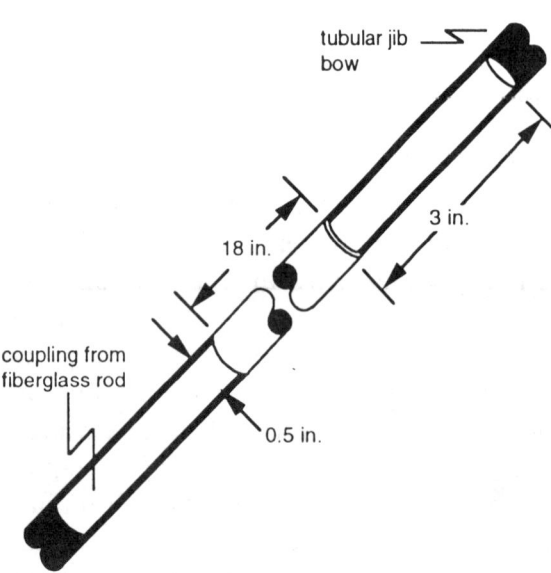

Figure 3-14: Tubular Sections of Jib Bow Coupled by a Rod

instead of aluminum for the bow coupling. The sides of such brass tubing are seven-eighths-inch wide and the tubing wall is 0.04-inch thick.

Rod-Shaped Couplings

To join the sections of a bow made from tubular carbon-fiber smelt poles, cut the sections to length and shape the ends of a piece of fiberglass rod to fit. The finished rod should lie snugly inside the larger ends of the tubes (Figure 3-14). A 24-inch-long piece of fiberglass rod having a half-inch diameter is suitable. The shaped sections of the rod are about three inches long. The finished rod need not be fastened to the tubing, but will be held in place by sail tension.

Coupling Spar Sections

In a skate sail as small as 55 square feet, each spar spans nine feet. Like a jib bow at just under 10 feet, such long spars are cumbersome to transport and handle inside an automobile. As a result, many sail makers divide each spar into two or three sections of equal lengths, and assemble the sections with couplings. Concentric lengths of aluminum tubing make durable couplings for tubular aluminum spars (Figure 3-15), as do the wooden plugs discussed below. Sleeves made from other metals and from plastics are also useful.

Metal Sleeves

Metal sleeves, usually made from brass or aluminum tubing with a wall thickness of 0.03 inch, join wooden spar sections (Figure 3-16). The sleeves run six to eight inches and their outside diameter equals the spar thickness so the assembled boom slides smoothly over your shoulder despite the coupling. Where each boom section fits into the sleeve, its diameter will have to be reduced. A screw fastens the coupling to one end of the wooden sections. Beveling the ends that fit into the sleeves prevents the

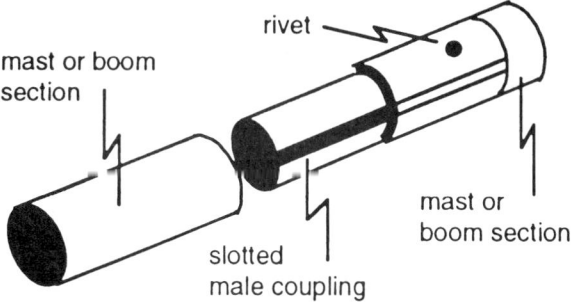

Figure 3-15: Split Aluminum Sleeve Coupling Mast and Boom Sections

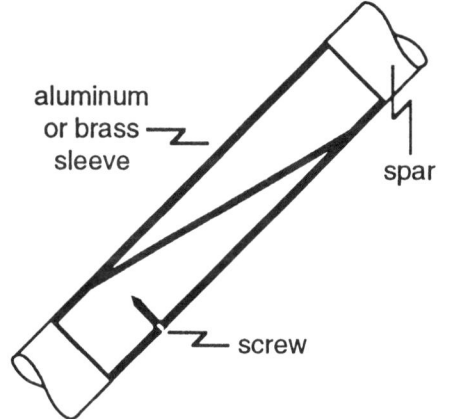

Figure 3-16: Metal Sleeve Coupling Beveled Spar Sections

ends from turning and gives the assembled spar a satisfyingly solid feel.

Wooden Plugs

An alternative method for joining sections of aluminum tubing uses round wooden plugs that fit inside the tubing. Each plug is about seven inches long, and one or two sheet-metal screws fasten one end of each plug to the tubing. The completed assembly resembles that used to join bow sections (Figure 3-14).

Fastening the Mast to the Boom

The mast and boom of a properly shaped, steerable skate sail must be fixed tightly to one another, and there are two popular methods for doing so. The older method ties the two spars together with a crisscrossed lashing, and the newer one joins the spars with a pair of interlocked hose clamps.

Lashing

Nylon line, a skate lace, a leather thong, or a one-inch-wide strip of rubber lashes the mast and boom together. Even bungee cords will work. In any case, the lash must be tight to avoid wobbling of the spars, which makes steering unresponsive. Wrapping adhesive tape around the mast and boom gives a good surface for the lashing. In cold weather, the lashing must be kept dry lest water freeze within it; it will have to be tightened if it becomes wet and stretches.

Hose Clamps

An ordinary lashing may loosen if it becomes wet, necessitating a halt to undo and tighten it. Wet or icy lashings are difficult as well as uncomfortable to work with, so several sailors prefer to fix the mast to the boom with hose clamps.

Two inexpensive, stainless-steel hose clamps will hold the mast firmly to the boom. The clamps interlock like the links in a chain. One clamp surrounds the mast and the other encircles the boom. In the final task needed to assemble a skate sail, a nut or screwdriver tightens the clamps. This is done last to avoid damaging aluminum spars. Either spar may crimp if the sail is stretched after the clamps are tightened.

Position the hose clamps properly each time you use them. The flat steel band, rather than the nut and bolt assembly, should lie against the sail. This arrangement prevents or minimizes abrasion of the cloth, which would benefit from reinforcement beneath the mast clamp.

Hose clamps tightened by hexagonal nuts fasten more securely than thumb screw clamps or lashings, which tend to loosen during use. Although nut-bearing clamps require the sailor to carry a tool, she can manipulate both the clamps and the nut-driver with gloved hands. Hardware and plumbing-supply stores provide thumb screw and nut-operated clamps.

Fastening the Boom to the Tail Bow

Skate sails always include a device to permit tightening the sail and lashing it to the tail bow. In Hopatcong sails (but not in the Swedish kite-shaped skate sails), these devices always lie on the aft end of the boom, requiring the boom to protrude behind the sail and exceed the sail length by six to 12 inches. Along this tailing boom segment runs an outhaul lanyard used to stretch the sail and to lash it to the boom.

Boom Cleats

Hardware stores sell inexpensive brass or galvanized iron cleats used for clothesline. They are suitable for tying the tail of a skate sail to its boom and require a light line, which can be $^1/_8$-inch nylon. A two- or $2^1/_2$-inch long cleat, screwed to the boom, works well. Stores specializing in boat or windsurfing equipment provide more expensive jamb cleats that do not require lashing. These cleats are also fixed with screws to the boom.

A simple wooden jamb cleat will also serve both aluminum and wooden booms. Figures 3-17a and -b illustrate the construction of this cleat as well as the method of using it, while Figure 3-18 gives its dimensions.

The jamb cleat is used with a belaying pin that serves dual purposes (Figures 3-17 and -18). Passing through the boom and lying forward of the cleat, the pin easily allows the sailor to lash the lanyard to the boom. However, the pin may already have served its other purpose. A seated sailor rigging her sail can set her feet on the belaying pin to give a good purchase and to free both hands, which can then be employed in stretching the sail. She can obtain a flatter sail and a firmer lashing than without the pin.

To adapt a tubular aluminum boom for a jamb cleat, the sailmaker prepares a wooden peg, one end of which fits into the tubing. The other end of the peg, or the tail end of a wooden boom, bears a $^1/_4$ by 1-inch jamb notch, which terminates in a hole (Figure 3-

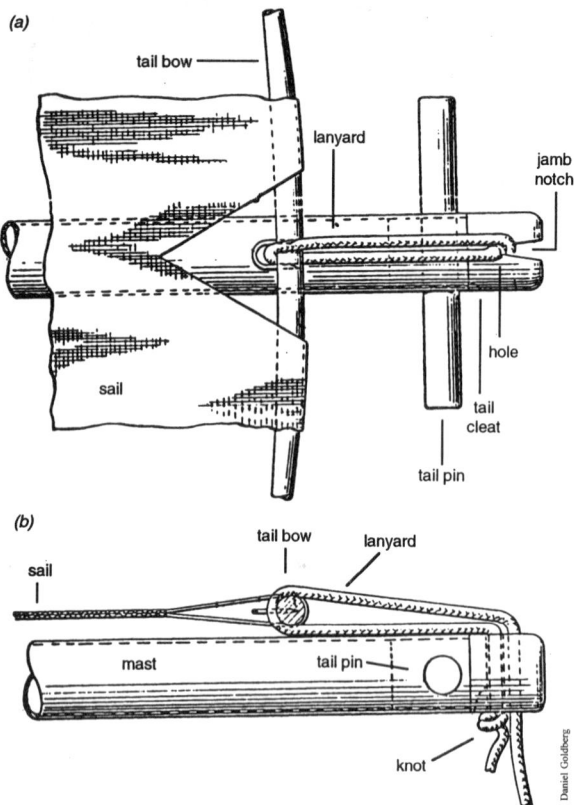

Figure 3-17: Boom Cleat at Tail: (a) Top View; (b) Side View

18, see also Figure 3-17). A glued belaying pin passes through a second, larger hole in the end. The belaying pin, made from a $5^1/_2$ by $^1/_2$-inch hardwood dowel, lies perpendicular to the notch.

The notch hole admits an $^1/_8$-inch nylon lanyard with a knot at one end. Larger than the hole, the knot keeps the lanyard in place. The lanyard runs from the hole to the tail bow, passes around it, and returns to the notch where jambing secures it. That provides a two-to-one mechanical advantage, when the sailor lashes the lanyard in a crisscross around the belaying pin.

Alternatively, the outhaul lanyard may pass twice around the tail bow and once around the belaying pin. Only then does the sailor jamb the lanyard into the notch and lash it to the boom. With this method, the tail bow and belaying pin act like pulleys, providing mechanical advantage in tightening the sail.

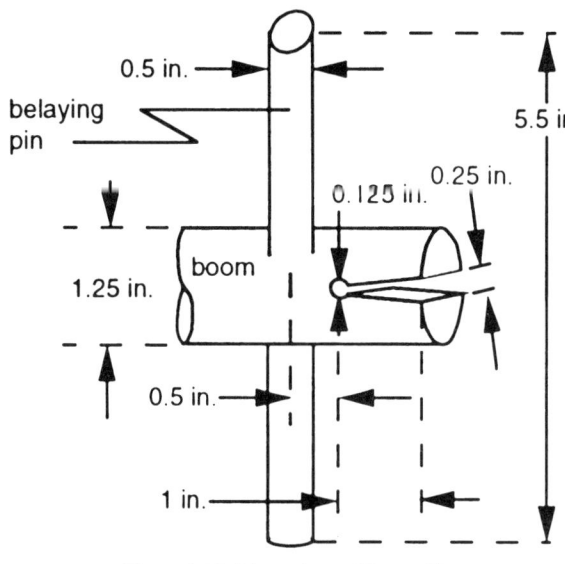

Figure 3-18: Dimensions of Boom Cleat

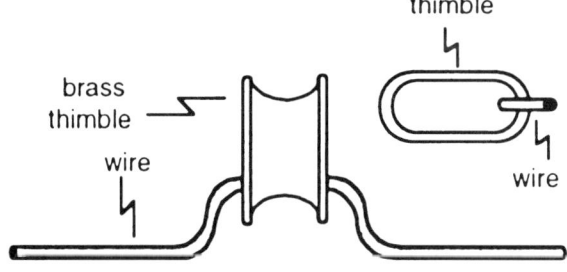

Figure 3-19: Wire and Thimble

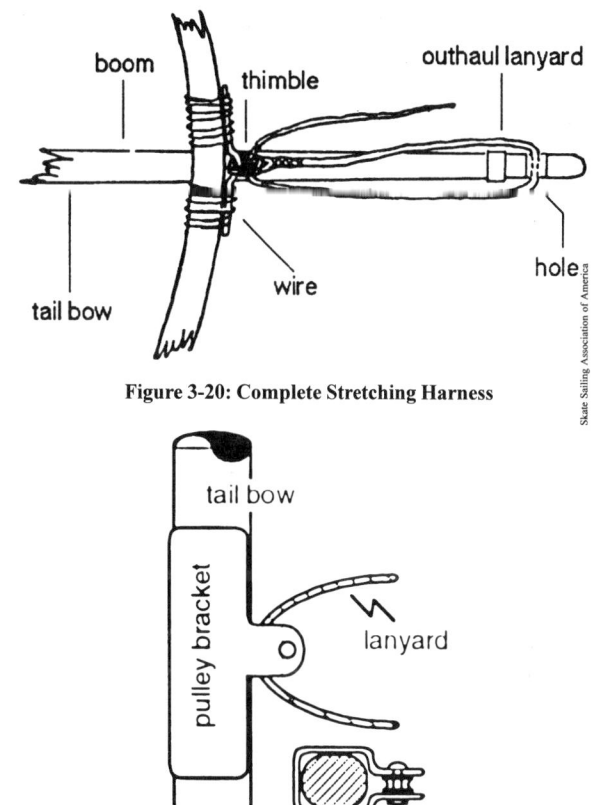

Figure 3-20: Complete Stretching Harness

Figure 3-21: Stretching Harness Made
from Pulley and Bracket

Stretching Harnesses

Dating from the 1930s, a method for making a stretching harness dispenses with the tail pin and jamb notch described above (Figures 3-17 and -18). This older method calls for a piece of heavy galvanized wire, a five-eighths-inch brass thimble, and a hole in the boom end (Figure 3-19). The wire has a U-shaped bend in its middle, and the hole admits the outhaul lanyard. The thimble passes around the heavy piece of wire, which lighter copper wire binds to the tail bow. One end of the lanyard surrounds the thimble; whipping secures the lanyard to it. The lanyard then runs to the hole, passes through it, and returns to the thimble. The lanyard passes through the thimble before being pulled tight and lashed securely; Figure 3-20 shows the complete stretching harness.

Another stretching harness makes use of a pulley, which a metal bracket holds to the tail bow (Figure 3-21). The bracket is made from 0.05-inch-thick steel.

SAIL GEOMETRY

Various plane-geometric features give a Hopatcong sail its characteristic overall shape, and determine its performance. These features comprise the shapes and sizes of the individual sail components, as well as their relative area proportions, fencing angle, and aspect ratio. The shapes of standard Hopatcong sails do not vary with their sizes, so it is possible to tabulate standard sail dimensions for a variety of sail areas. Table 3-4 presents these dimensions, but sailmakers should beware. Important factors other than sail area influence sail performance and will limit sail size. These

Table 3-4: Geometry of Several Hopatcong Skate Sails[a,b,c]

As	R_j	R_t	$2Z_j$	$2Z_t$	S_j	S_t	Y_j	Y_t	W	V_s	H	Q_{uf}
95	106.2	65.4	141.6	59.5	155	61.8	27	7.2	106.9	141.1	66.1	36.1
90	103.4	63.7	137.8	57.5	150.8	60.1	26.3	7	104.1	137.3	64.3	35.1
85	100.5	61.9	133.9	56.3	146.6	58.4	25.6	6.8	101.1	133.5	62.5	34.2
80	97.5	60	129.9	54.6	142.2	56.7	24.8	6.6	98.1	129.5	60.7	33.1
75	94.4	58.1	125.8	52.9	137.7	54.9	24	6.4	95	125.4	58.7	32.1
70	91.2	56.2	121.5	51.1	133	53	23.2	6.1	91.8	121.1	56.7	31
65	87.9	54.1	117.1	49.2	128.2	51.1	22.4	5.9	88.4	116.7	54.7	29.9
60	84.4	52	112.5	47.3	123.2	49.1	21.5	5.7	85	112.1	52.5	28.7
55	80.8	49.8	107.7	45.3	117.9	47	20.6	5.4	81.3	107.4	50.3	27.5
50	77.1	47.5	102.7	43.2	112.4	44.8	19.6	5.2	77.6	102.4	48	26.2
45	73.1	45	97.5	41	106.7	42.5	18.6	4.9	73.6	97.1	45.5	24.8
40	68.9	42.5	91.9	38.6	100.6	40.1	17.5	4.6	69.4	91.6	42.9	23.4
35	64.5	39.7	85.9	36.1	94.1	37.5	16.4	4.3	64.9	85.6	40.1	21.9
30	59.7	36.8	79.6	33.4	87.1	34.7	15.2	4	60.1	79.3	37.1	20.3
25	54.5	33.6	72.6	30.5	79.5	31.7	13.9	3.7	54.8	72.4	33.9	18.5

[a] Table 3-5 and Fig. 3-22 respectively define the symbols and illustrate the corresponding dimensions. [b] Areas A_s are in square feet; other dimensions are in inches. [c] Angles c_j, c_t, and a (the fencing angle) equal 83.6, 54.1, and 21°, respectively.

limiting factors are also geometric features, namely the position of the sail center of effort, and the sail height.

Sail Shapes, Sizes, and Proportions

Jib and Tail

The jib and tail sectors represent circle sectors corresponding to an imaginary circle segment, which includes a characteristic angle c (Figure 3-22: in the figure, only the shaded areas represent sailcloth. The white triangles are imaginary but complete the drawings of circle segments.) A straight line called a chord and drawn between any two points on the circumference of a circle forms a sector, which is a two-sided figure including the smaller of the two arcs defined by the points. The two chords $2Z_j$ and $2Z_t$ associated with the jib and tail represent the heights of these sail components. Connecting the two points on the circumference to the circle origin by straight lines completes a segment. The two straight lines defining the segment are circle radii R,

and they include the sector angle c between them. This angle adopts values that characterize the jib and tail components of the sail, and does not change as the total sail area increases or decreases. The area changes only in response to changes in radii. For a Hopatcong sail as modified by Jefferson, the jib angle c_j spans 83.6° and the tail angle c_t equals 54.1°.*

The lengths of the circle radii R_j and R_t, and the sizes of the sector angles c_j and c_t, establish the jib and tail areas A_j and A_t, respectively. The relation between jib or tail area, radius length, and angle size for a circle sector can be expressed as trigonometric formulas, in which the numerical factors reflect the constant values of the jib and tail angles:

$$A_j = 0.2326\ R_j^2$$
$$A_t = 0.0671\ R_t^2$$

The relation between area and radius is not a simple linear one because it contains a squared factor. In fact, a 10% increase in the jib radius would increase the jib and total

---

* No magic attends the numerical values of these angles, although they run to one decimal place. Jefferson chose the angles to make whole numbers of certain linear dimensions characterizing the four sails he described.

sail area by about 20% each. The same rise in radius would cause an equal percentage increase in the jib half-height Z_j.

The jib occupies 19% of the total sail area, and the tail area amounts to 2%. These proportions, derived from sail dimensions appearing in Jefferson's *Skate Sailing*, are standard and do not vary with changes in total sail area. Relative areas of sail components described in "Practical Suggestions for Making and Using Skate Sails", a publication of the Skate Sailing Association of America, differ only slightly. There the proportions of jib areas range from 16 to 21 percent.

Mainsail

In a Hopatcong sail, the mainsail is a parallel trapezium, a four-sided figure made from straight lines only. Two of its sides are parallel to one another but unequal in length, while its other two sides span equal distances but converge. As a parallel trapezium, the mainsail is symmetrical and so pairs of its interior angles have equal sizes. The pair of larger angles lies at the intersection of the mainsail with the tail, and each angle there has a value of 111°. The angles of the smaller pair have values of 69° and lie at the intersection of the mainsail with the jib. The longer and shorter of the two parallel sides respectively coincide with the jib and tail heights $2 Z_j$ and $2 Z_t$.

With the help of plane geometry, it is possible to derive a formula giving the area A_m of the mainsail in terms of its parallel sides and length W (Figure 3-22):

$$A_m = W (Z_j + Z_t)$$

This is a simple linear equation in which the mainsail area is directly proportional to the length W and to the sum of Z_j and Z_t.

The mainsail, which is almost four times larger than the jib, occupies 79% of the total sail area. This proportion, like the corresponding one in the jib, is constant and independent of sail size, at least in standard designs.

Skate Sail Areas

The total area A_s of a standard Hopatcong sail can be calculated from a formula representing a sum of terms, each one giving the area of one sail component.

$$A_s = 0.2326 R_j^2 + 0.0671 R_t^2 + W (Z_j + Z_t)$$

From the left, the first term in the above equation represents the jib area, the second the tail area, the third term the mainsail area. Values for R_j, R_t, W, Z_j, and Z_t appear in Table 3-4. This equation gives sail areas in square inches, if inches are the units for the other quantities. It permits comparing sizes of existing sails. For the equation to be useful, however, such sails must have jibs and tails that are circle segments. Also, they must adopt the standard values for the jib, tail, and fencing angles (Table 3-4). This last angle is discussed in a following section called Fencing Angle.

Standard Sail Dimensions

This book defines a standard Hopatcong sail as one that adopts values of angles c_j, c_t, and a respectively as 83.6, 54.1, and 21.0°; and that has proportions of jib and tail areas to total sail area of 19 and 2%, respectively. These specifications make it possible to compute and compare various dimensions in sails having the same shapes but different areas. For sailmakers' convenience, numerical values of 13 standard sail dimensions appear in Table 3-4. They come from the 13 sail equations presented in Chapter Seven. Included are 15 sail sizes, ranging from 95 to 25 square feet, and differing by 5-square-foot increments. The last two columns in the table give values of two variables discussed in subsequent sections entitled Distance from the Spar Crossing to the Sail Edge (H) and Center of Effort (Q_{uf}). Symbols used in Table 3-4 are defined in Table 3-5 and illustrated in Figure 3-22. To appreciate the tabulated sail sizes, note that the unfenced height $2 Z_j$ nearly

Table 3-5: Key to Symbols

area

A_s total sail area

angles

c   jib angle

c_t tail angle

a   fencing angle

lengths

R_j jib radius

R_t tail radius

S_j jib arc length

S_t tail arc length

Z_j jib half-height

Z_t tail half-height

Y_j greatest extent of jib bowing

Y_t greatest extent of tail bowing

X_j distance from jib circle center to mast

X_t distance from tail circle center to mast

W   mainsail length

V   overall sail length

H   perpendicular distance from lower edge of fenced sail to mast-boom intersection

Q_{uf} distance from center of effort to mast of unfenced sail

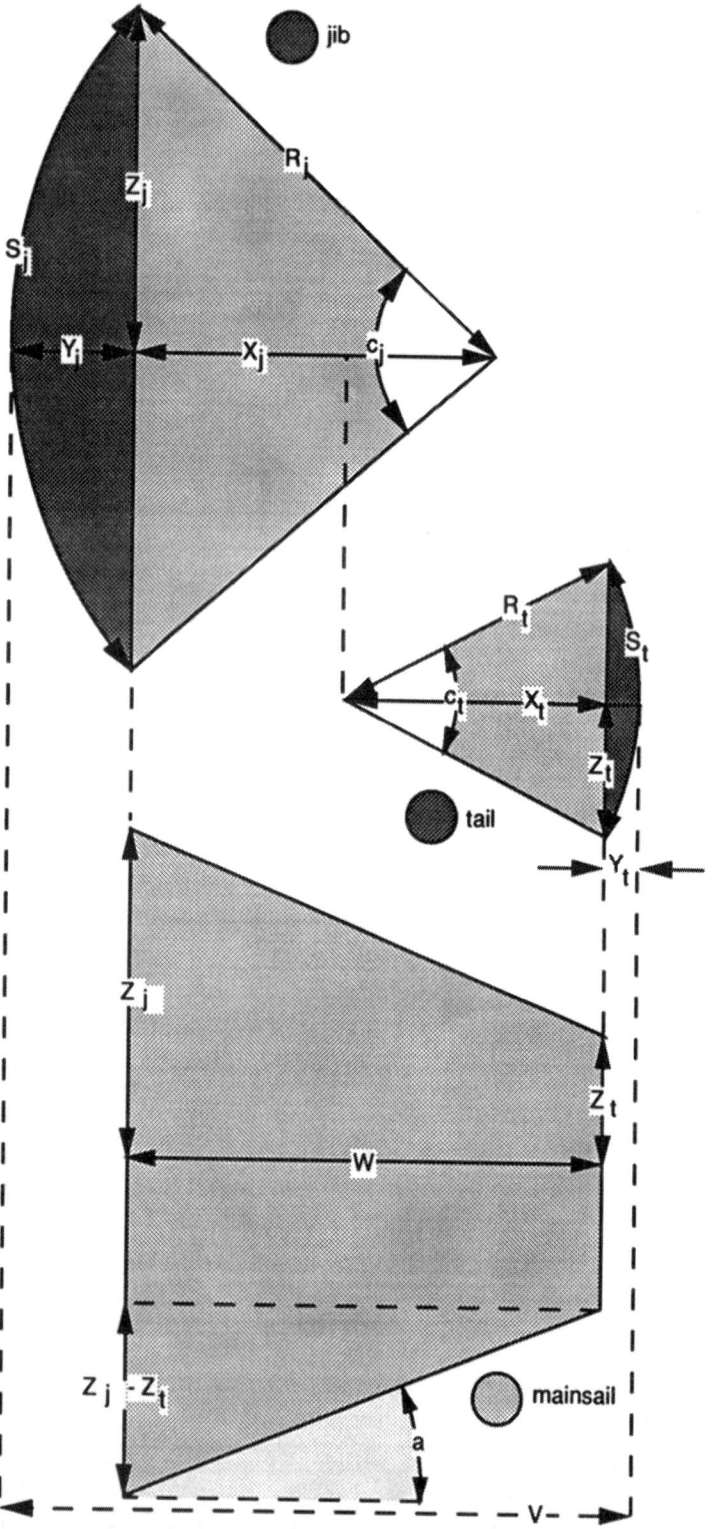

Figure 3-22: Geometry of a Standard Hopatcong Skate Sail

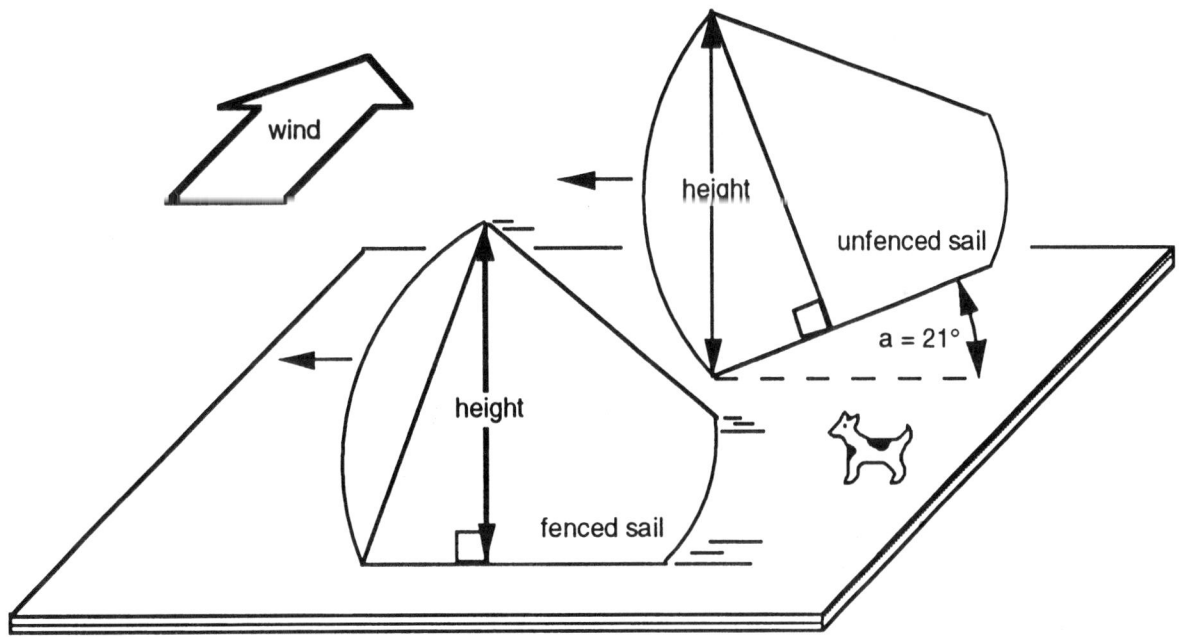

Figure 3-23: Fencing Angle and Heights of Hopatcong Sails

equals the overall length V.

A 95-square-foot Hopatcong sail, which would be the largest such sail ever known, would have the same area as the largest Dragon sail permitted in races sponsored by the Swedish Ice Sailing Association. The center of effort of such a Hopatcong sail would lie 36 inches aft of the mast-boom crossing. Steering the craft would require a tall sailor with a long reach. Held upright, a 95-square-foot Hopatcong sail would reach nearly 12 feet high, and would require the sailor's shoulder to be elevated in order to carry the boom. Unless the sailor's height were about 6-foot-6, this would in turn call for high skates, thick boom padding (not recommended), a double boom, or some other (unknown) device. Avoiding all these devices would necessitate redesigning the Hopatcong sail, probably by increasing the proportion of the jib area to the total sail area. A change in fencing angle might also be helpful.

North American racers usually choose smaller sails ranging from 55 to 70 square feet. They do not require the high skates

favored by Swedish skate sailors, nor do they require extraordinarily tall, long-armed sailors. The smallest sails included in the table are suitable for adults in strong winds, or for children.

Additional Factors Governing Performance

Fencing Angle

With a skate sail mast held vertically, the sail edge and an ice sheet form an angle known as the fencing angle (Figure 3-23). In a Hopatcong sail this angle takes on a value of 21°, which characterizes the design but does not vary with sail area. A skate sail is fenced when its position meets several conditions. Its boom must rest upon the sailor's shoulder, and its lower edge must lie parallel and close to the ice. Merely rotating the mast 21° from the vertical makes the sail edge parallel to the ice. However, for the edge to lie within an inch or two of the ice requires the largest sail that a given sailor's height and reach will allow her to handle. Other factors equal, sailing with a fenced sail increases speed compared to the velocity attained with an unfenced sail, because of an aerodynamic phenomenon

†Other, related definitions appear in Marchaj's book *Aero-Hydrodynamics of Sailing.*

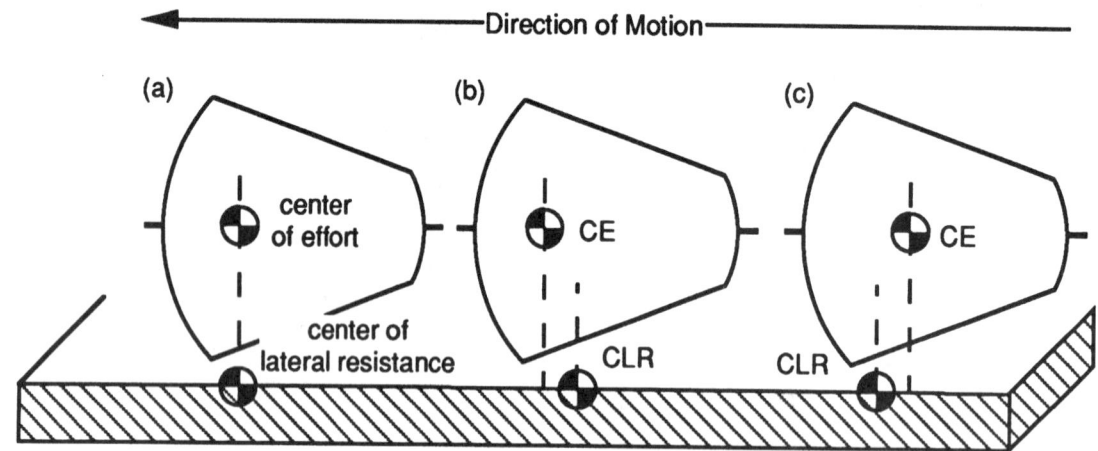

Figure 3-24: Helm Forces: (a) A Neutral Helm and a Straight Course; (b) A Lee Helm and a Downwind Turn; (c) A Weather Helm and an Upwind Turn

that Chapters Four and Five discuss and that sailors carrying the largest sails can exploit.

Aspect Ratios

Geometric aspect ratios compare some measure of height to area. In sails, this measure is often the square of the height divided by the area.† In an unfenced, 54-square-foot Hopatcong sail, which is 9 feet tall, the geometric aspect ratio equals 1.5 (Figure 3-23, background). In a fenced sail, this ratio drops to 1.3. The effective sail height decreases due to rotation through the fencing angle (Figure 3-23, foreground). For a given area, the higher the sail stands, the greater the aspect ratio. A higher ratio makes the sail a more efficient airfoil. Consequently, aspect ratios are important in all kinds of sailing.

Factors Limiting Sail Areas

Center of Effort

Like any other physical object, a skate sail has a center of effort (Figure 3-24). This one point on which all relevant aerodynamic forces act is similar to the center of gravity of a see-saw. Knowing the center-of-effort position is crucial to designing a sail. Misplacing it will make the sail difficult to steer, because the course taken by a skate sail depends partly on the center-of-effort

position. The sail turns downwind as the center moves forward relative to the sailor, when the sail develops a lee helm. The sail turns upwind when the helm becomes a weather one and the center moves aft. Moving the sail aft or forward is the means of steering.

If an unfenced Hopatcong sail is planar and stationary†, its center of effort lies on the boom because of symmetry. Since the jib area is small compared with the total sail area, the center of effort always falls aft of the mast. Furthermore, the distance Q_{uf} from the mast to the center increases linearly with the length V of standard sails. In 35-, 55-, and 75-square-foot, unfenced Hopatcong skate sails, the centers of effort respectively lie 20.7, 25.9, and 30.3 inches aft of the masts (Table 3-4). Fencing a sail increases the horizontal distance of the center from the mast by a few inches. The relation between sail length (or area) and center-of-effort position may cause large unmodified Hopatcong sails to be unmanageable because their centers are too far from the mast-boom crossing. Such sails would place the center of effort well aft of the center of lateral resistance, and might have a severe weather helm.

---

†In sail design, the center of effort of a stationary sail is used as a first approximation to the center of a moving one. Calculating the dynamic center-of-effort position for a moving skate sail distorted by the wind and the sailor's body falls outside the scope of this book.

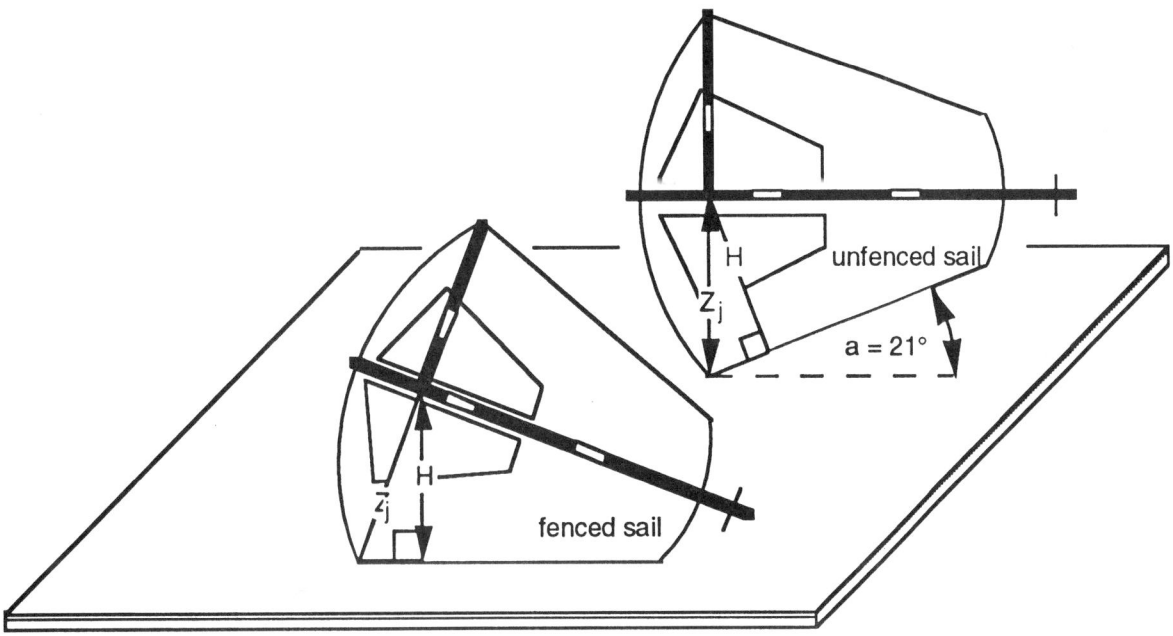

Figure 3-25: Distances Zj (background) and H (foreground) from Mast-Boom Crossing to Lower Sail Edge

Distance from the Spar Crossing to the Sail Edge

In the largest sail that a sailor can handle, the lower edge of the fenced sail should ride close to the ice. As a result, the perpendicular distance (H) from the mast-boom crossing to this edge is important (Figure 3-25, foreground). The H-distance determines the size of the tallest fenced sail that a sailor of a given height can use, since a moving sailor bends her knees for stability, which reduces the distance between her shouldered boom and her blade edges. Effectively, this reduces her height, which spans the H-distance. With decreased height, the mast will strike ice if the intersection-to-edge distance H is too great. Striking ice can splinter the end of a wooden mast or topple the sailor.

Merely knowing that the mast of a large, unfenced but shouldered sail does not strike ice does not suffice to fit the sail to the sailor. As the hypotenuse of a right triangle, the mast half-height Z_j always exceeds the H5 distance in an unfenced sail (Figure 3-25, background). The difference between Z_j and H equals 4 inches in a 70-square-foot sail and 2 inches in a 60 square-footer. Such differences can be enough to let the mast end touch the ice and to topple the sailor.

Expert sailors fence their sails; and with a fenced, shouldered sail, the sailor stands along the shorter H-distance, not along the longer Z_j-distance.

As a result, sailors who would fence their sails must take the shorter H-distance into account when buying a sail, and so Table 3-4 furnishes numerical H-values. To account for this distance, they should put on skates, shoulder the boom, fence the sail, and bend their knees. If the sail fits properly, the mast end and the lower sail edge will ride one or two inches above the surface. As a corollary, anyone building the largest sail that her height and reach can accommodate should give it the proper H-distance and a well placed center of effort. This can be done by selecting a sail that fits, using the dimensions in Table 3-4, and perhaps by changing one or more of the standard angles to reach the desired area. In either case, the sailmaker must estimate the distance by which she decreases her effective height in bending her knees when she sails. Bending one's knees is important not only in building a sail, but also in sailing one. It is an action that forms part of several sailing techniques explained in the next chapter.

CHAPTER FOUR: TECHNIQUE

"Many a first-timer who has been whirled across a sheet of ice to become entangled in a clump of brush on the far bank will vouch for the fact that a skate sail surely makes you travel, but not always in the precise direction in which you wish to travel." — E. H. Jessup, *Snow and Ice Sports: A Winter Manual*, 1923.

A scream of distant iceboat runners mysteriously accompanies a hush from nearby hockey players 8 years old, as two skate sailors reach the lake shore. The sound and silence promise extraordinary speed and intense excitement. As they change hats for helmets, the sailors read the ice and wind. They hear whispering crystals snatched from shifting snow patches, hurled low over the ice, and swiftly borne downwind. Geese aloft struggle beneath an austere but azure sky, against a far-off gray-brown shore, where complaisant trails of horizontal smoke emerge from tell-tale chimneys. From the lakefront rises a swaying flagpole, its halyard flailing and its flag rippling, snapping, and straining to fly free. The man and boy stand watching.

The flag evokes the old skate sailor's memory of last year's perfect day on this lake. The thick ice is hard, the steady wind high, and the long way clear — save for huddles of ice fishermen, their backs to the wind. During that unforgettable excursion, he sails seven miles crosswind without a stop or tack, nearing the farthest shore in little more than 10 minutes. Again he feels the satisfaction and trepidation of the voyage. Relief envelops him as he passes the mid-lake state border without crossing, skirting, or sighting a single pressure ridge, even where he knows them usually to lurk. But the relentless wind thrusts him north over an unknown surface invisible beneath snow dust. Kept safe by the rare uniformity of a single ice sheet spanning the whole lake, he reckons his instantaneous speed reaches 45 mph when the wind rises momentarily.

Over glass-smooth ice, his silent run startles hooded fishermen, who flutter like seagulls disturbed.

Today, 10 months later, the wind blows from the same quarter while the anemometer reads 12 mph, so a lust for sailing speed and freedom fills him. His hair rustles, his ears sting, his eyes tear. He feels exhilarated by the wind, the cold, and the winter landscape — and by the prospect of upwind runs sailed on ice skates at 30 mph. After tightening his helmet beneath his chin, the old sailor begins to rig his neighbor's son's sail.

"It'll be easy," he says as he works, "and fun, because you can skate. The snow patches are thin and few. There's ample wind to drive us, but not enough to thwart us."

"How do you hold the sail?" asks the boy, pulling on his skate laces.

"All you have to do is keep your hands on the vertical mast when you're underway," replies the man. "Hold them below the horizontal boom resting on your windward shoulder. If you get into trouble, don't brake until you raise the sail overhead. Remember to release the sail if you don't have time to lift it."

"And when you've buckled your life vest, show me your ice picks."

The boy grimaces, but the man continues to speak.

"Today's Saturday, and we have the whole day to learn and practice. If the snow holds off for 24 hours, we'll be sailing the Commodore's Cup Race tomorrow. Twenty of us — and you, too!"

Yes, one day's sailing can bring competence in most skate sailing techniques, and even a few hours' practice will give you much pleasure and some proficiency. Several seasons will transform a novice skate sailor into a competitive racer, but as little as a day's experience prepares good skaters to sail races. Imagined difficulties, therefore, should not prevent or delay you from taking up the sport. Skate sail now, because this sport is almost unimaginably easy to practice.

This chapter presents the one skill and few techniques needed to use Hopatcong skate sails. It confines the discussion to these sails because their booms lie on the sailor's shoulder and because such designs have been the most popular for almost a century. Summarized in Chapter Ten, special techniques are used to sail an icewing, a Windskate-Windski sail, and a parawing.

BASIC TECHNIQUES

Fundamentals

The Only Prerequisite Skill

If you can stand on skates — unassisted by the extension of your arms, by the rail of a rink, or by the arm of a friend — you can skate sail. This ability is the only prerequisite skill. Skating excellence, sailing experience, and great strength are unnecessary. Many skate sailors who have passed their 70th birthdays avidly practice the sport, and one graceful, recreational skater sailed until he was 81, living into his early 90s. Moreover, a 6-year-old child was a capable skate sailor. Obviously, age is no impediment to skate sailing.

Advice to a Novice

Openness to advice makes for a pleasant maiden voyage. Also contributing to a successful first trial are a light breeze; smooth, unobstructed ice; a small sail; and sharp, well fitting skates. A novice should choose a time, a place, and equipment that meet these conditions. "There is much to be observed just by watching," said quipster and former baseball player Yogi Berra, so sailing in the company of experts is also advisable. They have much to teach a beginner, not only about techniques and equipment but also about ice lore and safety.

Release of the Sail

If you get into trouble on the ice, release the sail. This tactic can help you escape harm and avoid obstacles. Distancing yourself from a fast-moving sail, for example, will prevent it from striking you and making a tumble worse. If you find steering momentarily difficult, prefer to free the sail than to disentangle yourself from a clump of brush on the far bank. Should the wind carry the sail away, so much the better. It will usually float gently to the ice, from which you can retrieve it after your troubles end. W. B. Van Claussen, the founder of the Skate Sailing Association of America, gave the following advice:

> Remember never to argue with your sail; if you carelessly let the wind get too far around in front of it, so that it suddenly jumps off your shoulder, don't attempt to hold it by main force. If you can't smoothly and deftly swing it into place, or into the overhead position, better let it go.

Lastly, judge well before you drop a wind-driven sail. Released near ice fishermen, a sliding sail will slice their tip-ups as cleanly as a sharp knife will chop carrots.

Geometric Relation among Wind, Sail, and Sailor

The relative positioning of wind, Hopatcong skate sail, and sailor differs from that adopted by windsurfers and ice boarders. For them, the order is wind, sailor, and sail. However, a Hopatcong skate sail underway generally lies between the true wind and the sailor. This ordered sequence of wind, skate sail, and sailor places the skipper in the lee of his sail. In heeling the craft, the sequence is advantageous because it makes for comfortable travel and reduces speed. However, it is possible to sail a

Hopatcong sail from its windward side. Instructions appear in this chapter at the end of the section called Advanced Techniques and in Chapter Ten.

Starting Well

Rigging a Skate Sail

Practice rigging a skate sail at home, inside if the weather is cold or outside if not. Learning on the ice wastes precious sailing time and can chill your fingers. With experience, however, the job of setting up the sail on the ice will take you only about five minutes and you can do it with warm, gloved hands. Wear lightweight undergloves for dexterity, rather than the heavy gloves or mittens used in sailing.

Rigging a skate sail is done with the sail lying on a flat surface, if there is any wind. Because the handiest surface is the ice or ground, the sailor must bend or kneel, which is easier wearing shoes than skates, particularly those with long blades. So, experienced skate sailors who assemble their sails on the ice do so before donning their skates. They prevent puncturing the sails with a misstep of a skate blade. Many sailors rig skate sails ashore to reduce the chance of mishaps, especially if the ground lacks snow.

The following procedure for rigging a Hopatcong skate sail contains several dependent steps, so take them in order. Begin by assembling the jib bow, mast, and boom; and by finding the wind direction. Now lay the mechanical assemblies upwind of the sail and downwind of any onlookers. Spread the sail, placing the jib upwind, the tail downwind, and the pocket-bearing side upward. Insert the jib bow into the forward pocket, center it there, and smooth any large wrinkles in the pocket. Next, lay the mast on the sail and fasten the mast ends to the jib with the grommets. Place the boom over the mast, and connect the forward boom end to the jib bow. If the wind threatens to take

Table 4-1: Picking Up a Rigged Skate Sail

- **Find the wind direction**
- **Arrange the sail**
  downwind of bystanders
  jib upwind of tail
  mast and boom on the ice, and sailcloth uppermost
- **Approach from upwind**
- **Bend, grasping jib bow with both hands spread far apart**
- **Straighten, extending spread arms to raise sail overhead**
- **Turn to face the oncoming wind**
  releasing the jib bow
  grasping the mast on both sides of the boom
  spreading hands far apart from one another

the sail, turn it until its tail lies upwind before inserting the tail bow. Otherwise, release the sail and walk to its aft end to center the tail bow in its pocket. Lash the tail bow to the aft end of the boom, passing the outhaul lanyard twice around the bow for mechanical advantage. Make the lashing tight enough to stretch and flatten the sail, which you should examine for wrinkles before you knot the lanyard. When you have smoothed any wrinkles and stretched the sail again, knot the lanyard. Return to the jib end of the sail, and finally reach across the jib along the boom to fix the mast to the boom at the point where they cross.

Picking Up a Skate Sail

A beginner's second lesson in techniques concerns picking up a skate sail in a breeze (Table 4-1). A firm grip is needed to prevent the wind from wrenching the sail from the sailor and flinging it downwind, to the onlooker's peril and the sailor's chagrin. Gripping the sail firmly requires a knowledge of which parts to seize and how and where to hold them. The parts in question are the jib bow and mast. Each time you seize one of them, you must initially use both hands, placing them as close to the ends of the spar as possible. Grasping either spar with only one hand, or with both hands held near the center, asks the wind to take the sail.

As a beginner, you will have to pick up the sail twice before you get underway. On

Table 4-2: Getting Underway

- **Choose a course running at about 90° to the wind**
- **Turn onto the chosen course,**
  lowering boom onto windward shoulder
  releasing grip of leeward hand on mast
  seizing mast below waist with both hands
  pulling mast to leeward
- **Set skates parallel to one another, windward foot leading**
- **Bend knees**
- **Raise toes of blades by placing bodyweight on heels**
- **Be alert!**

the first occasion you'll pick it up merely to flip it from one side to the other, and the second time you'll pick it up to raise it to the overhead starting position. Although the proper method for picking up a skate sail contains several elements, you'll find yourself flawlessly combining these tasks after a little practice.

To flip the sail when its tail lies downwind from its jib, approach the jib from a point situated upwind. Face the sail and seize the bow with both hands. Spread your hands as far as you can. Now straighten your body and turn the sail over, placing the side bearing the mast and boom on the ice. Beware, because the wind can easily steal the sail when it lies in this position.

You are ready to raise the sail to the overhead starting position once you have flipped it. But confirm the wind direction

Figure 4-1: A Skate Sailor in Stays

before raising sail, feeling for moving air with your face. When you know the direction, arrange the sail so the jib lies upwind of the tail and downwind of any bystanders. Again, skate downwind to the sail, which should still be lying with its mast and boom on the ice and its sailcloth uppermost. Face the jib and bend down to take the bow with both hands spread wide. Now rise, at the same time raising the jib overhead by extending your arms completely. Keeping the jib headed into the wind, pivot quickly to face the wind, and simultaneously change the positions of your hands. Releasing the jib bow, and holding your upraised hands well apart, grasp the mast on both sides of the boom.

If you carried out these maneuvers properly, then you and the sail should be facing directly into the wind, still standing but not moving. The sail should be overhead with the jib ahead of you and the tail behind you. Now you are in stays, with the wind pouring ineffectively past the sail (Figure 4-1). Regardless of whether you are moving or stationary, this is a stable position for the sail, which floats easily and lifts the tail far above the ice. You will place the sail in stays to begin sailing, to turn into the wind, to slow, and to stop.

Even the strongest sailor in stays must use both arms to hold the sail and spread them for stability when a wind is blowing. Otherwise, he will lose the sail, strike one of its harder parts, fall, or suffer all of these fates. A sail held loosely overhead will soon develop forceful oscillations, swaying frequently from left to right. Merely to hold the sail steady demands more technique than strength.

Getting Underway

To present a Hopatcong sail to the wind requires a series of maneuvers, which even a novice will make smoothly after a little practice (Table 4-2). With the sail in stays, choose an unobstructed course at about 90°

to the prevailing wind. Turn through 60-90° and place the sail at your windward side (left, for example) with the sail plane perpendicular to the ice. Lower the boom quickly onto your left shoulder, which should lie about 16 inches aft of the mast. At the same time, release your right hand from the mast above the boom, drop both hands, and grip the mast with both hands below the waist. In lighter airs you'll need only one hand to hold the mast, and the wind pressure will hold the sail securely on your shoulder without turning the craft over your head.

Placing Your Hands

With the sail on your left side, your right hand should then lie above the right one; and vice versa, if the sail stands on your left. Use both hands to pull the lower mast half toward your body close to your windward ankle (Figure 4-2). This grip gives the greatest control over the sail, but can be tiring because it cocks your windward wrist at an unnatural angle. It is better to use this grip only in coming about or jibing when you will need it to lift the sail overhead.

If you are sailing a straight course, you can use the leeward hand to pull the mast and the outstretched windward hand to push it. For example, with the sail on your right shoulder, you should place your right hand between the sail and mast, near your knee. Grip the mast only with your left hand held below the boom. Now push the mast toward you with your right hand while you pull it in the same direction with your left hand. The wind pressure will keep the sail securely on your shoulder.

Bringing the lower half of the mast toward you creates a necessary force equilibrium. Wind acting on the overhead part of the sail tends to rotate this part downward, producing a torque that you must oppose. Sailing in a stiff breeze or close to the wind will require both hands. Thrust between the mast and sail, your windward hand will

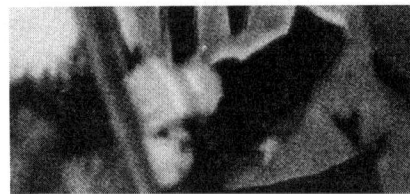

Figure 4-2: Proper Placement of Hands

suffice in light airs or after practice. It will not be necessary to squeeze or even encircle the mast with your fingers. The extended fingers and open palm of a spread hand will suffice to counter the sideforce when they push the lower mast half to leeward (Figure 2-37).

Too diffident to lean on the sail, many novices push the upper part of the mast to counteract the overhead torque. Insufficient leverage makes the counterforce exerted by the pushing hand and arm ineffective, so the first-timer loses control of the sail. Such a foredoomed effort squanders strength and sacrifices speed. The beginner can produce the needed counterforce by pulling on the mast with both hands, pushing with one hand only, or pulling with one hand while pushing with the other. In all cases, the hands lie below the boom. An experienced sailor combines one of these techniques with heeling or bracing, topics discussed in the following section.

Taking a Stance

To sail a straight course, position your feet with the windward foot riding four to five inches ahead of the leeward one. For example, with the sail on your left side, your left foot should precede your right one. Conversely, the left foot should follow the right one when your right shoulder bears the sail. You must take a stance long enough to provide stability in the plane of your sailing motion.

Your feet also should run parallel to one another, so that the tracks left by your blades fall a few inches apart. This distance represents the width of your stance, which should be great enough to prevent you from sliding to leeward. If you have to counter a powerful leeward torque from the overhead part of the sail, you will need to increase this width to 8-12 inches, unless you are leaning on the sail (leaning on the sail is discussed in the section entitled Advanced Techniques).

Bend your knees to absorb any shocks, and lean a little backward to raise the fronts of the blades. Raising the tips will allow the blades to pass more easily over small obstacles. In this way the blades act like the upraised tips of skis, and will carry you safely through a patch of rough ice or shallow, powdered snow. (However, sailing deliberately into any snow patch is inadvisable unless you know it to be shallow or loosely packed.)

Keeping Watch

If all has gone well, the sailor should now be sailing at a good clip. And he should be watching where he is going to avoid making landfall abruptly. Falls on land can damage flora and fauna there. To avoid collisions on ice, keeping watch on all sides is obligatory; and looking through the sail windows is a help. "Windows prevent deadheading into a sailing companion or lakeside dock," as noted in Jefferson's *Skate Sailing*.

Steering

Moving the boom forward or aft upon your shoulder steers a Hopatcong skate sail. Sliding the boom in small increments is best but, because of wind pressure, you'll need a little force to move it at all. Moving it forward turns you downwind. Conversely, shifting the boom aft turns you upwind. In both cases, you help by pivoting smoothly on your skates.

Back-and-forth movements of the boom change the ratio of forward to aft sail areas, and disrupt the balance of forces that allowed you to sail straight on your previous course. With a forward motion of the boom, the sail area lying ahead of you increases,

so the wind exerts proportionately more force on the sailcloth in front of your body than on the cloth in back of it. The increased force ahead turns you downwind to restore equilibrium. When you shift the sail backward on your shoulder you decrease the ratio of forward to aft sail areas, placing more sail behind you. So, you turn upwind in response to the corresponding force change.

A wise novice under sail should not attempt to turn sharply by using his skates alone. A successful turn, notably a sharp one, requires cooperation between the hydro- and aerodynamic forces that act on skates and sails. Trying to turn only with skates forsakes this cooperation. Without it, the fortunes of the sharply turning sailor will take a sudden downturn, leading to an all-points landing.

With a little practice, however, you can skirt nearby obstacles by steering only with skates, and so avoid the great course changes that shifting the boom brings. A skate sail is so maneuverable that small course changes are easy to make, and thus obstacle races are feasible. Seasoned skate sailors taking part in these races make minor course changes with their skates alone and make major changes with both their skates and booms.

Ending Well

Slowing

Spill the wind! Each time you want to slow down, you will have to accomplish this crucial maneuver.

To do so, raise the sail overhead so that its plane is parallel to the ice. Then, lest you lose the sail, grasp the mast with both hands spread far apart. One hand will then lie far to the left of the boom while the other will lie far to its right. You will still be moving, even though you are in stays, but braking like a skater will stop you gently or sharply, as needed. Without raising your sail, merely pointing it upwind will cause uncontrollable vibrations known as luffing but will fail to spill the wind completely. In this respect, a skate sail differs importantly from a sail or an ice boat, both of which dump wind by heading directly into it. Neither kind of boat changes the sail plane relative to the ice sheet, as a skate sailor does.

A skate sailor can also slow down (or speed up) by changing his angle to the wind, because course angle affects sailing speed. Sailing into the wind and as close to it as is possible without luffing will lower his speed. The slowest sailing results from running before the wind, when skate resistance reduces sailing speed to less than the real-wind velocity. Exchanging large sails for small ones in high winds sensibly reduces speed. So, experienced skate sailors usually carry sails of differing sizes to use in varying winds.

Stopping

Before trying to stop, every sailor must spill the wind, lest he land like an artillery round. Nature greets with indifference a novice's attempt to brake with his skates while the sail thrusts him forward. He falls as his feet stop and his upper body advances, so confirming Isaac Newton's First Law of Motion, stated more than 300 years ago. Only when the sail is in stays should a novice sailor brake like a skater. Slow stops, planned long in advance, are preferable; but fast, ice-shaving stops are feasible. The fastest stops require the sailor to turn upwind before placing the sail in stays and braking.

Approaching Bystanders

A skate sailor hurtling like a bowling ball must take care not to strike and scatter bystanders like duck pins. "A beginner sailing swiftly and uncertainly among crowded skaters will not immediately win unanimous popularity," wrote R. C. Jefferson, author of *Skate Sailing*. Good public relations demand safe approaches, which require planning.

In a safe, well planned approach, the sailor turns into the wind to sail upwind toward bystanders whom he wishes to greet. Downwind arrivals threaten collisions, and so they inspire fear. An approaching sailor who wishes to instill confidence in his judgment puts his sail into stays 50-100 feet ahead of his stopping point, which should lie downwind of the bystanders. After braking with his skates he lays the sail on the ice, jib heading into the wind. Leaving the tail facing upwind or releasing the sail at waist height risks having the wind hurl the sail away.

Laying a Skate Sail Down

When the winter sun is relatively high, its light will warm a sail lying on the ice and can cause a nylon model to stretch. A warmed sail in contact with ice will melt it and become wet. Wet nylon stretches three times more than dry nylon does, and a stretched sail is hard to handle. Extra sailcloth loose on the same mast and boom causes a skate sail to luff. Because the Hopatcong design does not necessarily provide for trimming a stretched sail along the mast, its sailor must tolerate luffing or stop sailing. Therefore, the side of a nylon sail bearing the mast and boom should be placed on the ice in February or March, to minimize wetting and stretching.

Wet Dacron sailcloth is not difficult to handle, because a wetting does not stretch this kind of cloth. So, such a skate sail can be advantageously placed on the ice with the mast and boom lying uppermost and the sailcloth contacting the ice. The wet windward side of the sail will not soak the sailor's clothing when he later leans against the sail, because he will then touch only the dry leeward side.

On colder, sunless days, the same side

K.G. Bauder

Figure 4-3: Coming About

of the sail should touch the ice, the mast and boom then lying uppermost. Then the wind cannot penetrate between the ice sheet and sail plane to steal the craft. If the mast and boom touch the ice, as they should do on a sunny warm day, they raise the sail from the ice and so invite the theft.

A young child learning to skate threatens sails lying on the ice. Drawn inexorably to such a sail, he can stumble when he nears it, fall forward, and put a skate blade through the sailcloth to save his balance. Adult skate sailors, therefore, must guard any sail they lay on the ice especially when children are nearby, and must also beware of adult onlookers wearing skates.

Anchoring a Skate Sail

When you lay your sail down, anchor it to the ice with any handy, heavy objects. Then watch the sail, wary of any unanchored sails if you are near them. A gust can easily fling an unsecured skate sail into bystanders' faces or open water, or onto thin ice. A laden duffel bag or heavy folding chair usually makes a suitable anchor in light winds, although an inexpensive, convenient all-winds anchor has yet to be devised.

A winter climber's ice screw makes a convenient, if pricey, all-winds anchor. An ice screw is a seven-inch-long, three-quarter-inch-wide titanium tube bearing sharp saw teeth at one end and an open, oval handle at the other. Threads run around the whole length of the exterior surface. The handle, which protrudes at a right angle from the shaft, allows the user to drive the screw manually. Turning the screw against an ice sheet easily cuts and crushes the ice directly below the teeth, while the thread pulls the screw into the sheet and sets it firmly. The handle opening will admit a lanyard to hold a skate sail even in a strong wind.

ADVANCED TECHNIQUES

Making Round Trips Under Sail

Softwater sailors, ice boaters, and skate sailors travel upwind by beating, and doing so makes round trips possible. To beat is merely to follow a zigzag course in which successive legs are sailed at different angles to the real wind direction. Each leg is called a tack. The distance sailed during beating exceeds the shortest distance back to the starting point.

Coming About

The easiest means to change course is to come about, which is to turn toward the wind (Figure 4-3). This maneuver requires the skate sailor to shift the boom aft, so beginning the turn. When the sail begins to luff and lose thrust, he raises the sail overhead spreading his hands far apart on the mast. He completes the turn using skates alone and, after passing through the wind, lowers the sail boom onto his other shoulder, departing on the new tack.

Experience is needed to choose the moment for putting the sail in stays. Doing so too early leaves the sailor to skate the turn, while leaving it too late invites the sail to luff and slow. With practice, however, coming about causes little loss of speed and no vibrations.

Jibing

Begin to jibe, which is to turn away from the wind, by pushing the boom forward. Then raise the sail only enough to roll the mast across your upper back and shoulders. Incline your head downward as you move the mast upward, and keep the tail low to the ice as the mainsail slides across your back (Figure 4-4). Assist the turn by skating, and finally lower the sail onto your other shoulder to sail on the new course.

Jibing is a more difficult maneuver than coming about. If the tail rises high off the ice during a jibe, the wind will catch and fling the sail overhead, an effect that does not attend coming about. Raising the tail through the proper distance requires good judgment, which results from experience in jibing. Thus, casual sailors who never practice jibing should expect to lose races that demand it. Reclaiming a winning position rarely occurs after recovering a lost sail.

Coming About or Jibing

A choice between coming about or jibing arises if you are sailing across the wind with a course angle of more or less than 90°. Whether you should jibe or come about now depends on the angle between your course and the wind direction. Jibe when you are sailing at an angle greater than 90° to the wind direction (Figure 4-5, top) to minimize the time needed to turn. Conversely, come about when you are sailing at less than 90° to the wind (Figure 4-5, bottom).

Figure 4-4: Jibing

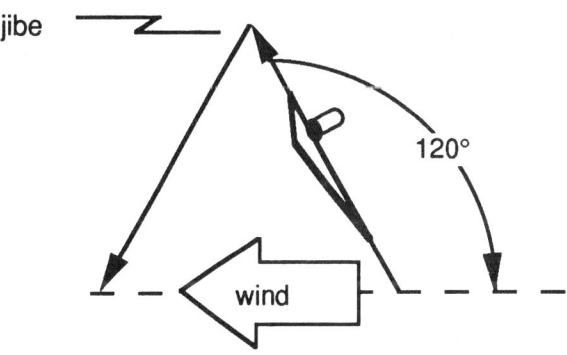

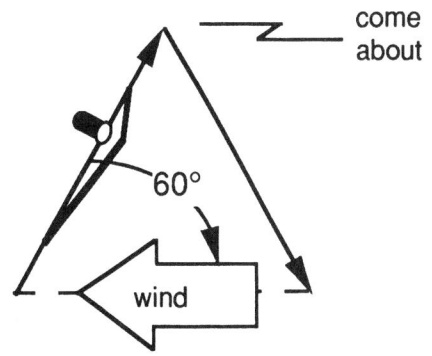

Figure 4-5: Jibing and Coming About

Increasing Speed

Positioning Your Upper Body

Sailing with one's body facing forward maximizes the bodily area presented to the air. Such a position decreases sailing speed by increasing drag unnecessarily. A skate sailor who twists his leeward shoulder aft and grasps the boom with his leeward hand reduces this drag and increases his speed.

The resulting cruciform position minimizes the bodily area moving through the wind as long as the sailor's thickness from side to side exceeds that from front to back. This position also allows the sailor to counter backwinding. With his extended arm grasping the boom behind him, he can easily resist the tendency of the mainsail and tail to twist downwind.

Fencing a Skate Sail

Once you learn the basic techniques, practice fencing your sail to increase speed. Fencing calls for tilting the forward part of the boom upward so that the lower sail edge parallels the ice. If the fenced sail is large, then the gap between its lower edge and the ice sheet will be small, amounting to no more than one or two inches. If the sail is small, then fencing it is pointless because so much wind will pour beneath the lower edge, which can ride a foot or more above the ice.

Opposing Sail Torque

Besides forward thrust, wind acting on a skate sail produces a strong side force that, if unopposed, would topple the sailor leeward. Skate sailors use three techniques to oppose this side force, which is a torque. Two of them, full heeling (Figure 4-6a) and body heeling (Figure 4-6b), make use of body mass. Full heeling, or lying on the wind, requires the sailor to angle both the sail and his body. In body heeling he inclines only his body, keeping the sail upright. The third technique calls for the sailor to brace himself with an out-thrust leg, to hold both the sail and himself vertical (Figure 4-6c).

Lying on the Wind

Full heeling, which demands a high wind from the weather and soaring confidence from the sailor, is the most common of the three techniques (Figure 4-6a). Lying on the wind reduces the effort needed to sail, is the least strenuous technique for countering the sideforce, and brings a thrilling ride. The sailor's graceful posture attracts onlookers, because it seems to defeat gravity.

"The particular point that one must learn is freely to lean the weight against the sail, and actually allow the wind to hold one up," according to *Practical Suggestions for Making and Using Skate Sails*. To lie on the wind, the sailor holds his body rigid and boldly leans on the sail, its lower edge lying close to his windward ankle. His windward hip and shoulder touch the sail and his hands haul the lower half of the mast toward him. Meanwhile the windward edges of his blades bite the ice, keeping him erect, thrusting him forward, and preventing him from drifting sideways. This position, stable even in a steady wind, enables the sailor's body mass to counter the side force of the wind. The more he leans, the stronger the wind is and the taller his blades are; and a good sailor can incline more than 45° from the vertical.

Heeling a skate sail requires sharp skates and is most comfortable in a steady wind. Sharp blades prevent slipping sideways to the course sailed, while a steady wind minimizes the number of times that the sailor momentarily dips to windward. Contrary to expectations, a heeled sailor wearing sharp skates rarely falls to windward. This is so because the wind does not often cease abruptly, although its speed does tend to change instantly. Thus, momentary dips to windward are common, but do not necessarily cause falls. Instead of falling, a proficient sailor recovers his balance by turning to windward, exerting force on his windward skate, which relieves the sail of his body weight.

Full heeling decreases sailing speed, which is directly proportional to effective sail area. Tilting a skate sail to windward reduces its effective area by a factor equal to the cosine of the heeling angle. This angle varies from 0°, when the sailor is perpendicular to the ice, to about 60° from the vertical, when he is heeling maximally.

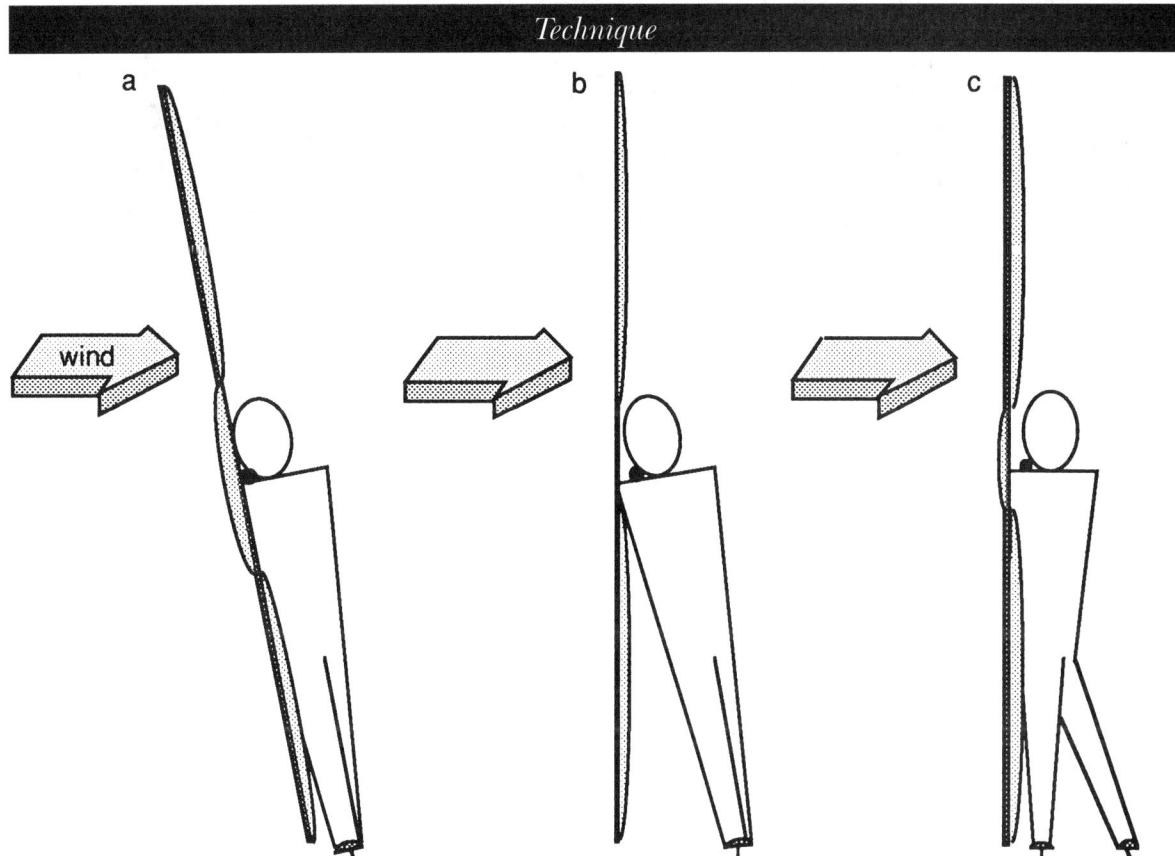

Figure 4-6: Opposing Sail Torque: (a), Lying on the Wind (full heeling); (b), Body Heeling; (c), Bracing

The corresponding cosines range from 1 to 0.5, and so can reduce the effective sail area by as much as 50%. This percentage represents a large decrease so, as one champion skate sailor said, "The more you heel, the slower you go."

Body Heeling

One agile race winner solves the problem of reduced speed by heeling only his body. His arms force the sail into a vertical position (Figure 4-6b). This increases his speed, compared with another sailor heeling both his sail and body, but the increase comes at the cost of comfort. Continuously forcing the sail upright is strenuous work.

Bracing

As a flying buttress keeps a cathedral wall upright, bracing holds the sail vertical (Figure 4-6c). To practice this sailing technique, hold your body vertical, stiffen your leeward leg, and thrust it sideways to counter the side force of the wind. Bend your windward leg to crouch slightly. Bracing is

advantageous because it entails no reduction in effective sail area. It demands, however, that you fight the wind, makes it difficult to recover from gusts, and impedes turning.

Divertissements!

Sailing on One Foot

Sailing on one foot is a thrill a minute. Perfecting this technique brings an adrenaline rush. Still, the Swedes also do it for more practical reasons. Proficient Swedish skate sailors sail cross-legged on one foot only, reportedly to minimize resistance and optimize balance (Figure 4-7). To adopt the imported technique, during which you will stand on the foot farthest from the shouldered sail, begin by sailing across the wind. Then stretch your leeward hand aft, grasping the boom as far behind your body as your arm reaches. This puts you in an outstretched, cruciform position that facilitates the impending transfer of body weight from your windward foot to your leeward one. The position also helps

Figure 4-7: Championship Form: Alexander Sahlin of Hägersten, Sweden, Lying on the Wind, Sailing Cross-Legged on One Foot, and Wearing High Skates, His Dragon Sail Occupies 95 Square Feet.

to maintain balance when one foot has been lifted off the ice. With your windward shoulder and hip against the sail, lift the upwind foot from the ice and cross it over the other skate. You are now sailing cross-legged on one foot, which originally was the leeward one, as well as lying on the wind.

To sail comfortably on one foot alone requires a long, straight obstacle-free course over smooth ice. The course should also be long and straight. Steering around obstacles like patches of rough ice obliges the sailor to release the grip of his leeward hand on the boom before he can shift the boom to turn the sail. Both skate blades must travel on the ice for stability in steering, in crossing rough spots, and in braking. But to lower the raised skate requires the sailor carefully to straighten his legs. These acts of changing stance and grip consume time, and call for more foresight and planning than sailing on both blades.

In a steady wind over smooth ice, a one-legged sailing stance is stable, comfortable, and extraordinarily thrilling. Changes in wind speed do cause the sailor to dip like a ballroom dancer, but the dips merely lend excitement to the experience. Indeed, the extra thrill of sailing cross-legged on what was the leeward foot may be a stronger reason for learning the technique than decreasing resistance or optimizing balance. Standing atop a single eight-inch-high blade, superb Swedish athletes maneuver 95-square-foot skate sails heeled 60° from the vertical!

Sailing on the Windward Side

Sailing on the windward side of the sail is feasible, and in this position the sailor's shoulders lie broad to the wind. His forward hand grasps the mast near the mast-boom crossing, and his aft hand holds the boom toward the tail. The sail then curves naturally, pressing against neither the spars nor the skater, but adopting a more efficient airfoil-like shape. Chapter Ten presents the details of maneuvering the sail from its windward side.

Two advantages offered by this technique

are the relative ease and speed with which the sailor can free himself from the sail. By contrast, the wind presses the sail hard against any sailor on the leeward side, and releasing the craft does not always free the him instantly. Sometimes it is necessary forcibly to raise the sail overhead before releasing it.

Carrying Passengers

Skate sailing "can be enjoyed alone, or one may take pleasant company along, either in tow or as a member of the crew of the captain's gig."* In a good breeze, a skate sail will give a thrilling ride to one or two extra persons, sitting on a sled or standing on skates. A tow rope leading to a passenger or a sled should be long enough not to interfere with the sailor. He holds the rope loosely in his leeward hand, and grips it so that he can release it instantly. For whip-cracking thrills, one skate sailor favors a nine foot length of thick bungee cord.

Lacking a rope, a towed passenger wearing skates grasps the sailor's leeward hand with a grip allowing either person to free himself. For example, each party contributes one hand and both parties interlock their curved fingers as railway cars couple. Lest the sail become unmanageable, the passenger should not grasp it; but should hold only the sailor's leeward hand. For the same reason, a tow rope should not be tied to the skate sail.

The thrills felt by a skate sailor and his passenger have a basis that Chapter Five explains.

---

*J.C. Dier, "Skate-Sailing" in *The Book of Winter Sports*, The Macmillan Co., New York, 1922, p. 101.

CHAPTER FIVE: DYNAMICS

"Those who fall in love with practice without science are like a sailor who steers a ship without a helm or compass, and who never can be certain whither he is going." — *Leonardo da Vinci.*

"The exhilaration of high speed under sail is a powerful emotive drive." — *C. A. Marchaj*

Hurtling at 70 miles an hour, a skate sail outpaces a 28 mile-an-hour wind by a factor of about two and a half. This explains much of the thrill of skate sailing, and understanding how it happens interests many skate sailors. So, part of this chapter extrapolates the well established theory of softwater sailing to skate sailing. Prospective skate sailors can learn from experienced sailboat skippers, but must mind the differences between the forms of travel. Softwater sailors hoist efficient sails over hulls slowed by drag from the resistant water. Conversely, skate sailors shoulder inefficient sails over skates largely unimpeded by drag from the almost frictionless ice. This lack of friction is decisive, so skate sailing speeds greatly surpass the wind speed. Driven by the same wind, skate sails on ice would overtake any sail boat in water.

To view skate sailing speeds in perspective, consider the ratios of sailing speed to true wind speed for other kinds of sailing (Table 5-1). These ratios, which are approximate, are a standard measure of performance applicable to all kinds of sailing craft. The table includes the figure for a catamaran because this multihulled craft is the fastest to sail in soft water.

Proficient skate sailing requires some knowledge of aero- and hydrodynamics, which respectively treat the forces of wind on sail and of skates on ice. To win races, expert skate sailors apply sailing dynamics, strategy, and techniques (Chapter Four). Complete ignorance of sailing dynamics would make skate sailing hapless, restricting

Table 5-1: Estimated Ratios of Sailing to True Wind Speeds

iceboats	
Skeeter	5
DN	4
skate sail on ice	
Hopatcong	2.5
catamaran	
International Tornado	1.4

a sailor to running before the wind and reducing her speed to less than the wind velocity. By contrast, an expert's sailing pleasures transcend those of slow motion and fixed directions, because she can sail anywhere fast.

Skate sailing dynamics comprise the physical interactions among wind, sail, sailor, and ice. Although a detailed understanding of this topic requires mathematics, this chapter avoids equations. Much of skate-sailing dynamics can be presented and grasped in the non-mathematical language used here. Indeed, an appreciation of the rest of this book does not require a reading of the present chapter.

MECHANICS OF SKATE SAILING

Points of Sailing

For novice sailors, Figure 5-1 presents the points of skate sailing, which describe the different courses that can be sailed relative to the wind direction and are somewhat analogous to compass points.

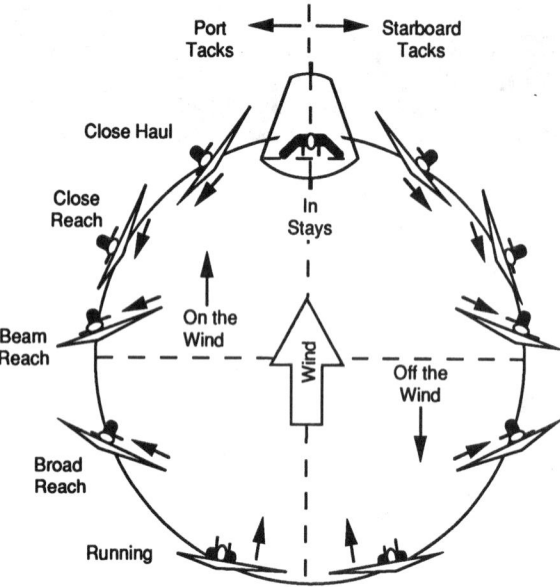

Figure 5-1: Points of Skate Sailing

appear on the right of the figure and feel the wind from their right.

At the top of Figure 5-1, a skate sailor stands facing the oncoming true wind and holding her sail horizontally overhead. In this position she is said to be in stays. She is motionless because the wind force has no effect on her sail. A sailor facing directly into the wind and keeping her sail vertical would also remain stationary for the same reason.

Two sailors running before the wind appear at the bottom of Figure 5-1, one sailing a port tack and the other a starboard tack. Both of them necessarily travel slower than the wind speed because of friction between the ice and the skate blades. This friction dissipates some of the wind energy as heat, which is not expressed as speed.

Note the similarity and difference between running (Figure 5-1, bottom) and sailing a beam or broad reach (Figure 5-1, middle). In all three cases, the sail plane is perpendicular to the true wind direction, or nearly so. In running, the sailor's blades point directly downwind in the direction of travel and are perpendicular to the plane of her sail. Her blades parallel the direction of travel on a beam or broad reach and lie parallel to the sail plane. The geometric relation parallel or perpendicular between the skate blades and sail plane partly determines the sailing direction relative to the wind.

Standard names taken from softwater sailing are given to these courses.

In the top half of Figure 5-1, all the sailors are traveling upwind and are said to be sailing on the wind. They are sailing off the wind, or downwind, in the bottom half of the figure. On the left of Figure 5-1, the sailors feel the true wind coming from their left sides: they are said to be sailing port tacks. Skate sailors on starboard tacks

Wind Pressure and Force on a Skate Sail

Air has mass, and any mass in motion produces kinetic energy, which imparts a force to a skate sail that is the product of the sail area and the wind pressure. It is possible to estimate the force acting on a skate sail because force equals area times pressure. A 54-square-foot skate sail held perpendicular to a fresh breeze (16-20 knots) produces a force of about 70.7 pounds, which equals 54 square feet times

Table 5-2: Wind Velocities and Pressures		
	Velocity (knots[a])	Pressure $\left(\dfrac{\text{lbs.}}{\text{square ft.}}\right)$
Calm	0	0
Light Air	1–3	0.01
Light Breeze	4–6	0.08
Gentle Breeze	7–10	0.28
Moderate Breeze	11–15	0.67
Fresh Breeze	16–20	1.31
Strong Breeze	21–26	2.30
Moderate Gale	27–33	3.60
Fresh Gale	34–40	5.40

[a] One knot, or one nautical mile per hour, equals 1.15 mph

1.31 pounds per square foot (Table 5-2). In this example, the fresh breeze represents the true wind. However, forces on the sail change during high-speed skate sailing because the apparent wind speed exceeds the true wind velocity. It is then the apparent wind defined in the following section that determines the force exerted on the sail.

True, Induced, and Apparent Winds

Winds are airs in motion, and sailors distinguish three types called true, induced, and apparent winds. A stationary sailor senses the velocity and direction of any wind striking her, which is known as the true wind.

When this sailor moved, however, the wind she felt differed from the true one both in direction and in speed. To appreciate the difference, recall skating on a windless day at a speed of, say, 10 mph. Then, even with no true wind at all, you will still have felt a 10-mph wind on your face. Such a wind is designated an induced wind because your motion partly caused it. The faster you skated, the greater the induced wind became. Its source always seemed to lie ahead of you like the end of a rainbow and did so regardless of the compass direction in which you skated.

Now suppose that you skate in a

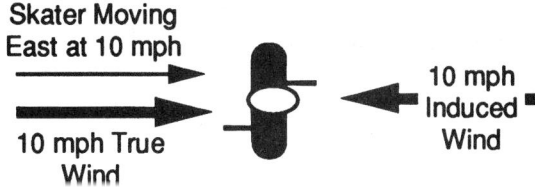

Apparent wind is zero.

Figure 5-3: Resultant Apparent Wind When Skating East with the True Wind from the West

northerly direction at 10 mph, and that a 10-mph breeze blows from the west. Your skating motion alone induces a 10-mph wind traveling south that adds vectorially to the true, 10-mph wind going east (Figure 5-2). Consequently, you now feel a 14-mph wind moving southeast, which is called an apparent wind. Its exact magnitude and direction, which differ from those of the true and induced winds, result from the vector addition. (Such a mathematical operation is different from arithmetical addition, and is explained in elementary textbooks of physics.)

Here is what happens when someone skates in other directions. Traveling east at the same speed and direction as the true wind causes the induced wind to cancel the true wind (Figure 5-3). Thus, the velocity of the apparent wind becomes zero. As the skater turns south, the vector summation

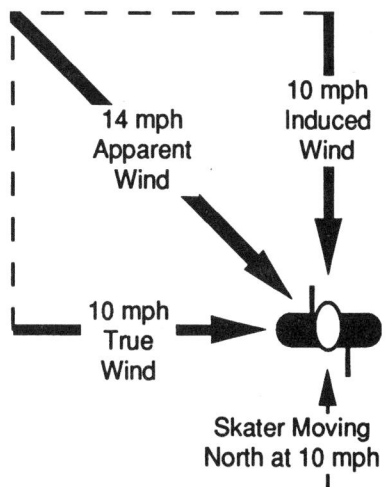

Figure 5-2: Resultant Apparent Wind When Skating North with the True Wind from the West

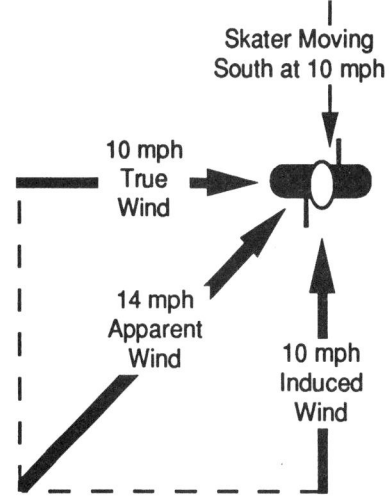

Figure 5-4: Resultant Apparent Wind When Skating South with the True Wind from the West

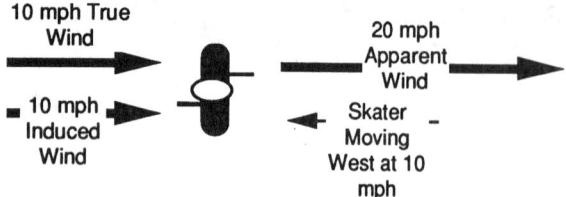

Figure 5-5. Resultant Apparent Wind When Skating West with the True Wind from the West

of the true and induced winds produces a 14-mph apparent wind from the southwest (Figure 5-4). Finally, the skater turns west to skate into the true wind. This causes the induced and true winds to add arithmetically, and results in a 20-mph apparent head wind (Figure 5-5).

For the ice skater, the apparent wind results from interaction of the induced wind and the true wind. Whenever the skater stands still, the induced wind is zero, and the apparent and true winds are the same. Similar principles hold when sailing. A skate sailor propelled by the wind is in motion and, therefore, induces a wind. That, in turn, adds vectorially to the true wind and makes the apparent wind act on the sail.

To persuade yourself of the physical reality of so-called apparent winds especially as they apply to sailing, make the following

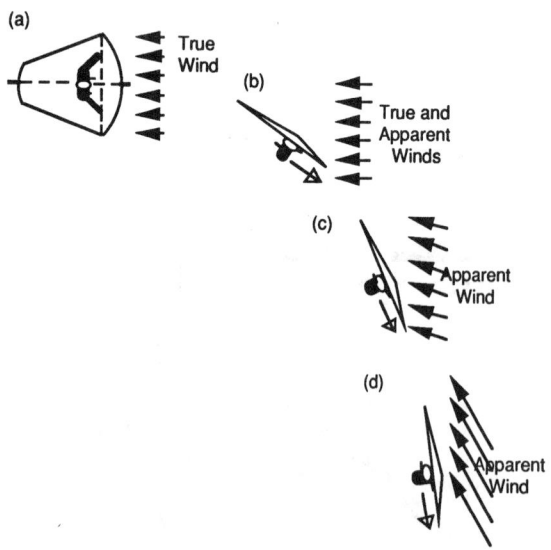

Figure 5-6: Wind Shifts During Acceleration: (a) In Stays; (b) Lowering the Boom; (c) Gaining Speed; (d) Sailing the Desired Course

experiment. When you are traveling as an automobile passenger, extend the fingers of one hand, holding them close together. With your fingers in this closed position, the surfaces of your hand will act like those of a crude airfoil. Keeping your palm horizontal and downward, cautiously thrust your hand through the open window and forward in the direction of motion. If you are moving fast, an irresistible force — the apparent wind — will act on your hand. It will drive inexorably upward, despite the forward motion that the car imparts and despite the backward push that the induced wind exerts. Your hand will soon adopt a stable position elevated some 45° above the horizon. Comparable forces due to apparent winds act on sails, wings, kites, and other air foils, and comprise the subject matter of aerodynamics.

AERODYNAMICS OF SKATE SAILING

Apparent Wind Shifts

The highest sailing speed depends upon the maximum thrust, itself a product of an optimum attack angle. Lying between a sailor's course and the apparent wind direction, this angle varies with changes in the apparent wind strength and direction. Shifts in the apparent wind, which a skate sailor feels as she accelerates, influence sailing speed. To understand that the apparent wind shifts during acceleration, look first at a sailor in stays (Figure 5-6a). The induced wind is zero so the apparent and true winds are the same. She starts by turning away from the true wind (Figure 5-6b). Gaining momentum, the sailor induces a wind that causes the apparent wind to act on the sail (Figure 5-6c). Now it appears that the wind changes direction and increases speed as the sailor changes positions (Figs. 5-6b to -6c). In Figure 5-6d the fast-moving sailor causes a high-velocity apparent wind. The angle between the apparent and the true winds increases from what it was in the sailor's earlier positions (Figs. 5-6c and -6b). At the same time, the angle of attack formed by the sail and the apparent wind remains fairly constant as the sailor accelerates (Figs. 5-6b through 5-6d).

Development of Forces on an Airfoil and a Boat Sail

Wind acting on a sail brings a simple, subtle law of physics called the Bernoulli effect into play. Pressure within a stream of moving air decreases as air velocity increases. A sail subjected to lower air pressure on one side is pushed by the higher pressure air on the other side. In effect, the pressure difference generates a force acting in the direction of least air pressure.

To understand how this force develops and thrusts sails forward, consider the most efficient kind of sail, an airfoil (Figure 5-7). Placed in an air stream, the airfoil divides the apparent wind coming from the left, some of it passing above the airfoil and some below. The lower air stream travels a fairly straight path and retains its original velocity. By contrast, the upper air stream travels farther and faster because of the curved path. This creates less air pressure above the airfoil, while the pressure below remains nearly normal. A pressure difference generates an aerodynamic force in the upward direction of the airfoil. The air is at its lowest pressure on the upper surface just forward of the position of maximum camber (the arching curve of an airfoil from the leading edge to the trailing edge). This position affects the amounts of thrust and side forces generated by the sail. When fast-moving air becomes turbulent (curved arrows in Figure 5-7), it immediately reverts to its original atmospheric pressure.

Conditions around a cloth sail are similar to those around the airfoil (Figure 5-8), despite the differing shapes of the two objects. The upper and lower surfaces of

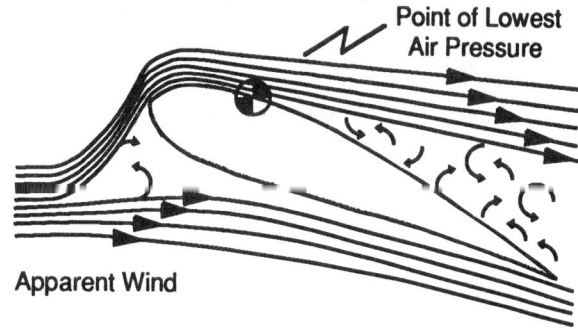

Figure 5-7: Air Flow Around an Airfoil

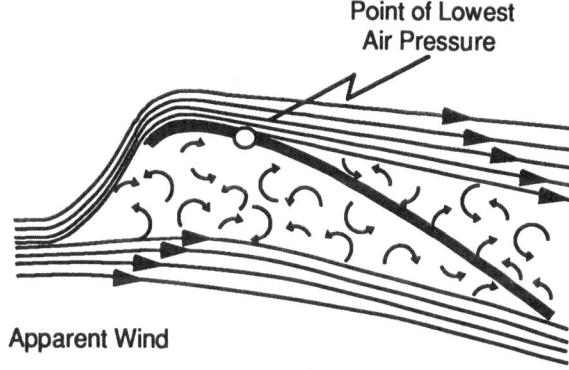

Figure 5-8: Air Flow around a Cloth Sail

the airfoil are curved and (nearly) flat, respectively, but both surfaces of the sail are curved. Another difference is that air flowing freely on both sides of a cloth sail must fill it to the designed shape.

Thrust and Side Forces

A sail generates thrust whenever the total force exerted on it points at an angle less than 90° to the direction of movement. This total force consists of component thrust and sideways forces that are perpendicular to one another (Figures 5-9a and -9b). The sizes of these forces determine how much of the total force serves to move the sailor forward and how much of it tries to tip her sideways. For a given total force, the side force increases as the thrust decreases.

If the total force is constant, thrust varies with the angle the sail makes to the apparent wind and the direction of movement. In Figure 5-9a the angle of attack and the thrust are greater than in Figure 5-9b. Small changes in the angle of attack cause significant changes in thrust, and thereby in speed.

Lift and Drag

Lift and drag are component forces that respectively increase and reduce the thrust that moves a skate sail. In the present context, lift has nothing to do with flying; although the term comes originally from aeronautics and has become conventional in aero-hydrodynamics. Drag not only acts to lessen thrust but also acts to increase side forces that tend to tip a sailor over.

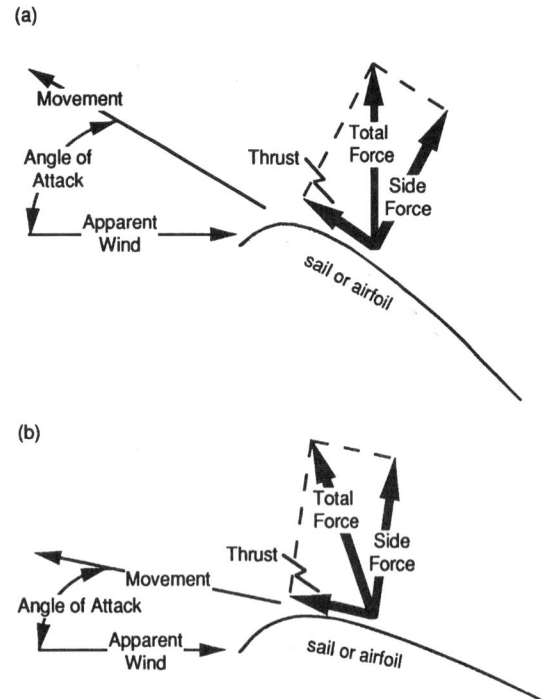

(a)

(b)

Figure 5-9: Thrust and Heeling Forces on a Sail or Airfoil; Top Views

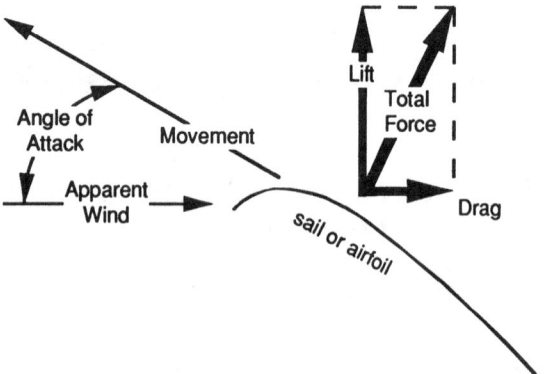

Figure 5-10: Lift and Drag Forces on an Airfoil or Sail; Top View

Aerodynamic total force can be resolved into two perpendicular parts, a desirable lift and an undesirable drag (Figure 5-10). Because thrust acts in the same direction as movement, aerodynamic lift lies perpendicular to the apparent wind. And because the side force is perpendicular to movement, aerodynamic drag is in the same direction as the apparent wind. Shifting the total force more in the direction of movement causes an increase in lift and a decrease in drag.

Both the aero- and hydrodynamics of skate sailing entail lift and drag. As a result, it is possible to distinguish four separate forces: aerodynamic lift, aerodynamic drag, hydrodynamic lift, and hydrodynamic drag. All four are important not only to an understanding of sailing physics, but also to sailing comfortably and winning races.

Center of Effort

Wind strikes the entire surface of the sail to produce forward thrust and side forces. Nonetheless, it is useful to make the simplifying assumption that the wind acts on a single point of the sail. This point is termed the center of effort, abbreviated CE.

Because a planar, stationary Hopatcong sail is symmetrical, its center of effort lies along the boom. The boom divides the sail into symmetrical halves related like an object and its mirror image. The center of effort also falls aft of the mast, but its distance from the mast increases with the sail area. The distance of the center of effort from the mast increases in direct proportion to the sail length. In a 54-square-foot, standard Hopatcong sail, the center of effort is 25 inches from the mast.

In a moving sail, the actual position of the center is displaced from the estimated position in a stationary one. The displacement is likely because the wind does not act uniformly on a moving sail. This is especially true for a skate sail. Distorted by

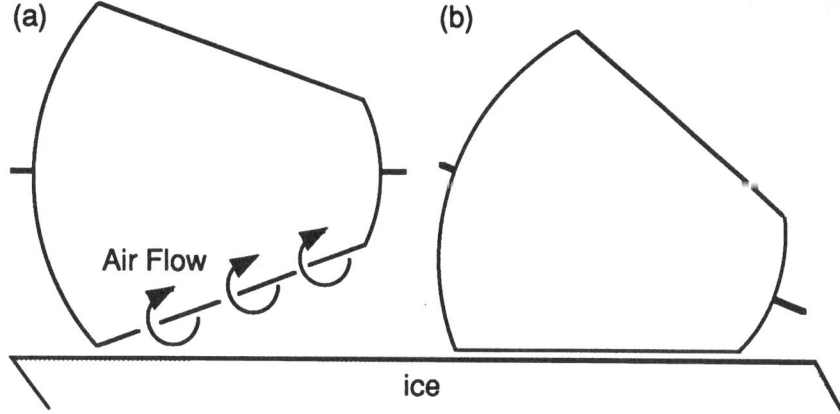

Figure 5-11: (a) Unfenced Skate Sail; (b) Fenced Sail

the sailor's body, its lower half exerts more side force on the sailor while its upper half generates more thrust.

The concept of a center of effort is not a fancy. The center-of-effort position determines whether a moving skate sail balances on the sailor's shoulder, necessary for the sailor to avoid falling. If it does not balance horizontally, the sailor slides the boom back and forth until it does. Adjustments to horizontal balance determine whether the sail follows a straight course. For balance on a vertical axis, the sailor can tilt the boom to raise or lower the tail until the sail feels right. Several other variables — among them the point of sailing, angle of attack, angle of heel, and the velocity of the wind — also influence these adjustments to balance.

Aspect Ratio

A high, narrow sail generates more aerodynamic lift than a low, broad sail of the same area, according to sailing theory.† This lift is directly proportional to the aspect ratio of a sail, which is one measure of its height to its area. The aspect ratio is defined as the quotient of the height squared and the sail area. This is applicable only with the sail well above the ice and air flowing freely from one side of the sail to the other (Figure 5-11a). A Hopatcong sail with an area of 54 square feet and a height of 9 feet

has an aspect ratio of 1.5, which equals (9 x 9) / 54. Given a constant sail area, the aspect ratio varies only with the height squared. Doubling the sail height then quadruples the aspect ratio.

Fencing

An aerodynamic phenomenon called fencing occurs when the edge of a moving skate sail lies close to the ice (Figure 5-11b). The sailcloth largely prevents free passage of air around the lower sail edge. Fencing almost doubles the effective aspect ratio, thereby increasing lift without affecting sail height or area. Exploiting this effect, experienced skate sailors position their sails close to the ice to increase speed.

Camber

The curvature of a sail, measured by the ratio $^{Q}/_{B}$ (Figure 5-12), is known as its camber — important in sail design because it, as well as other factors, influences the amount of aerodynamic lift a moving sail develops. Camber controls the distribution of wind pressure on the sailcloth. For high speed boat sailing when the angle of attack to the apparent wind is about 10°, the camber of an ideal cloth sail is about 3%.

Distortion of a Skate Sail

Alas, reality departs from theory, so a skate sail defies any simple aerodynamic analysis. A sailor lying on the leeward side

†A detailed exposition of this topic lies beyond the scope of this book, but interested readers may consult Marchaj's *Aero-Hydrodynamics of Sailing.*

of a skate sail distorts the sailcloth below the boom (Figure 5-13). Above the boom the sail shape is better, but is still imperfect. Therefore, the upper half of the skate sail has a higher lift-to-drag ratio, and provides most of the drive. Nevertheless, the distorted sail shape violates the principles of airfoil design.

Although the imperfect aerodynamic shape of a skate sail lowers thrust and raises side force, two other factors are vital to ice sailing because they tend to compensate for sail distortion. Ice-skate blades slide well over smooth ice and sharp ones resist sideways movement. High hydrodynamic lift and low hydrodynamic drag result, while the resistance allows a skate sailor to lie upon the wind.

LYING ON THE WIND

Aerodynamic side forces tend to tip a skate sailor to leeward, partly because the sail center of effort lies at shoulder height, well above the center of lateral resistance that falls on the ice. The sailor counters the tipping force by leaning on the sail, a form of heeling known to skate sailors as lying on the wind (Figure 5-14). Agile skate sailors can heel at angles more than 45° from the vertical, but pay a price for heeling greatly. Heeling effectively reefs a sail, which slows the sailor but reduces her workload.

The Effect of Heeling on Sailing Speed

A skate sailor's speed is directly proportional to the effective area of the skate sail, which decreases as the angle of heel increases. To understand the effect, consider two extreme but simple cases. With the sail lying motionless on the ice, the heeling angle is maximized at 90° and the wind passes ineffectively over the sail. In this case the effective sail area is zero. If the heeling angle is minimized and equal to 0°, the moving sail stands perpendicular to the ice, presenting the maximum area to the wind.

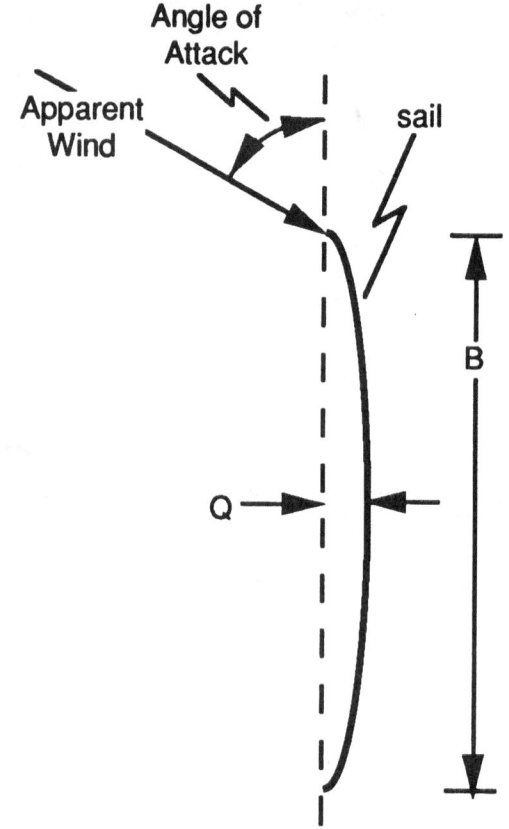

Figure 5-12: Cloth Sail Camber and Angle of Attack; Top View

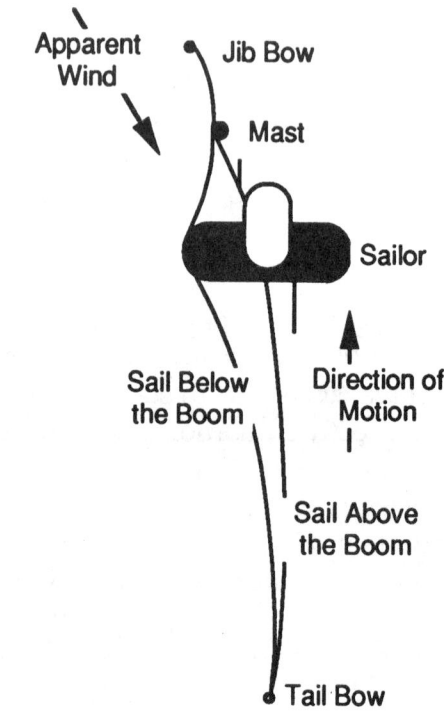

Figure 5-13: Distortion of a Moving Skate Sail, Top View

In this case, the effective area equals the sail area.

In intermediate cases, the effective sail area depends upon the product of sail area and the cosine of the heeling angle. This product, which we approximate by considering a simple rectangular sail, decreases as the heeling angle increases from 0° to 90°. As a result, we can calculate the amount by which the sail area falls due to heeling at various angles. Heeling a rectangular sail at an angle of 15° would reduce sail area about four percent. The reduction, however, is not directly proportional to the heeling angle. Doubling the angle to 30° brings a loss of effective sail area that amounts to 13 percent, considerably more than twice four percent. Heeling at 45° would reduce sail area by nearly 30 percent, a very substantial change.

The Effect of Heeling on Sideforce

The more you heel, the more easily you sail. This follows because the force exerted by the leaning sailor's body weight opposes the aerodynamic sideforce applied by the wind. As a result, the sailor does less work in opposing the sideforce, which supports her own body and permits her literally to lie on the wind. Countering the sideforce is necessary to prevent tipping or capsizing to leeward, and can require a strenuous effort if the sailor uses techniques other than heeling. Like the effective sail area, the size of the heeling force depends on the heeling angle. The size varies according to the product of the heeling angle sine and a numerical constant. Three factors determine this constant, namely the sailor's weight and two distances. One distance is that between her centers of gravity and lateral resistance. The other distance lies between her centers of gravity and effort.

The heeling force size varies with the sine of the heeling angle, in contrast to the effective sail area, which varies with the cosine. Sine and cosine respectively increase and decrease as the heeling angle increases from 0 to 90°. As a result, the heeling angle

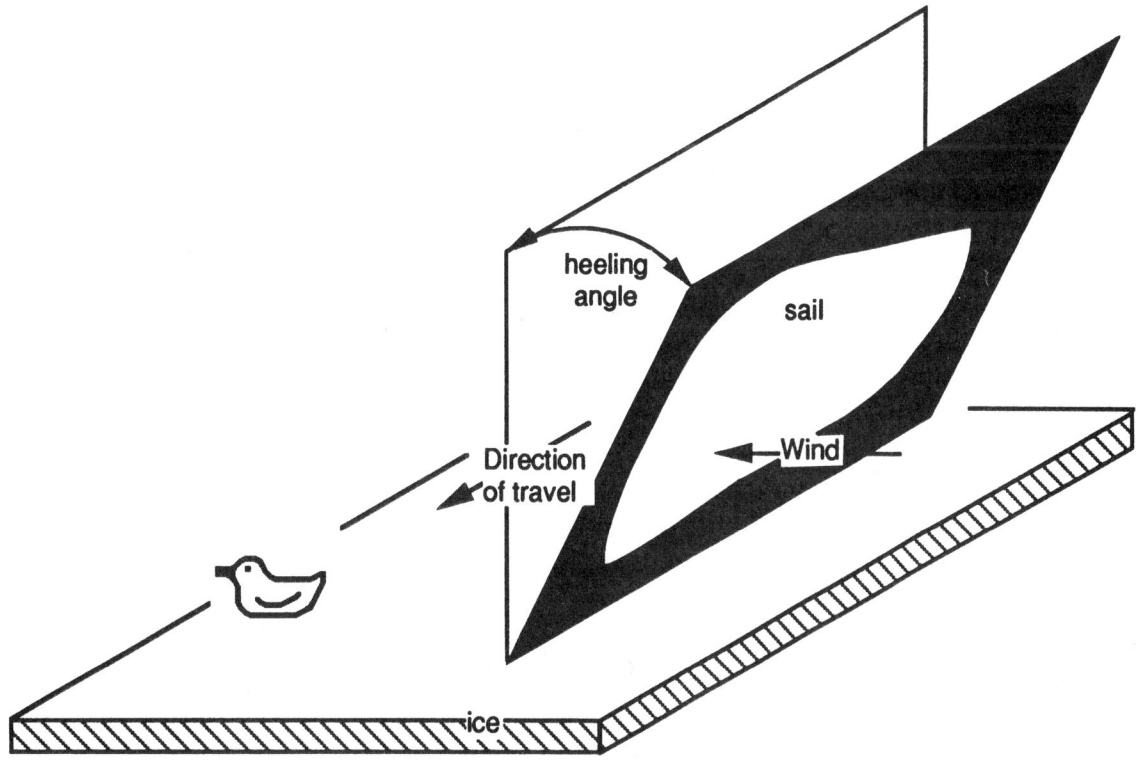

Figure 5-14: Heeling Angles

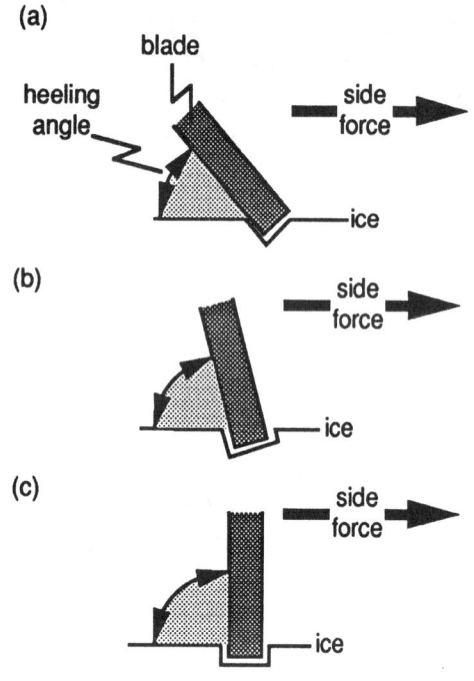

(a) blade, heeling angle, side force, ice

(b) side force, ice

(c) side force, ice

Figure 5-15: Blade Slippage Due to Heeling: (a) Extreme Heeling; (b) Small Heel Angle; (c) Heel Angle Zero

effects on force size and effective sail area oppose one another. Heeling at a larger angle decreases the effective sail area, but requires the sailor to exert herself less. Heeling a skate sail thus represents a compromise between speed attained and work done. Either the sailor buys speed at the cost of work or saves work at the cost of speed.

Heeling Angle Limit

The ratio of a sailor's boot width to her blade height sets an upper limit to her heeling angle. The edges of her boot soles will touch the ice at this maximum angle, and the impact will lever her blades from their grooves in the ice. Collapse to windward will result.

The maximum heeling angle that a sailor can attain without toppling varies with the ratio of boot width to blade height. The angle increases as the ratio decreases. In other words, enlarging this angle practically demands a blade height increase, since the sailor cannot comfortably narrow her boot width.

Wide boots call for higher blades than narrow boots do, if both pairs are to allow the same maximum heeling angle. This point need not concern novice sailors venturing forth on commercially available skates. Experts, however, who build their own skates from downhill ski boots should take it into account. Such ski boots are broad.

Typical Planert and Nestor Johnson racing skates allow a maximum heeling angle of 51°, for example. This value corresponds to a boot-width-to-blade-height ratio of 1.6 and a blade height of about two and a quarter inches. Heeling at 60° would require the blade height to rise only to three inches if the corresponding boot width were to equal three and a half inches. At this angle, the ratio falls to 1.2.

Reducing Heeling

Like a skier who tumbles uncontrollably down a slope, a skate sailor can take picturesque — but embarrassing — spills. Sometimes the cause is extreme heeling, which can entail ice-skate blade slippage. When a sailor heels at 45° or more, her blades ride only on their windward edges and can slip out of the ice grooves if they are dull (Figure 5-15). They can also escape the grooves if the edge of the sailor's boot sole touches the ice. A blade heeled at a small angle retains much of its resistance to lateral movement (Figure 5-15b), while an upright skate blade runs much more firmly within the ice groove (Figure 5-15c). The sharp edges of the blades hold to the grooves.

You can reduce heeling by bracing, a method that Chapter Four presents, by reefing the sail, or by changing to a smaller one. Depending on your weight, for example, a 54-square-foot skate sail might serve in winds up to a moderate breeze (15 mph). In breezes peaking 26 mph, you would be more comfortable and probably faster with a smaller skate sail of 48 square feet. Stronger winds would call for a 32-square-foot skate sail. Although aggressive sailors prefer to be overpowered rather than underpowered, the smallest sail might still be the best choice in a strong wind. It would afford the greatest control in handling and steering. Such a decision is important because it helps win or lose races, and because it averts or causes falls.

SAILING VELOCITY

Sailing Speed as a Function of Course Angle

Exhilarating speed results from good sailing dynamics and requires some knowledge of how speed varies with the points of sailing. Because the changes are complex, the simplest way to understand them is to inspect a plot (Figure 5-16). In the figure, lines radiating from the center represent sailing angles to the true wind. These angles comprise all the points of sailing, from a course close hauled at 40° to one running before the wind at 180°. Concentric semicircles express sailing velocity as a multiple of true wind speed. Speeds for courses sailed on port tacks have starboard tack counterparts, so the plot is symmetrical. Although the plot is hypothetical, it gives an idea of the speeds that an expert sailor with an efficient skate sail might reach.

Sailing a beam reach at a right angle to the true wind produces the highest sailing velocity. On such a course, an expert sailor can reach estimated speeds up to 2½ times the true wind speed. It is the apparent wind not the true wind that drives the sail, and in sailing a beam reach at high speed, the apparent wind speed is considerably higher than that of the true wind. The sailor, however, must always be slower than the apparent wind. So even when a sailor moves at 2½ times the true wind speed, she might be going only 90% of the apparent wind speed. Broad and close reaches bring slower speeds than a beam reach does, but still permit sailing at about twice the true wind velocity. A skate sailor slows down to near the speed of the true wind when she runs or sails close hauled. At less than 40° to the true wind, the angle to the apparent wind becomes too small to allow sailing and the sail luffs.

Running with the wind, when it blows on the sailor's back, is the least exciting way to sail. The sailor feels little wind because the induced and true winds almost cancel each other. Speed is then reduced to a maximum of about 90% of the true wind speed.

Making Best Time

To reach an upwind mark in the shortest time, you must fulfill several requirements. First, sail a zigzag course because you cannot

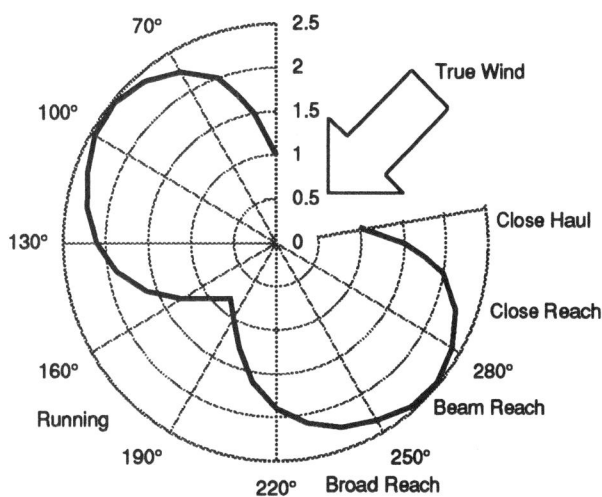

Figure 5-16: Estimated Ratios of Ice-Skate Sailing Speed to Wind Speed as a Function of Course Angle (deg.)

sail directly into the wind. (Each zig and zag is a tack, and sailing a sequence of alternate port and starboard tacks is called beating.) Second, keep the number of tacks small. Every course change takes time to execute, so each slows you down. One starboard and one port tack are the irreducible minimum; but a narrow course may require more tacks than two. Third, sail toward the upwind mark. Moving perpendicular to the wind brings no upwind progress, even though beam reaches are the fastest points of sailing. Sailing a fast course to the sidelines will not win a race to an upwind mark. The fourth factor dictates sailing at the smallest possible angle to the apparent wind while still making good speed. Sailing at angles between 40° and 65°

reduces the time upwind (Figure 5-16).

A good strategy for reaching a downwind mark in the shortest time also requires tacking. At any angle to the wind between 170° and 130°, tacking brings the best downwind progress. Furthermore, an angle of about 165° reduces the number of downwind tacks. Reducing this number is important because each tack involves jibing, an awkward and potentially dangerous maneuver especially in high winds. Running directly before the wind is a poor choice because the true wind speed would exceed your sailing speed.

Other potential dangers involve the quality of the ice surface, which the next chapter treats.

CHAPTER SIX: ICE LORE

Sail while the wind blows!

Many is the occasion when homebound novices query icebound skate sailors. With surprise and not a little disappointment they ask, "How did you manage to sail so often last winter?" The obvious answer, that the enthusiast sought and found sailable ice, usually elicits disbelief. More succinct than persuasive, it fails to dispel a misleading but widespread preconception concerning unfavorable sailing weather. This preconception, that any given winter was too mild or harsh to allow skate sailing, too often keeps novices at home.

Understanding such an answer — as well as sailing on skates — requires a grasp of ice lore. Therefore, the first part of this chapter defines sailable ice as the favorable result of capricious influences, namely weather, climate, and geography. These influences produce sailable ice over such a large part of North America that skate sailing is feasible in 45 states, provinces and territories (Table 6-1). The kinds of naturally formed ice determine whether a given ice sheet is passable. Also in this chapter we will deal with selected physical properties of ice and the processes that form it. We will explain certain familiar observations and lay a foundation for understanding Chapter Nine, which deals with safety. This chapter goes on to explain that ice sheet thickening and thinning are not instantaneous events but time-taking processes. Chapter Six ends advising how, where, and when to seek sailable ice.

SAILABLE ICE AS THE RESULT OF WEATHER, CLIMATE, AND GEOGRAPHY

Found by those who look, sailable ice is plentiful, smooth, and thick, yet free of drifted snow and puddled water. Such ice results from fortuitous cooperation among weather, climate, and geography, which are its only source. Nowhere do private or public organizations create or maintain outdoor ice, other than on rinks too small to allow skate sailing.

Weather and climate should contribute winds, freezing temperatures, and an ideally arid, three- or four-month-long winter. A dry winter is ideal because the widespread, heavy snowfalls of wet weather prevent sailing altogether. Even thin snow patches can cause skate sailors to tumble if wind has compacted the flakes. Sailing in falling rain or over ice obscured by puddles is not only soggy but unsafe. Practically, however, even a humid climate can provide the thrills of skate sailing as long as it brings variable weather.

Geography should add lakes, reservoirs, river bays, and estuaries that are large and numerous. Clustering of shallow and deep lakes, as well as low- and high-lying ones, tends to provide a long sailing season.

Weather

Winds

Moderate steady winds of 10 to 25 mph propel skate sailors nicely. Weaker winds make skate sailing sluggish, whereas none but Herculean sailors can manage much stronger winds. Nevertheless, gusts and gales are welcome to clear a lake of freshly fallen snow and leave sailable ice in their wakes.

Temperatures

Winter temperatures that form and maintain sailable ice range from about 32 to 18° F. Skate sailing is possible at a peak daytime air temperature as high as 55°, but not for long. The sun soon softens the ice surface, especially if it comprises snow ice. The softened surface of thick ice will impede a skate sailor's passage over it even though the ice will still bear his weight. Because melting occurs slowly, a 12-hour-long, 55°air temperature will not completely liquefy a thick ice sheet.

Skate sailing is easiest when the temperature is just below freezing. Then, even relatively dull blades retain their grip on comparatively soft ice. Harder ice surfaces require sharper blades, especially when the sailor tries to lie on the wind. Prolonged low temperatures — 14° F, for example — are undesirable because they harden the ice and allow snow to accumulate on it.

Ideal ice temperatures for skate sailing range from 18 to 23° F, where the friction between a skate blade and the ice surface falls to a minimum. Below this range, sliding friction increases as ice temperature decreases, and would prevent skate sailing altogether at minus 220° F. The blades would stick to the ice! (Figure 6-1)

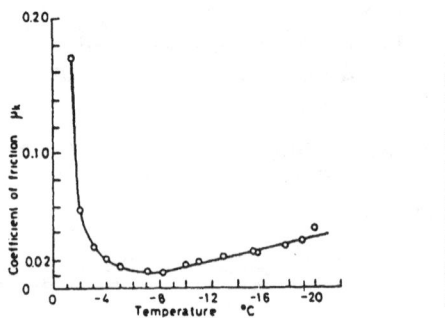

Figure 6-1: Variation of sliding-friction coefficient μ$_k$ with ice temperature, for the 0001 plane. As the temperature decreases, the coefficient falls to a minimum and the rises. (From *The Journal of Glaciology*, Vol. 19, p. 225, 1977)

Variability

Short thaws and even rains are desirable in a snowy winter if they alternate with cold spells. Neither light rains nor short thaws necessarily destroy an ice sheet, which takes time to melt as it does to form. Indeed, variable weather benefits skate sailors by dispersing snow and providing rain. Temperatures hovering around the freezing point convert impassable snow to sailable snow ice. Thaws accomplish this re-surfacing by hastening the physical processes that convert less dense snow crystals to the denser ice crystals. Winter rains, followed by cold spells, also re-surface rough or snow-covered ice. Rainy then cold weather on outdoor ice produces the effect of a Zamboni machine on indoor ice. As a result, variable weather and precipitation need not deter anyone wishing to sail on ice.

Climate

Sailing weather is a reward of climate, which results from exchanges of matter and energy between the surface of the earth and its atmosphere. Heat is the kind of energy that takes part in these exchanges, which transport masses of air and water. Climate dynamics, which vary all over the Earth, are complex yet one of their net effects is simple. Cooling occurs whenever outgoing terrestrial radiation exceeds incoming solar radiation. Fresh water then forms ice as a result of convective and radiant heat losses that reduce average surface temperature to less than 32° F.

Advent of Winter

Climate decides the advent of winter, as determined by the southward advance of the 32° F isothermal line in the U. S. Places north of this line and on it have already attained freezing temperatures, while sites south of the line are warmer than 32°. In North Dakota, the advent of winter is November 10. By contrast, the freeze does not normally arrive before mid-December in the Greater New York City area, which includes Long Island, New Jersey, and Connecticut. Although the coming of winter helps set the length of the skate sailing season, it is not the only cause.

Ice Cover

Winter temperatures help determine whether skate sailing is possible in a given location and regulate the length of the sailing season. Nearly 80% of the United States and Canada has the freezing temperatures needed to form ice. During a normal winter, these temperatures persist for about 100 days in a quarter of this area. Ice-forming temperatures occur in a wide band spanning 35 northern United States (Table 6-2) and 10 Canadian provinces and territories, and occur in another strip lying across northern Europe. In North America, the band is subject to periodic thaws and freezes, so ice sailors refer to it as the melt belt.

Snow Cover

Skate sailors long for arid weather, or for a rain and a cold spell to follow snow. Snow is the nemesis of their sport and at least 80% of North America is subject to regular snowfalls. From Massachusetts to northern Nevada, there are likely to be more than 40 days when the snow covers the ground. Points north of a line drawn between these states can have as many as 160 such days. Although these times seem ominously long in a three-month sailing season, snowfalls in any one season rarely prevent skate sailing altogether.

The amounts of snow and rain that fall in the sailing season concern skate sailors for opposing reasons. As little as one inch of accumulated snow, if it strongly resists the passage of a skate, can ruin the ice sheet surface for skate sailing. By contrast, rain dissolves snow and so tends to resurface an ice sheet without destroying it.

Table 6-1: Where Skate Sailing is Feasible in North America

- **in 35 States**
  - Alaska
  - Arizona
  - Colorado
  - Connecticut
  - Delaware[†]
  - Idaho
  - Illinois
  - Indiana
  - Iowa
  - Kansas
  - Maine
  - Massachusetts
  - Michigan
  - Minnesota
  - Missouri[†]
  - Montana
  - Nebraska
  - Nevada
  - New Hampshire
  - New Jersey
  - New Mexico
  - New York
  - North Dakota
  - Ohio
  - Oregon
  - Pennsylvania
  - Rhode Island
  - South Dakota
  - Utah
  - Vermont
  - Virginia[†]
  - Washington
  - West Virginia[†]
  - Wisconsin
  - Wyoming
- **in 10 Provinces and Territories**
  - Alberta
  - British Columbia
  - Manitoba
  - Newfoundland
  - Northwest Territories
  - Nova Scotia
  - Ontario
  - Prince Edward Island
  - Quebec
  - Yukon Territories

[†] Ice conditions are marginal in this State.

Table 6-2: Winter Temperatures (deg. F) in Various United States Cities

	December	January	February	March
St. Louis	35.6	32	35.6	42.8
New York	35.6	33.8	33.8	41
Salt Lake	32	28.4	33.8	41
Boise	32	28.4	33.8	41
Omaha	28.4	23	26.6	37.4
Denver	33.8	30.2	32	37.4
Elko	26.6	23	28.4	35.6
Milwaukee	24.8	21.2	23	30.2
Williston	17.6	10.4	14	24.8
Fairbanks	-7.6	-11.2	-2.2	8.6
Barrow	-11.2	-16.6	-18.4	-14.8

Table 6-3: Winter Precipitation (Inches) in Various United States Cities

	December	January	February	March
New York	3.3	3.3	2.8	4.0
St. Louis	2.0	2.0	2.0	3.0
Milwaukee	1.6	1.8	1.4	2.3
Salt Lake City	1.2	1.3	1.2	1.6
Omaha	0.8	0.8	0.9	1.4
Boise	1.3	1.3	1.3	1.3
Denver	0.5	0.6	0.7	1.2
Elko	1.0	1.1	0.9	0.8
Williston	0.5	0.6	0.5	0.7
Fairbanks	0.6	0.9	0.5	0.4
Barrow	0.2	0.2	0.2	0.1

Distribution of Winter Precipitation

One measure of the amounts of snow and rain that fall in the melt belt is total winter precipitation for selected cities. (Table 6-3) Precipitation values, although they can be multiplied by a factor of 10 to estimate snow amounts, require cautious interpretation. Relative aridity alone does not guarantee a satisfactorily long sailing season. Winter precipitation in Denver, for example, amounts to three inches. This is less than the 13 inches falling on New York in an average winter.

Furthermore, New York's December precipitation (three and a quarter inches) exceeds Denver's (half an inch) by more than six-fold. What little snow falls in Denver or its environs remains on the ice, however, restricting the sailing season there to about one month, usually December. By contrast, the three-month-long season in the Greater New York area is a consequence of the relatively humid climate and variable weather in the eastern United States. This winter climate provides frequent rains followed by freezes, which clear and smooth the surfaces of ice sheets. In Sweden near Stockholm, where winter temperatures are a few degrees lower than those near New York City, the sailing season sometimes lasts from mid-November to mid-March. The longer sailing season is partly due to the lesser amount of winter precipitation in Stockholm than the Greater New York City area.

Geography

The melt belt running from Maine to Washington contains thousands of bodies of water that are large enough for skate sailing because they equal or exceed 10 acres. A few examples include parts of the Piscataqua River (Maine), Lake Winnepesaukee (N.H.), Holly Pond (Conn.), Lakes Hopatcong (N.J.), and George (N.Y.); Sandusky Bay (Ohio), Lakes Mendota (Wis.) and White Bear (Minn.); as well as Dillon Lake (Colo.) and Burlington Bay (Ontario). New Jersey also offers skate sailing on salty Barnegat Bay, where the Toms River meets the Atlantic Ocean, and on two other estuaries. The Toms, Shrewsbury, and Navesink River estuaries are broad as well as relatively slow-flowing and shallow. Ice sailing on the Shrewsbury River has enjoyed popularity for nearly a century, while a good winter brings a spectacle to the Navesink River ice at Redbank on weekends. The lively, unscheduled ice events include not only skate sailing but ice boating, kite flying, pleasure skating, hockey games, iceboard sailing, and strolling.

For a satisfactorily long skate sailing season, suitable bodies of water should not only be numerous but should differ in altitude, depth, and salt content. This increases the chances of sailing and makes it more pleasurable. It extends the season, provides more days to sail during it, or furnishes more places to sail.

Effects of Altitude

High lying bodies of water tend to freeze early in the winter when low-lying ones remain open. These early freezes happen because atmospheric temperature decreases about 3.5° F for every 1,000-foot increase in elevation. (Unluckily, significant variations in the microclimate surrounding particular lakes diminish the accuracy of this rule in forecasting exact temperatures.) Low-lying lakes freezing later in the winter often escape the snowfalls that obstruct frozen lakes at higher elevations, adding sailing days to a season for an enthusiast willing to search for sailable ice.

Effects of Depth

Shallow lakes freeze earlier than deep ones. The shallow end of a lake can provide sailable ice when the deep end is still open. Freezing weeks later, the deep end will sometimes form sailable ice after snow covers the shallow, frozen end. Bodies of water like Dillon Lake in Colorado, Greenwood Lake in New Jersey and New York, and Lake George in New York, repay visits at different times in the sailing season.

Altitude and depth effects will guide a search for smooth, thick ice without guaranteeing a favorable result. Sailable ice forms on high-lying or shallow lakes early in the season. In mid-to-late season, low-lying or deep lakes offer it. Late in the season, look for sailable ice over slow-moving, shallow estuaries. Foretelling the development of passable ice sheets is difficult because varying weather, lake altitudes, and depths bring sailable ice to different lakes at different times.

Effects of Salinity

Estuaries often afford an opportunity to sail when lake ice is rough or snow-covered.

Salt ice forms over a comparatively long time. Consequently, an estuary will freeze later than a fresh-water lake. The estuarine ice, however, will often have escaped a snowfall that made lake ice impassable or rough. Skate sailors in New Jersey can therefore expect to find sailable ice on the Shrewsbury, Toms, and Navesink estuaries during February. This holds true even though sailing on freshwater lakes may have begun elsewhere in the state during late December or early January of the same season.

Even a snowfall can be advantageous, if it falls into salt water that requires a relatively low temperature to freeze. Snow can serve to cool open water or seed supercooled water, and can hasten freezing. As a result, New Jersey estuaries often become sailable when lakes become impassable. Holly Pond, which lies beside Long Island Sound in Stamford, Conn., is also salty and subject to the same effect.

Rainwater accumulated, then frozen, over salt ice can give a harder surface than that provided by the dry, mildly cold weather that first provides the salt ice. In New Jersey, for example, what descends as snow on northern lakes often falls as rain on southern estuaries. As a result, ice conditions in variable winter weather often change for the better, which rewards a tour of inspection.

Conclusion

Throughout the sailing season, the coming of ice differs from place to place, and the surface condition of an existing ice sheet changes from time to time. Both the differences and the changes — sometimes occurring in as little as a day — can be advantageous. The varying locations of sailable ice make it likely that an eager skate sailor will find it if he seeks it. A knowledge of water altitude, depth, and salinity will lead a sailor to appropriate bodies of frozen water, but will do so at different times in the sailing season.

KINDS OF OUTDOOR ICE

The notion that ice is just ice is completely wrong. Some ice can enhance your performance and let you rise above your standards; some can make you fall and take a seat on the ice. Indeed, ice can be a friend or a foe.

An examination of outdoor ice will reveal several types worth noting. An ability to recognize them helps determine which to trust and distrust, and when to do so. Most sailable ice comprises one or more of three types: black, snow, and salt ice.

Skim Ice

Few sights are more welcome or exciting to an eager ice sailor than the prospect of skim ice. Signifying the long-awaited departure of torrid summer, an ice skim on a pond foretells the imminent arrival of tolerable winter.

Skim ice, sometimes called sheet ice, is the thin film that forms first on any part of a lake. Winds will often break skim ice, which will be re-formed and re-broken several times before lasting cold weather establishes a thick, permanent cover. As skim ice ages, sustained cold will thicken it into black ice.

Black Ice

Treasured by skate sailors for exhilarating runs, thick black ice is precious as a gemstone, which it resembles in smoothness, hardness, transparency, and rarity. The early part of the skate sailing season often affords such ice, sometimes as the first durable ice cover. Black ice covering relatively shallow or high lakes is infrequently seen in mid-season or later.

The color (or lack of color, accurately) is a consequence of its purity. Free of contaminating air bubbles, it is transparent like an ice cube from a refrigerator. Black ice transmits incident light, absorbing little of it. Lake water and bottom absorb the transmitted light, returning none to the viewer and hence imparting no color to the ice, which appears black.

The relatively slight absorption of sunlight by black ice entails a practical benefit. Patches of black ice amid gray, snow ice can be sailably hard when the surrounding ice is impassably soft. Snow ice absorbs more sunlight than black ice, and this absorbed light becomes heat, raises the surface temperature, and softens the surface to make it impassable to skaters. But islands of hard black ice in an expanse of snow ice are commonplace on deep lakes during mid to late winter. They develop from open water in mid-lake unaffected by early freezes. The same freezes bring ice to the shallows that accumulates snow and gradually transforms to gray (or grayish white) snow ice.

Thick black ice promises smooth sailing, but thin black ice threatens cold bathing. This kind of ice lacks air bubbles when pure and lacks cracks when new. A skate sailor cannot judge its thickness without cutting or breaking through it. By contrast, the presence of air bubbles in snow ice, and of short shallow cracks in aged black ice, allows an ice sailor to estimate the sheet thickness. Such cracks run three to six inches in length, for example.

The cracks are a common feature of safely thick ice, and appear as short, opaque bands below the surface and perpendicular to it. They look white so they starkly contrast the surrounding blackness, making it easy to estimate their width and depth. With one crack lying above another, summing the estimated widths crudely measures the ice thickness near the cracks.

Special weather — including below-freezing temperatures, clear skies, and still air — favors the overnight formation of thick and smooth black ice. Ice sheet thickness increases as the surrounding air temperature decreases. Temperatures much below freezing allow a growing ice sheet to thicken fastest. Air temperatures are lowest at night when radiant heat loss is at a maximum. A clear night maximizes heat loss to the atmosphere; whereas an overcast sky minimizes the loss, reflecting some radiation to the earth.

Windless weather helps produce smooth ice over still water. It prevents new ice sheets from breaking into small, irregular pieces. Clumped together, such pieces fuse to yield jagged ice, which is called brash ice and can be impassable or difficult to traverse for anyone wearing ice skates.

Agglomeratic Ice

There are two kinds of agglomeratic ice, one formed from fusion of sheet ice pieces, and the other from a freezing mixture of water and snow. The first kind of agglomeratic ice displays a geometric pattern formed by the shapes of the small irregular pieces that froze together to form it. The second type arises when falling snow lands in freezing water to produce slush. Patches of slush initially accumulate, then solidify and link together. This kind of agglomeratic ice is also known as snow ice. (The term snow ice has two meanings, the present one and the following one.)

Snow Ice

The color of snow ice ranges from bright white through light green to stone gray. Entrapped air makes the ice opaque. The trapped gas bubbles reflect visible light striking the ice, accounting for its appearance. The white color results from mixing all the primary colors. Snow ice is also called white ice.

Probably snow ice is the most common kind traversed by skate sailors. It is aged ice, formed from snow accumulated on an ice sheet and gradually transformed into ice.

Several time-taking processes, hastened by the presence of liquid water and the prevalence of near-freezing temperatures, convert snow into ice. One of these processes is recrystallization, which may occur by local melting and refreezing on a microscopic scale. Recrystallization may also take place by sublimation, which entails no melting at all. Instead, gaseous water molecules diffuse from one crystal to another where they resolidify. The larger crystals then grow at the expense of the smaller ones, which ultimately disappear. In another important process, known as sintering, microscopic ice bridges form between existing crystals. All these processes change smaller, lighter snow crystals into larger, heavier ice crystals, which sometimes reach lengths of 20 inches.

Shell Ice

Shell ice is translucent, white and thin, attaining thicknesses of three-eighths of an inch or less. It lies over an air pocket that itself surmounts a thick, stable ice sheet. Shell ice forms in comparatively small patches over water pooled in temporary depressions. The pooled water drains off leaving ice as brittle as eggshells. Such ice shatters beneath skates, and the loud, crashing noises that result often precede a tumble. The broken ice drops the skater or sailor to the main ice sheet below the shell.

Salt Ice

Growing ice crystals physically reject impurities like air and salts that are suspended or dissolved in the water. Consequently, ice lying over an estuary contains little salt on a microscopic scale. The salt expelled by freezing, however, does form brine pockets in the ice sheet that are evident on a macroscopic scale. In effect the crystal lattice formed by water molecules excludes salt ions, which then concentrate near the edges of adjoining crystals. Unlike the water molecules, the salt ions and air gases are not essential structural components of the ice lattice.

Ice near the intercrystal boundaries contains more impurities than ice far from the edges. The impurities lower the melting temperature of ice at the boundaries, and the depressed melting point helps create unsafe, rotten ice that forms in springtime or during a prolonged winter thaw. Boundary ice lying over fresh or salt water melts first, leaving floes that can tilt or break beneath a sailor.

Pulled by gravity, the pockets of brine in salt ice migrate downward as the ice ages. The upper layer of new salt ice is therefore saltier than lower layers, its content attaining values of 2 to 4%. Toward spring, the macroscopic salt content due to brine pockets falls between 0.4 and 0.7% because of migration.

Because of concentration during crystallization, the clustered brine pockets contain more salt per volume unit than the estuarine water that formed the ice first. The saltier the solution at crystal boundaries, the less readily it freezes and thickens. In part, this explains why salt ice of a given thickness merits less trust than freshwater ice of the same thickness. A narrow strip of thin ice may border an expanse of thick salt ice.

Pressure Ridges

An ice mountain running for hundreds of feet and rising several inches or feet above the plane of an ice sheet is a pressure ridge. Such ridges, which can be dangerous to approach or cross, appear at the boundaries of two ice sheets and often connect opposite points of land where a lake narrows. In some places they are associated with currents created by streams emptying into a lake. Each sheet bends to form the ridge, one sheet rising above the other and above the water as well. The edge of the lower sheet dips below the water surface, and open water often extends a considerable distance along the lower sheet from the upper sheet edge.

Physical forces acting on ice produce pressure ridges, and these forces arise when water freezes and ice contracts. Water expands as it cools below 39° F and then freezes, so that a fixed mass of water fills a larger volume than the ice it forms. This expansive property of (liquid) water distinguishes it from ordinary substances. They show the opposite behavior, contracting as they cool and expanding as they warm. Ice is an ordinary substance in this sense, although it has the same chemical composition as liquid water.

The relatively low temperatures of winter nights contract an ice sheet, which cracks because the tensile strength of ice is low. (Fortunately for skaters, the shearing strength of ice is relatively high.) Cracks, sometimes forming to the accompaniment of booms, allow water to well between the resulting two ice sheets. Overnight, this water simultaneously freezes and expands, and new ice occupies the crack (Figure 6-2). The expansive force helps form pressure ridges.

The higher temperatures of the next day inexorably expand all the ice, which tends to grow in all directions. It does grow only in those directions that will physically accommodate its increased volume. But the ice cannot always expand horizontally

Figure 6-2: Developing Pressure Ridge

toward the shore, which may restrict growth. So, when only vertical expansion is possible, ice ridges arise from ice plains.

Large variations between day and night temperatures cause cycles of ice expansion and contraction. This explains the changeability of pressure ridges, which may contain no more than a six-inch gap of open water on one day, but a six-foot expanse on the next. Repeated expansions and contractions could, in principle, pump an entire lake onto the surrounding shore as ice. Indeed, massive ice boulders sometimes appear beside frozen lakes, exiled by the expansive forces of growing ice sheets.

Expansion and contraction cycles also cause damage near shores, which often offer little resistance to advancing ice. The force of expansion easily drives an ice sheet landward, where it can crush undefended boathouses and boats. To avert damage, lakeside property owners sometimes circulate the water near docks or boathouses to prevent freezing. The sight of boathouses should remind skate sailors to bear away because the boathouses may adjoin open water maintained by bubblers.

PROPERTIES OF ICE AND WATER

Because of their importance to skate sailing, certain physical properties of ice and water inform this section. For ice, they comprise the freezing point, crystallinity, heat of freezing, thermal conductivity, coefficient of friction, and density. This section also presents the extraordinary relation between the temperature and density of liquid water. All these properties bear on ice formation, safety, and slipperiness, and they explain certain familiar observations:

♦ Lake water must cool to 39° F before any of it freezes even when the surrounding air temperature is below freezing

♦ A shallow body of water develops ice sooner than a deep one, which dissolves

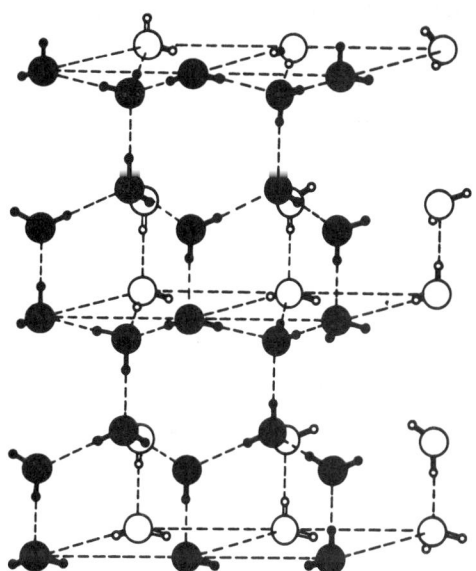

Figure 6-3: Crystal Structure of Ice. Large and small circles designate oxygen and hydrogen atoms, respectively. Dark circles project toward the viewer and light ones away. Dotted lines indicate hydrogen bonds or the horizontal planes occupied by certain oxygen atoms.

ice later than a shallow one

♦ Ice floats atop water

♦ Deep water below a thick outdoor ice sheet remains liquid despite prolonged sub-freezing temperatures in the air above a lake

♦ Skate sailing and skating take place at optimum temperatures established by the varying coefficients of sliding friction between steel and ice.

Finally, an acquaintance with these properties will facilitate understanding of the section dealing with the time required for ice to form or melt.

Selected Physical Properties

Freezing Point

Under ideal conditions, fresh water solidifies at 32° F, a temperature that represents a characteristic physical property known as its freezing point. For water (as well as for other liquids), the freezing and melting temperatures are the same. Neither freezing nor melting is instantaneous, so freezing water and melting ice can and often do co-exist in the same place.

The brackish water freezing point differs from the fresh water one, and depends on the salt content. Increasing concentrations of dissolved salt depress the freezing point. The Baltic Sea, which contains about 1% of salts by weight freezes at 31° F, a drop of one degree. By contrast, the Atlantic Ocean freezes at a lower temperature of 29° F because it contains as much as 3.5% of salts.

Latent Heat of Freezing

Freezing water liberates measurable heat to colder surroundings, while melting ice absorbs heat from a warmer environment. The two amounts of heat equal one another when the mass of liquid water equals the weight of the ice. The quantity of heat released when a fixed amount of water forms ice is a constant called the latent heat of freezing. A pound of freezing water liberates 144 British thermal units (btu) of heat. This quantity is characteristic of water, other liquids showing different heats of freezing.

Freezing water liberates heat, and melting ice absorbs it. Both influence how long it takes an ice sheet to appear or disappear. The time required to disperse or supply the heat of freezing increases with increasing quantities of ice. It depends partly on the rate at which heat flows through ice.

Thermal Conductivity

Heat flows at different, characteristic speeds through different materials. The time taken to form or melt an ice sheet depends in part upon this rate. Ice is not an exceptional substance, and the rate of heat flow through it is not infinitely fast. The time taken to form or melt ice is finite, not instantaneous.

The rate that heat travels across a temperature gradient is known as the thermal conductivity of ice. It has a measurable, constant value under specified conditions. The numerical value refers to fixed amounts of heat, a set temperature difference, and to a certain distance between the surfaces representing the warmer origin and the colder destination of the heat journey. Exactly 0.000358 btu per second will pass through a one-foot-thick ice sheet with its surface temperatures differing by one degree Fahrenheit.

An ice sheet conducts heat so slowly that it insulates the underlying water as a rug does a floor. As a consequence, even a shallow lake rarely if ever freezes completely, despite prolonged stretches of cold weather. Instead, slow heat transport establishes comparatively durable temperature differences, which run from the air to the ice, across the upper and lower ice surfaces, and from the lower ice surface to deep water. For example, with the air near the ice at 0° F, the ice temperature might range from 0° to 32°. The 0° ice would lie near the top of the sheet, and the 32° ice near the bottom of it. The water temperatures would span the gap from 32° to 39°. Water at 32° would be found near the underside of the sheet, and water at 39° would appear at the lake bottom.

Water Volume and Density

Liquid water is extraordinary because of the way its temperature affects its volume (Figure 6-4, upper curve). The volume of a fixed mass of the liquid can increase or decrease as its temperature falls. If the temperature rises, the volume can also increase or decrease. Furthermore, the dependence of volume on temperature shows a minimum value. Water volume is least at 39.2° F. By contrast, ordinary substances contract only as they cool, expand only as they warm, and show no minimum volume.

Whether water expands or contracts as it cools depends upon its initial temperature. At temperatures between 39° and 32° F, liquid water expands on cooling, whereas ordinary materials shrink. Liquid water contracts on cooling if its temperature initially exceeds 39° F, and its volume is least

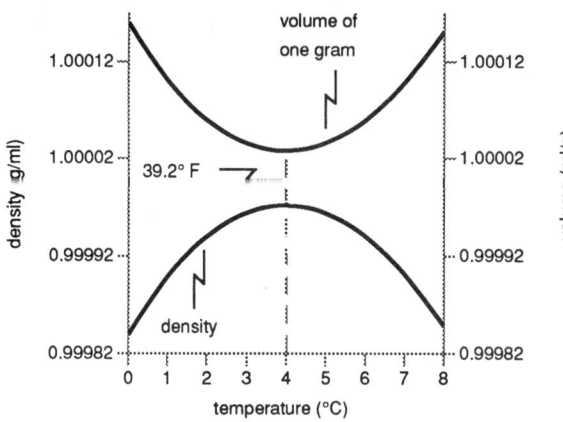

**Figure 6-4: Effects of Temperature on the Density
and Volume of Liquid Water**

at 39.2° F. In other words, a pound of water cooled from 50° to 40° fills a smaller space after cooling than before it. In this respect, water resembles ordinary substances. Because the volume of liquid water changes with temperature while its mass is unaffected, the density of the liquid, defined as the ratio of mass to volume, also varies (Figure 6-4, lower curve).

The effects of temperature on volume determine the density of water, which is greatest when its temperature is 39.2° F (4° C). (Figure 6-4, lower curve). Above this temperature, the density regularly increases, from a smaller initial value, as the water temperature decreases. But from 39° to 32° F, temperature drops smoothly decrease density. If a 50° layer of water at the surface of a lake cools to 38° F, it sinks because its density rises. The falling, 38° water displaces any warmer layer near the lake bottom, and the displaced layer rises toward the surface where it can be cooled. Displacements like these create a top-to-bottom current that exchanges overlying, recently cooled layers with underlying, warmer layers. Because of such currents, no lake water freezes until all of it cools to 39° F, and until some of it reaches 32° F. Ice formation in a lake is a relatively slow process since so much water must be cooled before any freezes. The time required

explains why ice on shallow lakes forms and melts faster than that atop deep lakes. More heat must leave deep lakes, which contain more heat because they contain more water than shallow ones.

A lake freezes from the top down because the coldest, 32° F liquid water forms and remains at the surface. Heat loss from a lake to its surroundings occurs largely at the interface between water and air, so the coldest water appears first at the surface. As water cools from 39° F to 32° F, its volume increases while its density decreases. Water at 32° is the least dense.

Ice Density

Ice floats because it weighs only 92% as much as water, when equal volumes are compared at 32° F. A sheet of ice formed from 32° F water at the surface of a lake remains uppermost. This welcome quirk of nature makes skate sailing possible in the northern climes. If ice were denser than water, the frozen solid would sink below the liquid surface and lakes would freeze from their bottoms up. No one could skate sail until the ice thickened enough to reach the surface, and fewer opportunities for skate sailing would arise. Complete solidification of a deep lake would take much longer than formation of a relatively thin ice sheet.

Ice density is not a constant, but varies with temperature. It decreases as the temperature increases. A fixed weight of ice at a higher temperature therefore occupies a greater volume. For example, ice at 32° F occupies about 8% more space than an equal mass of water at the same temperature. Such a volume increase occurs during daytime warming, and, like the expansion associated with freezing, can cause damage to lakeside structures.

PROCESSES FORMING ICE

In the formation of ice, five processes are important: heat loss and transfer, supercooling, nucleation, and growth. An appreciation of these effects is needed to understand the next section of this chapter, which deals with the time needed to thicken an ice sheet.

Heat Loss

Ice formation requires that lake water cool to 32° F and that the atmosphere absorb the heat elevating the temperature of the lake above the freezing point. The atmosphere must also disperse the heat liberated when water freezes. The consequent heat loss occurs at the surface of a lake, largely through air convection and infrared radiation. To a lesser extent, a lake also loses heat by evaporation from its surface, a process more important in summer than winter. Precipitation and an influx of cold ground water contribute to a lowering of water temperature, but less so than convection in the fall and winter.

Heat Transfer

Freezing requires not only heat loss from the surface but heat transfer from the depths. Indeed, there is a peculiar dependence of liquid water density on temperature: Density increases as temperature decreases from a higher value to a limiting value of 39.2° F.

Heat loss produces relatively cool, dense water near the top. Grown denser than the underlying water because it is cooler, this water sinks, displacing warmer water lying at greater depths. The risen warmer water, like the original water at the surface, requires cooling before freezing. The arrival of a cold air mass above a warm lake creates upwelling currents in the lake depths, which effectively carry heat from the bottom to the top. Heat transport by such a mechanism requires that the whole lake cool to 39.2° F before any of it freezes. This phenomenon partly explains why deep lakes freeze comparatively slowly: More water must travel between the surface and the deep. A deep lake takes more time

to accomplish this than does a shallow lake, where the mass of water and the amount of heat borne by it are smaller.

Oppositely, the volume of a fixed weight of water expands as the water cools below 39.2 degrees. Such water remains at the surface, or floats to it; so the exchange of water masses ultimately slows and stops. The top layer of water continues to lose heat to the air, while its temperature drops below the freezing point before any ice forms.

Supercooling

For water to form ice, it is necessary but usually insufficient for the liquid to attain its freezing point. Supercooling is also necessary, as is nucleation (read on). The term supercooling refers to the attainment of a water temperature less than the 32° F freezing point of fresh water.

If ice were to form exactly at the freezing point, the liberated heat of freezing would raise the remaining water temperature over 32°, so preventing more freezing. As a result, continued heat loss to bring the liquid water temperature below the freezing point is necessary to dissipate the latent heat of freezing.

Nucleation

Ice formation rarely takes place in isolation unless the degree of supercooling is very great, when spontaneous crystallization does occur. Instead, crystallization usually begins with seeding, which occurs when a falling particle of snow strikes supercooled water, or when such water physically touches some other solid particle. Crystallization of one substance induced by a particle of another is known as nucleation. Suitable seed particles must resemble ice in crystal structure (Figure 6-3) but need not possess the same elemental composition.

Ice Growth

Seeding supercooled water can

instantaneously begin an ice sheet, and simultaneously advance it in three dimensions. Growth is fastest in the surface plane where the latent heat of fusion is most quickly dispersed, and such growth produces skim ice. The skim can cover a large area within a short time. The crystals grow much more slowly on the underside, partly because of the time required to disperse the liberated heat of freezing. The time course of ice-sheet thickening without snow is a well studied phenomenon, described by a simple equation that appears in the next section.

THE TIME NEEDED TO THICKEN ICE

Puzzled onlookers often press skate sailors to explain two paradoxical observations. First, ice formed during a short cold spell can be thick and safe in late November or early December. Second, safe lake ice can last as late as March or April, despite a string of several warm days. Both observations have a single explanation with a basis in simple physical chemistry. Time is needed to form or melt ice because heat conduction through it is not instantaneous. How much time is needed is the subject of this section, which must concern anyone who ventures onto naturally formed, outdoor ice. Long times and low temperatures bear directly on ice thickness. This and the preceding sections consequently form the basis for an understanding of ice safety, which Chapter Nine presents.

Relation among Time, Thickness, and Temperature

A simple equation governs the time needed to form ice. It relates the time (t, in hours) to a numerical constant, to the square of the ice sheet thickness (x, in inches), and to the reciprocal of a temperature difference ($T_0 - T_a$):

$$t = \frac{21.2\,x^2}{T_0 \cdot T_a}$$

In the denominator of this expression, T_0 represents the freezing point and T_a represents the surrounding air temperature. Both temperatures are expressed in degrees Fahrenheit. T_0 equals 32° F for fresh water, 31° for Baltic Sea water, and 29° for the saltier Atlantic Ocean. The constant of 21.2 is determined by three physical properties of ice and water, namely thermal conductivity, latent heat of freezing, and ice density.

This equation is applicable only under certain conditions that are rarely met except in the controlled setting of a laboratory. These conditions are (a) physical contact between the water and ice, and between the ice and air; (b) still water; (c) calm air; (d) constant air and water temperatures; and (e) water temperature equal to or less than the freezing temperature.

The first of these requirements, for contact between ice and air, prevents applying the equation to ice covered by snow. Accumulated snow slows or halts growth on the underside of an ice sheet. The thermal conductivities of snow and ice differ, so heat travels more slowly through the snow than it would through the ice. A blanket of snow insulates warmer ice from colder air, retarding heat transport from the water through the ice to the air. Therefore, snow-covered ice is untrustworthy because it may be thin despite cold weather.

In nature, moving water is often warmer than still water, so the equation does not accurately describe the time needed to freeze it. Indeed, the time needed to form ice over lakes and reservoirs is usually unpredictable,†† partly because they contain springs, inlets, and outlets of moving water.

†† Predicting the advent of permanent ice cover has been the object of much research, and the mathematically adept reader may wish to consult a standard Russian work: *Manual of Forecasting Ice-Formation for Rivers and Inland Lakes*, ed. L. G. Shulyakovskii; published for the U. S. Dept. of Commerce and the National Science Foundation by the Israel Program for Scientific Translations, Jerusalem, 1966.

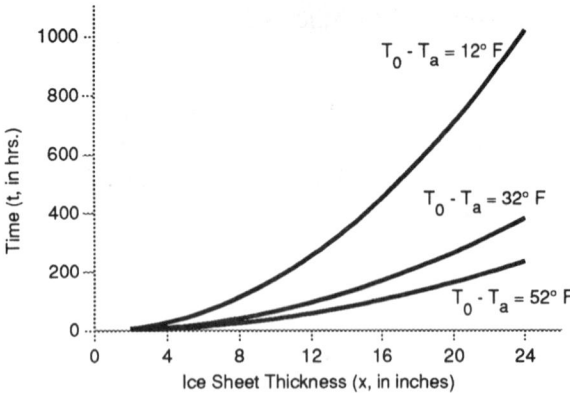

Figure 6-5: Time Course of Ice Sheet Thickening in Fresh Water: Variation of Time with Thickness at Constant Air Temperature

Certainly the needed time cannot be forecast by our equation because lake water lacks the steady thermal state that the equation assumes. The motion of air over a lake also disrupts the thermal equilibrium in which water releases or absorbs heat. Moving air can quickly carry heat away from the water, and decrease freezing times beyond what the equation would predict.

The requirement for constant air temperature means that our equation becomes inaccurate when applied to lakes warmed by day then cooled by night. As a result, use of the equation must not supplant direct measurement of ice thickness for safety's sake.

Times to Form Varying Ice Thicknesses

That said, consider how ice sheet thickness x and temperature difference $T_0 - T_a$ affect the time for ice sheet thickening (Figure 6-4). At constant thickness, freezing time decreases as the temperature difference increases. In other words, the lower the below-freezing temperature is, the faster an ice sheet reaches a given thickness. This decrease is a linear one proportional to the reciprocal of the difference, as long as the surrounding air temperature is nowhere near 32 degrees F. As the air temperature approaches the freezing temperature, however, the times required to form sheets of any thickness abruptly become large.

The effects of changing thickness at a constant temperature difference (Figure 6-5) and of changing difference at constant sheet thickness (Figure 6-5) oppose one another. An increase in thickness brings an increase in time, but an increase in difference leads to a decrease in time. Cooperation of time and temperature changes is needed to account for a familiar observation. The greatest ice sheet thickness arises from a prolonged stretch of the coldest weather

Freezing time increases as thickness increases. The increase occurs in proportion to the square of the ice-sheet thickness. For example, a two-inch-thick ice sheet forms in seven hours when the air temperature equals 20° F. This sheet doubles its thickness in 28 hours, four times longer than the previous seven-hour period. Doubling again, this time to an eight-inch-thickness, needs 113 hours, which is nearly five days. Doubling of the sheet thickness requires quadrupling of the freezing time, so plots of these variables do not show straight lines but smooth curves instead (Figure 6-5). Inspect Figure 6-5, which presents three plots of the equation. The curves show that, in cold weather and under ideal conditions, comparatively little time is needed to form safe, thick ice. At air temperatures ranging from -30° F to 10° F, a seven-inch-thick sheet will form in one to three days, respectively. A foot of ice results from two days at -30° F or six days at 10° F. Even shorter times create ice two inches thick. Cold snaps often bring these temperatures and times. Hence, the sight of skate sailors in early December or late November should come as no surprise.

From Melting to Breakup

Even at air temperatures above 32° F, a thick ice sheet does not melt instantly. It requires time to disappear because heat transport from the warmer air through the

Table 6-6: Finding Sailable Ice — A Prescription

By telephone

Whom to call
- Skate-Sailing Association hot line
- Other skate sailors
- Ice board sailors and associations
- Ice boat sailors and clubs
- Ice fishermen
- Shore dwellers

When to call
- 12-48 hours before an outing

By inspection

What to visit
- lakes
- ponds (10 acres or more)
- reservoirs
- estuaries
- river bays
- clusters of the foregoing

When to visit
- mid-November to mid-March
  depending on geographic location
- early season
  shallow, high-lying lakes or ponds
- late season
  — deep, low-lying lakes, ponds, or
    reservoirs
  — estuaries and river bays

How far to travel
- an hour's drive often brings success,
  especially among clustered sites

Such ice, however, can be treacherously thin at crystal boundaries where melting occurs first because of concentrated impurities.

Spring brings ice floes, which form near ice sheet boundaries like shores, pressure ridges, and other cracks. Melting is fastest near such boundaries because near them lie impurities expelled during freezing and trapped afterwards. Impurities like salts and entrapped air lower the freezing point of the surrounding water, and so weaken the sheet. Furthermore, ice over shallow water melts first. A greater proportion of the heat from the sun serves to warm the ice over shallow water than over deep water. Where the water is deep, more of the thermal radiation warms the water than the ice. Even a thick ice sheet may prove unsafe at its boundaries in spring temperatures.

FINDING SAILABLE ICE

Anyone who desires to sail on ice should seek sailable ice, so this concluding section prescribes methods to employ in the search. These methods, presented in Table 6-6, can be summarized briefly. Telephone interested parties because they are likely to know the whereabouts of sailable ice, and repeatedly inspect suitable sites at different times in the sailing season. If you find sailable ice, act soon on your knowledge because ice surfaces change quickly.

Tours of Inspection

Venture forth often if you would sail on skates, knowing that most arguments in favor of staying home are too flimsily based. Neither the snow of harsh weather, nor the rains and thaws of mild weather, necessarily end the skate sailing season. Admittedly, such weather prevents sailing in comfort or safety when it arrives, yet wet weather does not preclude an outing after it ceases. Useful knowledge of its effects on pre-existing ice must form the basis of a successful outing, however. An inspection tour or a few phone

colder sheet is not instantaneous. Melting on a lake begins when the surrounding air temperature averages 32° F. From the first appearance of surface water, 10 to 30 days follow before ice breakup. Thick ice sheets formed over the whole winter consequently last through the comparatively warm days of late February and early March. And in some places, lakes retain thick ice into April.

calls often reveal sailable ice within a 50-mile radius from home, even when current forecasts or a recent history of wet weather make the prospect seem remote.

Whom to Ask

A call to skaters, other skate sailors, ice boarders or boaters, ice fishermen or shore dwellers may be rewarded even when local weather seems to preclude skate sailing. The condition of an ice sheet is of greatest concern to skaters and to other skate sailors who need smooth ice that is free of snow. It concerns ice boaters and ice boarders to lesser extents because they can sail on rougher or snowier ice than skate sailors. Shore dwellers and ice fishermen are also likely to know the whereabouts of sailable ice. State highway patrols and local police forces are often willing to report lake ice conditions, but their assessments of ice safety can be more conservative than helpful. Seeking information is most important after snow or rain, and a short call may save a long drive leading to disappointment.

Several ice-sailing organizations maintain telephone hotlines for members and other callers during the sailing season. Their scouts make ice information available by Thursday or Friday, in preparation for weekends when most sailing takes place. Such information usually covers the condition and location of sailable ice, and sometimes gives driving directions for reaching the spot and the whereabouts of suitable launching places. Often the scout will include his judgment of the prospect for good weekend sailing. The organizations devoted to ice sailing are listed in the *Encyclopedia of Associations*, available in public libraries. For another introduction to these groups, visit a lake, find an ice sailor, and ask him.

Acting Soon

If you come upon sailable ice or learn of its whereabouts, act promptly. Weather and ice conditions change fast, so postponing an outing for more than a day courts disappointment. Skate sailors cannot expect more than 12 to 48 hours' notice of sailable ice and must seize the moment. "You have a short season and maybe no season at all if the weather refuses to cooperate," warns one avid skate sailor.

Mid-week Illnesses

Not only uncooperative weather but work and other duties restrict the number of sailing days available to many skate sailors. When working days have been subtracted from a sailing season rarely longer than three months, the remainder is some 12 weekends and a few holidays comprising about 28 days in all. Snow, thaws, and a lack of ice sometimes ruin half of these days. As a result, many sailors can enjoy only about 14 good skate sailing days during some seasons. Understandably, then, the small number of good sailing days in a bad season makes skate sailing pleasures keen and sailors eager to seek them. Enthusiastic skate sailors who are gainfully employed thus fall prey to obscure mid-week illnesses. Complaints include the mysterious Lake Bottom Fever and the notorious Salt Ice Craving, affecting those who sail on estuaries in New Jersey. Treatments — there are no cures — call for victims to return promptly to the sites where they fell ill. Healing pilgrimages take place on what otherwise would be working days. "I've had a seizure; I'm deathly ill; I can't make it in today," they say.

Augury

There are lies, there are damned lies, and there are weather forecasts. Forecasts, although they are well meant, are often useless to skate sailors because they apply to large geographic regions. Despite their ready availability, they do not accurately predict conditions in the diverse microclimates surrounding scattered bodies of water. Like weather close to home, weather predictions do not reliably foretell the condition of a distant ice sheet. As a result, armchair judgments of the likeliness of sailable ice, if they are based on forecasts or existing local weather, are often inaccurate and always untrustworthy.

Misplaced trust in predictions and judgments needlessly disappoints novice skate sailors.

Another needless disappointment — lack of a skate sail — is prevented by the next chapter, Sailmaking.

CHAPTER SEVEN: SAILMAKING

"Measure twice and cut once." — proverb

There are three reasons for building a skate sail in preference to buying one: to earn the satisfaction of accomplishment, to lower costs, and to meet your own specifications for the finished craft. If you make a skate sail, you will be free to choose its color(s) as well as other elements of its graphic design. You can select its fabric and its window size and placement, all of which contribute to its performance. Finally, you will have the chance to make your sail as large or small as you like. If you are the least bit handy, read on to learn what the work entails.

Chapter Seven explains how to make a Hopatcong skate sail at home. Having chosen the desired sail area, you will need to know the dimensions of the planned sail, the length and width of sail cloth required, and the dimensions of the needed sailcloth panels. The sail is made by cutting a length of sailcloth into five panels of three shapes, heat-sealing the edges, sewing the cut pieces together, finishing the edges, making the jib and tail bow pockets, and installing the grommets, windows, and reinforcements.

To help choose the sail size, the chapter reviews the different ways in which a skate sail can serve its sailor, and indicates how varying sail areas do this. It also examines the limitations to sail size imposed by a sailor's physique and proficiency, by the prevailing wind, and by sail design. A knowledge of the sail area alone will yield the dimensions of a standard Hopatcong sail, from the set of simple sail equations in Table 7-1 or from Table 3-4 in Chapter Three. The latter table eliminates the need to evaluate equations; instead of doing so, a sailmaker need only select the desired sail dimensions from the table. Numerical values of the required sailcloth length and width appear in Table 7-2 as functions of sail area. The panel dimensions appear there and in Tables 7-3 and 7-4. Other tables list the tools (Table 7-5) and materials (Table 7-6) that sailmaking requires.

CHOOSING THE SAIL AREA AND FINDING THE SAIL DIMENSIONS

Skate sailors use differently sized sails for varied purposes: to sail in a storm, to introduce a child to the sport, to sail in all winds except gales, to race, to sail in a calm wind, and to go fast. As a rule, small sails ranging in area from 35 to 45 square feet are useful to adults in high winds and to children in low winds. A 35-square-foot sail, for example, will propel a 190-pound sailor at a breath-taking speed in a 20- to 25-mile-an-hour wind. As this section explains, seven factors — wind speed, sailing expertise, body size, sailing posture, and sail design determine the optimum sail area. Body size includes height, weight, and reach.

Eager to Start?

You can make a 54-square-foot Hopatcong sail without reading the first half of this chapter. Get 10 linear yards of sailcloth 36 inches wide, and consult Tables 7-5 and -6 for the tools and other materials you will need. Then turn to the section heading CUTTING and SEWING THE SAILCLOTH and follow the step-by-step procedure given there.

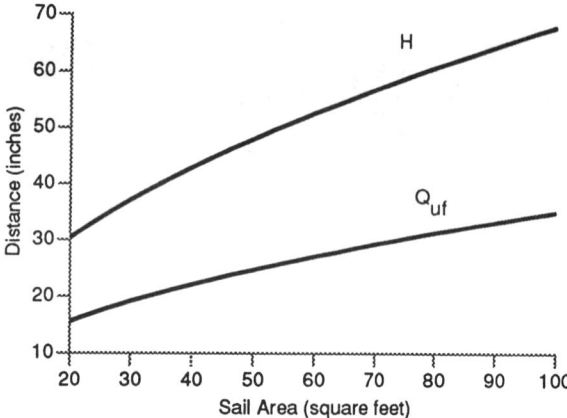

Figure 7-1. Variation of H and Q_{uf} with Sail Area in the Standard Hopatcong Design. (H and Q_{uf} are defined in the text.)

Area

The 55-Square-Foot Sail

Sails of 50 to 60 square feet are often regarded as all-weather, all-purpose sails, with the 55 square footers the most popular in the United States for more than 75 years. They are good for adult beginners, who will soon become proficient enough to race them in heavy winds. Expert sailors, however, frequently adopt these sails as their storm sails, which are useful and safe in strong winds. So, if a beginner persists in the sport of skate sailing, her initial investment will not be lost because she can continue to use her first-made sail in high winds. Even if a sailor gives up the sport, she can expect readily to sell a well made, used, 55-square-foot sail.

Racing Sails

Ice skate sails of 65 square feet or more are racing sails that become desirable when a beginner acquires an expert's sailing skills. Such sails are most often seen in the hands of racers, heavyweights, or ardent speed lovers. They will propel an adult sailor even in a light wind. One graceful, expert, and lightweight sailor deploys an 89-square-foot Hopatcong sail to pass his becalmed companions. Larger Hopatcong sails than his are presently unknown, although Table 3-4 in Chapter Three gives the dimensions of an unmodified 95-square-foot Hopatcong

sail. Identically sized skate sails of the Dragon plan are commonly used by Swedish experts even in high winds.

Fitting the Sail to the Sailor

For fun and safety, a skate sail should be correctly sized to serve its intended purpose. Its size should complement the wind-speed range as well as its sailor's proficiency and body size. In winds exceeding 20 mph, for example, an inexpert sailor weighing less than 150 lbs will do well to choose a 35-square-foot sail. These three factors — wind speed, sailing proficiency, and body size — set a lower limit to useful sail size. However, there are other criteria for choosing sail area. Body fit determines the largest sail that a sailor can handle. A skate sail fits if its mast passes an inch or two above the ice when it is properly shouldered and fenced by a sailor wearing ice skates and comfortably bending her knees. Shoulder height, sailing posture and, to a lesser extent, arm length determine how well the sail fits. These factors limit the largest useful size of sails made according to the standard Hopatcong plan. A sail is overlarge if its mast strikes ice, when it can capsize the sailor. It is also too big if holding the mast and maneuvering the sail require her fully to extend her windward steering arm. Finally the sail is overlarge if it develops a weather helm, turning uncontrollably upwind.

To estimate the area of the largest sail that you can handle, match its H-distance to the distance between your shoulders and skate blades (Figure 3-24). The H-distance is the perpendicular line between the sail edge and the mast-boom crossing; it lies along the (vertical) mast only when you shoulder your sail without fencing it. It is partly determined by the sail plan and area, and increases as the area does (Figure 7-1). The H-distance decreases with the angle between the sail edge and the ice sheet. As a result, it diminishes when you fence your sail, setting its lower edge parallel to the ice

(Figure 3-24). With your legs slightly bent, the distance between your shoulders and blades should exceed the H-distance by at least one inch. Otherwise, the mast will strike ice and the collision may topple you. Although your height partially determines the distance between your shoulders and blades — and thereby sets the area of the largest sail that you can handle — it is only one of two factors that influence this distance.

Sailing posture is the other factor. For stability, a proficient sailor bends her knees when she gets underway, reducing her effective shoulder height by several inches. In choosing sail area, therefore, a sailmaker should comfortably bend her knees when she measures the distance from her shoulders to her blades. Otherwise, the largest sail seemingly suitable for someone as a beginner may be too large for the same person as an expert. Novice sailors, who often stand straight without fencing their sails, risk overestimating the area of the largest sail that they can maneuver.

The tendency of an overlong mast to strike ice can be eased — although the best remedy is to choose the sail size properly in the first place. The next best treatment is to pad the boom or increase the distance between the sailor's blade edges and boot soles. A cylindrical shoulder cushion wrapped around the boom will raise this spar an inch or so above the sailor's shoulder. Spacers made from square aluminum tubing can be fixed between the boot soles and skate blades. They will elevate the sailor's feet above her skates, lifting her shouldered boom. Either device will permit her mast to clear the ice. The worst therapy is a beginner's attempt to hold the boom above her shoulder. It surrenders control of her craft.

Your arm reach also limits the size of the largest sail that you can handle, especially if the sail exceeds about 70 square feet and

follows the Hopatcong plan. Steering the sail requires you to hold the mast so that the center of lateral resistance of the sailing craft lies close to the center of effort. But, the distance (Q_{uf}) along the boom between the center of effort and the mast-boom crossing increases with sail size, which forces you to stand farther from the mast (Figure 7-1). This increasing distance demands a greater reach but provides less control.

Fortunately, arm reach is relatively unimportant in Hopatcong sails under 70 square feet. Such sails can readily accommodate an adult's reach. However, arm length was crucial in handling the 60-square-foot triangular Erie sails at the turn of the 19th century, and undoubtedly caused their popularity to decline. Their centers of effort lay 52 inches aft of the mast along the horizontal boom. This long distance exceeded virtually everyone's arm length, and made for strenuous sailing.

Dimensions

Sail Dimensions Tabulated

After deciding the sail area, you must find numerical values for the various sail dimensions. This is easily accomplished by selecting the values from Table 3-4 in Chapter Three. The table gives dimensions for sails ranging in area from 25 to 95 square feet, in steps of five square feet. To help you choose a sail area, Table 3-4 lists values of the perpendicular distance (H) from the sail edge to the mast-boom crossing and the horizontal distance (Q_{uf}) from this intersection to the center of effort.

Standard Sail Equations

For builders who seek to make intermediate-sized Hopatcong sails not covered by Table 3-4, Table 7-1 presents a dozen simple equations that relate the desired area A_s to the needed dimensions. These dimensions, illustrated in Figure 3-22 of Chapter Three, are respectively the jib and tail radii (R_j and R_t), the jib and tail

Table 7-1: Sail Equations†*

$$R_j = 10.902 \sqrt{A_s} \qquad S_j = 15.906 \sqrt{A_s} \qquad W = 10.974 \sqrt{A_s}$$

$$R_t = 6.714 \sqrt{A_s} \qquad S_t = 6.339 \sqrt{A_s} \qquad V_s = 14.482 \sqrt{A_s}$$

$$Z_j = 7.266 \sqrt{A_s} \qquad Y_j = 2.774 \sqrt{A_s} \qquad H = 6.781 \sqrt{A_s}$$

$$Z_t = 3.053 \sqrt{A_s} \qquad Y_t = 0.734 \sqrt{A_s} \qquad Q_{uf} = 3.687 \sqrt{A_s}$$

† Areas are in square feet and other dimensions are in inches. * Symbols are defined in the text.

half-heights (Z_j and Z_t), and the arc lengths (S_j and S_t). They also include the depths of jib and tail bowing (Y_j and Y_t), the mainsail length (W) and the overall sail length (V). The last two equations give the horizontal distance Q_{uf} and the perpendicular distance H from the sail edge to the mast-boom crossing. In an unfenced sail, the distance Q_{uf} lies along the boom between the center of effort and the spar crossing.

These simplified equations require the builder to extract the square root of the desired sail area, and to multiply this root by a numerical constant. Each equation accepts the sail area in square feet and yields the desired value in inches. All the equations apply only to standard Hopatcong sails with the characteristic jib, tail, and fencing angles, respectively of 83.6, 54.1, and 21°.

Other conditions must also be understood. Values of the numerical constants are given to three decimal places only as an aid to further calculations. Sailcloth is not cut to a tolerance of a thousandth of an inch, and cutting to within a quarter of an inch is adequate. The equation giving the H-distance assumes that the sail is fenced. By contrast, the equation furnishing the value of Q_{uf} refers to an unfenced sail carried with the boom horizontal. The center-of-effort position changes by a few inches when the sail is fenced. This last equation considers only the sail, not the physical system of sailor, spars, and sail. It treats the sail as a geometrical object that is planar, stationary, and rigid. The calculated position of the center of effort relative to the spar crossing therefore represents a first approximation to its actual position in a cruising skate sail.

HOW MUCH SAIL CLOTH TO BUY

This section analyzes the lengths of cloth needed for Hopatcong sails of various areas according to the layout detailed in the section entitled Making the Sail. Because sailcloth comes only in standard widths of 36 or 48 inches, the required length primarily depends upon sail area and the width of the purchased cloth. The layout calls for cutting the length of cloth initially into three panels. Two are equal in area (panels A, Figure 7-2). The third (panel C, Figure 7-3) will be smaller. The two larger panels, each of which will form one half-sail, will be cut into two pieces. The smaller of these pieces will be right triangles (panels B, Figure 7-2) for the V-shaped inserts characterizing the Hopatcong sail plan. The larger pieces (panels A) will have the shape of an irregular pentagon. Cloth from the third panel (C) will go into the jib and tail pockets, and this panel will be a simple rectangle until it is cut into four curved strips. (Figure 7-3). In summary, the work of cutting the one strip of purchased sailcloth yields five panels: two pentagonal panels A, two triangular panels B, and one rectangular panel C. Further subdivision of panel C furnishes four curved strips of two sizes.

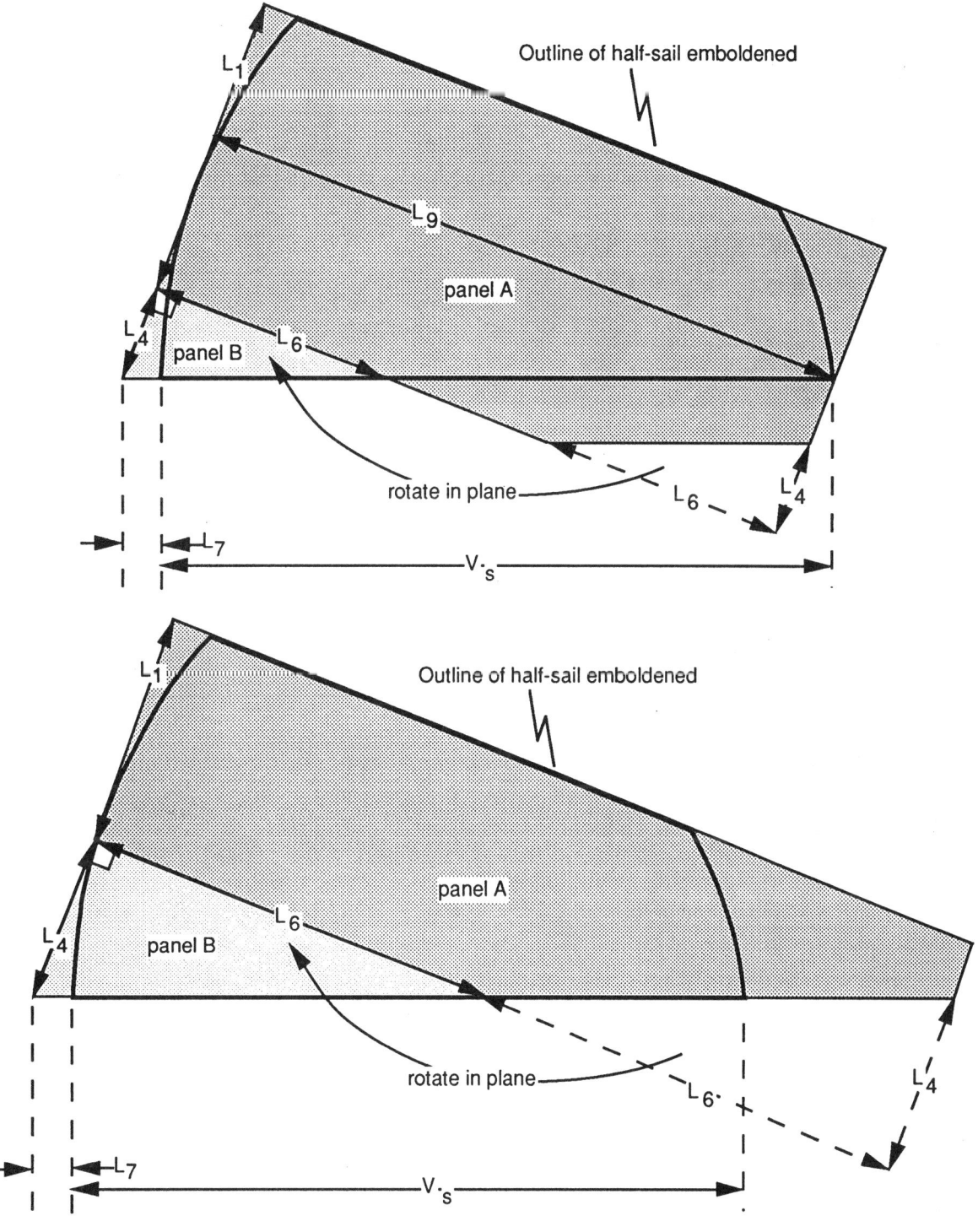

Figure 7-2: Layout of Half-sails; Top, Half-sail Made with Wide (48-inch) Cloth; Bottom, Half-Sail Made with Narrow (36-inch) Cloth

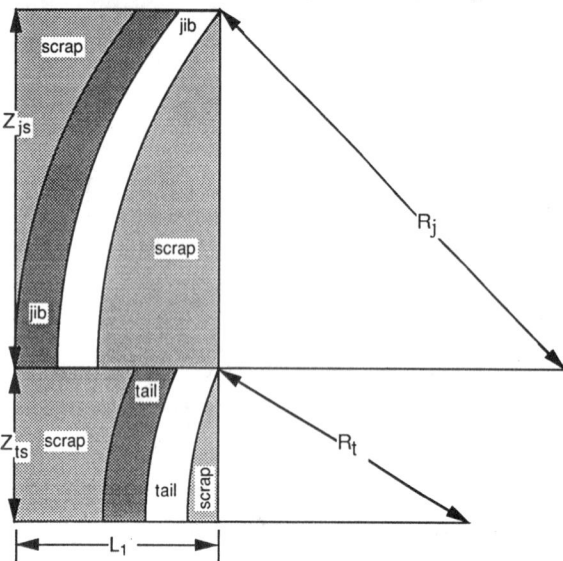

Figure 7-3: Panel C: Cloth for Jib and Tail Pockets

Cloth for the Half-Sails

Figure 7-2 shows that the needed length of sailcloth depends on its width (L_1). For a given sail, the triangular panel B will be smaller in area if the cloth is wide (Figure 7-2, top) than if the cloth is narrow (Figure 7-2, bottom). With narrow (36 inches) cloth, the length needed for the two half-sails will equal four times the length (L_6) of the triangular panel B (Figure 7-2, bottom). With wide (48 inches) cloth, the required length equals twice the length L_9. This equality follows from an inspection of the half-sail shown at the top of Figure 7-2; it includes a factor of two because two half-sails are needed.

In general, the length of sailcloth needed for two half-sails will be the larger of $4L_6$ and $2L_9$. These lengths are shown in Table 7-2 where this quantity is called "Twice the Length of Panel A." The table lists values of this quantity as functions of cloth width and sail area. The values apply to two widths, 36 and 48 inches, and to 13 sails differing by increments of five square feet. Table 7-2 requires no mathematics, but only a choice of the desired sail area and the corresponding length for panels A and C.

Cloth for the Jib and Tail Pockets

The length of sailcloth to make panel C

also depends on the sail design, dimensions, and layout. The layout in Figure 7-3 calls for cutting a rectangular piece of cloth into two long curved strips for the jib pockets and two short ones for the tail pockets. It requires that the jib and tail strips be longer than the jib and tail by 6 and 4 inches, respectively. The layout gives the sailmaker freedom to determine the widths of the jib and tail strips, which in turn establish the fullness of the corresponding pockets. In all cases, a width of 5 inches should be more than enough.

With the aid of simple mathematics, the foregoing requirements and equalities furnish the needed length of cloth to make panel C. This length represents the sum of the length (Z_{js}) needed to make the jib strips and that (Z_{ts}) required for the tail strips. Called "Length of Panel C" or $Z_{js} + Z_{ts}$, 13 values of this sum are presented in Table 7-2. All of them are correlated to sail areas. Separate values of Z_{js} and Z_{ts}, which will be needed to make the corresponding strips, appear in Table 7-4.

Cloth for the Complete Sail

The amount of cloth needed to make a sail equals the sum of the amounts for two half-sails and for the jib and tail strips.

Total Length of Sailcloth =
2 x (Length of Panel A) + (Length of Panel C)

This total appears in Table 7-2 under the heading "Total Length of Sailcloth." Throughout the table, it is correlated to sail areas.

The sailmaking method presented in the following section calls for a fabric area at least 50% greater than the nominal sail area. Regardless of whether you use 36- or 48-inch-wide sailcloth, you will have fabric left over. For example, an 80-square-foot sail would require 119 square feet of cloth, and would leave a remnant occupying 39 square feet. If you select 48-inch-wide cloth for a 40-square-foot sail, then you will need a strip

Table 7-2: Lengths (Yards) of Sailcloth Needed for Complete Hopatcong Skate Sails

Sail Area [a]	Total Length of Sailcloth [b]		Twice the Length of Panel A [c]		Length of Panel C [d]
	Width = 36 in.	Width = 48 in.	Width = 36 in.	Width = 48 in.	
95	—	11.8	—	8.8	3
90	—	11.1	—	8.2	2.9
85	—	10.5	—	7.6	2.9
80	13.2	9.9	10.4	7.1	2.8
75	12.5	9.6	9.8	6.9	2.7
70	11.7	9.2	9.1	6.6	2.6
65	10.9	8.9	8.4	6.4	2.5
60	10	8.6	7.6	6.2	2.4
55	9.2	8.2	6.9	5.9	2.3
50	8.3	7.8	6.1	5.6	2.2
45	7.4	7.4	5.3	5.3	2.1
40	7	7	5	5	2
35	6.6	—	4.7	—	1.9

[a] Sail area A_s in square feet. [b] Length (L_{11}) in linear yards. [c] Length ($2 L_{10}$) in linear yards. [d] Length ($Z_{js} + Z_{ts}$) in linear yards.

Table 7-3: Dimensions (Inches) of Right Triangular Panel B

Sail Area [a]	Height [b]		Length [c]	
	Width = 36 [d]	Width = 48 [d]	Width = 36 [d]	Width = 48 [d]
95	—	30.5	—	79.3
90	—	28.4	—	73.9
85	—	26.2	—	68.3
80	36	24	93.8	62.5
75	33.7	21.7	87.8	56.6
70	31.3	19.3	81.7	50.4
65	28.9	16.9	75.3	44
60	26.4	14.4	68.7	37.4
55	23.7	11.7	61.7	30.5
50	20.9	8.9	54.5	23.2
45	18	6	46.9	15.6
40	14.9	2.9	38.8	7.6
35	11.6	—	30.3	—

[a] Sail area A_s in square feet. [b] Height L_4 in inches. [c] Length L_6 in inches. [d] Sailcloth width in inches.

of sailcloth occupying 84 square feet. Of the 36-inch and 48-inch cloths, less is required of the former for sails ranging from 70 to 40 feet. For example, a 40-square-foot sail requires only 63 square feet of 36-inch-wide fabric. For the 40-75 square-foot sails in which 36- or 48-inch-wide cloth is useful and in which different quantities are needed (Table 7-2), the narrower fabric is more economical. In these and the other five cases, you may have enough cloth left over to make a sail bag, depending on how you fold the finished sail.

The lengths of cloth calculated here exclude certain allowances. The values in Table 7-2 do not deliberately allow for extra cloth to make an optional sailbag. Nor do they include the cloth used by the various seams, so the finished sail will be somewhat smaller than the planned one, a result that will detract little from sailors' pleasure or speed.

Rise and Run of the Triangular Panel B

As expected, the rise (L_4) and run (L_6) of the triangular panel vary with sail area and cloth width (Figure 7-2). Values of the rise and run appear in Table 7-3. Although a complete sail requires two panels B, making them uses no more sailcloth than two panels A. Whether the sailcloth is narrow or wide, the acts of cutting panels B yield panels A (Figure 7-2).

MAKING THE SAIL

A Hoptacong skate sail is easy to make because of its vertical symmetry and flatness. Symmetry allows the sailmaker to lay out the sail in halves, so she has to handle only one half at a time. The bottom half is constructed as the mirror image of the top part, which reduces the labor considerably. A flat sail requires no darts or tucks. (Darts are wedge-shaped inserts that increase fullness, while tucks produce camber.) A Hopatcong skate sail does

Table 7-4: Heights of Jib Z_{js} and Tail Z_{ts} Strips[a]

Sail Area [b]	Z_{js} (yds.)	Z_{ts} (yds.)
95	2.1	0.9
90	2	0.9
85	2	0.9
80	1.9	0.8
75	1.9	0.8
70	1.8	0.8
65	1.7	0.8
60	1.7	0.7
55	1.6	0.7
50	1.5	0.7
45	1.5	0.7
40	1.4	0.6
35	1.3	0.6

[a] Fig 7.2-2 defines these heights. [b] Sail area A_s in square feet.

require curved pockets to hold the jib and tail bows, as well as two pocket openings to admit the boom, but these items and the needed windows can be readily made.

The other important components of a skate sail, discussed in Chapter Three, are the mast, boom, and jib and tail bows. All should be made to fit the finished sail, not vice versa. Therefore, a sailmaker should finish the sail before completing the spars. Making spars to fit an existing sail is easier and wiser than making a sail to match existing spars. More labor goes into the sail than the spars, and the material for the spars is often less costly.

Preliminaries

Workplace

Just as a boat sail maker needs a loft, a skate sail maker requires a proper place to lay out the cloth. For a 54-square-foot sail, which is nine feet high and a little more than nine feet long, an unobstructed area that is 10 feet by 10 feet will do. Where space is tight, a five-by-10-foot area will serve to make the sail one half at a time. You will

---

**Table 7-5:
Sailmaking Tools**

ironing board
improvised, string compass
hot glue gun
clear or white glue sticks
pressing iron
hot knife
sewing machine
#90 needle
medium lead pencil
8–9 inch scissors
straight-edges
   1 × 2 inch × 6–8 feet lumber
   yardstick
25-foot, steel measuring tape
punch and setting tool

---

obviously need more area for a larger sail.

Sailmaking calls for a smooth working surface like a wood or composition floor. No harm will come to the surface, because the layout calls only for taping the cloth to it. To protect the floor from heat damage, however, it is advisable to lay thin plywood or pressboard over it if you are heat-slitting the sailcloth. Carpets are difficult to work on and should be avoided.

Tools and Materials

Except for a sewing machine, the tools needed to make a skate sail are inexpensive and readily available (Table 7-5). Look into renting or borrowing a sewing machine if you do not own one, perhaps practicing using it with scrap materials. The resulting sail will be durable and fast, even if its stitching lacks expertness. A sewing machine that stitches zig-zags is preferable, although straight stitches will suffice. For smooth operation, oil the machine according to instructions. A No. 90 needle works well with the No. 40, three-ply, polyester sewing thread recommended for the stitching.

Scissors that are sharp and tightly jointed will make cuts smoothly and easily. Most of the cut edges will be turned under and sewn, so some fraying is tolerable. Any exposed

edges, however, should be cut with a hot knife to seal the threads. Marine suppliers and hobby shops sell hot knives. You need not buy one solely to make a skate sail because you can improvise one by fastening a metal edge to the tip of a soldering iron. As an alternative, use an electric soldering gun with a sharpened tip. Never use an open flame for sealing because of fire hazards and the bulky, unsightly masses of plastic that accumulate on the edges.

Laying out the cloth will require long straightedges, and drawing the arcs will call for an improvised compass. You will need a yardstick and a six- to eight-foot piece of one-by-two-inch lumber as straight-edges. To rig a compass, fasten a pencil to a length of

---

**Table 7-6:
Materials for a 54-Square-Foot Sail**

sailcloth
Dacron, 2.4-ounce, American; 9 linear yards, 36-inch width

window sheeting
optically clear, press polished, 0.016- to 0.020-inch gauge, one square yard

tapes
Dacron, 1 inch wide, 6 linear yards
paper, light adhesive, one inch wide

thread
number 40, 3-ply polyester, white, one spool

grommets
brass, $\frac{3}{8}$ inch inside diameter, four

paper
heavy brown, for pattern making

---

string looped over a pivot nail. Drive the nail into a one-by-four-inch scrap of wood, one to two feet long. This scrap will protect the floor you are using.

A hot-glue gun comes in handy for tacking panels of sailcloth together in preparation for sewing. (Tacking, a sewing term, means temporarily attaching pieces of cloth to one another.) Small spots of glue about four inches apart work well. The double-sided, $1/4$-inch-wide adhesive tape that a professional sailmaker uses serves the same purpose as gluing.

Design Choices and Changes

The sailmaking method described in the next section lets sailmakers choose among several specific designs or invent others. As a result, Hopatcong sails will differ from one another in certain details, even though the sails will have been made by the same method. The differing details include the devices that fasten the boom to the jib and tail bows, the openings to admit these devices into the pockets, and the shapes and sizes of the windows.

Design choices and changes must be considered beforehand. They dictate how and where the sailmaker cuts and sews the cloth. The boom-to-jib-bow connection, for example, determines the size and construction of the jib-pocket opening, which must admit the connecting device. In particular, the pocket-opening design of Figure 7-13 accommodates the metal S-hook used in the Icicle skate sail. Other connecting devices, however, demand different pocket openings not shown here. This book cannot illustrate or anticipate each sailmaker's modifications of this or any other skate sail design, so the sailmaker herself should draw or model those portions of the sail that she is changing.

Modeling the pocket openings where the ends of the boom meet the bows is prudent. Strong brown paper wrapped around the hardware will yield three-dimensional models of these critical areas, and the models will act as templates for cutting the sailcloth accurately. To represent the jib pocket, for example, you can wrap paper around the intersection of the boom and jib bow. Then the paper will act as a template for the jib pocket opening.

For unobstructed viewing sideways and forward, a skate sail needs good-sized, well-placed windows. Suitable dimensions of a four-sided, plastic window for the 54-square-foot sail are 24.7 x 5.8 x 30 x 18 inches (see Figure 7-8). For sails exceeding 54 square feet, the larger the skate sail area, then the larger the windows should be. One sailmaker recommends a window that projects into the jib and surpasses the span of his outstretched arm. Windows for sails under 54 square feet may be smaller, but not proportionately so. Sailing with only small windows, or with none at all, should be a cause for concern.

If you do change the window size, shape or placement, make a paper template of the proposed window before cutting the plastic sheeting. The finished template will serve to outline the plastic for cutting. The window should ordinarily fit within panel B, with its sides parallel to the seam and edge.

The Purpose of Panel B

The right-triangular panel B (Figure 7-2) is essential to a properly shaped Hopatcong skate sail made from simple woven cloth like Dacron or nylon. In the finished sail it angles the sailcloth panels A relative to the boom and mast (Figure 7-4). Hence, it fixes the directions in which the sailcloth stretches relative to the directions in which the tail lanyard and mast halyard exert tensile forces. Simple sailcloth, woven from mutually perpendicular fibers, stretches least in the fiber directions (Figure 7-4, bottom left). It stretches most on the 45° diagonal between the warp and fill fibers, which respectively run lengthwise and crosswise. Woven sailcloth also stretches in other directions, albeit to lesser but still useful extents.

In a standard Hopatcong sail the lengthwise warp fibers of panels A lie at 21° to the boom and at 69° to the mast. The crosswise fill fibers respectively form angles of 69° and 21° with the boom and mast. The fibers of panels B have identical relative orientations. As consequences of these

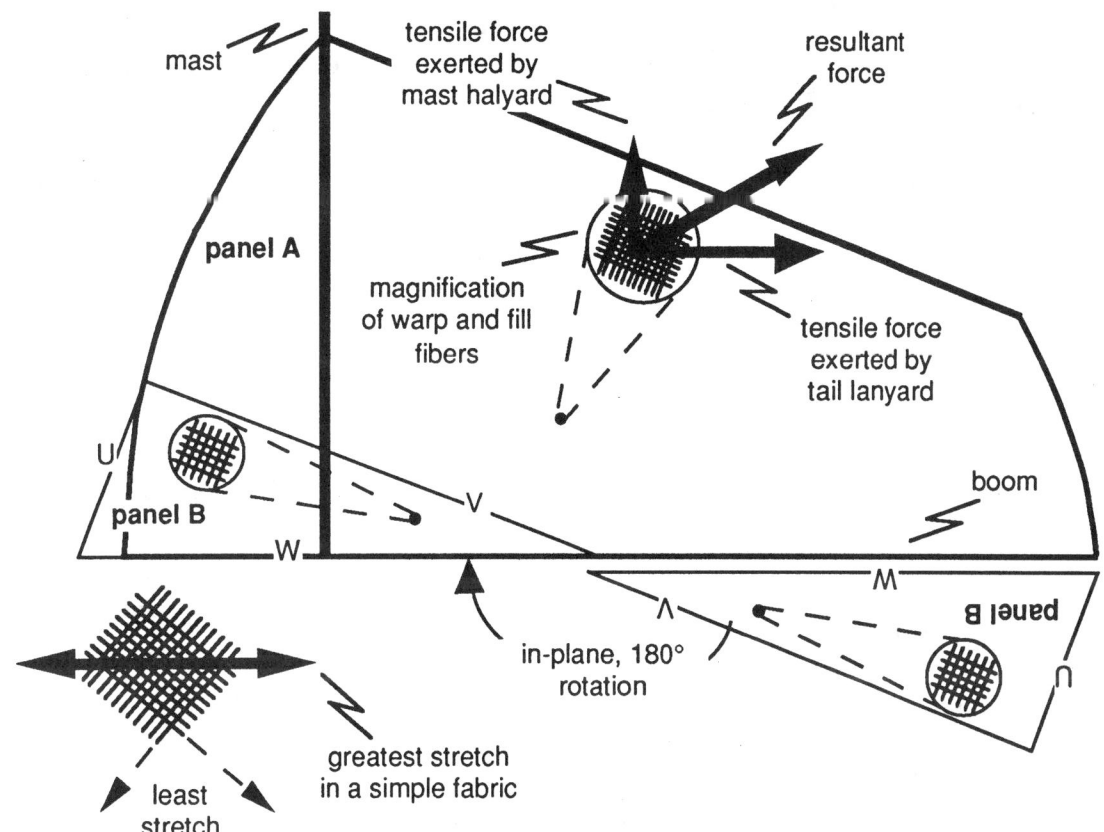

Figure 7-4: Proper Relative Inclinations of Sailcloth Fibers and Tensile Forces

angles and the stretchiness of woven sailcloth, a properly made skate sail can be tightened in the mast and boom directions. Tugging the mast halyard creates a tensile force stretching the sail in the mast direction, while pulling the tail lanyard yields a force that tautens the sail in the boom direction. Because of the relative inclinations of sailcloth fibers and tensile forces, the resultant force always tautens the sail. It never acts in any direction of least stretch. Tautness prevents luffing and makes the moving sail more controllable.

Using wide cloth to make a small sail, even some experienced sailors mistakenly omit panel B. Consequently, the warp fibers in the sailcloth parallel the boom, while the fill fibers lie in the same direction as the mast. A pull on the boom lanyard creates a tensile force acting in one of the directions of greatest resistance — namely, the warp direction — but the force scarcely stretches

the sailcloth. Similarly, hauling on the mast halyards does little to flatten the sail. The rigged sail consequently hangs loosely from the mast and boom, and may require pleats to prevent luffing. They can be effective, but initially introducing panel B avoids pleats altogether.

Sail Symmetry

Stand a Hopatcong sail on the jib end of its boom, and you will see that its right half is identical to its left. As oriented, the sail evidently has vertical symmetry, which should be preserved for a good appearance. To create this look while you are assembling the halves, make sure the pocket flaps, plastic windows, corner reinforcements, and tabling lie on the same side of the completed sail. Putting them on opposite sides of the two halves would detract from the appearance of the finished sail and perhaps from its performance as well.

Sewing Guidelines

For sewing the sail parts together, zig-zag stitching is preferable, and about 10 stitches per inch is suitable. This value corresponds to five zig-zag cycles per inch. To ensure that your stitches are smooth, tight, and regular, you may wish to practice making them; and this is best done with scraps of the sailcloth you plan to use. Some adjustment to the thread tension may be necessary to produce acceptable stitches, and the sewing machine manual should show how to make it.

Keep the half-sails separate as long as possible before sewing them together. This precaution will delay the moment when you have to manipulate the large assembled sail. It will ease the work.

The still popular Hopatcong sail dates to 1917. Despite the age of its design, no complete procedure for making such a sail has been published until now. Although simple, the method is not commonly known, is tedious to re-invent, and sometimes misunderstood even by advanced sailmakers. Therefore, this section describes the entire procedure, and summarizes it in Table 7-7. The steps from this table and the dimensions listed in the following paragraphs will provide a 54-square-foot sail. The dimensions belong to the serviceable

Table 7-7: Successive Steps in Making a Hopatcong Skate Sail

1.	cutting panels A and B
2.	sewing panels A and B together
3.	cutting the half arcs of the jib and tail
4.	finishing the mainsail edges
5.	reinforcing the corners
6.	installing windows
7.	cutting the jib and tail strips from panel C
8.	sewing the jib and tail strips to the half-sails
9.	finishing the jib and tail pockets
10.	joining the half-sails to one another
11.	making the pocket openings
12.	placing the grommets
13.	inspecting, trying, and adjusting the finished sail

Icicle model, a slightly modified Hopatcong sail with jib, tail and fencing angles of 84.9, 49.7, and 21.8°, respectively. Larger and smaller sails will result from using different sets of sail dimensions taken from Tables 3-4, 7-2, 7-3, and 7-4.

Cutting and Sewing the Sailcloth

Cutting Panels A and B

To make panel A of a 54-square-foot sail, cut a length of cloth that is 122 inches long and 36 inches wide (Figure 7-5). Flatten and fasten the cut cloth to the floor with tabs of paper tape. Draw a line across the lower right corner to generate a 61- by 24-inch right triangle, that will become panel B. Cut off triangle B with a hot knife to seal the edges. Flip panel B and place it on the lower left edge of panel A, allowing the two panels to overlap by half an inch. Tack panels A and B together with tiny dots of glue from a hot-glue gun, spacing the dots about four inches apart. Flatten each of the molten dots with your finger to reduce their bulk, and allow the glue to cool before moving the cloth.

You will need another set of panels to make the second half-sail, so you will have to cut another 122-by-36-inch piece of sailcloth. Laying one half-sail over the other will verify that the two have the same sizes. If they do, then you will repeat the work described in the preceding paragraph, making the two halves mirror images of one another.

Sewing Panels A and B Together

With two rows of zig-zag stitches, first sew panels A and B together, remembering to flip panel B before joining it to A (Figure 7-4). The row of stitches should be placed next to the cut edge of the uppermost panel (regardless of whether it is A or B). Then turn the sail panels over and stitch the second row next to the other exposed cut edge. Try to place all stitches within the overlap area. Repeat this procedure for the second half-sail, and then begin making the

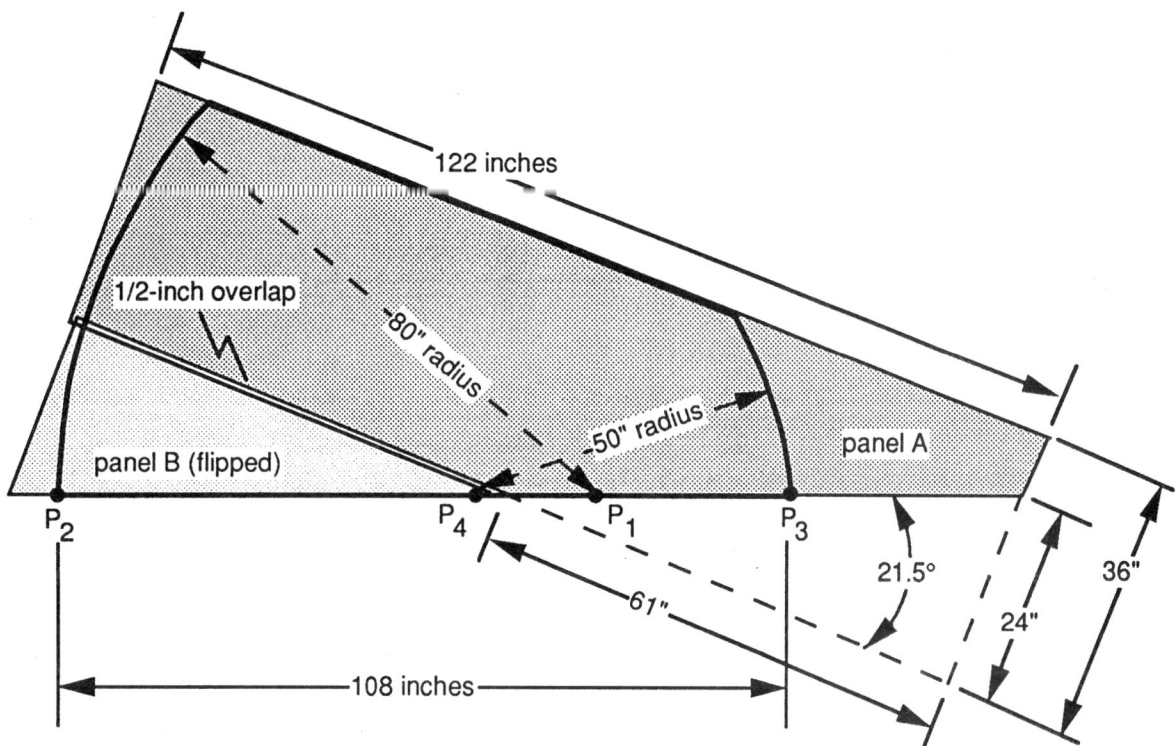

Figure 7-5: Cutting Panels A and B of a 54-Square-Foot Icicle; Outline of Half-Sail Emboldened

jib and tail curves.

Cutting the Jib and Tail Half-Arcs

Adjust your string compass to draw a curve with an 80-inch radius, that will become half of the jib arc in the finished, 54-square-foot sail. Position the pivot point P_1 on the cut edge of panel A so that the compass pencil is about one-half inch inside the left edges of panels A and B (Figure 7-5). Draw the curve so that it intersects the lower edge of panel B, and mark the point of intersection as P_2. From P_2, measure a distance of 108 inches to the right along the lower cut edge and mark P_3. Measure a distance of 50 inches to the left from P_3, and mark P_4 on the lower cut edge. With the string compass set for a 50-inch radius, and with P_4 as the pivot point, draw a curve from P_3 to the upper edge. This curve represents half the tail-bow arc. With scissors, cut the sailcloth on the two drawn curves. Repeat these operations on the other half of the sail to prepare the second set of jib and tail half-arcs.

Finishing the Mainsail Edges

Next, install tabling on the uncut top edge of panel A to strengthen and stiffen it. Figure 7-6 shows how to make a two-fold tabling. With the half-sail lying on an ironing board, turn down a ³/₈-inch flap and flatten it with a hot pressing iron. Turn another fold that is ¹/₂-inch wide and press it to make it easy to handle. Sew the folds together with two parallel rows of zig-zag stitches, keeping the stitches on the tabling. Repeat these steps with the other half-sail.

Reinforcing the Corners

For the sail to withstand the stresses developed when it is underway, the corners need strengthening. Sailcloth remnants, of which you should now have enough, will serve as reinforcing patches. The patches are often the same color as the sail, although sometimes they show contrasting colors.

Each set of reinforcements consists of two overlapping circle segments with four- and five-inch radii. Four sets are required and, in the finished sail, all the patches are

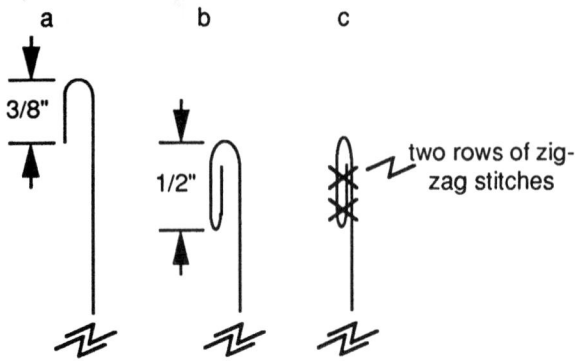

Figure 7-6: Steps in Making a Two-Fold Tabling: (a), Folding; (b), Pressing and Folding; (c), Pressing and Stitching

to lie between the sail and the pockets. Consequently you will sew the patches to the sail before attaching the pockets.

To reinforce the sail halves, sew the larger patch to each corner, using a double row of zig-zag stitches. Then sew a smaller patch over the larger one, again with a double row of zig-zag stitches. Repeat this work at the other three corners of the two half-sails (Figure 7-7).

Installing the Windows

Position a plastic window on panel B, and trace the window outline on the sailcloth with a pencil. Draw a second outline placed one inch inside the window outline on all sides. Cut an opening on the smaller outline. Then make half-inch-long slits at the four corners, beginning each slit at the opening. Fold the cut sailcloth edges to reach the outer pencil outline and press them down with a hot iron, leaving a half-inch overlap all around (Figure 7-8). Clip off the sharp corners of the plastic. Now sew the window to the folded edges of panel B with two rows of zig-zag stitching, making sure that both half-sails bear the windows on the same side.

Cutting the Jib and Tail Strips

Lay out panel C, that, for a 54-square-foot sail, is a strip of cloth 75 inches long and 36 inches wide. Let P_1 represent the point on the cloth that is shown at the bottom middle of Figure 7-9; it designates one of the spots where the sides of the cloth

intersect. Measure 21 inches along the right side of the cloth, from P_1 to a new point P_2, and mark P_2. On paper tape, draw line L_d that coincides with the bottom side of panel C, and extends about 50 inches to the right of P_1. Now place the compass pencil at P_2 and, with a 50-inch string, make the pivot touch L_d at point P_3. Pencil the tail-strip arc on the cloth, and mark the point P_4 where the arc crosses the cloth bottom.

To define the widths of the tail strips, measure five and 10 inches to the left of P_4, and mark the ends of the measurements as P_5 and P_6. Draw two arcs with 50-inch radii, one from P_5 and the other from P_6. Then cut the tail strips away from panel C, and set them safely aside. Trim the upper part of panel C in preparation for making the jib strips according to Figure 7-10.

The trimmed remnant provides the strips of cloth needed for the jib pockets. Its dimensions are 36x54 inches, the latter representing the height of the jib strip. Values are also needed for the jib radius (80 inches) and the jib-strip width (five inches). To cut the cloth, follow the procedure given for making the tail strips, and begin with point P_7 (Figure 7-10). This and the other points $(P_8$-$P_{12})$ in Figure 7-10 correspond respectively to points P_1-P_6 in Figure 7-9.

Sewing the Jib and Tail Strips to the Half-Sails

Lay the curved jib strip over the head of the half-sail (Figure 7-11a), and sew them together with a single row of straight stitches. Space the stitches $1/2$-inch from the front. Leave about three inches of excess jib strip hanging off each end.

Turn the half-sail over, spreading apart the short ends, and press them flat with a hot iron (Figure 7-11b). Also press a $1/2$-inch-wide tabling on the free side of the flap. Turn the half-sail over again and sew a one-inch-wide piece of Dacron tape over the seam. Use two rows of zig-zag stitches (Figure 7-11c). The half-sail will look

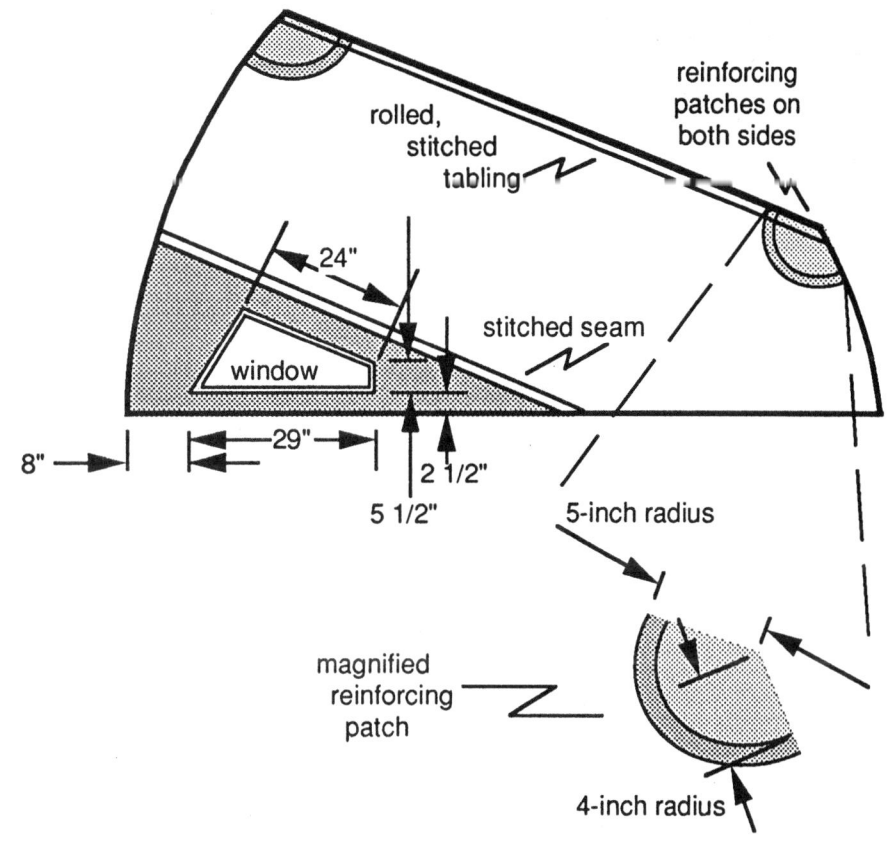

Figure 7-7: Half-Sail Assembly

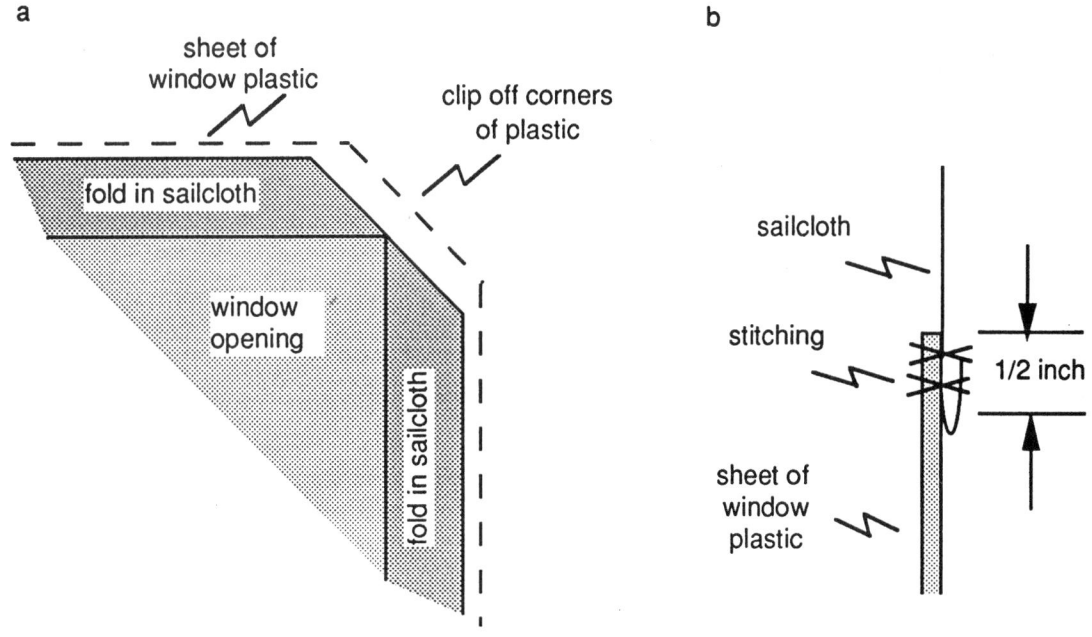

Figure 7-8: Window Detail: (a), View from Leeward Side; (b), View of Edge

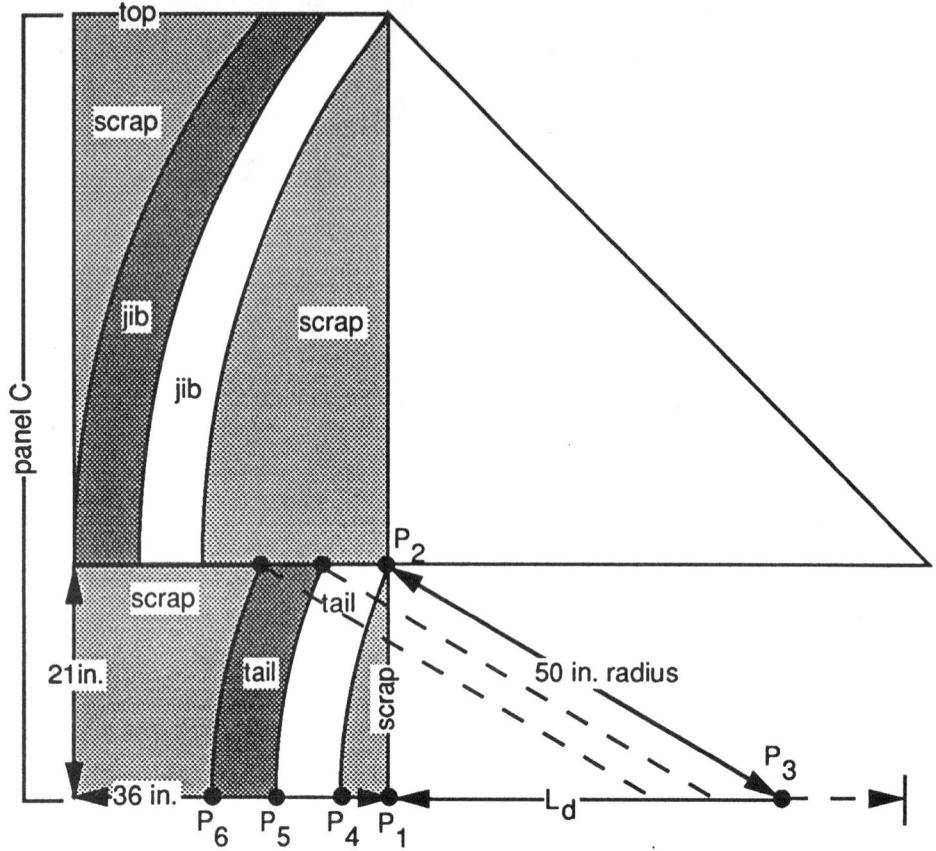

Figure 7-9: Cutting the Tail Strips

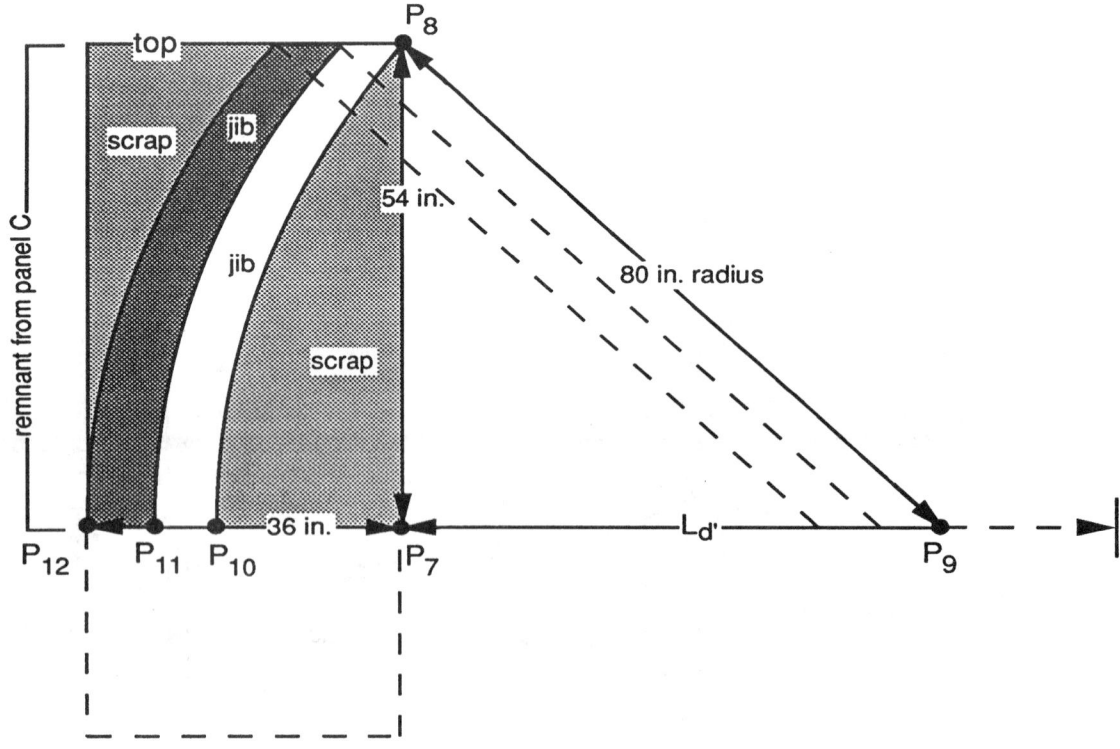

Figure 7-10: Cutting the Jib Strips

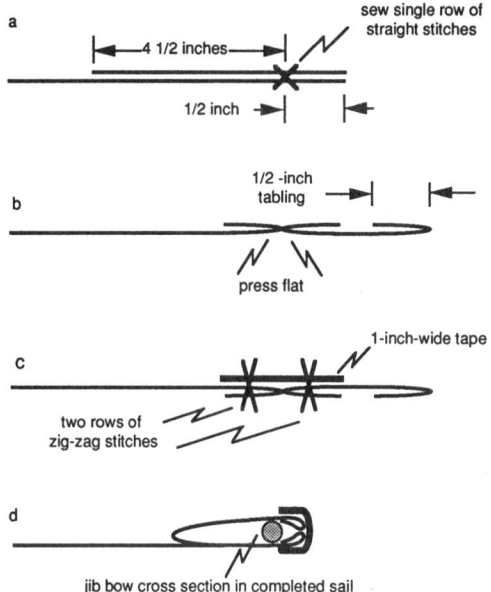

Figure 7-11: Steps in Making the Jib and Tail Pockets

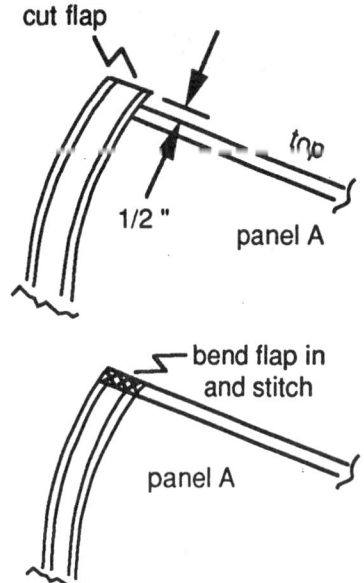

Figure 7-12: Finishing the Pockets

crinkled, because the curves of the sail and strip oppose each other. Turn over the half-sail again (Figure 7-11d) and fold the flap onto it, but leave it unsewn. The half-sail will relax to a flat state when the curves no longer oppose one another.

Make the tail-bow pocket similarly, from the tail strips of cloth cut from panel C. The drawings of Figure 7-11 and the method described above can be adapted to the task of making the smaller tail pockets. Until these pockets have been finished, the strips should extend beyond the half-sail by about two inches on either end.

Finishing the Pockets

The rough ends of the pocket strips extending beyond the top and bottom edges of the half sail need finishing. To complete them, begin at the mast (top) corner and draw a pencil line on the strip parallel to the edge of panel A and ½-inch beyond this edge. Next, cut off the excess strip along the pencil line (Figure 7-12, top). Open the flap and make a ½-inch tabling on the newly cut edge. Sew the tabling with two rows of zig-zag stitching (Figure 7-12, bottom), remembering to leave the top end of the

pocket open to accept the jib bow. Fold and smooth the jib strip over the sail and tack it with glue spots only on panel A. Leave the flap unattached to panel B for the moment.

Joining the Half-Sails

Now join the two halves of the sail. On one sail half, draw a pencil line ½-inch away from, and parallel to, the center edge. Overlap the other sail half and bring its center edge to the pencil line. Tack the two sail halves together. Join the sails with two zig-zag lines of stitches on the overlapping areas to make the center seam. For now, do not stitch into the jib and tail pocket areas.

Making the Pocket Openings

The device that connects the boom to the jib bow determines the size and shape of the pocket opening. However, the planned device may vary in size and shape. So, giving step-by-step instructions for preparing the pocket opening is impossible. Instead, this section presents two alternative designs for jib pocket openings and offers some general advice. The design of Figure 7-13 accommodates the boom-to-jib-bow connection found in the Icicle skate sail. Here a metal S-hook permanently fastened

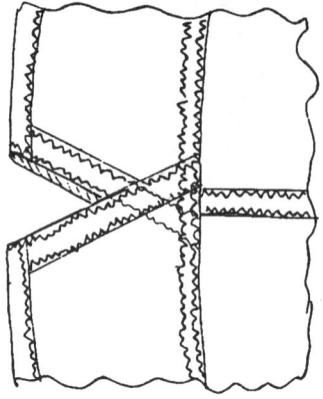

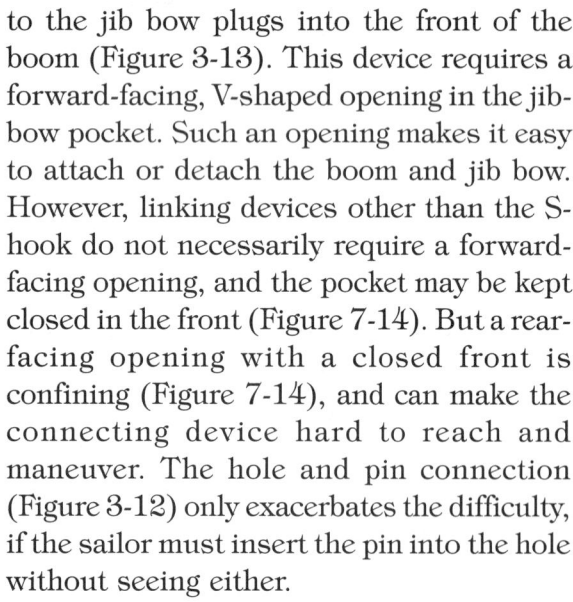

Figure 7-13: Finished Jib or Tail Pocket Opening; Open Design

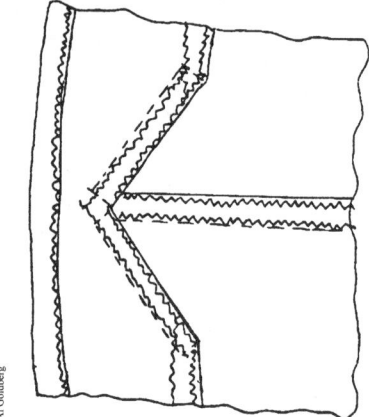

Figure 7-14: Alternative Jib Pocket ; Closed Design

to the jib bow plugs into the front of the boom (Figure 3-13). This device requires a forward-facing, V-shaped opening in the jib-bow pocket. Such an opening makes it easy to attach or detach the boom and jib bow. However, linking devices other than the S-hook do not necessarily require a forward-facing opening, and the pocket may be kept closed in the front (Figure 7-14). But a rear-facing opening with a closed front is confining (Figure 7-14), and can make the connecting device hard to reach and maneuver. The hole and pin connection (Figure 3-12) only exacerbates the difficulty, if the sailor must insert the pin into the hole without seeing either.

Whatever design you choose, lay out and mark the pocket parts. Allow enough fabric to sew ³/₄-inch single-fold tablings to frame the opening. Make sure that the inside of the pocket remains unobstructed. The pocket opening that fastens the tail bow to the boom can resemble the jib-pocket opening in shape, but doesn't have the same width. In this case, the diameter of the tail bow should dictate the size of the tail-pocket opening.

Placing the Grommets

Pairs of ³/₈-inch brass grommets belong at each mast corner of the sail, and you will need four grommets in all. They should lie centered ³/₄ of an inch from the corners, to accept either mast-halyard lines or mast

hooks. All the grommets should fasten separately to the sailcloth, and each pair should possess a common axis. The grommets should be in place before the jib strip is sewn to the sail. Otherwise, the narrowness of the pocket hinders the work of installing the grommets.

To install the grommets, mark their locations on the jib pocket, and then punch an awl through both sides of the flattened pocket. Install individual grommets in each hole. Repeat this process at the opposite mast end of the sail. With the installation of the grommets, you have completed your sail, which will look sleek when its spars, bows, and lanyard have stretched it.

Installing the grommets may create traps for the jib bow ends, depending on the grommet locations and other factors. The grommets themselves and the leading jib edge form the sides of the trap. When it closes around the bow ends, the bow will remain in place even when the sailor loosens the tail lanyard. To remove the still-bent bow from the pocket will require the sailor to bend the bow even more. Extra bending risks breaking the bow or a ferrule. One solution to the problem caused by existing traps is to isolate their sides from the bow ends. A diagonal row of stitches through the pocket will accomplish this. The row should run between the leading and trailing pocket edges, tangent to the grommets. Traps can be avoided altogether if the diameter of the bow end is large compared with the distance between the trap sides.

Inspecting, Adjusting, and Trying the Finished Sail

A day with a low wind will help you spot any floppiness in the assembled sail. For an initial inspection, the skate sail should stand vertically against a wall or a tree and you should step back a few paces to examine it. Ideally it should be flat, lacking sags due to gravity and puckers due to tension. Drumhead tightness, however, is unnecessary.

If puckering or sagging is evident, it may be helpful to sketch its position first. Adjusting the tension on the axis of the mast will correct puckering. Loosening or tightening mast halyards makes this job easier compared with the hooks or bolts sometimes used to fix the sail to the mast. Varying the pull on the tail bow will change the tension on the boom axis.

If the sail center sags while the top and bottom edges are taut, then the jib or the tail bow is too stiff at its ends and is failing to stretch the sail uniformly. Such a bow lacks adequate taper. (The section entitled Traditional Wooden Bows in Chapter 3 describes how to taper a bow.) Conversely, if the center of the sail is taut but the top

and bottom edges are slack, then the bows are too flexible, perhaps because they taper excessively. In either case, you will need to modify one or both bows.

Flip the skate sail over and check it for similar flaws by looking for a lack of symmetry. A flawless sail should look the same when flipped. If you note a defect, you will have to decide whether it is worth correcting: many faults are not. They are merely cosmetic and will not affect sailing performance.

With a wind of about 10 miles per hour at your back, examine the skate sail to determine its camber. Hold the boom with outstretched arms, and observe the fullness of the sail. Ideally, the sail should not separate more than five inches from the boom. Much more of a separation indicates that the sail needs retensioning.

Experienced sailors invited to examine the finished, rigged sail can offer valuable advice concerning any needed corrections. Act on their advice, but remember that the proof of a skate sail lies in the sailing. So take your creation to a lake: black ice, steady winds, and sharp skates to you!

Which skates you should bring and how you should sharpen them are explained in Chapter 8.

CHAPTER EIGHT: SAILING SKATES

Depend on yourself for ... the maintenance of your equipment, and be patient and extremely careful when working on the blades. — Diane Hollum, Olympic medallist and coach, *The Complete Book of Speed Skating*, 1984.

Excited by the promise of a new-found sport, anxious skate sailing newcomers may feel compelled to rush out and buy new skates. Big mistake. New isn't always better, and in this case it would be better to stick to old reliable skates. New skates of an unfamiliar kind simply would compound one task with another: learning to sail and re-learning to skate. It is best to stick with what you know at first, using what you have on hand.

Just as there are many skill levels of skate sailors, there are several kinds of skates suitable for skate sailing. This chapter addresses that topic, beginning with skates best for a maiden voyage.

Foremost among serviceable kinds are racing skates, which have recently become costly. Subsequent sections offer advice on choosing used racing skates, which cost less and are plentiful, and on maintaining them. The next section sets out the little-known technique for manually sharpening skate blades that are ground flat. Knowing and using this method are essential to choosing and maintaining sailing skates. The ill-advised alternative of machine sharpening damages or destroys expensive flat-ground blades. Chapter Eight concludes with a section presenting methods and materials for making the ski-boot skates that many ice-skate sailors prefer.

If a novice's closet offers a choice among the commercial types of skates, racing skates are preferred. If the closet is empty, a novice should try a skate sail before buying new skates for sailing and, if necessary, borrow skates needed for the trial. A new pair of beginner's racing skates costs upwards of $250, while a used pair runs about $25. The $225 difference approximates the cost of a skate sail, so a $250 expenditure would purchase a new sail and used skates. If you must buy skates for a first sail, look for an inexpensive secondhand pair. After one or more trials, you may want to obtain a pair of skates specifically for the sport. Skates with comparatively long (at least 16 inches for an adult) and flat blades are recommended. Whether you invest money or labor in buying or building these skates, you'll garner the rewards of sailing safety and speed for decades afterward.

Three kinds of skates have suitably long, flat blades and are readily available: racing, custom-mounted, or ski-boot. Hockey and figure skates are less suitable for a first trial and unsuitable for prolonged skate sailing year after year. Their short blades vibrate at high sailing speeds, and vibrations usually precede a fall. They prevent a racer from attacking long straight courses fast, and force him to sail slower than winning may demand.

Sailing straight is more difficult with the short, curved blades of hockey and figure skates. These blades allow more sideways drift, regardless of sailing speed. Drifting sideways handicaps a racer by forcing him to sail a longer course, and could be dangerous near open water, passersby, or shore. Not only are the blades of figure skates too short and curved, but they carry picks at the toes. If these picks engaged an obstacle in the ice, the sailor would risk falling forward. Because of debris on outdoor ice that no one grooms, figure skates seem dangerous in sailing. Grinding the picks smooth, however, will abolish the hazard posed by the picks catching on debris or even on rough ice.

CHOOSING ICE SKATES FOR SAILING

Kinds of Available, Suitable Skates

Racing Skates

Traditional racing skates (Figure 8-1) are suitable for sailing because their blades are comparatively long and flat. These skates include an ankle-length boot of stiff leather that is nearly an eighth of an inch thick. The boot contains a stiff counter that surrounds the skater's heel and supports the arch of his foot. Other rigid components are made from chrome-plated steel: cups, toe supports, sole plates, tubes and blades. On each skate, two cups and a toe support permanently link two plates beneath each

boot sole to the tube housing the blade. The blades are about 0.08 inch thick and 16 inches long, which approximates the minimum length needed to avoid high-speed vibrations during sailing.

In speed skates intended more for recreation than indoor racing, the blades lie along the center lines of the boots. Short-track, indoor racing skates have offset blades that facilitate turning counterclockwise. Such offset skates are not suitable for skate sailing.

Three modern developments in the manufacturing of racing skates are detachable blades, ubiquitous plastics, and semi-rigid boots. The French-Canadian firm La Berge was the first manufacturer to replace permanent cups and toe supports with blade assemblies bolted to production boots. Detachable assemblies make it easy to replace a blade or boot that is damaged or worn. They also allow the blade to lie

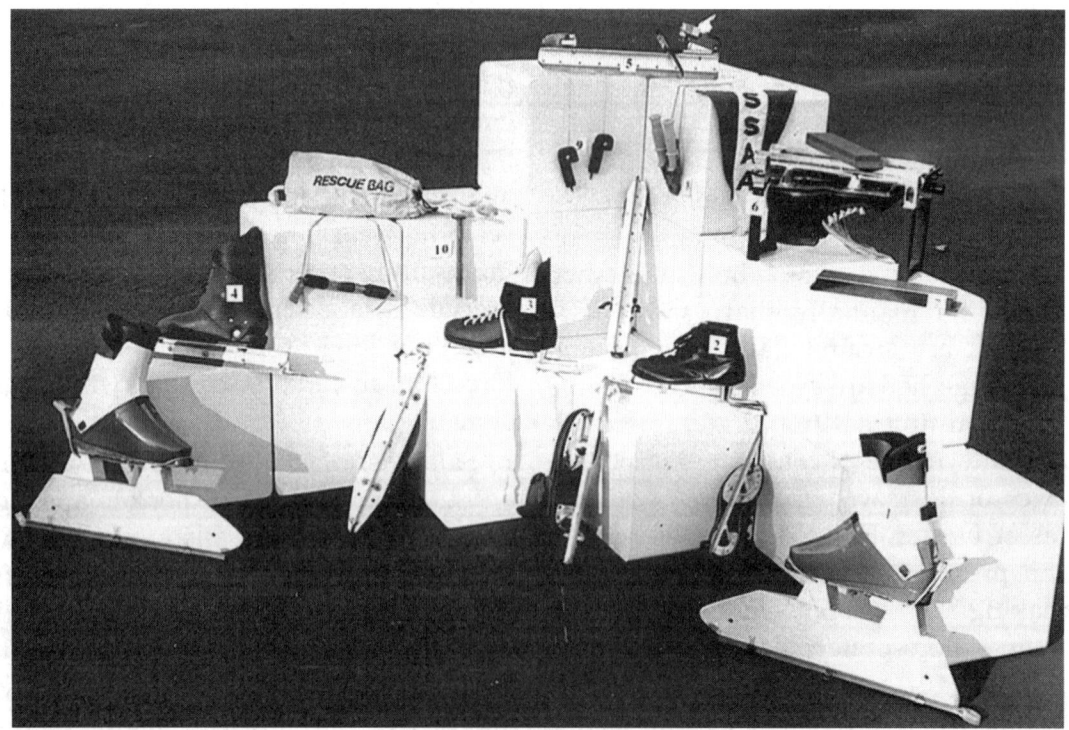

Figure 8-1: Sailing Skates; and Safety Gear: (1) Ski Boot Mounted on 8-Inch-High Swedish Sailing Skate; (2) Traditional Racing Skate with Leather Boot; (3) Modern Plastic Boot Mounted on Outdoor Racing Skate Blade; (4) Homemade Ski Boot Skates; (5) Skate Made from Hacksaw Blade and Aluminum Angle. (6) Sharpening Jig with Whetstone; (7) DMT® Diamond Whetstone; (8) Ice Picks with Whistle and Compass; (9) Ice Picks; (10) Rope Rescue Bag with Homemade Ice Picks; (No Number) Pennant of the Skate Sailing Association of America.

along the center line or to angle from it, desirable for indoor racing. Finally, longer or shorter blades bolted onto the same boots adapt the skates for recreation indoors or outdoors. Darkstar and Bont skate boots, which are described below, also bear detachable blades.

Like skiers, many modern skaters prefer semi-rigid or rigid boots. Lightweight, long-lived plastics impart rigidity to the boots of certain custom-made and assembly-line racing skates, and appear even in the cups of skates. Handmade in Australia, Bont skate boots are a popular, comfortable union of pliable leather and rigid fiberglass, which is a plastic. The manufacturer forms the semi-rigid boots around plaster casts of the skater's feet. A Utica, N.Y., manufacturer, Built for Speed, also makes semi-rigid boots containing leather and fiberglass. Named Darkstar, they resemble the La Berge Rouge but represent improvements over the Canadian ones. Zandstra skates from the Netherlands combine relatively rigid, all-plastic boots with strong plastic cups.

Dedicated racers as well as a few skate sailors favor these modern skates. However, they can cost as much as $450-700, blades included. Many recreational skaters seek less costly equipment, which is necessarily secondhand, custom mounted (but not custom-made), or homemade.

It is difficult to know if boot flexibility in skate sailing is a merit or a flaw. Some race-winning skate sailors swear by the soft, thin, under-the-ankle boots that the Dutch manufacturer Viking provides on its racing skates. They claim the boots provide greater control of steering. Other expert sailors prefer the rigidity of modern plastic boots that afford more support in heeling and greater comfort in traversing rough ice. Anyway, the leather boots of traditional racing skates are comparatively flexible and remain so even at below-freezing temperatures.

The traditional boots of racing skates readily radiate heat, however, and they let a sailors feet grow cold. Cold feet — no pun meant! — are less problematic in skating outdoors than in skate sailing, which demands little foot exercise. While a sailor's body moves continuously over the ice, his feet remain almost motionless relative to his body. And in steady winds he uses his feet even less than in variable winds. His comparatively motionless feet produce heat more slowly than they lose it through poorly insulating leather.

Various remedies cure the condition of cold feet. Some sailors skate to increase circulation in their feet; or they remove their skates to run in place on their sails. Others who take off their skates don shoes, slipping heat packs inside them and over their toes. The packs contain chemicals that release controlled amounts of heat when the chemicals dissolve in or react with one another. On the coldest days, experienced sailors combine speedskaters' foam-rubber overboots with traditional racing skates. Skate shops catering to racers sell overboots. Similar footwear can be adapted from bicyclers' winter overboots or skin divers' boots. Homemade from women's bedroom slippers, fuzzy overboots place a sportsman in the avant garde of skate-sailing fashion. All these remedies notwithstanding, other kinds of modern sailing skates are warmer than traditional racing skates.

Custom Mounted Skates

Mounting outdoor racing blades onto rigid hockey or in-line roller skating boots yields one type of modern sailing skates (Figure 8-1). Several manufacturers offer the blades in varying thicknesses and in 20-inch lengths. Alternatively, blades homemade from industrial hacksaw blanks can be mounted onto various kinds of commercially available skate boots. (The following passage dealing with ski-boot skates describes these blades.)

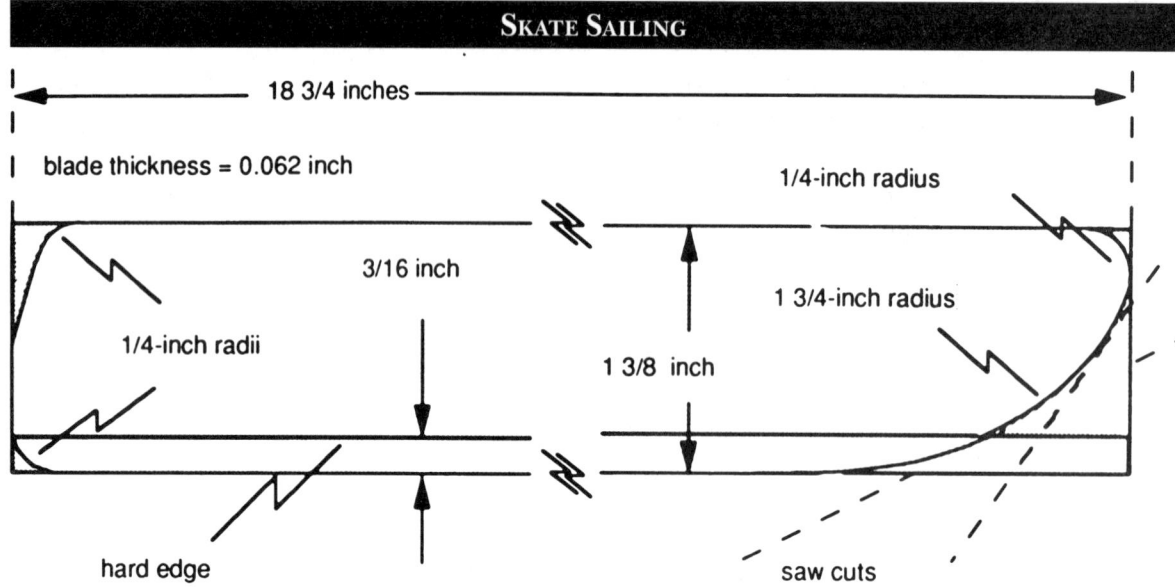

18 3/4 inches

blade thickness = 0.062 inch

1/4-inch radius

3/16 inch

1 3/4-inch radius

1/4-inch radii

1 3/8 inch

hard edge

saw cuts

Figure 8-2: Bi-Metal Skate Blade Emerging from Industrial Hacksaw Blade Blank

Rigid plastic hockey boots, which are comparatively inexpensive if they are used ones, cram the shelves and bins of secondhand stores and skate and ski exchanges. Unlike leather, the plastic of these boots requires no maintenance such as polishing. Skates made from outdoor blades and hockey or in-line boots are lightweight, and offer a good compromise between heeling support and steering control.

The rigid plastics of modern hockey and in-line roller boots require liners. The liners encase the skater's feet, prevent abrasion, and make the boots warm even in near-zero temperatures and despite only a single pair of socks. Rigidity also makes over-tightening the laces to impede blood circulation in the skate sailor's toes almost impossible.

Compared to used skates with leather boots, there are three disadvantages associated with new skates having plastic boots: increased rigidity, greater width, and added expense. First, lower temperatures make plastic boots more rigid. This can be disadvantageous when the sailor tries to don cold skates outdoors. Warming the boots ahead of time — in a heated automobile parked nearby, for example — may be necessary. Nonetheless, they remain flexible

in sailing, so that cold weather does not greatly affect the ease or difficulty of removing them. Admittedly, the relatively rigid boots can be harder to don than leather ones in any weather. Second, plastic boots are wider and higher than the boots of traditional racing skates of the same foot size. Consequently, such boots may not fit into the same sharpening jig. Third, such skates may call for the services of a skate shop to mount the blades on the boots, which adds to the cost.

Homemade Ski-Boot Skates

Ski-boot skates comprise high, rigid, Alpine ski boots fixed to continuous mounting brackets. Blades that are usually handmade from industrial hacksaw blanks are held in the brackets. These skates give the greatest comfort in crossing bumpy ice, and may be the warmest skates ever (Figure 8-1). Those made from one-buckle, rear-entry downhill boots more easily admit and fasten the sailor's foot than any other kind of skate. Ski-boot skates can be inexpensive because new power-hacksaw blanks are mass-produced, as are boots. Secondhand boots can be even less costly.

Although bolts penetrate the soles to hold the boots to the blade assemblies, the ski boots need not be reserved for skate sailing.

Removing the bolts and plugging the holes with set screws restores the usefulness of the boots in skiing. Making the blade assemblies for ski-boot skates does require plans and power tools as well as metal-working skills.

Ski-boot skates or other rigid plastic boots can exploit heavy-duty, industrial hacksaw blades (Figure 8-2). Sold by the Skate Sailing Association of America, the blades are manufactured as toothless blanks. They cost about a quarter as much as purposely made outdoor skate blades of the same length. Produced by the Armstrong-Blum Mfg. Co. in Agawam, Mass., the blanks have dimensions of $0.062 \times 1^{3}/_{8} \times 18^{3}/_{4}$ inches. The edges of the hacksaw blanks contain the metal titanium, which is harder than ordinary steel. Such blades require only infrequent sharpening, remaining sharp enough for a dozen or more outings. For the same reason, sharpening these blades with an ordinary whetstone can be a long-lasting job. However, a diamond-coated stone speeds the work.

Ski-boot skates have two disadvantages, restricted forward lean and awkwardness. The high, rigid boots incline the wearer forward but prevent him from leaning as far forward as ordinary skates permit. This restriction, however, which initially surprises skaters accustomed to low, flexible boots, is virtually unnoticeable in sailing. The awkwardness of ski-boot skates becomes conspicuous only when the sailor must stop sailing. The all-too-heavy and rigid boots then transform graceful skating to elephantine lumbering. Many skate sailors change from ski boots to other skates when they seek to skate during a calm.

Buying Used Racing Skates

Finding Secondhand Racing Skates

Plentiful secondhand skates await buyers, even though large Canadian and United States manufacturers no longer make inexpensive racing skates. Garage sales, flea markets, and thrift shops are likely sources of Planert Northlight and Nestor-Johnson racing skates. Skaters sometimes advertise these as well as Dutch (Viking, Zandstra) and Canadian (La Berge) brands in the classified pages of newspapers. Other advertisements appear in skaters' publications including the *Speedskating Times* and *The Racing Blade*. These publications are respectively a Pompano Beach, Fla., magazine and the newsletter of the Amateur Skating Union of the United States. Both also advertise skate shops offering new racing skates, sharpening jigs, and blade-mounting services, as well as everything else that an ice skater could want.

Blade Condition

If used skates are worth buying, they should satisfy six criteria. (1) To serve skate sailors, the blades should run along the center line of the boots. Offset blades are useful to short-track, indoor racers who must turn counterclockwise, often, and fast. But you'll sail in circles if your blades lie to the left of the center line. (2) The metal parts should be intact and should lack rust and cracks. A careful inspection of the plates, cups, tubes, and blades will repay itself. Be sure to look inside the convex toe supports where rust often lurks. Don't be easily put off because fine steel wool will readily remove a little rust on the metal parts. Do confirm that any rust spots are shallow. (3) Skate blades should be straight. To check for straightness in used blades, pick up each skate, invert it, and site along the length of the blade. This inspection quickly will reveal any collision-induced bends.

(4) Well treated racing skates should always have been sharpened manually. So, to strike a good bargain, examine racing-skate blades for undulations caused by improper machine sharpening. Hold the skate broadside to you, with the heel and

toe on your left and right, and look for short waves in the blades. You can check your findings by placing one edge atop the other, with one boot bottomside up and the other topside up. Pressing the edges gently together, hold the skates to a light and look for leaks. No light will leak between the edges, if the previous owner sharpened the blades properly. A straightedge will also detect improper sharpening in the form of waves and hollow or flat sections.

(5) The blade thickness should be adequate for the stresses of skate sailing, for which manufacturers never intended their racing skates. Racing or casual skating doesn't require as much stress, so some thin blades are too weak for skate sailing. These blades bend during each outing and require straightening before the next excursion. Other blades are thin enough to break in two. An adequate thickness need not exceed $\frac{2}{32}$ of an inch.

(6) The remaining depth of used blades should be enough to allow many more sharpenings. Although sharpening removes only comparatively little metal at one time, many sharpenings ultimately grind away all the useful blade.

Boot Condition

The boots of used racing skates should be satisfactory in the following respects. Metal eyelets should still be present. Stitching should still be intact, especially that holding the tongues to the boots. To support the skater's arches, the counters should remain firm. The boot leather should be supple and should lack cracks, holes, and badly worn spots. Worn spots are sometimes apparent on the outside edges where the uppers meet the soles midway between toes and heels.

Fit

Finally, leather skate boots should fit snugly, otherwise they won't transform leg and ankle movements into course changes. Loose boots are those large enough to be worn over two pairs of thick socks.

A snug fit — but not an uncomfortable one — is as important for a growing child learning to skate as it is for an adult learning to sail. Parents whose children will soon outgrow expensive new skates might provide used skates to save money, and might replace them to accommodate growth. Secondhand skates are available at ski and skate exchanges held each fall, when parents regularly trade outgrown for well fitting equipment.

For control at the expense of comfort, some skaters who wear traditional racing skates without socks choose boots one size smaller than their shoes. They claim that skate boots must be tolerable, not pleasant. (These skaters are competitive if not also heroic.) Happily, undersized leather boots worn without socks are unnecessary for skate sailing.

CARING FOR SKATES

Obeying a three-part rule will help preserve your skates: Apply the blade edges only to ice, and afterward dry the metal and polish the leather. Wearing unsheathed skates over hard surfaces blunts the blades, wastes the labor of sharpening, and can ruin an outing. On a cement sidewalk the noise of an adult's skate blades (grik, grik!) is more appalling than the screech of a child's fingernails on a blackboard.

Sheathing the Blades

Long scabbards of leather or plastic available through skate shops serving racers will protect your blade edges. Serviceable scabbards can be made simply from strips of old bicycle tire or the soft transparent plastic tubing for sale in hardware stores. Yet another source of scabbards are the plastic sheaths used to guard the blades of carpenters' handsaws.

Drying Skates

Skaters who wish to preserve their skates

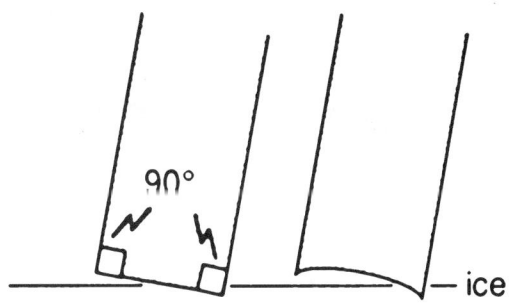

Figure 8-3: Flat (left) and Hollow-Ground (right) Skate Blades; in Cross-section

dry the metal parts with a rag immediately after every use on fresh-water ice. Although the metal parts of racing skates rust slowly because they are chrome-plated, the plating does wear off in spots. These corrode, and the rusted spots spread like measles among the unvaccinated. A dry rag is therefore an essential item in a skate sailor's equipment.

Sailing on salt ice inevitably deposits solid salts on the skate blades and boots. Both the blades and boots should be washed off with fresh water before they are dried. Otherwise, the deposited salts, which chemically catalyze rusting, will accelerate blade corrosion. The deposits may be thin enough to be invisible or thick enough to be white, but will be present regardless of visibility. Brushing off white deposits will not remove all the salt, and the minute remaining amounts will suffice to hasten blade pitting.

Coating Skate Blades

Before putting your skates away until the next sailing season, coat the metal parts to protect them from moisture and air. This will prevent rusting, which requires both water and oxygen. Suitable coatings for the metal components are paint, heavy oil, and petroleum jelly as well as transparent acrylic resin sprayed from an aerosol container. Wax, car polish, and polyurethane will also do.

Storing Skates

For long-term storage, skates deserve a dry place. A closet is suitable, but a garage

is not. Opening the doors to admit an automobile exchanges moist outside air for dryer inside air. The water accelerates rusting.

SHARPENING FLAT-GROUND SKATES

Sharp blades are indispensable to lying on the wind, and capsizing is often the consequence of dull blades. Moreover, most sailing skates often require sharpening after each day's outing because outdoor ice is usually much harder than indoor ice, and because of the long distances sailed on a windy day. In only four hours a skate sailor travels 100 miles at an averaged speed of 25 mph, and the grinding action of such a journey dulls skate blades. In a snowless winter, a fine, windblown grit often covers the ice near sandy beaches, and such a surface will soon dull your skate blades. So, skate around sand-covered ice, but also prepare to sharpen your skates often. Experienced sailors making two-day, weekend excursions completely sharpen their skates each week, and touch up their edges on Saturday evenings or Sunday mornings.

This discussion of sharpening applies to those well matched blades that are to be ground flat, that lack hollows and flat spots, and that already possess proper curvature (called rock or rocker). Ordinarily, racing and sailing skates are ground flat by hand, while hockey and figure skates are ground hollow by machine (Figure 8-3). Although a few skate sailors grind their blades hollow, with a round, rat-tailed file or a Dremel tool, any advantages for skate sailing are little known.

Machine sharpening, which is appropriate for figure and hockey skates, frequently ruins racing blades by gouging short waves in them. Improper sharpening, often by an electric grinding wheel, is sometimes the only technique offered by

Table 8-1: Manual, Flat Grinding of Sailing Skates: Guidelines

General

- sharpen both blades simultaneously
- set skates same way in jig each time
- scratch blades to confirm settings
- follow the existing blade curvature
- let whetstone weight be the only force applied to blades
- grind with whole whetstone area and overlapping strokes
- rotate stone and jig in plane
- raise a burr everywhere on each edge

Coarse Sharpening

- stroke along diagonals
- stroke back and forth

Polishing

- stroke parallel to blades
- stroke back and forth
- sight along blades to confirm absence of cross scratches

skate stores and cobblers' shops. There the importance of manual sharpening may be unknown to the proprietors, unspoken to the customers, or both. The destruction of old blades and the expense of new ones are among the consequences of machine sharpening.

Rocking new, expensive blades, which refers to the task of curving them properly from heel to toe, is a laborious task perhaps better left to skate shops serving racers. So is the repair work of grinding the blades to remove hollows and flat spots caused by improper manual sharpening.

At best an oily and gritty job, sharpening skates demands a work bench that is remote from one's living room. Frequent trips to a distant workplace, however, may elicit comment like this one from a spouse. "Life with a skate sailor resembles that in a Gothic novel: a demented relative inhabits the cellar."[†]

Equipment

Straightedge

Sharpening sailing and racing skates requires a straightedge, which serves several purposes. It detects undesirable blade bends, flat spots or hollows; and it confirms proper curvature. If the running surfaces of your blades contain hollows, then your skates may need the attention of a skate shop dedicated to speed skaters. Otherwise you face the laborious task of manually sharpening grossly mismatched blades.

A straightedge will also detect a depression in the whetstone center. A whetstone wears away faster at its center than at its edges, in a process known as dishing. Attempts to sharpen skates with such a rutted stone would round the blade edges. Instead of trying such a stone on your skates, replace or reface it.

Whetstones

Sharpening flat-ground skates, including racing skates, calls for a large stone. Both blades are sharpened simultaneously and lie about four inches apart during the work, so the whetstone must occupy about 12 x 2 x 1 inches to make room for the user's hands. Shorter, narrower stones are more common and less expensive, but hollow the blades and themselves. Such stones also lead the user to pare his fingers like carrots. Finger paring occurs because of the short distance between the blades and because of the needed two-handed grip on the stone. This grip brings the user's fingers close to the newly sharpened edges.

Traditional whetstones used for racing skates are two-grit Arkansas or India oilstones. One side has a coarse grit, while the other is fine. The coarser side does the work of grinding and the finer side polishes

[†]To learn more about skate sharpening, consult *The Complete Book of Speed Skating*, Diane Hollum, Enslow Publishers, Inc., Hillside, N.J., 1984; ISBN 0-89490-051-x.

the resulting surface. A typical whetstone suitable for skates is the 85851 India Giant Combination IM2, made by the Norton Co. of Worcester, Mass. Coarse silicone carbide stones wear too easily to represent a good investment in a whetstone, which should last for years.

Efficient diamond sharpening stones are available nowadays, thanks to chemical synthesis (Figure 8-4). As diamond is the hardest known material, a sharpening stone made from it is very durable. By the same token, a diamond stone must be used carefully; otherwise, it will remove too much steel from the blades and shorten their lifetimes. Expect to pay about twice as much for an industrial diamond whetstone, and to use the diamond stone with water, not oil. Diamond whetstones are manufactured by Diamond Machining Technology, Inc., in Marlborough, Mass.

For the smoothest edges, apply a polishing stone to your newly sharpened blades. Recommended to competitive skaters, this use seems uncommon among skate sailors, perhaps representing an unnecessary refinement. Anyway, a polishing stone should possess the same dimensions as the combination stone mentioned previously. It should also present a harder, smoother finish.

Finishing Stones

A finishing stone will remove the burr raised by sharpening and polishing your

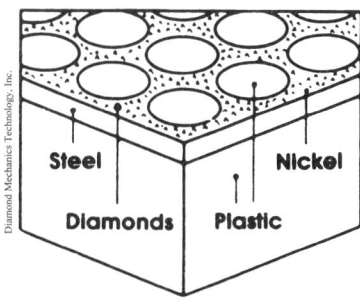

Figure 8-4: Construction of a DMT® Diamond Whetstone

blades. Such a burr lies perpendicular to the blades and is a minute, jagged strip of metal. To de-burr or not is as contentious as sharpening with figures-of-eight strokes. A skate-shop proprietor writes, "Some say the edge will last longer if a little burr is left on. These people use hedge clippers to cut their hair." After 40 winters' experience a certain skate sailor says, "I never bother with this refinement, but then I don't race." Diane Hollum, a skater who did race in the Winter Olympics, recommends de-burring to the racers whom she now coaches.

Deburring requires a stone having a smoother, harder surface than either of those on the whetstone. A suitable deburring stone is the Norton 85570 India Stone FB14. Its dimensions are 4 inches x 1 inch x $^{1}/_{4}$ inch. Some skaters prefer a much smaller, square stone that spans only one inch on the larger sides. Supposedly, such a small stone more effectively tracks and smoothes the tiny bumps that compose the burr, and is less prone to develop hollows. A one-inch-square stone can be awkward to use, however, and may be more likely than a longer burrstone to let the user slice a finger.

Lubricants

Conventional whetstones and burrstones require non-aqueous lubricants, so you'll need a mineral oil or a light household oil. Almost any oil will do, but certain solvents are better avoided. Volatile solvents, which evaporate readily, should be used only with good ventilation. Breathing such a solvent over many years is unwise because it may be unhealthy. A solvent that is both volatile and flammable makes a doubly poor choice of lubricant. Not only is inhaling it foolish, but a flame or spark can ignite a little or explode a lot of it.

Some solvents can also take fire without any visible source of ignition. Spontaneous ignition can occur during grinding because the accompanying friction heats the surrounding air and because the flashpoints of some solvents are low. The flashpoint of a solvent, which varies as its composition does, is the temperature at which it spontaneously ignites in air. The surrounding heat that this temperature measures is a sufficient source of fire.

Although one writer recommends kerosene as a whetstone lubricant, others reserve it for cleaning a stone. This represents a precaution taken because kerosene is flammable and volatile. To avoid any double threat that it poses, it is wise to go outdoors to use it.

Cleaning Materials

You'll need to clean your whetstone after sharpening your skate blades several times. A small steel brush, available in hardware stores, will remove the grindings from a sharpening stone. A solvent-moistened rag will eliminate grindings and lubricant from your blades, while an old newspaper placed beneath your skate stand at the outset will avoid dirtying the surface of your work space.

Jigs

The standard method for sharpening flat-ground sailing and racing skates calls for a skate stand, also known as a jig or a sharpening stand (Figure 8-1). Indispensable, and usually made from aluminum, a jig lightly but firmly holds both boots. Skate stands often accompany skate sailors to a frozen lake, because the jigs are lightweight, collapsible, and small. Skate shops catering to racers sell them, as do individuals advertising in *The Racing Blade* and the *Speedskating Times*.

Principles

What a Skate Stand Does

A jig holds the running surfaces of skate blades coplanar to one another while the whetstone travels over them. The arrangement permits simultaneous sharpening of both blades, and ensures that the newly ground surfaces will be flat. The

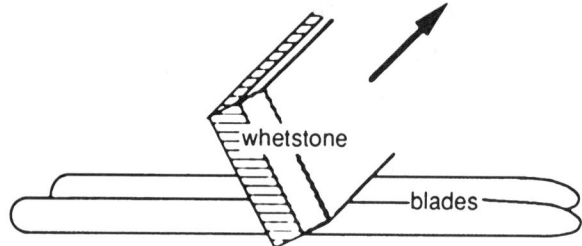

Figure 8-5: Scratching the Blades

person sharpening skates must properly place them in the skate stand and convince himself that he did so. Afterward, he must keep the blades correctly positioned, and confirm that they retain their place throughout the work. Negligence or failure to heed these guidelines will waste time, labor, and metal.

Relative Positions of Skates and Jig

For working convenience, the boots hang upside down in a jig set on a waist-height work bench. During each sharpening, they also lie side by side, toe to toe, and in the same positions relative to the skate stand. For example, the outside edge of the left boot should always abut the right side of the jig (when the jig is seen from above) while the toes lie near the jig front. Relative positioning must be reproducible to obtain consistent results, and calls for defining and permanently marking the front and right sides of a symmetrical jig. As well, you must note or remember which way the skates lay in the jig during the last sharpening. Unnoticed changes in relative positions will prolong each sharpening job and will tend to remove too much metal from the blades.

Starting from Scratch: A Test for Coplanarity

To establish that the running surfaces lie in the same plane, incline a whetstone and, holding its long axis perpendicular to the blades, draw its edge lightly across them in the axis direction (Figure 8-5). This will produce a pair of shallow, visible scratches running across the whole thickness of each correctly aligned blade. Several pairs of complete scratches at short, regular

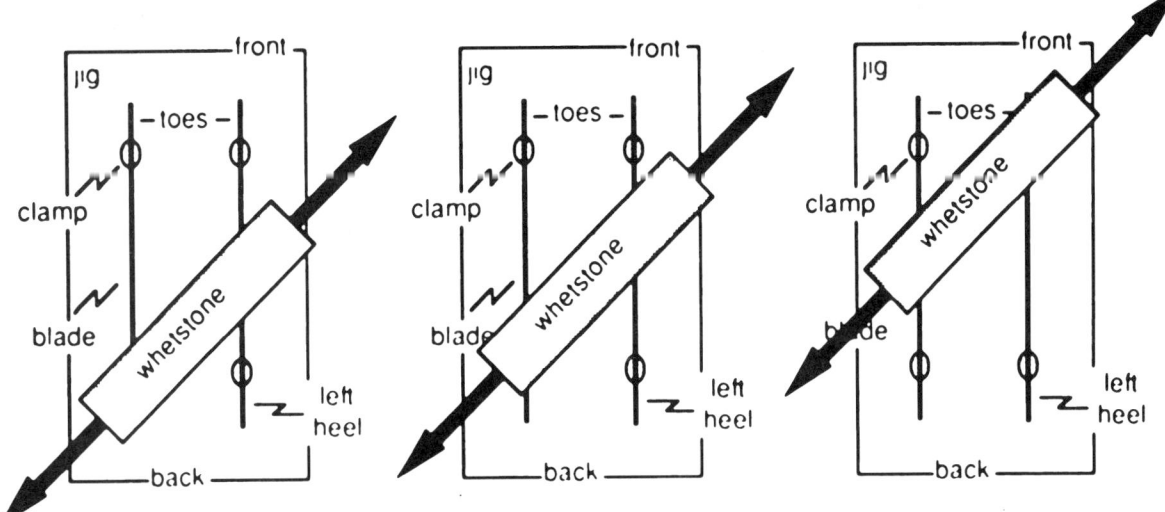

Figure 8-6: Diagonal, Successive (l. to r.) Strokes with the Coarser Side of a Whetstone; Top View

intervals along the blade length demonstrate satisfactory alignment. If no scratches appear on a blade that lacks hollows, then it is misaligned and should be raised in the jig. If the scratch fails to span the full width of a blade, then the edge lacking the scratch is likely to be very dull. In this case a somewhat more difficult but still feasible grinding task lies ahead.

When coarse grinding is complete, the blades are polished. Polishing with the finer surface of a two-grit whetstone will remove the test marks, producing a gleaming, mirror-like finish on the running surfaces. This finish will be evident in a bright light when you sight down the blades. Polishing will also prepare the blades for the next sharpening, which should start from scratch.

Holding a Curve

The whetstone must follow the existing blade curvature, removing only enough metal to yield sharp edges. Taking away more than this produces flat spots. They result from too much pressure or too many strokes deliberately given the middle blade portions, which sailing dulls fastest. Another source of middle flat spots or hollows is inadvertent relief of whetstone pressure near the toes or heels, where the blade curvature is

greatest. Continued grinding of flat spots converts them to hollows, and both can be very difficult to repair.

Laying Off the Whetstone

Throughout the coarse grinding, the whetstone weight should provide the only force applied to the blades. The greater force that forearms or shoulders can exert on the stone is self-defeating. Bearing down on the stone removes too much metal from the wrong sites on the blades. Also, such a force is harder to control than the number of strokes (which some sharpeners deliberately count).

Overlapping Strokes

Two principles should govern the choice of stroke path: each stroke should use the entire whetstone area and successive strokes should overlap one another. Using the whole whetstone area in overlapping strokes prevents dishing the stone and avoids developing ridges in the blades. For coarse sharpening, the whetstone may follow any of a variety of paths in traveling over the blades, straight lines as well as small and large circles. Although some sharpeners swear by figures of eight, others favor straight strokes along a diagonal. Straight, back-and-forth strokes along a diagonal use the whole whetstone area (Figure 8-6). They minimize dishing, which instantly rounds the blade edges and ultimately ruins the stone.

The whetstone should contact a previously untouched blade area during each stroke. The stone should also pass over a part of the area covered by the previous stroke. Overlapping strokes (except near the toes and heels) thus ensure that the stone traverses the whole of each running surface without creating flat spots or ridges.

Testing for Sharpness

Coarse grinding initially sharpens each of the four blade edges until any of them will pare a fingernail anywhere along its length. This grinding finally raises a burr everywhere. Feeling the new burr with a finger nail is a practical test of sharpness. Indeed, burr raising is a better test than nail paring because a semi-sharp edge will lack a burr but will pare a nail. Also, removing the burr after one sharpening prepares for the next sharpening. As a result, a change from burrless to burred edges demonstrates that the more recent sharpening was effective.

Turning the Stone and Jig

Frequent turns of the stone and jig minimize the chances of dishing and uneven grinding (Figure 8-7). To accomplish this, the sharpener lifts the whetstone from the blades and rotates it through 180°. The rotation takes place in a plane parallel to

the running surfaces. Turning the jig through 180° in the work bench plane is also commendable, because it places the far ends of the blades near the sharpener, and the near ends far from him. It helps to grind the running surfaces evenly.

Techniques

Positioning Skates in a Jig

To begin the job, place the skates in the jig and raise the blades into the clamps. The tube flanges are allowed to rise until they abut the clamps. (If your jig has upstop devices, let them regulate the maximum blade elevation.) The blades are clamped to finger tightness only. To test whether the running surfaces are coplanar along the whole blade length, scratch the blades with a whetstone as described previously. As necessary, readjust and re-test the blade positions before sharpening.

Tightening the Clamps

When the blade positions are satisfactory, tighten the clamps using only your fingers to turn the thumb screws. The relatively light whetstone weight provides force enough to sharpen the blades and will not displace the blades from the jig. Furthermore, tightening the clamps with a wrench will damage a soft jig. The steel in the thumbscrews, or in the nuts and bolts that work the clamps, is stronger than the aluminum that composes most metal jigs. The softer aluminum can break under the torque transmitted by the harder steel. Clamp tightness should be checked during sharpening so that neither of the blades slips downward in the jig; otherwise, mismatched blades may result if grinding continues.

Coarse Grinding

Lubricate your whetstone, using a finger to spread the oil over the coarse surface. Lay this side of the stone diagonally across the blades. One end of the stone should lie near the heel of one blade (Figure 8-6, left). Lightly grasp both ends of the stone between

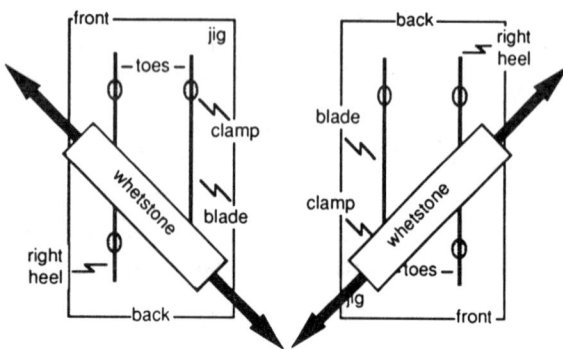

Figure 8-7: (a) Relative Positions after a 180°, In-Plane Turn of the Whetstone; (b), After a 180°, In-Plane Turn of Skates and Jig

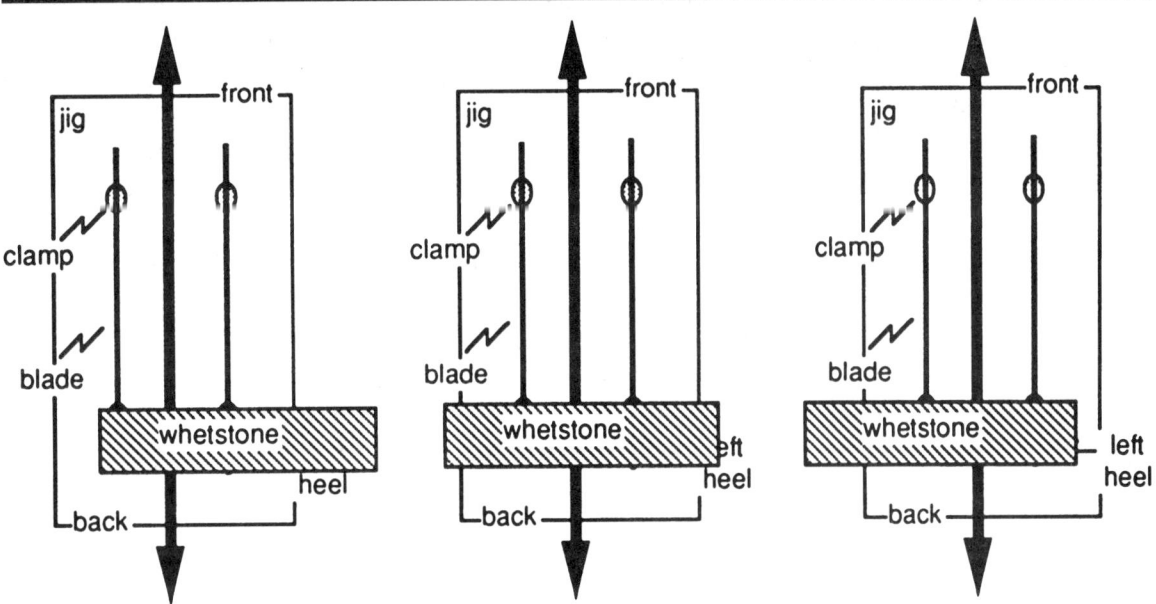

Figure 8-8: Straight, Successive Strokes with the Finer Side of a Whetstone; Changing Relative Positions of Blades and Whetstone (Top View)

thumbs and fingers, and gently slide the stone along a diagonal. At the end of this stroke, return the stone to its starting position along the same path. Moving the stone ahead, begin the next back-and-forth stroke (Figure 8-6, middle). Successive strokes should continue at least until the stone has traversed the whole blade area (Figure 8-6, right). Monitor sharpening progress by feeling for burrs.

When you have covered the blades with the foregoing strokes, rotate the whetstone in plane until its other end lies near the other boot heel (Figure 8-7a). The resulting position serves as a new starting place for another series of successive, overlapping strokes along the second diagonal. At the end of this series, turn the whole jig through 180° until the boot toes are nearer you. Then complete a third series of strokes as illustrated (Figure 8-7b), covering the whole blade area. Again rotate the stone in plane to begin the final series with the toes nearer to you. The four series of strokes are repeated until they raise a burr everywhere along the four blade edges.

The number of strokes per series may be larger than needed merely to cover the blade

area, of course. Neither the number of strokes nor the length of time needed to raise burrs is predictable, however, so sharpening demands patience. Sharpening old skates in an old jig is quickest.

Polishing and De-Burring

To polish the running surfaces, place the fine side of the whetstone on the blades, hold the whetstone at a right angle to the blade length, and push the stone back and forth in the direction of the blades. The last few strokes with the coarse whetstone surface, and all those with the fine surface, should be made only along the blade lengths. These straight strokes remove the test scratches and the cross scratches left by diagonal strokes. Sighting down the blades readily detects the presence and absence of all such scratches.

In successive polishing strokes, the whole area of the stone should be used. To accomplish this, change the starting position of the stone in each stroke as shown (Figure 8-8). Changes in the starting positions, as well as in-plane rotations of the stone and jig, avoid ruts in the whetstone.

If you remove the burr from your skates, remove them from the jig, and lay one blade flat on a workbench edge. Holding the skate with one hand, use the other hand to run a burrstone across the blade. The burrstone working surface should be perpendicular to the blade running surface. Pick the edge with a fingernail to monitor progress, doing so often and examining the whole blade edge.

Flattening a Whetstone

A dished whetstone should be replaced or ground flat, lest using it damage the blades being sharpened. Rubbing the stone over powdered, 60-mesh silicone carbide mixed with mineral oil and spread on plate glass will restore flatness. Machine shops often possess the equipment to flatten a whetstone and express willingness to do the job. However, such work may cost more than a new stone.

MAKING SKI-BOOT SKATES

Shaping and Drilling the Blanks

Hacksaw blanks, as manufactured, take the shape of a rectangle, and all four corners need shaping to serve as skate blades (Figure 8-2). Three of the corners require rounding to a radius of about $1/4$-inch, which prevents injury to the sailor and damage to the sail in a tumble. The other corner will

---

Table 8-2: Saws into Skates — Tools and Materials

power tools
 miter or portable saw
 grinding wheel or disk sander
 electric drill
 stationary belt or disk sander

hand tools
 center punch
 jig, or clamps and flat surface
 burrstone

materials
 aluminum oxide cut-off wheel
 220-grit sandpaper
 drill bits
  high speed steel
  $\frac{5}{64}$- and $\frac{9}{64}$-inch diameters
 coarse and fine sanding belts or disks

---

ultimately form the leading part of the skate blade, so it must have sufficient curvature to pass smoothly over rough ice. It requires a radius of about $1\frac{3}{4}$-inch, beginning $\frac{3}{8}$-inch from the top of the blank. This top, which must be identified in the case of a bi-metal blade, lies opposite to the long edge bearing the harder metal. The strip of harder metal is typically $\frac{3}{16}$-inch-thick and readily apparent to a visual inspection.

A powered miter saw or a portable saw equipped with an aluminum oxide cut-off wheel will make the cuts indicated (Figure 8-2). Their positions are drawn on the blank, which is cut outside the drawn lines in one or two efforts. With these straight cuts completed, a grinding wheel or a disk sander serves to smooth the newly cut edges. Fine sandpaper removes the burn marks left by the cut-off wheel. Cutting the angle irons according to a pattern drawn on them requires a powered saw or a hacksaw. In either case, the saw should have a fine-toothed blade. An electric sander rounds the angle-iron corners.

Some precautions are advisable in using the cut-off wheel, which emits sparks and heat. The workplace should be free of flammable materials and debris. The saw should possess a metal guard, not a flammable and low-melting plastic one. Gloves, goggles, and long sleeves will prevent injuries.

Drilled holes in the blade tops admit about 15 sets of $\frac{1}{2}$-inch-long machine screws and nuts. The screws that hold the blades to continuous mounting brackets (Figures 8 -9 to -11) are of number 6 wire. Numerous machine screws, as well as the smaller angle iron in the bracket, prevent the blade from bending in use. They act as the long tube of a conventional racing skate does.

A center punch and an electric drill equipped with a high-speed bit mark the spots and make the holes. Drilling begins and ends with $^5/_{64}$- and $^9/_{64}$-inch bits, respectively. The bits squeal when they become dull, calling obviously for replacements. Unlubricated new bits working at 500 to 600 revolutions per minute bring the best results. A faster speed of 1,000 revolutions per minute is also effective, but requires oiling the work.

Mounting the Blades

The continuous mounting brackets, designed by R. H. Pace, past commodore of the Skate Sailing Association of America, resemble certain devices used to fix ice boat runners to the planks. Pace's brackets consist of differently sized angle irons, which hold the blades to the boots with the help of $^5/_{16}$-inch bolts, hexagonal nuts, T-nuts, and washers (Figures 8-9 to -11). Extruded (6063-T5) or structural (6061-T6) aluminum makes serviceable angle irons. The smaller irons are $^1/_2$-inch x $^1/_2$-inch x $^1/_8$-inch, and the larger span $1^1/_2$-inch x $1^1/_2$-inch x $^1/_8$-inch. The T-nuts are set into the soles of the ski boots, and lie flush with the surfaces of the soles.

Sharpening the Blades

To sharpen the blades, a jig is needed to hold the running surfaces in the same plane and ensure that the surfaces will be flat when the edges are sharp. A flat plank of plywood, for example, makes a suitable jig. It should bear four holes to accept the bolts that otherwise would fix the blade assemblies to the boots. The blade assemblies, comprising the continuous mounting brackets and the blades, are bolted to the plank. The blades should lie $2^1/_2$ to $3^1/_2$ inches apart from one another in the jig. An alternative to making a jig is clamping the blade assemblies to a flat surface.

A disk or belt sander fitted with a coarse belt will sharpen the blades. The blades are moved to the machine, which is allowed to remain stationary. To retain curvature, the blades should be rotated during sanding from heel to toe and back. The running surfaces should then be angled at about 30° to the plane of the sanding belt. After the sander raises a burr everywhere along each blade edge, the belt should be changed for a fine one used to polish the surfaces. Used manually, a finishing stone will smooth the burr left after polishing.

Ground Round or Left Flat

An ice skate blade is not ordinarily flat but is curved along its entire length. This curvature, known as rock or rocker, allows figure skaters and hockey players to turn sharply because their blades act as pivots. Rock also lets short-track racers maneuver for advantage. Indoor racing skate blades have a more pronounced curvature. Blades on outdoor racing skates usually have radii of curvature in the range of 62 to 82 feet. Olympic racers prefer blade radii of 69 to 76 feet. Only skate sailors' blades are sometimes left flat, not ground round.

Leaving the blades of sailing skates flat advantageously sacrifices skating maneuverability to sailing stability. Skating on flat blades is clumsy because they do not permit sharp or fast turns. At best, their flatness allows only awkward (but effective) kinds of skating motions. Sailing on flat blades, however, is not awkward at all. Fast, sharp turns are rarely needed, except in obstacle-course races. Indeed, flat blades help prevent side slipping and facilitate sailing the desired course. The chances of being blown off one's course increase with the wind speed, so many sailors welcome flat blades in strong winds.

The flatness of many sailors' homemade blades arises partly by default, not entirely by choice. Blades made from hacksaw blanks are flat as manufactured. Grinding them round requires knowledge, skill, and a suitable machine; and few sailors possess all of these prerequisites. Alternatively, a sailor wanting rocked blades on his sailing skates can take them to a skate shop specializing in racing blades. Such shops routinely grind blades round for a fee, although paying it makes skate sailing somewhat more expensive. Leaving the sailing blades flat often represents the easiest and least expensive course of action.

The courses and actions to avoid are the subjects of Chapter Nine, which deals with safety.

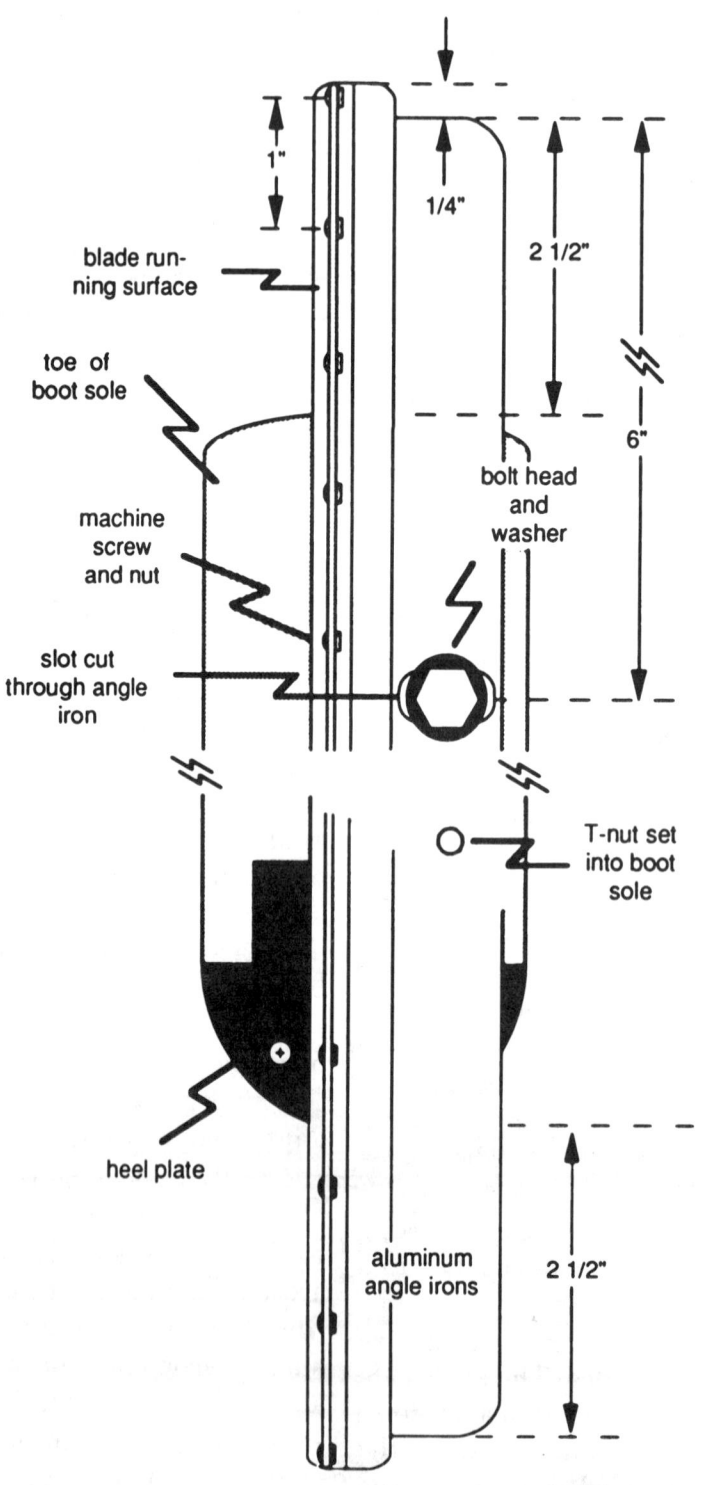

1"

1/4"

2 1/2"

6"

blade run-
ning surface

toe of
boot sole

bolt head
and
washer

machine
screw
and nut

slot cut
through angle
iron

T-nut set
into boot
sole

heel plate

aluminum
angle irons

2 1/2"

Figure 8-9: Bottom View of Continuous Mounting Bracket for Left Boot

(a) right blade assembly

(b) left blade assembly

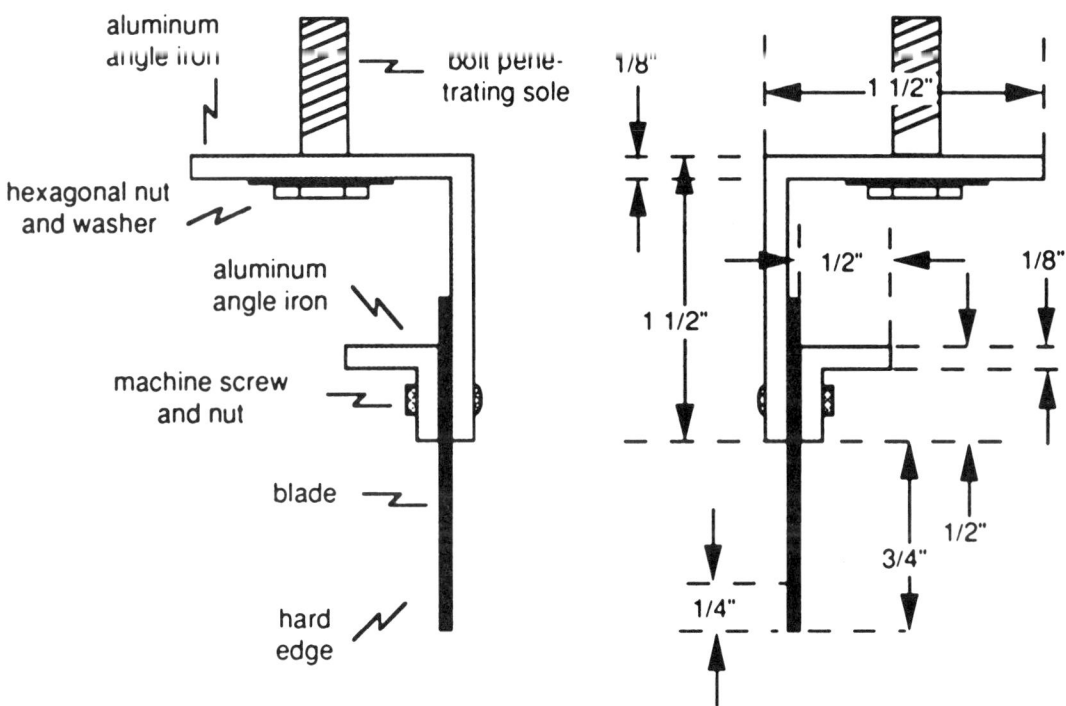

aluminum angle iron

bolt penetrating sole

hexagonal nut and washer

aluminum angle iron

machine screw and nut

blade

hard edge

1/8"

1 1/2"

1 1/2"

1/2"

1/8"

3/4"

1/2"

1/4"

Figure 8-10: Front View of Continuous Mounting Brackets

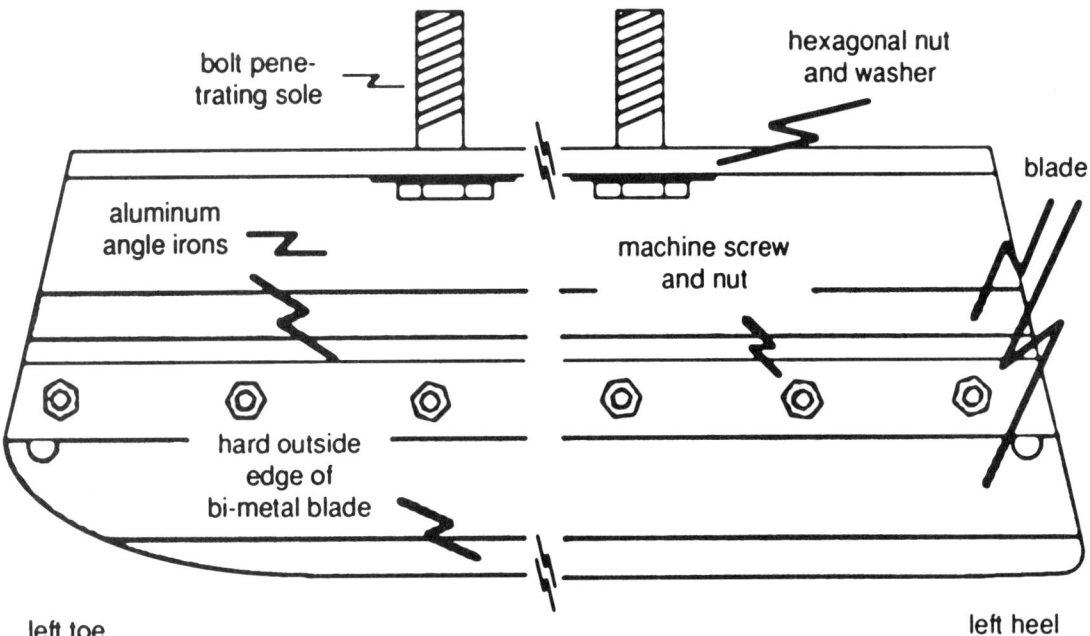

bolt penetrating sole

hexagonal nut and washer

blade

aluminum angle irons

machine screw and nut

hard outside edge of bi-metal blade

left toe

left heel

Figure 8-11: Continuous Mounting Bracket: Left Side View of Outside Blade Edge

CHAPTER NINE: SAFETY

"Praise no ice until it's crossed." — from a Viking saga of the 10th or 11th century

You could hear [the ice] groaning and heaving in a dozen different places; and a spot that would offer safe transit one day would be a gaping crevasse by the next. — Admiral Richard E. Byrd describing the Bay of Whales, Antarctica, on Jan. 17, 1934.

They may not inspire fear like lions and tigers and bears in the woods, but dogs, goose droppings and rocks on ice can pose a danger for the uninitiated.

Still, because most skate sailing accidents are neither frequent nor serious, the sport is safe. Indeed, dogs, goose droppings, rocks and other perceived obstacles needn't be a nuisance at all. Avoiding accidents and escaping harm are keys to safe skate sailing. They require constant vigilance combined with ice knowledge, as well as evasive techniques combined with safety gear.

Falling onto solid ice — not colliding with obstacles and certainly not falling into water — is the most common accident (Figure 9-1). Usually such tumbles merely result in morning-after muscular soreness, if they bring any aftermath at all. Sometimes, however, falls onto ice scrape skin, but rarely do they break bones. Even spills taken at high speeds are comparatively safe for either of two reasons. Heavy winter clothing protects a falling sailor's body, or a long slide over slick ice harmlessly dissipates her energy of motion, making her safer than a lightly dressed rider catapulted from a speeding motorcycle and stopped short by abrasive pavement. Falling into icy water is a potentially serious accident but in skate sailing actually is an infrequent and usually harmless one. Such a fall is readily avoided; yet if it does occur, its victim is easily rescued.

Skate sailing can be a safe venture by following the guidelines of this chapter, broken into sections on vigilance and knowledge, techniques and gear.

HAZARDS

Sailing on ice skates generally presents two kinds of hazards, falling down and falling in. You must recognize the causes of falls onto ice or into water to avoid them. Improper equipment, collisions, and impassable ice are the main causes of falling down (Table 9-1). Sharpen your skates to sail without falling, and watch constantly on all sides to avert collisions when you are under sail. If you find yourself unavoidably crossing rough or snowy ice, make the maneuvers outlined (Table 9-3). To avoid falling into water, you should learn the circumstances associated with thin ice and open water (Table 9-4), and follow guidelines for skirting untrustworthy ice (Table 9-2). Getting out of the water calls for special techniques.

Figure 9-1: Whoops!

Table 9-1: Causes of Falling onto Ice

● **Improper equipment**
  dull blades
  loose skates
  too large a sail
	● **Impassable surfaces**
	  shell ice
	  shallow cracks
	  soft surface

● **Collisions** with
  snow-covered ice
  shore
  skaters and bystanders
  dogs
  iceboats
  fellow skate sailors
	rough ice
	  ice pocked by geese
	  ice holed by fishermen
	
	  snow patches
	  pressure ridges

Falling Down

Improper Equipment

Sailing skates are unsafe if they are dull or loose. Sharp blades worn beneath tightly fitting boots allow a sailor to keep to a course, prevent capsizing to windward, and stop quickly when she has spilled the wind. Sharpness is especially important when the ice surface is hard during extraordinarily cold days. Because a day's sailing over hard ice will dull skate blades, they will need sharpening before the next outing. Tightly fitting boots rapidly translate foot movements into blade maneuvers, so they are essential to steering a skate sail. The remedies for dull blades or loose boots — sharpening skates and choosing them knowledgeably — are among the subjects of Chapter Eight, Sailing Skates.

For various reasons, a skate sail may be too large to be safe. An adult's sail of 54 square feet, for example, will be too tall for a child to handle, regardless of wind velocity. As a result, the mast will strike ice, needlessly toppling the sailor. Any sail, even when a tall sailor handles it, may be too large for the combination of wind speed and sail area. Cautious sailors exchange oversized skate sails for smaller ones, or they skate until the wind drops or steadies.

Collisions

Collisions, although they occur rarely, cause falls. They can happen for any of several reasons: too small a sailing area or an overcrowded one, carelessness or poor evasive technique. Skate sailing requires a minimum sailing area of about 10 acres, which corresponds to a circle having a 745-foot diameter. (A one-half-mile diameter, sometimes cited as the minimum, corresponds to a circle encompassing 126 acres.) If sailing speed equals twice the wind velocity, then a skate sailor driven by a 15 mph wind on a beam reach will cross a 10-acre pond in 17 seconds. Under these conditions, sailing on a 10-acre pond repeatedly calls for turning or stopping merely to avoid the shore. Therefore, a sailing area large enough for a small sail boat but less than 10 acres may be too small for a skate sailor. With a greater speed, she travels a longer distance than a boat in the same time.

Larger sailing areas have longer, safer courses. Many lakes provide long, straight courses, even though they are irregularly shaped. Consider a lake large enough to provide a half-mile-long run. Such a run taken at 30 mph gives you a little under four minutes before you have to turn, enabling you to watch where you are going as you cross the lake and plan your turn as you near its shore. Not surprisingly, then, experienced skate sailors prefer lakes to ponds, because the greater size of lakes makes sailing safer and more enjoyable.

It takes only a few skaters or bystanders to crowd a small pond or a favored portion of a larger lake, which increases the chance of collisions beyond a sailor's control. For example, a good approach to the ice from shore causes skaters, skate sailors, ice fishermen, and ice boarders to congregate nearby. Escaping such a crowd calls for a cautious departure made by skating with the sail held overhead. Taking leave by sailing amid skaters and others makes the sailor persona non grata, because such a course risks injuring someone. Stay away from crowds or stop sailing.

Because of crowding by boats and skaters, looking around is particularly important on Navesink River ice at Red

Bank, N.J. All ice boats there follow the same course in departing or approaching the shore where they moor. Their course carries them past the public wharf that attracts skate sailors because of nearby parking despite congested access to the broad expanse of open ice. To avoid collisions with ice boats and other crafts, skate sailors must also know and heed the established rights of way.

Lapses of vigilance result in collisions, so skate sailors must keep a constant watch, deliberately on the windward side where the sail restricts visibility. Sail windows should, of course, be large enough to give good windward visibility. Windows no larger than 36 square inches are too small. Sail plans calling for such windows date to shortly after World War I when only a few transparent plastics were available and all were expensive. Because 36-inch-square windows restrict visibility, prospective skate-sail buyers or builders may wish to buy or make sails with windows three or four times as large as these. A completely transparent sail made from Mylar is another suitable alternative.

With good visibility, sailing on skates through a gentle snowfall is a tranquil experience. But, the sailor must keep her bearings. Let her leave the ice if she risks losing either her bearings on a large lake or her visibility on any lake. On one occasion, the author fled to shore to wait out an advancing snowstorm that had reduced visibility on the lake to 50 feet. Soon after, he noted a walking ice boater emerge from the swirling snow, dragging and carrying the fragments of an expensive mast. A collision between ice boats shattered it.

Only rarely do motionless ice fishermen seem to leave or reach the ice. They resemble timeless landmarks like the ruined columns of a Toltec temple standing still amid ancient rubble. So sail around the clustered fishermen, who create impassable ice domains with radii of 25 feet or more. Their ice holes and excavated debris destroy the sailing surface, while their huts and gear clutter it. Even in cold weather, crashing through a fishing spot can ignite hot controversy (Figure 9-2).

Figure 9-2: Crashing through a Fishing Spot

Shun dogs, which view skate sailors as vultures see carrion, unerringly from afar. Some dogs seem as eager to capsize sailors on ice as they are to topple bicyclers on pavement. They chase the sailors and lunge at the sails. Fast sailing turns leave dogs behind, but once their prey escapes by this means they anticipate her turns afterward. Perhaps the best method of dealing with a dog on ice is to skate until it leaves.

Impassable Surfaces

Besides fishermen's debris, there are eight other common sources of impassable ice surfaces: shell and cracked ice, pressure ridges and soft ice, rough ice and tracked-up ice, dropping-littered and snow-covered ice. A cautious skate sailor must be alert to the presence of all of them.

(1) Shell Ice

Large or numerous patches of shell ice make a frozen lake unsafe for skate sailing. Shell ice breaks readily under the touch of skates, and drops the sailor onto solid ice. The drop ranges from about a quarter inch to an inch or more, and the impact can hurl the sailor to the ice. Circumnavigate such patches if they are small or few, or go home if they are large or many. Ice boats or boards sail safely through shell ice because their runners are deep and widely spaced, unlike the blades of ice skates. The presence of these crafts on a frozen lake, however, does not guarantee the absence of shell ice. When freezing weather follows a rain storm, a cautious skate sailor should be wary of newly formed shell ice. Look for it on a frozen lake even if ice boats are sailing there.

Shell ice is recognizable because it is white, but treacherous because it is opaque. An approaching sailor or skater cannot tell what she is getting into, even though she suspects something is amiss. Whether the brittle ice will support her or drop her an unknown distance downward onto thick ice is unpredictable. Skate sailing through patches of shell ice is always inadvisable, not least because it is tiring and somewhat frightening.

If you plow into a small patch of shell ice, your best bet to emerge standing is to lean back on the heels of your skates and to bend your knees. Leaning lifts the front of the blades, which would otherwise catch. Bent knees help leg muscles absorb the shocks of a rough passage. If the patch is large, you can hedge your bet by raising your sail overhead and coasting to a stop. Braking like a skater amid shell ice makes falling a near certainty. Broken ice beneath your skates arrests them, while your upper body moves on. Stepping out of shell ice, rather than attempting to skate or sail through it, will save much grief.

(2) Cracked Ice

Shallow cracks in the surface of thick ice pose little danger, if their widths are less than about half a blade length and if the sailor crosses them perpendicularly. Crossing them diagonally or sailing parallel to them, however, risks trapping a skate blade. In crossing a crack, raise the toes of your skates by leaning a little backward on

your heels. Cracks wider than half a blade length are likely to be pressure ridges.

(3) Pressure Ridges

Be wary of all pressure ridges, which sometimes present rough ice edges. Look for these overlapping ice layers especially between opposing spits of land or at mouths of streams. Pressure ridges can run for hundreds of feet and be treacherous for reasons set forth in the section entitled Falling In.

(4) Soft Ice

Look out for soft surface ice in late February or early March when the sun is higher and the earth can be warmer than in December and January. The sun softens ice surfaces without melting the underlying ice sheet. Consequently a solid, thick ice sheet sometimes has a soft surface that makes a whole lake or estuary impassable to a skate sailor. A soft surface slows your feet while the wind continues to move your upper body fast, resulting in falls. Skating over soft ice is possible when sailing is foolhardy; faced with soft ice, skate or leave.

Thick ice over salty estuary water also tends to be superficially soft, even when ice over fresh lake water is hard at the same temperature. Ice forming over salty water encloses pockets of brine, which lower the freezing point. Early in the season, ice on an estuary is similar to rock salt on icy steps: both leave a granular surface, which offers greater resistance in skating and increased traction for walking. Later in the season, the brine pockets migrate downward, leaving hard, salt-free ice on the surface.

At the same time of year, skate sailing over salt ice is safest early in the day before the sun has softened the surface. One skate sailor arrives shortly after dawn, as did his father before him. Both sailed in the company of iceboaters. Arriving early, however, risks sailing alone. Bring a friend,

Table 9-2: Safety Guidelines for Skate Sailors

- exchange information about ice conditions
- measure ice thickness
- inspect the whole expanse of ice to be sailed on
- confine sailing to the inspected area
- sail in company
- wear a helmet
- carry ice picks
- wear flotation gear
- bring a complete set of dry clothing

or track an ice boater.

Sailing late risks falling down. Ice on estuaries softens by early afternoon in February, unless that month is unusually cold. A prudent skate sailor should leave salt ice by mid-afternoon. A good sailing day sees most skate sailors packing up at three o'clock.

If you find yourself sailing through a small patch of soft ice, lift the toes of your skates and bend your knees. If the patch is large, or if you are unsure of its size, raise the sail overhead to slow yourself. Don't try braking inside the patch unless you are barely moving, but preferably glide to safety outside the patch. Skating safely out of soft ice is sometimes feasible when sailing through it is impossible or dangerous.

(5) Rough Ice

Rough ice probably causes the greatest number of falls. Indeed, you are heading for a fall when your blades chatter and your legs vibrate. Sometimes mistaken for warnings of advancing age, muscle tremors associated with skate sailing genuinely signal rough ice. To avoid rough ice altogether, you must search for it where it is likely to appear. Look near shore, pressure ridges, and other boundaries between ice sheets.

Slow down to cross a small patch of rough ice, raising the skate sail overhead, or

releasing it if necessary. Otherwise, lean a little backward on your skates and bend your knees to let your thigh muscles absorb the shocks. If you cannot glide to escape a rough ice patch, coast to a stop without braking. Then step gingerly out of the patch, or crawl through it. Long stretches of sailable rough ice demand a smaller sail, a different angle to the wind, or a rest until the wind abates. A smaller sail or a different course angle reduces speed, giving better control as well as more time to maneuver.

(6) Tracked-Up Ice

Not only weather but also people and birds roughen ice, sometimes making it impassable to skate sailors for weeks. Snow followed by rain and mild temperatures often create a thin layer of slush over a thick sheet of ice, which, despite the slush, attracts visitors even as it repels skaters and skate sailors. Ice boat skippers, off-road vehicle drivers, bicyclers, and pedestrians occasionally crisscross large areas of slush-covered ice. In their wakes remain blade ruts, tire tracks, and footprints that afterward freeze without flattening. Sailing over these frozen wakes provides a tooth-chattering experience better forgone. Look elsewhere for smoother ice.

(7) Dropping-littered Ice

Scores of Canada geese flock on the ice of some lakes and reservoirs, leaving their own dark hazards behind them. Goose droppings absorb sunlight, becoming warm

Table 9-3: To Avoid Falling on Rough Ice or Snow

If you can
- steer away from it

If you travel on it
- lean back on skate heels, lifting toes
- bend knees to absorb shocks
- raise sail overhead to slow, or
- release sail

and melting ice. They make hundreds of narrow, shallow holes in thick ice. As the geese flock, so do the closely spaced holes, which may cover thousands of square feet. These holes are deep enough to trap a skate, and any fall among them would be ignominious.

(8) Snow-covered Ice

More than two inches of snow makes skate sailing hazardous, although sailing through one or two inches of powdered snow is feasible but slow. Even a light snowfall brings several other disadvantages. It obscures shell ice as well as wind-packed snow remaining from a previous storm. A snow covering hides narrow cracks and ice boundaries, and it conceals suspect differences of appearance between adjoining ice sheets, or between parts of one ice sheet. Perhaps the only advantage of a light snowfall is to emphasize the presence of any open water by starkly contrasting black water against white snow. The contrast is advantageous because open water and snow-free, solid ice are sometimes visually indistinguishable even at a short distance of 50 feet or less. The lack of distinction can be especially important to a viewer sailing at 40 mph, who must bear away within two seconds to avoid a dunking!

The sight of ice boats or boards crossing a snow-covered lake should not encourage you to forgo inspecting the ice. These sailing crafts will readily sail through snow deep enough to make the lake impassable to skate sailors. More snow than one to two inches causes them to fall even if it is powdered, so pay attention to the snow thickness and to its hardness as well.

Even thin patches of wind-swept snow can be hard enough to be impassable to a skate sailor. The hardness of snow patches cannot be predicted from any visible characteristics, so that these patches are treacherous. Looking passable, they allow you to advance a few feet before they deposit enough snow beneath your boots to trip you. If you find yourself sailing through a snow patch, raise the sail overhead and lean a little backward on your skates to avert a fall. Better still, find a lake lacking patches of wind-swept snow, sail only where the patches are far apart, or go home.

To summarize, you must know the hazards and practice the techniques described here. Above all, look out for obstructions and impassable ice. Sail around them to prevent falls, whether onto thick or thin ice, or into water. Slowing or stopping before reaching obstructions is advisable. If you meet rough or snow-covered ice, lean backward on your skates and bend your knees, and raise the sail overhead or release it altogether. Brake only when your sail is safely overhead, and do so only on smooth ice. To escape patches of rough, shell, or snow ice, coast to a stop without braking. Then, without gliding, step attentively out of the patch, or crawl cautiously through it. Circumstances, especially ice quality and snow depth or hardness, determine which of these maneuvers should be tried and the order in which to try them.

Falling In

Falling into water is an infrequent skate-sailing accident, and most sailors never go in. Furthermore, no member of the Skate Sailing Association of America has become a fatality as the result of sailing on skates. A conservative estimate is that Association members have sailed about 5 million miles in the last 70 years and bathed fewer than

Table 9-4: Causes of Falling In

• breaking thin ice near	• sailing into open water
bridges dams docks inlets outlets rivers shores springs water	over springs at ice sheet boundaries
	• crossing pressure ridges
• sailing over rotten ice	• crossing ice floes

140 times as a result of skate sailing. These figures represent fewer than one ducking for every 36 thousand miles sailed. By this reckoning, the chance of going in is small, but nonetheless the consequences can be severe. Knowing the causes of unwanted baths will help a skate sailor avoid them (Table 9-4).

Thin Ice

An unaccompanied skate sailor weighing 200 pounds or less should seek freshwater ice at least two inches thick. A single adult can crack an ice sheet thinner than this. Such thin sheets appear over slowly moving or shallow water and extend some distance from it. Ice formed early in the winter can also be thin, regardless of whether it lies over still or deep water. To know if ice is dangerously thin or safely thick, cut through it and inspect the depth of the hole. Make holes in many, widely spaced places to gain a representative knowledge of the ice thickness. When you know where the ice is safely thick, confine your sailing to the inspected spots, or make new measurements.

Use a proper tool to cut through the ice you want to measure, for your own and other's safety. Don't drive the heel of your skate blade into an ice sheet, which is analogous to sawing a tree limb on which you are sitting! If you can force your blade through the sheet, the ice is too thin and you are likely to follow your blade. Indeed, a sailing companion once forcefully demonstrated his conviction that the ice underneath him would shatter beneath a blow. When he drove in his blade heel, the ice opened below him and the waters closed above his hips. He made his point, fortunately over shallows from which he soon extricated himself. With ice picks.

To determine the safety of an ice sheet, people sometimes throw rocks onto it. Throwing rocks, however, creates a hazard when it proves nothing. If the rock fails to break through, the experiment yields no knowledge of ice safety but the missile obstructs the surface. Often the obstruction remains throughout the whole winter, particularly if the rock lands in slush that freezes and remains solid. Striking a protruding rock can transform skate sailing to flight training.

Do not believe signs proclaiming ice safety or danger until you inspect and test the ice yourself. Posted signs are often as obsolete and ice-encrusted as Siberian mammoths. Such signs frequently spend whole winters beside lakes, rarely if ever changing to reflect current ice conditions. Trusting posted invitations and warnings has two likely results. The outcomes are falling in when a sign proclaims thick ice, and missing a day's sailing when a sign announces thin ice.

Posted to shun legal liability, signs forbidding skating are common and those permitting it are rare. Few government authorities frequently inspect lake or estuary ice, with one exception. Certain park rangers faithfully measure ice thickness on lakes in their charge, so consult a ranger about ice conditions. Be aware, however, that conservative park rules sometimes allow a flyweight visitor only to venture on ice that would safely hold a laden freight car. In New Jersey, park rules and rangers' attitudes differ from lake to lake and from reservoir to reservoir. Some rules or rangers permit skate sailing at one site and forbid it at another, even when the ice is safely thick at both places.

The locations of thin ice on a given lake change as the sailing season progresses. Early in the season, ice near shore quickly becomes thick, while the center of a still lake remains liquid or forms thin ice. Late in the season, mid-lake ice has grown thick, but open water or thin ice has appeared between the shore and thick ice. These changes in the location of ice result from heat transport to and from the water. How much heat is transported and how fast it moves depends partly on the height of the sun above the horizon and the volumes of water irradiated. Transmission of heat through the small volumes near shore is fast, but is slow through the large volumes in mid-lake. In a still lake, little heat moves sideways from the depths to the shallows, or vice versa. November or December, then, will see ice sailors hugging the shore, but February or March will show them keeping to the center of a lake. By late February even the task of reaching thick ice can be problematic. Often, it requires a long plank to bridge the liquid water lying between the shore and the mid-lake ice sheet. A 2-inch x 10-inch x 12-foot plank is a good size under these circumstances.

Transparent black ice formed during the still, cold, and snowless nights of late November or early December can be deceptively and dangerously thin. Cut through it to determine its thickness, and do not rely on visual inspections. Because a sheet of new black ice lacks cracks and trapped air bubbles beneath its surface, merely looking does not suffice to gauge thickness. Later in the season, however, air bubbles and cracks appear beneath the surface of aged black ice. These helpful cracks are small, occupying an approximate area of six inches by six inches, for example. They look white against a black background. The cracks and air bubbles serve as a visual guide to ice thickness, which can be estimated by their depth.

New black ice is the strongest kind of ice because it is pure. It excludes impurities like air and salt when it forms. Weather and time, however, age and weaken black ice, cracking it and often transforming it into white snow ice, after snow falls onto it. This kind of ice includes microscopic air bubbles,

which detract from its macroscopic breaking strength. If you sail on snow ice, it is wise to look for more than three inches of it and is foolish to trust less than this thickness. Cut through it to see its depth.

Signs of Thin or Weak Ice, and of Open Water

Beware of an ice sheet bending or visibly cracking beneath you. In the winter of 1989-1990, a companion unexpectedly found himself on a bending ice sheet but sailed to safety without stopping. An unnoticed pressure ridge, which he crossed on his outbound journey, signaled the end of a thick ice sheet and the beginning of a thin one. On his return a few minutes later, the thinner sheet gave way at the pressure ridge, where he bathed one foot. Despite the washing, his momentum carried him safely onto the thicker sheet.

Several years ago, another companion found himself sailing on thin ice near an ice-to-water boundary. The presence of open water escaped notice because the ice and water looked black in the prevailing light. A crack moving parallel to the sailor's course gave warning when the fissure overtook and passed him; and he bore safely away. Bending and cracking are danger signs that must be heeded by sailing swiftly off the sheet.

To keep safe, a skate sailor must know and look for boundaries between ice and water, different ice sheets, or between ice and shore. Visible discontinuities mark boundaries. For example, contrasting colors warn of boundaries, as does the sight of rough ice amid smooth ice. Strips of rough ice mark pressure ridges. Patches of black ice in a sheet of gray-white snow ice suggest that the former are new and possibly thin. Thin patches form over lake-bottom springs and creek mouths, where turbulence delays freezing and hastens melting. Ice over shallow water thins first because less underlying liquid must be warmed before any of the solid melts. Indeed, ice near shore may be thinner than elsewhere, so arrival and departure points require distrustful examinations.

Drama and farce sometimes conspire to lave the unwary ice farer. After a day's fishing from thick ice in mid-lake, an unobservant but conscious fisherman surprisingly approached shore along an ice ridge. The pressure ridge began at the mouth of a stream and tracked the underwater current for a distance of several hundred feet. Astonishingly, the fisherman followed the ridge from mid-lake until it neared land. When the ice sheet predictably collapsed beneath him, he slogged to shore in water topping his knee-high boots. His avoidable footbath resulted from the concurrence of three obvious hazards: a pressure ridge lying over water that was shallow and turbulent

Wherever you sail, be alert to the warning offered by birds perching on the ice sheet or flying over it. Aquatic fowl — especially ducks, geese, and swans — gather in and around patches of open water. The appearance of birds sometimes signals the presence of water. The patches often persist in the middle of deep or spring-fed lakes until mid-winter, despite severely cold weather. The birds' silhouettes are visible on the ice from a great distance: look for them to skirt any open water. Note also the destinations and origins of the birds' flights, which may be taking the birds to or from open water.

Bridges tend to accelerate water flow, producing thinner ice than might be expected. The supporting pillars effectively constrict the channel, and its water therefore flows faster. Thus, looming bridges signal danger because the relatively fast-moving water beneath them is warmer and makes the overlying ice thinner.

The mere presence of docks on lake shores warns of thin ice, so wharves are suspicious. Lakeside property owners often install air bubblers to prevent ice damage to their docks. Air passing constantly through the water prevents freezing near the dock, allowing only a thin sheet to form at the ice-to-water boundary. Cast a cold eye on the ice around a pier before sailing or skating toward it. Pass by if you see open water or hear bubbling sounds. Alas, you are too close if you see the bubbles.

Docks and other large dark objects warn of thin ice for another reason. Dark objects absorb sunlight to become warm and transmit heat to the surrounding water. So thin ice may lurk beside pilings and docks, around swim rafts and boats frozen into the ice, and beneath piles of leaves atop the ice sheet.

Look out for large air bubbles beneath an ice sheet. Such bubbles can be three to four feet long and two feet wide, and they tumble ominously as you sail over them. They warn that the sheet lacks support from the underlying water that ordinarily buttresses it. These bubbles can result from falling tides in an estuary or from lowering the water level in a lake or reservoir. Lowering the level can provide water for drinking, irrigation, or electrical power, or permit dredging of a channel or harbor.

Salt Ice

After a sunny spring day, salt ice near shore is especially untrustworthy. Many a homeward-bound skate sailor has bathed her feet in salts, assuming that safe ice in early morning would last until late afternoon. Don't depend on it! You may have to leave the ice from a spot different from the one where you stepped onto it. Leaving from either spot calls for an inspection and a thoughtful choice among alternative departure points.

Tilting ice floes, for which the Shrewsbury River in New Jersey is noted, develop on the shores of salty estuaries in late February or early March. Floes appear in late afternoon, aided by warming, abetted by fast melting at crystal boundaries, and helped by tidal motion. A six-inch-thick floe that is six by 15 feet will tilt under an adult's weight, and slide her into the water. Look for floes, and test a floe for tilting before crossing it to reach shore. Better still, cross to the Shrewsbury River shore by means of plank bridges.

On the tidal Navesink River estuary at Red Bank, N.J., the difference between high and low water can be as much as two to four feet at the public wharf. Because ice floats, it is often easy to descend to the ice at high tide. The ice sheet rises on the swelling tide to meet the bottom of the wharf ladders. It can be harder to ascend from the ice at low tide. The sheet falls on the ebbing tide, receding far beneath the lowest rungs and leaving them inaccessible. The height difference between the ice sheet at high and low tides may thus require different arrival and departure points. If so, the new point of departure deserves a careful inspection, especially at day's end. Consult an iceboater at the nearby yacht club, where the shore slopes gradually, if your own inspection turns up no safe departure point.

Skate sailors will do well to follow the practices of ice boaters who sail on salt ice. Ice boater and author Jack Andresen says,

> *[Salt ice] is unreliable until it's almost a foot thick. Tides rise and fall, and currents crack and undermine salt ice, making it hazardous. While perfectly clear, saltwater ice requires about 3 to 3½ inches for sailing [an ice boat], the usual gray ice should not be used at less than 6 to 7 inches.*

Rotten Ice

Late in the sailing season, the air and water surrounding an ice sheet become comparatively warm. This melts the sheet and pocks its underside in a process known as candling. Candled ice is rotten, so candling tends to convert stable sheets to

tilting floes. Be wary of sailing in late February or early March, particularly if the preceding weeks were warm. As a rule, the New Jersey sailing season ends by mid-March, which antedates ice-out. Avoid sailing on the ocean side of a salt ice sheet, where the higher salt concentrations make melting easier and freezing harder.

Pressure Ridges

Turn away from pressure ridges to avoid the following three hazards. The ridges often accompany open water, slope toward it, and change daily. Falling into the open water of a pressure ridge was a doubly chilling experience that befell an acquaintance in the 1987-1988 winter. He survived the experience — a solitary, nocturnal one — crawling uphill on an ice sheet to extricate himself. Ice picks saved him, he thinks. Approach pressure ridges only with a companion and cross them only if you must. Given a choice, make a crossing where others did so safely. It is also wise for one person at a time to make the crossing, and to do so during the plentiful daylit hours.

Ice ridges can widen or narrow within a day, so inspect them daily. For example, a ridge appeared unbidden on Greenwood Lake, N.J., in the winter of 1988-1989. During about 10 days' varied weather, the ridge opened and closed daily, like an umbrella in spring. The width of the gaps was variable, ranging from two to three inches to one to two feet. Such frequent changes soon make knowledge of a pressure ridge obsolete. Such knowledge is unreliable if not dangerous.

Pressure ridges advantageously serve as early warnings of changing ice sheets. They rise above the ice plane so they are easily seen from a distance, and they mark ice sheet boundaries. Sailing safely on one ice sheet does not guarantee that an adjoining sheet is safe. A crossing to an unfamiliar sheet calls for a distrustful inspection of its ice, and the sight of a ridge alerts a sailor to look carefully around. This grows more important the greater the distance you sail.

Long-distance skate sailing has been popular for more than a century. To be safe as possible, it would ideally require foreknowledge of the whole expanse of ice to be traversed. Such cruising repeatedly entails crossing pressure ridges, traversing different ice sheets, and overcoming other hazards. All of these hazards may span a distance of many miles, so discovering them could be difficult or impossible without closely approaching them from the ice. Although back-and-forth sailing over familiar ice may be relatively safer than cruising over strange ice, long-distance skate sailing can nonetheless be safe enough. Bill White of Schenectady, N.Y., who has sailed on Lake George for decades, said: "When the wind is right I can go 25 miles out and turn around and come back 25 under the right conditions."

TECHNIQUES

Ceding Rights of Way

To avoid collisions requires sailors to allocate rights of way according to written rules. Collisions can arise in any of three circumstances, in which (a) a sailing craft approaches a stationary craft or person, (b) two sailing crafts converge on directly opposed courses, and (c) two sailing crafts converge on courses that incline toward one another, but are not co-linear. The rights of way determine which of the approaching parties bears the duty to turn aside. Covering the first two circumstances, which are comparatively simple, requires only two rules. But the third case is somewhat complex, needing four rules. In two of these four rules, the tack sailed decides the right of way. In the other two rules, the sailors' positions relative to the wind are decisive. None of the six rules demands that the

yielding sailor stop, but all of them require her to change course. In no instance do the rules oblige her to turn in a particular direction; instead, they allow her to choose the new course freely. The rights of way governing ice-sailing crafts are sensible and long-established. Ice-boat skippers expect that the same rules will govern skate sails and ice boats alike, so the skippers plan their own courses accordingly. Skate sailors must do so, too.

Sailors use six standard terms to discuss rights of way. The terms, which describe the sailing motion of any craft relative to the true wind, are *off the wind*, *on the wind*, *a port tack*, *a starboard tack*, *windward*, and *leeward*. An understanding of the six phrases underlies an appreciation of the traditional rules conferring the right in differing circumstances.

Off the wind refers to a course sailed at 91-180° with respect to the true wind direction. Someone sailing off the wind is traveling downwind, moving in the same direction as the true wind. *On the wind* means sailing a course lying at 1-90° to the true wind. Sailing in this direction moves you toward the (imaginary) point

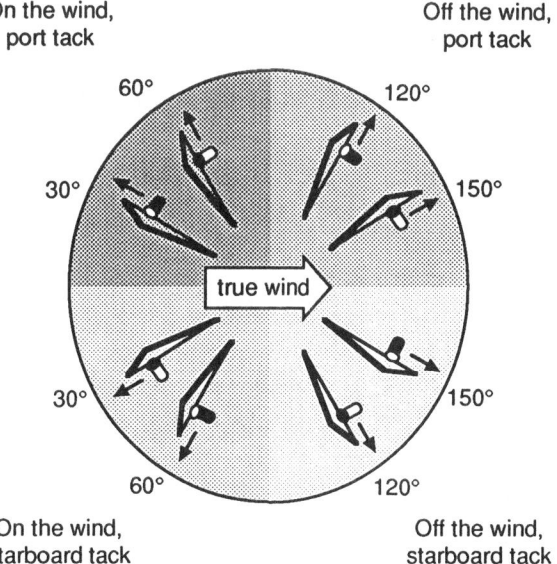

**Figure 9-3: Port and Starboard Tacks Sailed
On and Off the Wind**

representing the source of the wind. Figure 9-3, which represents a top view of skate sailors and sails, illustrates some of these courses sailed on port and starboard tacks. A triangle stands for the skate sail, and an oval adjoining a U-shape represent the sailor's helmet and one of her shoulders. Arrows indicate the directions of motion. On the right of Figure 9-3, all four sailors are traveling off the wind. Those on left are sailing on the wind.

The phrase *a port tack* refers to a course on which the wind comes from the sailor's left side. With the wind coming from her right, she is said to sail *a starboard tack*. The sailors shown in the top half of Figure 9-3 have taken port tacks, while those in the bottom half are traveling on starboard tacks. The meanings of *port* (left) and *starboard* (right) are easy to remember. The words port and left contain four letters each, whereas starboard and right contain five or more letters each.

Finally, the terms *windward* and *leeward* refer to a position relative to the source of the wind, respectively closer to it and farther from it. One sail stands to windward of another if the first lies closer to the wind source. The position of the second sail in this example falls to leeward of the first one. To take another example, a Hopatcong skate sail in motion always lies to windward of its sailor, while the sailor stands to leeward of the sail. Finally, each of the four sailors on the left of Figure 9-3 lies upwind of all the sailors on the right. The latter sailors' positions are downwind.

Sailing Crafts in Motion

The first of the six rules allocating rights of way pertains to the situation in which a moving craft approaches a motionless craft. (1) A sailing craft in motion shall keep clear of a stationary one. Skate sailors unfamiliar with the other rights of way would be wise to follow this one. Putting a skate sail into stays and stopping will prevent striking an

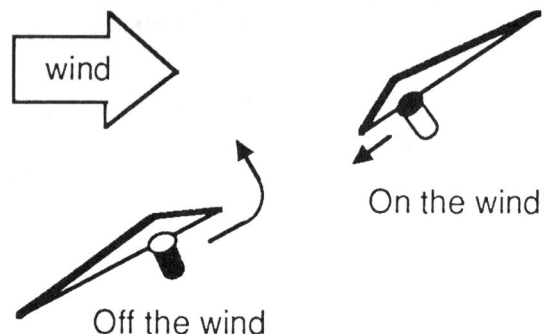

Figure 9-4: Right of Way for Skate Sailors on Converging, Co-Linear Courses: Decisive Upwind Direction

ice boat or pacifying its skipper after a near miss. Ice boaters are generally good humored, but narrowly averted collisions between ice boats and skate sailors justifiably anger them. Ice boats are unmistakably large, so close approaches to them are easily avoided.

Sailing Crafts Traveling Directly Opposed Courses

(2) A sailing craft traveling off the wind shall keep clear of one traveling on the wind (Figure 9-4). This rule applies whenever two sailors approach one another on directly opposed courses. Shown in the figure, the sailor traveling downwind is obliged by this rule to turn aside. But the rule does not prescribe the direction she must follow, so she is free to turn to starboard (right), or to port (left) as illustrated.

Skate sailors who move to avoid an approaching ice boat should heed this rule in fleeing. They must not scatter in several directions, but for simplicity should depart on one course only. Otherwise they create confusion, leaving the ice-boat skipper a multitude of choices. According to the first rule, however, stationary skate sailors have no obligation to move out of the way of the boat. They often do so, especially if they have unwittingly sailed onto a race course.

Sailing Crafts Converging on Inclined Courses

This section presents four rules covering two sets of circumstances (Table 9-5). The four rules apply in common to sailing crafts converging on inclined courses, not to those on directly opposed paths.

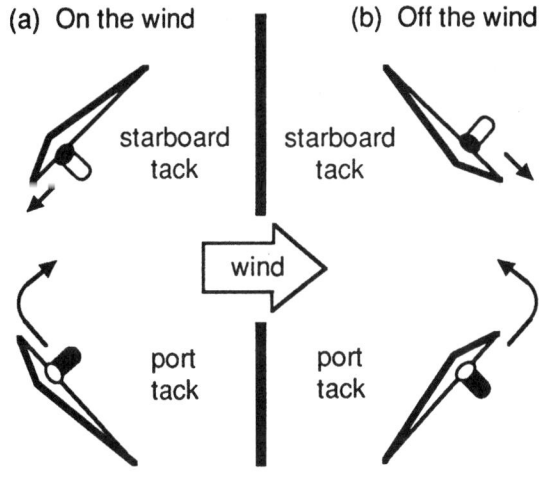

(a) On the wind   (b) Off the wind

starboard tack   starboard tack

wind

port tack   port tack

Figure 9-5: Rights of Way for Skate Sailors on Converging, Inclined Courses: Decisive Starboard Tack

(3) If two sailing crafts are advancing on the wind, the craft on a port tack shall keep clear of the craft on a starboard tack (Figure 9-5a). In the figure, the sailor wearing a black helmet continues on her original course, while the other gives way. Again, the rule does not prescribe the direction of the turn made by the yielding sailor.

(4) A craft on a port tack shall keep clear of a craft on a starboard tack, if both are sailing off the wind (Figure 9-5b). Rules (3) and (4) both give the right of way to the sailor proceeding on a starboard tack.

On the left of Figure 9-5, both skate sailors are proceeding upwind on converging courses. Their situations differ, however, because one of them has the wind from starboard while the other has it from port. The skate sailors on the right of Figure 9-5 also have the wind from different sides, although both are heading downwind on converging paths.

(5) If two crafts on the same tack are sailing on the wind, the windward craft shall keep clear of the leeward one (Figure 9-6a and -6d). The two skate sailors at the top left are advancing with the wind from their starboard sides. Those at the bottom left have the wind from port. In both cases, the sailor wearing a white helmet lies upwind of the other and is turning to give way.

(6) If two crafts on the same tack are sailing off the wind, the leeward craft shall keep clear of the windward one (Figure 9-6b and -6c). At the top and bottom right of Figure 9-6, the downwind sailor wears a white helmet and is turning to avoid the favored sailor in a black helmet. The latter is continuing to sail on her original course. Both have the wind from their starboard sides at the top right, and from the port at the bottom right.

Saving Yourself

Avoiding injury, whether from falls through thin ice or into open water, calls for rescue techniques and safety gear. These techniques include means for getting one's self or another person out of water surrounded by an ice sheet. Rescuing others, which can be done in a variety of ways, deserves a separate discussion that follows. Safety gear helps a skate sailor evade the effects of falling down and in.

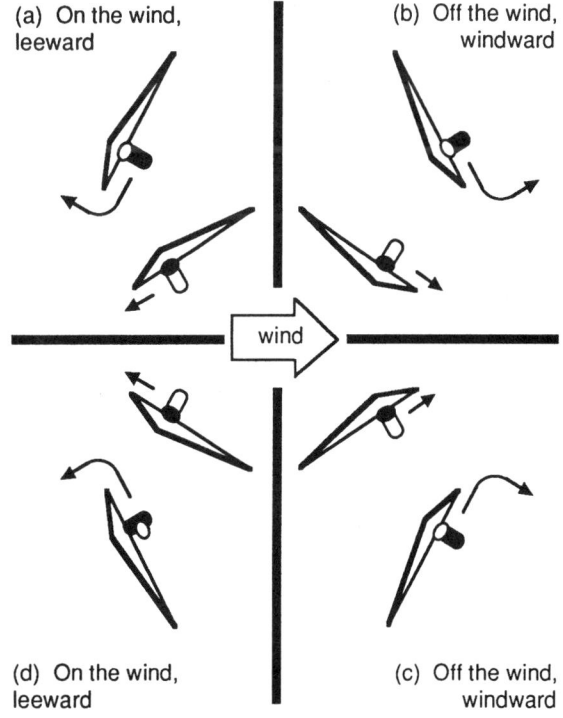

(a) On the wind, leeward   (b) Off the wind, windward

wind

(d) On the wind, leeward   (c) Off the wind, windward

Figure 9-6: Rights of Way for Skate Sailors Converging on Inclined Courses: Decisive Downwind (a,d) or Upwind (b,c) Positioning

Table 9-5: Rights of Way for Two Sailing Crafts on Converging, Inclined Courses

Tack	Course	Position Relative to Other Craft	Action
port	on the wind	—	turns
starboard	on the wind	—	continues
port	off the wind	—	turns
starboard	off the wind	—	continues
—	on the wind	windward	turns
—	on the wind	leeward	continues
—	off the wind	windward	continues
—	off the wind	leeward	turns

Finding Thick Ice from Open Water

Getting out of open water requires climbing onto an ice sheet thick enough to support the victim's weight. Surrounded by ice, she can choose only one edge to try first, and must select one that is safely thick. Which edge to choose, then?

Common sense dictates first trying the ice sheet sailed off or broken through, regardless of whether it is the closest to shore. Nearby must lie the thick ice that supported you before you went in. If a flight, a wind, or a current carried you away from this edge, you should swim toward it. Breaking this ice, if it proves too thin, will advance you toward thick ice. If your advance lies in the direction of shore, then so much the better. A chance to walk to land may soon reward your attempts to touch bottom.

Touching bottom with one's feet, however, does not guarantee a successful self-rescue. On a recent occasion, an ice boat plowed through thin ice on the Shrewsbury River, N.J., estuary. This accident left its skipper standing on the bottom, his head above the shallow water, but situated hundreds of feet from shore. Bereft of ice picks, he was unable to pull himself onto the slippery ice. He kept his grip on the ice sheet, called for help, and was salvaged by a skate sailor with a rope. The rescue demonstrates the value of sailing in company.

When you reach the edge of thick ice, cling to it and call for help. Clinging is important to prevent a current in an estuary or a large lake from drawing you beneath the ice sheet or away from the thick edge. You should not try to remove your skates or any item of clothing lest you lose your grip.

Escaping Open Water with the Help of Ice Picks

During each voyage, every skate sailor should carry ice picks to rescue herself from water surrounded by ice. They offer three advantages. First, picks support an immersed sailor on the edge of an ice sheet. Ice is slippery and grows more so when water is splashed onto it. As a result, grasping it is difficult with gloved or bare hands. Properly inclined ice picks firmly grip ice even when it is wet. They act like anchors, digging into and holding onto a surface.

Second, ice picks help an immersed sailor pull herself out of the water onto an ice sheet. Mounting the sheet is less difficult than often imagined, because it lies at water level. The victim has only to level herself in the water by kicking her feet before slithering onto the ice surface. Clambering onto the horizontal sheet is easier than getting onto a pier or into a boat from the water. In the latter two cases, the victim must climb vertically.

Third, ice awls rapidly move the prone sailor from thin to thick ice, while she spreads her weight over a relatively large area. Spreading her weight, which a prone position allows her to do, minimizes the

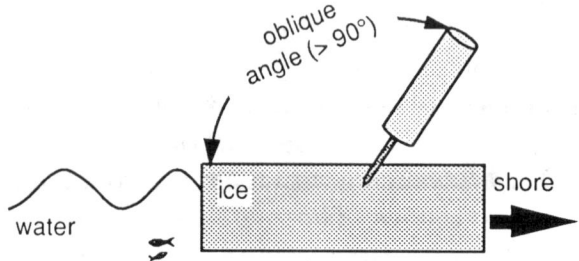

Figure 9-7: Ice Pick Set at a Proper Angle to Help a Swimmer Move from Water over Ice to Shore

chance that she will break through any thin ice that she crosses. All in all, ice sailing with ice picks improves the already high odds of a successful self-rescue.

To haul yourself out of open water onto an ice sheet requires a four-part technique, if your ice picks are to be of assistance. These parts, in the needed order, are (1) driving both picks into the ice you face, and (2) gripping them as you level your body in the water. (3) You pull on both picks to draw your whole body onto the ice, and (4) re-set, then pull on one pick while you free and advance the other. These last actions, carried out from a prone position, comprise a series of hand-over-hand motions. They will rapidly distance you from the hole.

To set the picks, incline them in your fists so that their points angle toward you (Figure 9-7). Then drive the picks downward into the ice to fix them at an oblique angle to ensure that they continue to hold when you pull on them. They will detach themselves when you pull on them if they are set at an acute or a right angle.

Still gripping the set picks, kick your legs as if you were swimming. This will raise your lower body to the surface and place your entire body and the ice sheet in the same plane. Co-planarity, which is easily achieved, is a prerequisite for self-rescue.

Now pull yourself onto the ice sheet, using both hands. Keeping your grip on one pick, loosen the other ice pick, advance it, and drive it into the ice ahead of its mate. Pull yourself ahead with the hand holding the newly set pick. Repeat these actions, alternating one hand and pick with the other pair until you are well away from the hole and any thin ice near it, or until you reach shore. The hand-over-hand motions resemble those used to climb a ladder or a rope.

Getting out of water and rolling away from thin ice is possible without picks. If you go

Table 9-6: If You Do Go In...
always
• stay calm
• call for help
• swim to the ice sheet you left
• face the ice sheet to help rescuers
with ice picks
• draw picks
• tilt handles forward, blades backward
• extend arms and drive picks into ice
• kick feet to level body, gripping picks
• pull body onto ice with picks
• spread legs and arms
• pull away from hole with picks
without ice picks
• lay forearms on ice sheet or grasp it
• kick feet to level body
• swim and wriggle onto ice sheet
• spread legs and arms
• roll away from hole

in but lack ice picks, use any handy tool to get a grip on the ice edge. A sharp metal object makes a suitable tool. A pocket knife will help you, as will a key or even a belt buckle.

Getting Out with a Skate Sail

A sail can also help a sailor extract herself from open water. Its mast or boom offers something to grip that is not slippery and it spans enough ice to distribute her weight. With a sail spar lying upon solid ice, the sailor grasps the spar, and raises her upper body over the sail, as if she were doing a push-up. She tilts forward onto the ice sheet, kicking her feet to level herself. Having drawn her whole body onto the ice, she rolls quickly away from the edge.

Rolling or Crawling to Safety

Rolling away from open water rather than

walking away can be essential to a rescue, if the sailor lacks ice picks. The victim who lies prone and rolls to safety spreads her weight over a larger ice area than one who tries to stand and then to walk. Body weight spread over a larger area creates less pressure on the ice. Consequently, the ice is less likely to break beneath the lesser pressure than it is beneath the greater one. Remember that rising to one's feet calls for concentrating body weight on them. And when they are clad in skates, the pressure will be enormous because the blade area contacting the ice is minuscule. In a sense, skate blades magnify the pressure exerted by a person standing on one foot. This is so because of the relation between pressure, force, and area:

$$\text{pressure} = \frac{\text{force}}{\text{area}}$$

This equation asserts that the exerted pressure equals the quotient of applied force divided by the area over which the force is distributed. With a constant force, the smaller the area is, then the larger the pressure will be. Therefore, it's even more important for a skater to roll away from a hole than for a pedestrian to do so. Compared with a boot, a skate has a small contact area, so the skater exerts a greater pressure than a pedestrian of equal weight.

Rescuing Others

Methods for extricating people from open water have as many as three features in common, depending on the equipment, which could include ropes, floats, skate sails, extension ladders, rescue crosses, human chains, and small boats. All give the victim something to grasp and keep the rescuers out of the water. Most of them help haul the immersed person to shore.

Regardless of the rescue method and equipment, a victim stands to benefit from using certain techniques. When she reaches the ice edge, she should kick her legs to raise her lower body to the ice level. This will prevent her body from catching on the ice edge, as it must do if she tries to advance when her trunk lies on the ice sheet and her legs dangle in the water. Once the victim is on the ice sheet near the water, she should lie prone upon the sheet. Attempts to stand may drop her through it again. Finally, rescuers should instruct the victim to roll away from the hole, lest the act of walking away break ice.

Throwing a Rope

In rope rescues, the helpers stand on shore or solid ice, toss a rope to the victim, and haul her to solid ice or land. Rescuers who venture onto slippery ice should wear skates or ice fishermen's creepers for a firm stance, otherwise they are likely to join the victim in the water when the thrown line takes her weight. In 1932, experiments carried out by the Skate Sailing Association of America established the likelihood that a rescuer without skates would be dragged in. Rescuers who lack skates or creepers must lie down on the ice to avoid being pulled into the water. In a dire emergency, a rescuer attached by a rope to helpers on thick ice or shore may crawl to the immersed person, entering the water to help.

Rope rescue bags may be the best devices to rescue someone who has gone in. Unlike a simple line, the rope in a rescue bag need not be coiled before it is thrown to the victim. The rescuer holds the free end of the rope and underhandedly pitches the rope-stuffed bag to the victim. As the thrown bag travels, it pays out the rope from its opening; as it lands, the victim grasps a loop protruding from the bottom of the bag. Throwing the bag accurately requires only a little practice. If a first throw misses, re-stuffing the rope into the bag takes less than a minute.

Rescue bags typically contain 75 feet of three-eighths-inch polypropylene rope and a polystyrene float. The float supports the bag in the water, while the rope itself floats. The breaking strength of the rope is 1,800 pounds; and the bag, rope, and float weigh only $2^{1}/_{4}$ pounds. The mouth of the bag contains a drawstring, and the length and diameter of the bag measure 15 and six inches, respectively. Kayaking suppliers, among others, sell rope rescue bags, which cost about $25 to $35.

Rescue ropes are preferably 75 feet long and at least 50 feet. Shorter lines may bring the rescuer too close to thin ice. Modern synthetic fibers make flexible ropes, so even a long one will fit in a pocket or in a pouch strapped around a skate sailor's waist. Ring buoys or loops secured with bowline knots sometimes terminate the ropes. If a loop ends the rope, it should be large enough to pass around an adult's upper body and beneath one arm.

Using Extensions

Two bolted-together eight-foot pieces of 2- x 4-inch lumber make a simple rescue cross (Figure 9-8). The victim grabs one arm of the cross, and a line tied to the other end of the same arm allows a rescuer to haul the sailor out of the water. The cross-piece distributes the sailor's weight as she emerges onto an ice sheet.

Ladders or rescue crosses, because they are comparatively short, may require that someone pushing them venture onto the ice to aid the victim. Both devices, however, distribute the victim's weight over a comparatively large area of ice, in contrast to ropes. The rescuer using a ladder or cross must distribute her weight, too, and so should lie on the ice near the victim.

Forming a Human Chain

If no equipment other than willing hands is immediately available, a human-chain rescue can succeed. Human chains venture onto the ice, with each participant lying prone. They wriggle forward, using elbows, knees, and toes to do so, until the leader

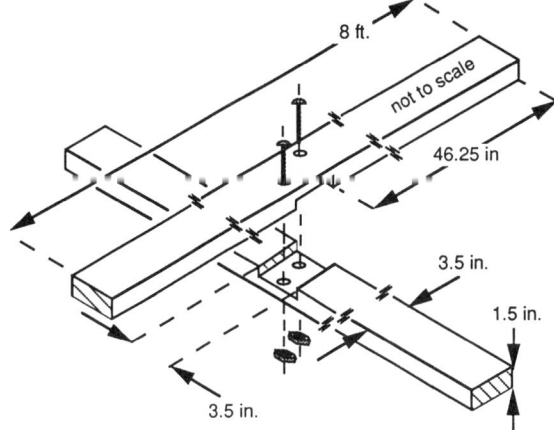

Figure 9-8: Construction of a Rescue Cross from Lumber, Bolts, and Nuts

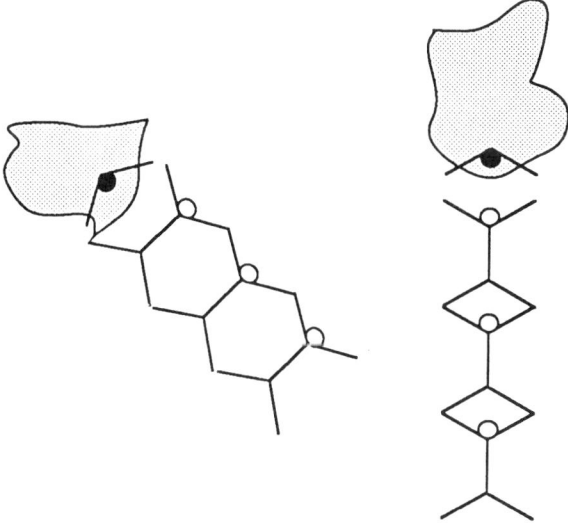

Figure 9-9: Hands-to-Hands (left) and Hands-to-Feet (right) Rescues Seen from Above

can grasp and pull the victim out of the water. To be successful, this method requires that the leader lie on a safely thick edge and that the victim move to this edge. That all the rescuers remain prone is crucial, both to distribute their weight and to prevent the victim's weight from dragging the leader's body into the water. The two kinds of human chains are hand-to-hand, and hands-to-feet (Figure 9-9). In both kinds, each participant spreads her arms and legs to distribute weight over as great an area as possible. The chain extends a greater distance in the hand-to-hand method. To a first approximation at least, both methods distribute the same weight over equal areas.

SAFETY GEAR

Safety equipment reduces the risk of injury during accidents. Personal protective gear, which is mostly worn over outer clothing, averts injury from falls onto ice, floats a sailor who has fallen into open water, gets her out of it, and warms her afterward. Such safety equipment should accompany you on every voyage, so it is wise to take inventory before leaving home.

Using Tools to Inspect Ice

Ice Sticks

Suspect the ice whenever and wherever there are no other people on it, and cut through to measure its thickness. Perhaps the best cutting tool is an ice stick, which is standard gear among Swedish skate sailors and long-distance skaters (Figure 9-10). These sticks are four to five feet long and comprise a long wooden shaft ending in a short, stepped metal dart. The bottoms of the sticks contain lead weighing about a pound. To use the stick, drive the metal shaft into ice, and note the depth of penetration. Thick ice stops the shaft at the first step, while thin ice allows the point to go in as far as the second step. An ice stick enables the user to stand farther away from the ice she is cutting compared with someone wielding a drill or an ax. Such sticks are available from a Swedish sporting goods store at the address given later.

Ice Spuds

Favored by ice fishermen, an ice spud is a massive chisel long enough to cut ice at a distance, as an ice stick does. It will easily cut through eight inches or less, thanks to its 2½-inch-wide beveled blade and its weight. The blade is six to seven inches long and lies at the end of a long iron shaft. Together the blade and shaft span 65 inches, a distance suitable for a 5-foot-10 person. Ice spuds are available from sporting goods

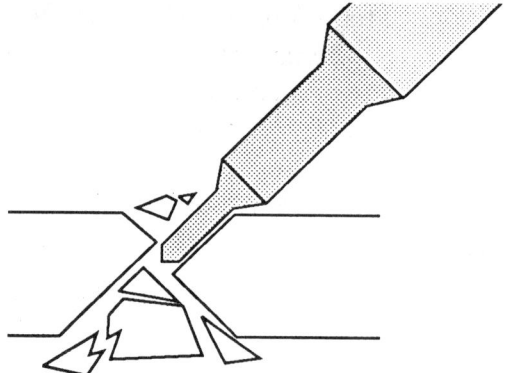

Figure 9-10: An Ice Stick Stopped by Thick Ice

stores that cater to ice fishermen.

Ice Screws

A climber's ice screw also serves to measure ice thickness, but is shorter and lighter than an ice stick or spud. This screw is a six-inch-long metal tube bearing saw teeth on one end and threads on its exterior. The top carries a short handle set at 90° to the longer shaft. The screw easily cuts a hole as deep as it is long, and requires no great strength to use. As it descends through the ice sheet, it crushes the cut ice, which ascends the interior of the tube. An inspection of the hole below the withdrawn screw then tells the ice thickness. Before withdrawing the screw, the user can also note the depth to which the shaft penetrated the ice when all resistance ceased. Ice screws, which are small enough to fit in pockets, are available from stores serving mountain and ice climbers. As Chapter Four notes, an ice screw will also anchor a skate sail to the ice.

Equipping Yourself

Helmets

Helmets are widely used by sportsmen and -women to prevent head injuries, and skate sailors are no exception. Indeed, the hardness of ice makes helmets indispensable for skate sailing. The consequences of head injuries are severe even though the likelihood of injuries may be small. On one occasion, nevertheless, a helmetless companion unexpectedly awoke in a hospital because of a fall taken while skate sailing. Landing on his head did him no permanent damage, but served as a warning that now he heeds. Today when he sails, he wears a helmet. So should you.

Skate sailors most often wear bicycle, hockey, or motorcycle helmets. Bicycle and hockey helmets contain ventilation holes and are colder to wear than motorcycle helmets. They are comfortably warm when placed atop a balaclava or a knitted cap drawn over the ears. Bicycle and hockey helmets are lightweight and short, so they do not affect hearing or catch on the skate sail boom.

The warmer and somewhat heavier motorcycle helmets extend farther down the head, covering the ears and the back of the skull. These helmets give greater protection against injuries than the shorter bicycle and hockey helmets. Various face shields are available for motorcycle helmets; some protect the wearer's lower jaw, others guard her eyes from the wind, and some do both. Shields that cover the wearer's eyes prevent the tearing and blurred vision that an unprotected face can experience during very strong winds. Goggles can substitute for a face shield.

Motorcycle helmets present two disadvantages. First, they reduce the wearer's ability to hear because they are thick and cover the ears. Sounds coming from beside and behind are nearly inaudible. Even speech coming from straight ahead is muffled. Second, the bottom sides of some motorcycle helmets, because of their design or length, tend to catch on the sail boom. This impedes steering the sail, cocks the sailor's head to leeward, and brings sore neck muscles after a day's sailing.

Flotation Gear

One reason alone compels a skate sailor to wear approved flotation gear. It supports a sailor in the water, perhaps helping to save her life. A life vest adds protective padding and thermal insulation, and is worn over ordinary winter clothing. Flotation jackets contain buoyant material between their outer fabric and inner lining, and hang well below a sailor's waist. They are warm enough to substitute for a heavy outer jacket.

Some skate sailors favor a life vest over a flotation jacket, unless the latter stops water from rising along an immersed sailor's chest and back. A firmly strapped vest reduces the rate at which water permeates clothing below the water line. This lowers the risk of shock and the discomfort of immersion, which occurs quickly when cold water dissipates body heat. Clad in a life vest tightly fastened by all four straps, the author emerged from a quick lake bath with three inner layers of clothing dry above the waist. Despite immersion to mid-chest, the vest excluded water, preventing discomfort and shock afterward. By contrast, some flotation jackets hang loosely about their wearers' waists, and admit water readily. The design of other jackets prevents this. But whether you choose a vest or jacket, do wear flotation gear, lest the want of it add injury to embarrassment.

Ice Picks

Ice picks of proven effectiveness come in pairs. They have sharp points on stout, stubby, cylindrical blades, and bear handles thick and long enough to afford a good grip.

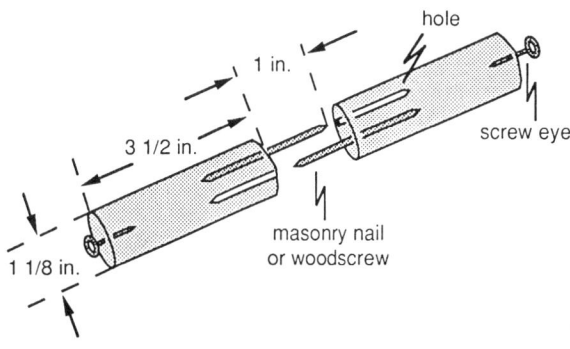

Figure 9-11: Ice Picks Made from Dowels

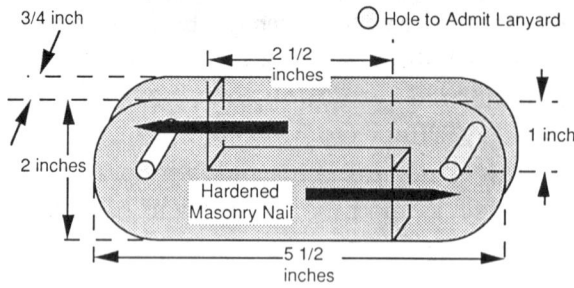

Figure 9-12: Polar Bear Ice Claws

whistle are available from a Swedish sporting goods store, which also furnishes ice sticks. Picks of a different design (Figure 9-12) can be purchased as Polar Bear Ice Claws from a Long Island business:

Firma S. Skyllermark	Polar Bear Co.
Terrassvägen 14	6 Nesaquake Avenue
13141 Nacka	Port Washington
Sweden	New York 11050

The width of the hand, measured at the palm (about four inches), plus the length of the blade (one to 1½ inches) make a total length that gives good leverage. A length of line connects one pick to another, so that dropping one pick does not entail losing it, provided that the immersed sailor retains the other pick. The line must be long enough to let the sailor extend both arms simultaneously and fully.

Skate sailors and ice boaters make ice picks from readily available materials or adapt commercially available tools, like screwdrivers or carpenters' awls. Buying ice picks abroad or from a domestic manufacturer represents a third alternative.

Driving stout screws or masonry nails into dowel segments, cutting off the heads, and sharpening the ends furnishes useful picks (Figure 9-11). The handle of one pick serves to sheathe the blade of the other. A lanyard passes through screw eyes driven into the butts. You can also make ice picks from a pair of screwdrivers, by cutting off the blades and sharpening the cut-off ends. The pick blades should be one inch long and have a one-eighth-inch diameter. An electrically powered grinding wheel makes cutting and sharpening easy. (Because screwdrivers have case-hardened blades, using a hacksaw is tedious). A short length of plastic or surgical-rubber tubing sheathes the blades, linking them to one another. Screw eyes can be driven into the handle butts to hold a lanyard, or the lanyard can pass through drilled holes in the butts.

Sheathed ice picks combined with a

Most skate sailors carry their ice picks over their outermost layer of clothing, below their collarbones, and in the center of their chests. The picks are readily drawn and the sailor can reach them without having to lower her hands into the water. Sheaths for picks are sometimes sewn to a life vest or flotation jacket reserved for skate sailing. In this case, one cord holds each ice pick on either side of the chest. Each cord spans an arm's length and fastens to the flotation vest or jacket, so dropping a pick does not entail losing it in the water.

Glasses and Goggles

Skate sailors who wear spectacles would be well advised to choose lenses made from plastic or safety glass. These lenses are shatter-resistant or shatter-proof. An extra pair of glasses will be welcome if one pair suffers damage in a fall. Spectacles, as well as goggles and shields on motorcycle helmets, prevent tearing. Yellow lenses in goggles or shields reduce glare and improve visibility.

Pads

Knee padding averts injuries and reduces the discomfort of kneeling on ice. Elbows are also vulnerable to bruising, and might benefit from padding. Basketball players', skate boarders', or roller skaters' knee and elbow pads are suitable. Knee pads also prevent the dampness that sometimes comes from rigging or disassembling a skate sail on a relatively warm day. Either job entails kneeling on ice, and woolen trousers (for example) readily absorb some of the

Richard E. Myers

Figure 9-13: Finnish Sailing Skates

superficial, but often invisible water present during mild weather.

What to Wear After Bathing

Dry clothing, a bath towel, and a space blanket usually complete a skate sailor's assembly of safety gear. Sold inexpensively at sporting and camping goods stores, a metal-coated space or survival blanket will add much to a sailor's physical comfort après le bain, yet will occupy only four or five square inches in her duffel bag. A generously sized bath towel will not only absorb water but conceal the hapless bather from any gathering crowd of eager spectators.

Assembling a complete set of spare clothing is a bit of a nuisance if the job is left to the last minute before the season's first voyage. Once gathered, however, the apparel can lie in a car trunk for the rest of the winter. Spare, dry clothing is a comfort because it prevents the misery of going home wet, and it can be a consolation. Be aware, however, that even a dry sailor attracts a spouse's notice when she arrives home wearing clothing different from what she wore when she departed. The change of clothing can inspire questions, comments, and sanctions; and one grandparent, who flew from ice through air into water, was grounded like a teenager.

You'll think *you're* flying if you sail the icewing described in the next chapter.

CHAPTER TEN: RELATED SPORTS

With good ice, a 30-knot breeze, and an icewing sailor made of the right stuff, 100 mph should be within reach.

— Anders Ansar, icewing inventor, writing of planned improvements, Jan. 12, 1990.

Would you like to sail upwind without a boat, to outrun the wind without a motor? If so, you can await winter, pull on ice skates, and mount a Hopatcong sail on your windward shoulder. But these choices aren't your only ones. Other options, presented in Chapter Ten, offer variety in technique, design, footgear, surface, and season. For example, you can learn here to maneuver a Hopatcong sail from its windward side. Discover other sail designs favored at home and abroad, which are the icewing, Windskate-windski, Roller sail and Skimbat.

You can sail them all on ice once you know the techniques specific to each craft. These crafts arose to serve three sports: ice skate, roller skate, and ski sailing. All three sports possess two defining features: namely footgear fixed to runners or wheels, and sails closely held by the sailors.

Chapter Ten will also acquaint you with parawing sailing. This sport is a distant relative of ice skate sailing, possessing only one of the two defining features, which is special footgear. Parawing sailors use footgear fixed to runners or wheels, but do not directly hold the sails that bear them. Instead, they loft cloth parafoils to propel themselves, and manipulate lines leading to these wing-like sails. Somewhat like kite flying, parawing sailing represents the newest form of ice sailing.

Yet you needn't confine your winter sailing to hard, smooth ice, if you change from skates to skis. Safe ice too soft to allow skating will permit ski sailing, and most of the crafts described here will let a proficient

Table 10-1: For More Information

Icewing Sailing:

Mr. Anders Ansar (a fluent English speaker)
Kungsholms Strand 183[3]
S-112 48 Stockholm
Sweden
Tel.: intl. + 08-650 21 72

Roller Skate Sailing:

Mr. James D. Budge
Windskate, Inc.
P. O. Box 3081
Santa Monica, CA 90403
Tel.: 310-453-4808

Sport Sail Inc.
5763 Arapahoe Ave., Unit D
Boulder, CO 80303
Tel.: 303-447-9094

Ski Sailing:

Mr. William Tuthill
World Ice and Snow Sailing Association
Box 414
Jamestown, RI 02835
Tel.: 401-423-3030

Oy Tech Center AB
P. O. Box 55
SF-02231, Finland
Tel.: intl. + 358-0-803-8290
http://www.otech.fi/otech/skywings

Parawing Sailing

Mr. George Theriault, President
North American Parawing Co.
P. O. Box 1693
New London, NH 03257
603-827-3115 (phone or fax)

Mr. Wolf Beringer
Noldeweg 1
73547 Lorch, Germany
Tel.: intl. + 07-172-5472

skier sail fast over snow. In Minnesota, for example, an off-duty policeman once clocked a Hopatcong ski sailor speeding at 50 mph. No arrest or fine ensued because the wind was driving the sailor on snow-covered lake ice, not a speed-limited highway. Equipped with a parawing, such a skier can make 30-yard broad jumps. He can sail uphill and upwind at the same time, defying gravity and wind force alike.

Other changes of footgear will extend the sailing season to the year around. With ordinary in-line skates, sailing on pavement is feasible with a variety of sails. Parawing sailors in the United States and Europe adopt long roller skates with tall, thick wheels of the in-line or side-by-side variety. These skates make it possible to sail a parawing across the grass of a meadow or lawn, or over the hard-packed sand of a beach or desert. And the powerful thrust of a parawing occupying 100-200 square feet allows water ski sailing!

ICEWING SAILING

The greatest practical innovation in ice skate sailing during the last 100 years is the extraordinary icewing (Figure 10-1). Looking somewhat like an airplane wing tip

Figure 10-1: An Icewing

on end, this Swedish craft encloses the sailor, who wears ice skates. Anders Ansar, a Stockholm writer and photographer, designed and built the first icewing in 1976. Also a marine inventor, Ansar sought to promote ice sailing races and to develop an ice sailing craft superior to conventional skate sails.

Ansar recognized that excessive turbulence is the outstanding flaw of a conventional, moving skate sail. The physical system of the sail and the sailor creates turbulence and decreases laminar flow as the sailor's body deflects the air around the lower sail half. This deflected air, which would stream smoothly over the isolated sail, increases aerodynamic drag. The combination of the windward skate sail and the leeward sailor therefore represents a relatively inefficient airfoil.

Devising and building a vessel that isolated its sailor from the air flowing over its sails were Ansar's valuable, practical contributions to ice sailing. His icewing, which realized this segregation, enclosed the sailor on all sides except the bottom. Isolation abolished the turbulence of a conventional skate sail, prolonged the desirable laminar flow of air over the icewing sails, and reduced aerodynamic drag. Greater airfoil efficiency should have rewarded lessened aerodynamic drag — and icewing sailors benefited as expected. An icewing is twice as fast as a conventional skate sail in the ratio of sailing speed to true wind speed.

On one occasion, an icewing sailed as fast as 56 mph in a 15-mph breeze, almost four times the wind velocity. "It doesn't seem as if you are going fast," said Basil Kamener of his first voyage in an icewing. Kamener, a former commodore of the Skate Sailing Association of America, went on: "But then you realize you're beating everything else on the ice." Racing an icewing in 1979, the Swedish developer Ansar beat DN and

Skeeter ice boats in an informal contest held on Peach Lake near Brewster, N. Y. Ansar's craft sailed to within 28 to 30° of the wind, pointing higher than an ice skate sail.

Original Design

An icewing comprises a rigid, curved front piece, two sails that make up the sides of the craft and meet in its rear, and a solid cap (Figure 10-1, compare Figure 10-2). A single, transparent plastic sheet forms the front piece, which is sometimes brightly painted, and contains a window. Viewed from the top, an icewing has the symmetrical shape of a (projected) teardrop. The original design called for synthetic cloth and windows in the port and starboard sails. Stiffened by aluminum battens and ribs, the sails occupied 50 and 69 square feet in junior and senior models, respectively. Newer sails are 75 to 80 square feet.

The interior of an icewing contains a steering handlebar made from aluminum

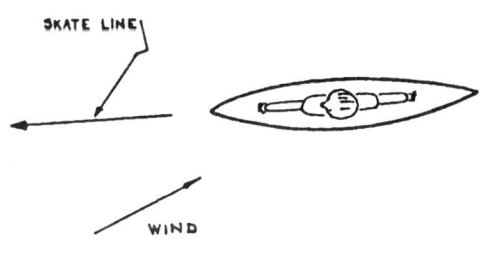

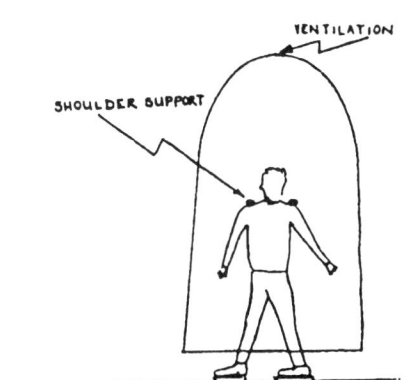

Figure 10-2. W. Garnett's Improved Skate-Sailer

tubing. It also contains cloth straps that support it atop the sailor's shoulders. All told, the icewing components weigh a total of 20-30 pounds. For transport, its sails and rigging fold against the front piece, and fit on a car-top rack.

Although Ansar realized the concept of enclosing an ice skate sailor within his craft, the same notion had occurred to other sailors. The concept appears in the published correspondence of two Britons, William Garnett and John Morwood.† In 1968, Garnett wrote, "I would like to try an improvement on my skate sailer in the form of a plywood and perspex airfoil made to fit over the body almost down to the knees and internally supported in the shoulders..." (Figure 10-2).

The Icewing Cabriolet

The newest development in icewing sailing is another Swedish craft that encloses the sailor only partially (Figure 10-3). Covering him from shoulder to ankle, the new wing is called the Cabriolet. Like the original model, the new one closes around the sailor's body at the front and back. The sail projects about two feet behind the sailor, but lies close to his body in front. It looks like a segment of an airplane wing, not like a wing tip. The Cabriolet is the invention of Ansar.

Ansar says, "[the] Cabriolet is a practice sail with good efficiency but is not as fast as the competition sail due to its smaller sail area. In a moderate breeze it moves as fast as a skater. In strong winds you can sail faster [and] it is easy to regulate the speed." The Cabriolet occupies only 21.5 square feet, about $1/2$ to $1/3$ of the original areas. The new model weighs 4.4 to 6.6 pounds and folds into a 4-inch x 4-inch x 47-inch package. It largely comprises fabric and aluminum tubing.

†The Garnett-Morwood letters can be found in *Foils, Ice Yachts & Sails*, publication number 66A of the Amateur Yacht Research Society, ed. J. Morwood, Woodacres, Hythe, Kent, 1968, pp. 81-85. They give no evidence that anyone ever sailed or built Garnett's craft.

recommends smooth ice and light winds not exceeding 4 to 7 mph. He writes, "bad ice and strong winds will most likely put you in a situation you cannot handle. Suddenly you are sailing at 50 miles per hour, wondering where the brake is and how to make a turn." Braking a moving icewing is feasible but, like turning one, requires practice and technique (read on).

Entering an Icewing

To enter an icewing, the sailor first places it on the ice facing upwind. He squats and, with a friend's help, raises the craft overhead. As he lowers the wing over himself, he shoulders the straps, adjusting them to place the sail edge about one foot above the ice. A proficient sailor carries the wing with the sail edge closer to the ice (Figure 10-1). Lowering the wing increases sailing speed and exploits the fencing effect Chapter Five explains.

Getting Underway

A wing sailor begins a voyage by turning until the wind strikes the port or starboard sail at a 90° angle. With wind from this angle, an icewing moves off as smoothly as a dancer. Once the sailor is moving he adjusts his course to head toward a chosen destination.

Choice of course angle is as important in icewing sailing as it is in ice skate sailing because it partly determines speed. The slowest sailing speeds result from sailing directly downwind, when one's angle to the wind is 0°. Icewing racers as well as softwater sailors avoid such courses and tack downwind. Their sailing speeds then exceed the wind velocity, and they reach their downwind destinations faster than if they sailed there directly.

Steering

Changing body position relative to the wing steers the craft, and to change position the sailor must pull or push the handle bar. Pulling moves the wing aft of the sailor,

Figure 10-3: Icewing Cabriolet

Skates

Like other skate sailors, an icewing sailor requires long blades to keep to a set course. Racing skates are suitable, as are skates made by mounting blades to Alpine ski boots. Ski-boot skates are more popular among Swedish icewing and ice skate sailors. High skates are unnecessary because icewing sailing owes its great speeds to aerodynamic efficiency, not to large sail areas.

Sources of Icewings

Amateur builders can make icewings and cabriolets with simple tools. Building plans for 50- and 69-square-foot wings are for sale, and they include dimensions, a list of materials, and most of the needed construction techniques.

Finished wings are for sale from Sweden (Table 10-1). Prospective buyers of plans or complete wings should write or telephone the developer, Anders Ansar, who speaks English.

Techniques

Trying an Icewing

For a first voyage in an icewing, Ansar

displacing the sail center of effort relative to the center of lateral resistance, which lies near his skates. This places a greater sail area behind the sailor, creating a weather helm. The wing then turns to windward as the sailor pivots on his skates. Pushing the handle bar moves the wing ahead of the sailor. It increases the forward sail area, and brings a downwind turn.

Turning toward the wind is more difficult than steering away from it, when the wind is strong. In this case, the sailor applies his shoulder to the sail as an aid to steering. Beginning a windward turn with an icewing must not be left until the last possible moment, according to Ansar; and such a turn requires practice to succeed. In this respect the ice wing differs from an ordinary skate sail that easily turns upwind but demands a special technique for turning downwind.

Slowing and Stopping

Turning directly into the wind eventually slows and stops an icewing. In this respect, an icewing differs markedly from a skate sail. The latter luffs and vibrates uncontrollably when sailed directly upwind, and must be moved overhead to stop.

A passive stop is not the only possible kind, and experienced wing sailors exploit air resistance to brake their vessels. Keeping to a direct upwind course, they rotate the wing slightly so that it develops a braking action. Braking by means of the sailing craft itself is a tactic employed by sailors on the windward side of Roller Sails.

As in ice skate sailing, the sailor must not use his skates to brake until he has spilled the wind. Doing so risks a headlong fall that might injure the sailor or damage the wing, costly because of the labor needed to fabricate the piece, and likely because of the somewhat brittle piece. For example, one sailor struck soft ice and crashed near the windward mark during a 1989 race held north of Stockholm. In the fall, one of his knees holed the front of his icewing. Speaking of his downfall, he allowed later that winning a National Championship while wearing a "hot-dog kiosk" was not dead simple.

Leaving an Icewing

To get out of an icewing, its sailor squats as he did to enter it. He lifts the forward part overhead, keeping the rising wing clear of his shoulders by grasping the lower battens through the sails. Once the wing is overhead, the sailor lowers it to the ice and rises to his full height.

Keeping Safe

Icewing sailors follow the safety guidelines offered in Chapter Nine, with one exception. A moving wing sailor ends comparatively minor troubles by sitting down on the ice without leaving the wing. Escaping a moving wing may be difficult; and leaving a sunken one is crucial but may be harder still. The wing design allows the enclosed sailor to flee in only one direction, through the opening at the bottom of the craft.

SKI SAILING

For more than 75 years, a covering of snow and a passion for sailing have led skiers and sailors to unite their sports. Ski sailing, the offspring of this marriage, originated in or before 1914, when it was practiced in pre-Revolutionary Russia. The European practice of ski sailing continues today, for example in Finland where the Skimbat, a sail designed by Sami Tuurna, is manufactured (Figure 10-4). The Oy Aerodynamics Co. makes this 42-square-foot sail from transparent fabric and an aluminum frame. The sail is bent in the middle to resemble a bird's wing, so that the two sail halves form a dihedral angle. From the intersection of the halves hangs a rigid rod that the sailor holds. The rod lies

Figure 10-4: A Skimbat Sailed on Snow

William Tuthill

a few inches away from the wing and runs perpendicular to the wingspan. The assembled sail spans 12 feet and weighs 14 pounds and, to use it, you stand on the windward side of the craft. You can sail it in winds ranging from 12 mph to 46 mph (!), and reach speeds exceeding 50 mph. If you want a Skimbat, which can also be used with ice skates instead of skis, write or call the manufacturer at the address or number listed in Table 10-1.

Other kinds of sails are also suitable for use over snow, and include the Hopatcong, the Windskate-Windski, the Roller Sail, and the parawing. The following discussion of ski sailing refers to Hopatcong sails or covers all these sails.

Advantages

Ski sailing offers four advantages over skate sailing, if the weather cooperates. (1) The sport extends the winter sailing season wherever snow falls early or stays late. For example, sailing on skis is feasible in Minnesota throughout March and, in a recent season, two Minnesotans sailed as late as April 10. Northern lake ice permits ski sailing in spring but forbids skate sailing

then. Although it can be one to two feet thick, its surface is covered by snow or softened by sun. Skis, however, because they are broader than skates, will cross a slush-covered ice surface. Consequently, sailing on skis remains possible when slush makes the ice impassable to skate sailors.

(2) Ski sailing brings more places to sail than skate sailing, which in the U.S. confines sailors to frozen lakes or estuaries. Snow-covered golf courses, fields, and untraveled roads allow ski sailing. The abundance of such places can reduce the travel to find a suitable sailing spot. Then, ski sailors can spend more time sailing and less time driving. (3) Sailors prepared to use either skis or skates can find more sailing days within any winter. Opportunities to sail on skis follow snowfalls, while chances to sail on skates follow thaws and re-freezes.

(4) Snow, because it adopts the contours of rolling terrain, allows out-of-plane ski sailing. An exciting variation of the sport, sailing uphill or downhill is impossible over horizontal ice sheets. Ordinary ski sailors can climb and descend gentle slopes while adventuresome sailors can leap from steeper grades and jump obstacles. Minnesota ski sailors launch themselves from natural drifts or artificial platforms and make jumps as broad as 20 feet. Dr. David Wiencke of White Bear Lake, Minn., wrote, "jumping 3-foot-wide expanses of open water brought us to smoother ice." On Jan. 11, 1990, the Minneapolis *Star-Tribune* pictured the leaping Jim Oakes descending safely in a 20-30 mph wind (Figure 10-17).

(5) Ski sailing holds a considerable advantage over skate sailing because of equipment differences. Ski sailing footgear is commercially available. Moreover, the market for inexpensive secondhand gear is vast, and skis and boots can be rented. The equipment needed for ski sailing is easier to acquire.

Ski sailing, if it is confined to land, is

less hazardous than skate sailing in one respect. It presents little or no risk of falling into water. Arguably, any falls will be cushioned by the snow, not exacerbated by the hard ice. The lower ski sailing speeds, compared with skate sailing speeds, will lessen the severity of any tumbles. A skier falling onto a flat surface, however, tends to stop short while a long, harmless slide gradually dissipates a skate sailor's energy of motion.

Sailing Speeds and Wind Velocities

Ski sailing requires higher winds than skate sailing, because a snow surface resists the passage of a ski more than an ice sheet impedes a skate. High sailing speeds are possible, however, despite the greater friction of snow. On a recent occasion in Minnesota, a ski sailor's speed was 50 mph, measured with an off-duty policeman's radar gun.

Another difference between ski and skate sailing concerns the sailor's angle to the true wind when he uses a Hopatcong sail. This angle is always larger in ski sailing. In the former sport, an estimate of the closest possible angle to the true wind is 55-65°. In the latter sport, the angle is about 35-45°.

Snow Conditions

Ski sailing requires a firm base of snow about two inches thick. Snow density, temperature, and age all influence ski sailing speeds. At 10 to 25° F, snow packed by wind offers an ideal surface. With properly waxed skis and an 18 mph wind, warmer snow is sailable despite its stickiness.

Experienced ski sailors find deep fresh snow difficult or impossible to sail on. Ski sailing over shallower but still fresh, powdered snow demands winds of about 20 mph that may permit only slow speeds. However, sun and wind age snow, advantageously changing its physical characteristics. In a few days, they can transform unsailable or slow snow into a

Figure 10-5: Ski Sailing on Lake Saratoga, N.Y., about 1920

Figure 10-6: Sailing Skier

sailable fast surface. Temperatures above the freezing point of water hasten such changes.

Sails

Lateen sails (shown in Figure 2-3) find use in ski sailing; but Hopatcong sails have largely supplanted the Schenectady sails popular with ski sailors in the 1920s (Figure 10-5). Winds blowing at 18-35 mph require sails of 60 to 35 square foot areas.

With a Hopatcong sail, the choice of size must be judicious. Ski sailors need a larger sail for a given wind speed than do skate sailors: snow resists skis more than ice hinders skates. Paradoxically, ski sailors require smaller sails because ski sailors depend on a semi-seated posture for stability. Skate sailors do not need to take this position, nor do they adopt it for any other reason.

A semi-seated posture lowers the mast-boom crossing and the sail edge. The mast end, however, must clear the surface to avoid striking it and capsizing the sailor. Whether the mast end will clear the ice or snow depends on the perpendicular H-distance (see Figure 3-24) between the spar crossing and the sail edge. This distance, which is proportional to the sail area, will be adequate for clearance if the sail is comparatively small.

Skis

Proficient ski sailors recommend downhill skis made from modern synthetic materials. Synthetic materials reduce resistance and speed the sailor. Downhill skis bear sharp metal edges, which allow a sailor to control his direction. These edges prevent the side slipping that would otherwise occur irresistibly on ice or crusted snow. A ski sailor encounters more side forces than a skier, so cross-country skis are unsuitable for sailing because they lack metal edges.

Longer skis are preferred because they spread the sailor's weight over a greater area. This distribution prevents or reduces his tendency to sink into soft snow. Long skis also increase stability on rough, crusted snow or a series of rolling snow drifts.

Waxed skis can be indispensable to a day's sailing. Glide waxes reduce the resistance offered by slow snow; and different waxes are useful in different temperatures. Waxing skis at home avoids wasting sailing time. Out-of-doors, the heat needed to melt and spread ski wax can diffuse quickly.

Boots

Alpine ski boots equipped with quick-release bindings make suitable footwear for ski sailing, in contrast to the flexible boots and bindings used by cross-country skiers. Like skate boots, ski boots must fit well, so that foot motions translate readily into ski movements. An inexpensive pair of secondhand ski boots can be adapted to ski sailing and ice skate sailing. Release bindings, recommended for safety, only rarely free the skis during falls, which are less severe than in downhill skiing.

Posture

Sailors bend their knees for stability, but a ski sailor bends them more than a skate sailor. The former lowers his center of gravity more than the latter for the greater stability needed to cross bumpy snow. The ski sailor looks like a person seating himself. It lets leg muscles absorb the shock of rough passages.

Ski sailors lie on the wind like skate sailors, countering the sideforce. To do this, a ski sailor bends his upper body from the hips and, keeping his entire body stiff,

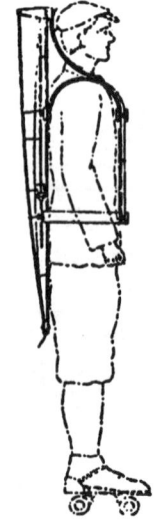

Figure 10-7: Collapsible Roller Skate Sail

Casper Hardt

Figure 10-8: Windskate Sailing in a Desert (left) with In-line Skates; (right) with All-terrain Skates

rotates it slightly aft to lean on a Hopatcong sail. He leans farther aft than a skate sailor.

Turns

Ski sailing techniques resemble skate sailing techniques, with one exception. On skis, directional changes made in deep, dense, or crusted snow may require a special, stepped turn. The sailor lifts one ski at a time, rotating it slightly in the desired direction, and replacing it on the surface. Repetitions with alternating skis complete the turn. A fast-moving sailor can carry out the stepped turn without stopping, but must take care not to cross his feet. "The Swedish crossed-foot skate sailing technique [is] impractical on skis," says an experienced Minnesotan ski and skate sailor.

ROLLER SKATE SAILING

The earliest date found for the origin roller-skate sailing is 1935, when the U. S. Patent and Trademark Office granted Patent No. 2,018,062 to Casper Hardt of Detroit. He invented a frame to support a collapsible sail on a skater's back (Figure 10-7). Hardt also sought means to spread the sail, hold it in an extended position, and release and collapse it. His collapsible sail took the shape of a parallel trapezium. The longer of the two parallel sides rested near the sailor's head and lay horizontally.

Roller-skate sailing became popular in the late 1970s with the advent of Windskate® sails. Then the part-time sail maker, Jamie Budge of Santa Monica, Calif., sold a thousand sails. Roller skate sailing also attracted an international following, and Budge soon shipped Windskate sails as far away as Europe and Asia.

Enthusiasts come from Germany, Switzerland, France, Sweden, Japan, and the United States. The Skate Sailing Association of America counts several declared roller skate sailors among its members, in Ohio, New Jersey, and Wisconsin. The Wisconsinite recently tried out an 80-square-foot Hopatcong sail on a newly paved Madison parking lot.

Like ice-skate sailing, roller skate sailing rewards a liking for speed: 45 mph, measured by a tracking car, is the highest reported velocity attained with a Windskate sail. True wind speed and angle to the wind on this occasion went unreported. A Roller

Sail user reports a sailing speed of 50 mph.

Places to Sail

Roller skate sailing, like ice skate sailing, unsurprisingly requires a suitable surface. New pavement that is flat, smooth, and hard is ideal if it lacks obstacles. Paved playgrounds, parking lots, and airport runways offer suitable surfaces. Certain bikeways and piers in Southern California are wide enough to allow sailing, remarkably. Paved streets can also be used if they are wide and uncongested.

Daytime automobile and pedestrian traffic turns some roller-skate sailors into nighttime athletes. One of them sails on the parking lots of shopping malls, befriending patrolling policemen who stop to wonder. He recruits them to the sport by loaning them his sail and skates. Another nocturnal roller-skate sailor prefers sailing on the road before his home. Headlights of oncoming vehicles light the night sky, warning him of their approach.

In one respect roller-skate sailors resemble ski sailors, who sail on snow or superficially soft ice. Roller-skate sailors, although they must avoid ice and snow that afford little traction, are not restricted to a single kind of surface, whether artificial or natural. They can even sail on dry lake beds or in deserts (Figure 10-8). El Mirage, a dry lake with such a natural surface, presents plenty of chalky, flat land hard and smooth enough for roller skate sailing. Favored by some heat-loving sailors, the lake lies in the Mojave Desert of California and occupies about 25,000 square miles. It attains daytime temperatures as great as 117° F.

Skills and Strengths

Beginning roller-skate sailors require the same skills and strengths of ice skate sailors. They are balance and the ability to skate, as well as some arm and upper-body power. Once acquired, these skills make roller-skate sailing techniques easy to learn. The

techniques needed with a Windskate sail or a Roller Sail differ from those required by a Hopatcong sail, so this chapter presents the basic Windskate and Roller Sail sailing techniques.

Skates

Both conventional and modern skates find use in roller-skate sailing. Conventional skates possess four wheels arranged in two pairs, one beneath the skater's toes and one beneath his heels. The permanent mounting of wheels to boots makes the skates differ from the detachable roller skates of years ago. Modern roller skates possess four or five wheels in a straight line, and became available in the mid 1970s. Such skates, for example Rollerblades® and UltraWheels®, combine support from rigid plastic outer boots with comfort from soft inner boots. Although they are preferred to side-by-side skates for speed and stability, they are not used exclusively. Unlike many ice skate boots, Rollerblade boots can be tightened or loosened in an instant. These comparatively rigid boots present a welcome contrast to flexible ice skate boots: over-tightening the rigid boots is difficult or impossible, so skating in them is painless. Other in-line, roller skate boots have quick release catches, not laces. In choosing in-line skates, the buyer must attend to the number and hardness of the wheels, and to the size and quality of the bearings. These factors influence performance of the skates.

Safety

Safe sailing of any kind demands eternal vigilance, and roller-skate sailors must keep alert to avoid obstacles. Those to avoid include holes, trees, and posts; parking meters, light stanchions, and stationary vehicles in parking lots; and moving vehicles anywhere. Obstacles in parking lots can be hazardous not merely because they obstruct the sailing surface, but because they cause air turbulence and pressure drops.

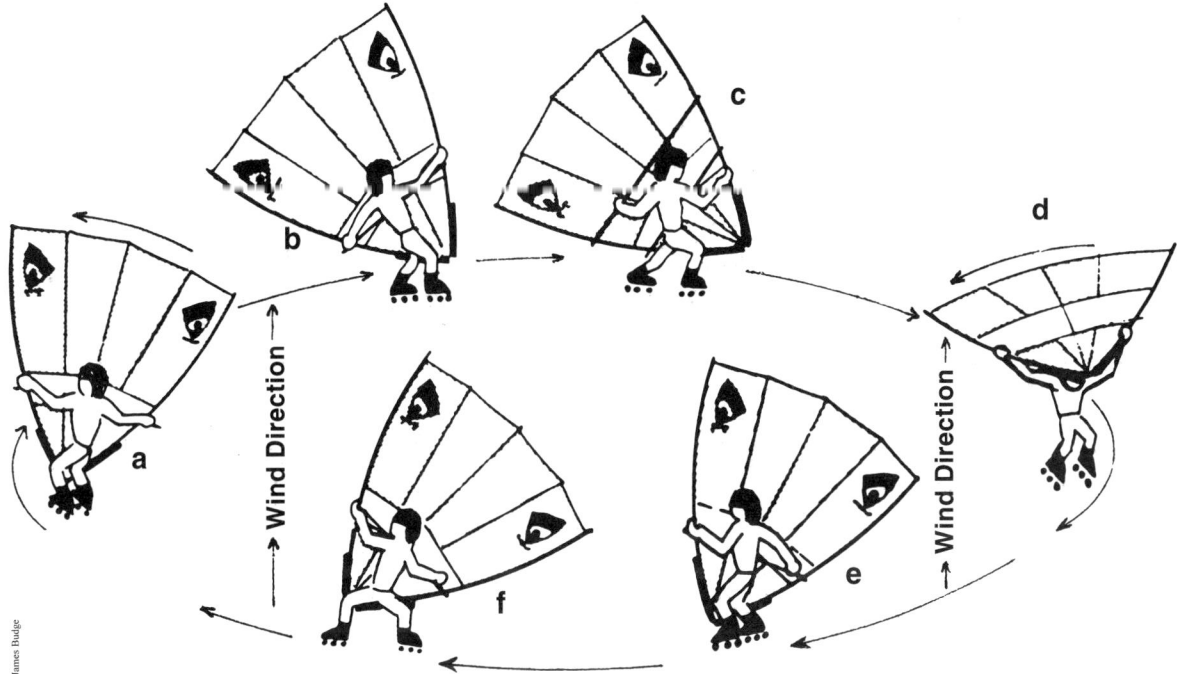

Figure 10-9: Roller Skate Sailing with a Windskate Sail

James Budge

Turbulence arises when, for example, light poles stand between the wind and the sail. Pressure drops occur beside automobiles, and can unexpectedly cause a sailor to lose thrust as he passes to leeward of a parked car. Loss of thrust can cause a fall if the sailor is heeling a sail that lies on his windward shoulder. Other obstacles that deflect wind, and that should be circumvented or approached carefully, are buildings, walls, hills, and groves of trees.

The sailing surface should be dry and free of debris like fallen leaves. Wet pavement, or pavement covered by moist leaves, offers poor traction. The whole sailing area deserves a close inspection. Clearing any debris from the area to be sailed on is advisable; and a newly paved surface, because it reduces friction, is preferable to old pavement.

Protective clothing and equipment for roller-skate sailing are indispensable. The intolerant surface that the sport requires — pavement, for example — can be harder and more abrasive than the relatively soft snow or slippery ice used by ski and skate sailors. Windskate and Sport Sail both recommend gloves, helmets, and knee and elbow pads. One experienced roller skate sailor suggests wearing a helmet that has a chin guard, while another suggests leather clothing for high speed sailing.

Sails

Although Hopatcong sails are sometimes used by roller-skate sailors, most of them use Windskate sails or Roller Sails. Consequently, the following sections concentrate on Budge's Windskate sails and Ansteensen's Roller Sails.*

WINDSKATE SAILS

Windskate, Inc., offers roller-skate sails in two sizes, 39 and 36 square feet. Both sails possess windows, use nylon sailcloth, and roll into a small package. They are colorful, and essentially take triangular shapes. The larger 39-square-foot sail, called

*One sailor who does use a Hopatcong sail recommends protecting the jib against abrasion of the sail. He covers the jib bow with a long piece of flexible plastic tubing slit along its length and snapped into place. Without the tubing, a falling sail will suffer damage when it strikes the pavement. Hardware stores sell such tubing in a variety of diameters.

the High Performance Roller Windskate-Windski, is a bellied sail having a bowed rig that is 9 feet by 9 feet. Fast and powerful in light to moderate winds, according to the manufacturer, this sail weighs 7 pounds including spars.

The smaller, 36-square-foot sail carries adults in stronger winds and children in lighter winds. This triangular sail, known as the High Wind Roller Windskate-Windski, also weighs only 7 pounds. It resembles the lateen sails used for ice skate sails at the turn of the 20th century. Modern Windskate sails have the advantage over earlier lateen sails (Figure 2-3) because the former are not lashed to the sailor. Escaping trouble is therefore easier now because today's sailor can instantly release the sail to spill the wind and free himself.

Windskate sails are smaller than those favored by American and Swedish ice skate sailors. For them a 35-square-footer — or even a larger one — is a storm sail only. Indeed, Minnesotan ski sailors recommend their smallest, 54-square-foot sail during blizzards. By contrast, the largest ice skate sails deployed in sponsored Swedish races reach 95 square feet.

Getting Underway

A sailor using a Windskate sail stands on the windward side not touching the sail with his body, a position that does not distort the airfoil shape (Figure 10-9a). To take off, he grasps each of the two outer spars. When movement begins, the sailor shifts the sail until one spar takes up a nearly vertical position. Then he supports the sail by resting the lower spar and sail edge on his upper thigh. His upper body twists a little, so that he faces in the direction of travel. Both skates point in the direction of travel, and parallel one another with the windward skate ahead of the leeward one. Figs. 10-9b and -9e show the positions adopted in opposing tacks sailed at 90° to the true wind.

Heeling

Roller-skate sailors with Windskate sails heel by leaning backward, which is exciting and tiring (Figure 10-9f). During heeling, the two skates face in opposite directions, with only the forward, windward skate pointing in the direction of travel.

Holding the Sail in a High Wind

To sail in relatively high winds, the sailor changes the sail attitude and the position of his arms (Figure 10-9c). He rotates the sail until one spar is parallel to the ground. His leeward hand then grasps the spreader, while the windward hand holds the forward spar.

Coming About

A two-part maneuver is needed to come about. One part, known as putting the sail in stays, is useful for stopping as well as turning upwind (Figure 10-9d). The sailor raises the sail overhead, holding the sail plane parallel to the ground. In the second part, the sailor lowers the sail to the other side of his body to begin sailing on another tack.

Jibing

Turning downwind is advisable only in light winds (Figure 10-9a). The Windskate jibing technique calls for rotating the forward spar from its position in Figure 10-9f. When the rotation is complete, the spar occupies the position shown in Figure 10-9b. In the intermediate position, the spreader lies parallel to the ground and above the sailor's head (Figure 10-9a).

Sailing on One Foot

Sailing on one foot is feasible, as it is in ice-skate sailing. In the one-foot position, the roller-skate sailor keeps the leeward skate on the ground. This position is the same as the popular one adopted by Swedish ice-skate sailors, who sail with the windward skate elevated and crossed over the other one.

Figure 10-10: Roller Sail with Transparent Jib

ROLLER SAILS

"I landed in a pile of bushes at the end of a parking lot," said Erik Ansteensen, remembering an ill-fated Florida voyage with an early roller skate sail. "Lying upside down, I said, 'This thing has potential.'" And now, a few years later, Ansteensen presides over Sport Sail, Inc., a Boulder, Colo., start-up company that sold over 1,000 Roller Sails (Figure 10-10 and Table 10-1).

His sail merits discussion here for five reasons. (1) Of all the traditional hand-held skate sails used in North America during the last 100 years, only the Roller Sail design balances the sail. These other crafts include the Hopatcong, the Schenectady, the kite sail, the Erie, the Nyack, and the Cape Vincent models. Although the independently invented Roller Sail resembles the older Cape Vincent skate sail in shape and construction, the latter craft is tail heavy. Cape Vincent sails tend to turn upwind because their centers of effort lie relatively

far from their masts that the skaters must hold. Depending on the Cape Vincent sail area, the distance along the boom between the center and the mast would range from 18 inches in a 25-square-foot model to 36 inches in a 95-square-foot model. In a 61-square-foot Cape Vincent sail, the center of effort lies in the mainsail 28 inches aft of the mast-boom crossing (Figure 10-11, top).

By contrast, the Roller Sail center of effort lies 10 times closer than that to the intersection of the mast with the boom. It falls 2¾ inches aft of the mast-boom intersection in a 61-square-foot model (Figure 10-11, bottom). The distances between the center and the crossing would equal two inches in a 25-square-foot Roller Sail but only four inches in a 95-square-foot sail. Because the skater must handle the mast in some maneuvers, he must stand within arms' reach of it. Therefore, the center of lateral resistance between the skater's moving feet must also lie close to

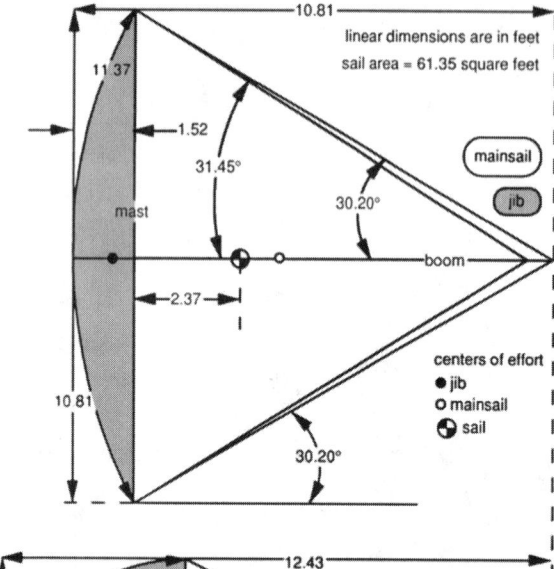

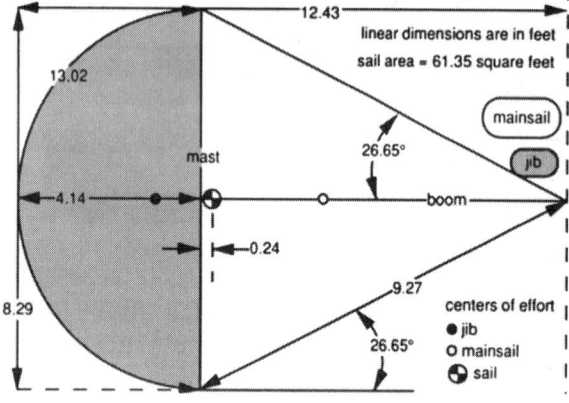

Figure 10-11: Centers of Effort in 61.4-Square-Foot Sails. Top, Cape Vincent Sail; Bottom, Roller Sail

the center of effort (Figure 10-11). A short distance between the two centers makes possible a large but balanced sail. To achieve balance, the innovative Roller Sail design places 44% of the sail area in a jib twice the size of that in a standard Hopatcong model of equal area. As a result, the sailor of an 81-square-foot Roller Sail requires only one hand to make certain maneuvers, despite the enormous power of the huge craft.

(2) A comparison of the Roller Sail and Cape Vincent designs demonstrates the principle needed to make a large balanced sail. The proportion of the sail devoted to the jib must be increased so that the center of effort shifts forward to establish or maintain a short distance between this center and the mast-boom crossing. With 44% of the sail area devoted to the jib, the

Roller Sail achieves this increase, but the Cape Vincent design fails to do so. The latter sail design allots only 18% of the sail area to the jib. Without an increase in jib area but with an initially tail-heavy design, a sailor whose stance aligned the centers of effort and lateral resistance to sail straight would not be able to reach or comfortably hold the mast.

This principle of suitable proportions served to make a useful 89-square-foot Hopatcong sail (Figure 2-37). The sail center of effort lay about 30 inches aft of the crossing of mast and boom, thanks to an increase in the jib area. However, the tail-heavy Erie sail design (Figure 2-23) violated the principle, perhaps accounting for the obsolescence of such sails.

(3) Customarily, a skater maneuvers a Roller Sail from its windward side. The techniques used to do so apply to skate sails of related designs like the Hopatcong. Sailors of the latter crafts can stand to windward, although they usually take a leeward stance.

(4) The Roller Sail represents a rare and perhaps unique example. It may be the only hand-held skate sail to have been produced with help from a computer program. Computer-assisted sail design usually benefits only costly softwater boats.

Finally, (5) one Roller Sail model exemplifies good use of modern sailcloth. It contains a generous window instead of parsimonious peepholes. Transparent fabric forms part of the mainsail and nearly all of the jib. In a 61-square-foot model, this large Roller Sail window would occupy over 27 square feet, more than 40 times the area of the windows recommended for a comparable Hopatcong sail..

Selected aspects of the Roller Sail materials, construction, and design inform the following subsections, as do performance characteristics and sailing techniques. The subsection dealing with design compares the heights and lengths of

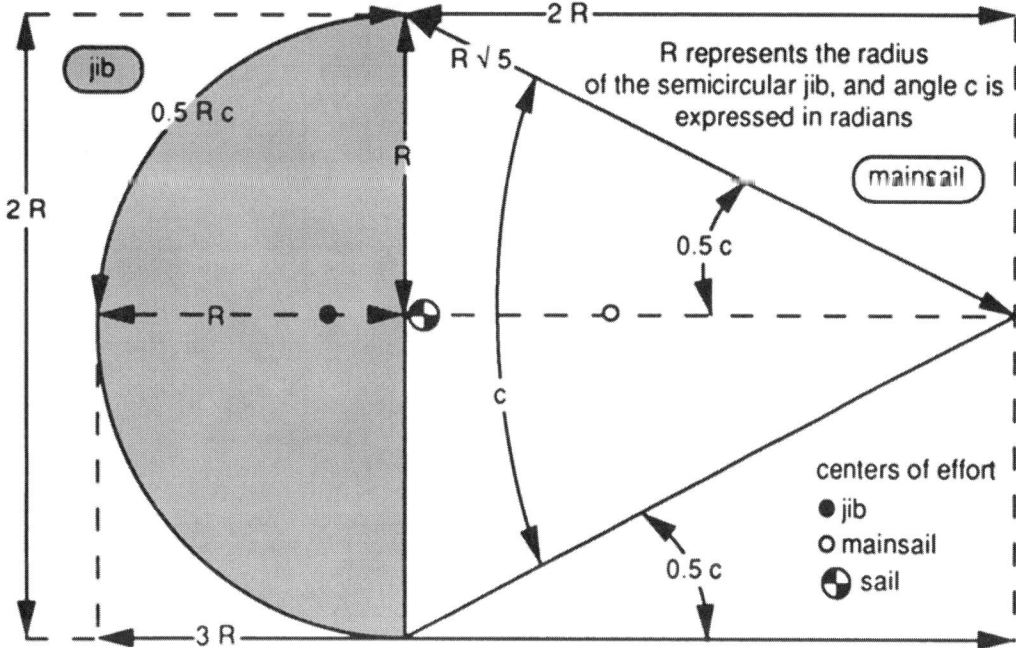

Figure 10-12: Characteristic Dimensions of a Standard Roller Sail

selected skate sails and the distances between their centers of effort and mast-boom crossings.

Design

Dating from 1989, the profile of a Roller Sail in use resembles an ice cream cone lying on its side (Figure 10-12). A semicircular jib contains the curved leading edge, and the diameter coincides with the short leg of an isosceles triangle having two long sides. This triangle represents the mainsail. The angle enclosed by these two sides equals 53.3°. The height of the sails equals the semicircle diameter, and the length spans three radii. The sail center of effort always lies upon the boom and close to the intersection of the mast and boom, although the distance between these points does vary with sail size. This distance increases slightly in proportion to the square root of the Roller Sail area (Figure 10-13).

Certain aspects of the Roller Sail design are claimed in a 1995 U. S. Patent. Another, related patent application is pending before the U. S. Patent and Trade Office.

The Roller Sail resembles the Cape Vincent sail in three respects. The jib and mainsail of each comprise a circle segment and an isosceles triangle, respectively. The chords of the segments serve as the bases of the triangles. The two designs differ in the proportion of the total area allocated to the two sail components. The Cape Vincent mainsail occupies 82% of the total area, while the Roller Sail mainsail takes up only 56%.

The Roller Sail design makes this sail the best balanced of all those traditional skate sails that are hand-held and that bear jibs.

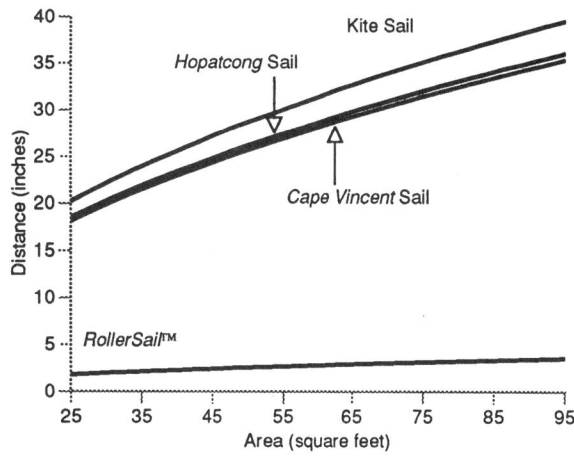

Figure 10-13: Distance along Boom between Center of Effort and Mast-Boom Crossing versus the Areas of Selected Skate Sails

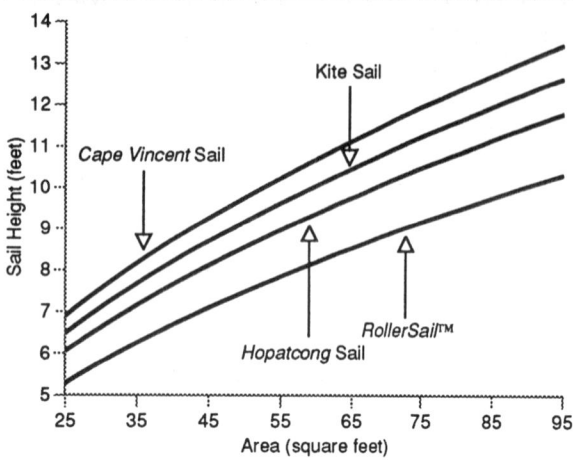

Figure 10-14: Heights of Selected Sails Increasing with Sail Areas

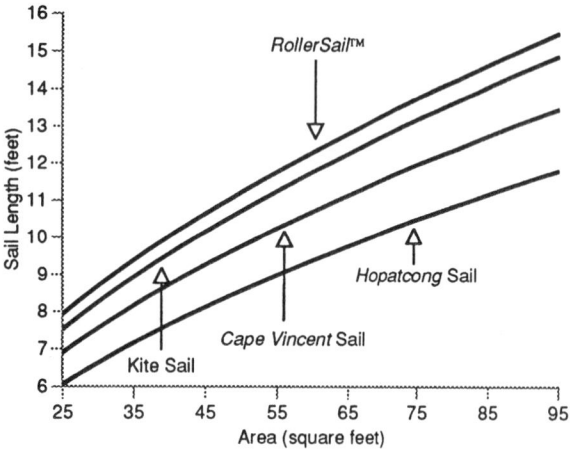

Figure 10-15: Lengths of Selected Sails Increasing with Sail Areas

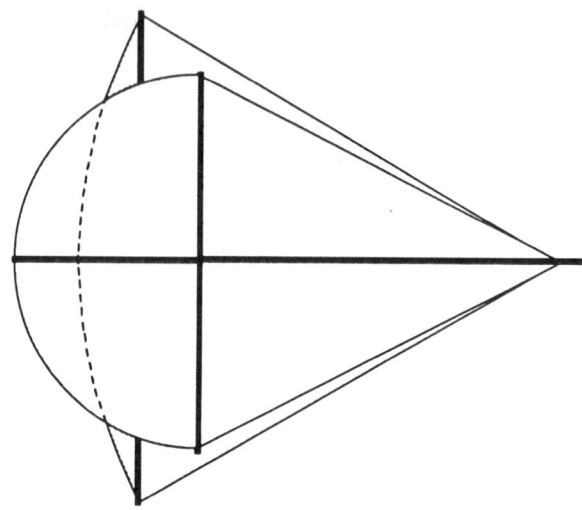

Figure 10-16: Comparison of the Heights and Lengths of Selected, 61-Square-Foot Sails: Top, RollerSail; Bottom, Cape Vincent Sail

(This comparison excludes the Windskate model because it lacks a jib, although it is hand-held). Because of its center of effort position, the Roller Sail is a relatively short sail (Figure 10-14). Although its height would increase with the square root of the sail area, it would rise only little more than ten feet in a 95-square-foot version, an area adopted for comparison to Swedish Dragon sails. Standard Roller Sails with varying areas would accommodate sailors with a broad range of body heights. Roller Sail sails are relatively long. For any given area, the Roller Sail is longer than other comparable sails (Figure 10-15). In all cases considered, the sail lengths are proportional to the square roots of the sail areas, as their heights are.

Production models occupy any of three areas: 21.5, 43. 1, and 61.4 square feet. The smaller sails are useful to adults in strong winds or to children in weaker winds. The largest Roller Sail ever made — never a production model but an experiment instead — occupied 81 square feet. It rose 9.5 feet and ran 14 feet.

Performance

A beginning sailor who is already a competent in-line skater will easily learn to use a Roller Sail, often in a single lesson. Practiced sailors can travel as fast as 50 mph on pavement, and 45-50 mph on ice, reports the manufacturer. With such a sail, a skater will find himself sailing faster than the wind: an estimate of the ratio of sailing speed to wind speed over pavement is $2^1/_2$. As in other kinds of sailing, the greatest speeds are attained in sailing upwind, not downwind, and a Roller Sail can travel as close to the wind as 15-20°. The sailor's windward position gives him certain advantages, one of them the ability to sail off curbs. To do so, both of his feet momentarily leave the pavement, even though his sail remains driven by the wind. With a Hopatcong sail thrust by the wind against its sailor on the leeward side, such a flight would ensure an all-points crash landing.

Materials

Thanks to modern spar and sailcloth materials, a Roller Sail weighs only about five pounds. It contains three spars: a jib bow located in a cloth pocket at the leading edge, a vertical mast, and a horizontal boom. These spars, depending on the sail model, are made of fiberglass or carbon fiber. The sailcloth used also depends on the model offered, and may be 3.9-ounce, brightly colored Dacron or a Kevlar-reinforced synthetic, laminated fabric. Reinforced Mylar makes up the transparent jibs in those sails having such jibs; other sails contain two or three windows.

Construction

The leading edge of the Roller Sail contains a solid jib bow lying in a long pocket. The jib bow bends to adopt the curved shape of the pocket when the skater rigs the sail. The bow flattens the sail, as does the jib bow of Hopatcong sails, for example. Although the jib bow length of a 61-square foot Roller Sail equals 13 feet, the bow comes in shorter sections for ease of transport and assembly. Each jib bow includes four flexible rods linked in pairs.

The Roller Sail features hole-and-pin devices novel to skate sails. They fix the jib bow to the mast and to the boom, and they also secure the mast to the boom. The jib bow passes through each end of the mast, and through the boom as well. Holes drilled in the boom admit the rods that form the jib bow. To connect the mast to the boom, aligned holes in these spars accept a short pin passing through both spars. Holding the pin in place, links like key chain rings pass through either end of the pin.

The number of sail panels in all the Roller Sail models exceeds that in most shoulder-borne sails, except in certain Dragon sails. For example, one Roller Sail model contains 11 panels, one of them common to the jib and mainsail. Centrally located, this panel is the longest of all. The jib sports seven panels while the mainsail bears five. With the exception of the central panel, all those in the jib resemble circle segments or pie wedges. The many panels in the sails offer numerous combinations of colors.

A stretching harness tightens the sail, which, despite flattening, adopts a three-dimensional airfoil shape when presented to the wind. The harness includes three straps and buckles. It lies at the aft end of the sail, as it does in many other designs.

Rigging

A Roller Sail must be assembled before it is stretched. To avoid damage by pavement or gravel, its components are laid out on a soft surface like grass. Assembly takes about 5 minutes for a sailor proficient in the task. He begins by joining the jib bow sections to one another and continues by inserting their (four) ends in the mast and boom. This job flexes the jib bow, and is aided by use of the sailor's knee as a stop. With the jib bow in place, the pin links the mast to the boom, and the harness stretches the sail.

Taking a Stance

To begin sailing, the skater ordinarily stands to windward of a Roller Sail, holding the boom horizontal. This sail can also be used from the leeward side like a Hopatcong sail, although the craft itself then obscures the skater's forward view. In sailing from the leeward side, the sailor's body interrupts laminar air flow, which may reduce the aerodynamic sail efficiency.

In any case, a skater with a Roller Sail to leeward enjoys a distinct advantage if he encounters trouble. Releasing the sail lets him escape difficulty, and creates no new hazard. The wind will fling a freed Roller Sail downwind, away from the sailor. By contrast, a Hopatcong sail released from its leeward side travels toward its sailor, and the fast-moving mast or boom can strike its erstwhile master.

A skate sailor's posture should allow the large muscles of his legs to absorb the shocks offered by rough sailing surfaces. So to use a Roller Sail he must keep his legs bent at the knees, with his feet spread about 18 inches from one another and both pointing in the direction of travel. His hips and head also face in the same direction, although his trunk twists toward the sail. This twist allows what would have been the sailor's leeward hand to grasp the boom.

Sailing Straight

For cruising, the sailor takes a two-handed grip on the horizontal boom, keeping each hand palm down. With the sail on his left side, his right hand seizes the boom forward of the mast. His left hand grips the boom aft of the mast. The positions of both hands reverse when the sail lies to the sailor's right. In either case, both his hands fall within a few inches of the sail center of effort, which rests upon the boom line just aft of the mast. For higher winds, the forward hand shifts toward the leading edge, reaching a point midway between the edge and mast-boom crossing. The aft hand then slides ahead to grip the boom forward of the mast. When the skater sails a straight course, he can hold the craft with one hand only.

Steering

To steer the sail, a skater uses his feet more than anything else. But fine adjustments to course angle can be made with the sail. Shift it forward to turn downwind and backward to move upwind. Whether you turn left or right depends on the sail location, on your left or right. If the sail lies to your right, for example, a forward shift of the craft will turn you to your right. Some windward-side in-line sailors claim that side-slipping with four-wheeled skates is never problematic. Others, however, argue that five-wheeled skates are superior because they prevent drifting downwind.

Turning through 180°

When a sailor ends his run to return to a starting point, he must jibe or come about to reverse direction. With a Roller Sail, turning downwind is no more difficult than turning upwind, which is an advantage that these sails have over Hopatcong or Dragon sails. The last two sails come about more easily than they jibe. With any of these three sails, a 180° turn takes place in three stages, raising the sail, placing it in stays overhead, and lowering it to the sailor's other side. Here is how to turn 180° from the windward side of a Roller Sail.

The sailor's forward hand raises the sail by the boom, as the aft hand releases its grip. The sailor transfers his aft hand to the mast, seizing it about one foot below the mast-boom intersection. He continues raising the sail until it lies overhead, when it spills the wind. At this instant the sailor's motion persists only because of conservation of momentum. The sailor completes the turn using his skates alone, and begins to lower the sail to his other side. The aft hand releases the mast and once again grips the boom in preparation for the coming descent. It reaches ahead, becoming the forward hand, and seizes the boom near the intersection with the mast. The forward hand now grips the boom palm down, while the aft hand momentarily retains a palm-up grip. To complete the turn, the sailor twists his trunk away from the sail to face in the new sailing direction.

Braking

Any skater proficient with a Roller Sail can brake it in either of two ways. As with other kinds of skate sails, the skater may place the Roller Sail in stays and brake with his skates alone. This technique makes fast, short stops possible. But there is another braking technique available to Roller Sails

Figure 10-17: Turf Skis for Sailing a Parawing over Grass (left), Snow Skis for Sailing over Snow (right)

and icewings, but not to skate sails maneuvered from leeward.

The sailor can use his own moving Roller Sail to brake himself. This maneuver, which calls for a 180° turn, ends when the sailor presents what is normally the leeward sail side to the wind. He never places the sail in stays to make the turn, which begins with his feet and face pointing in the direction of travel and at a right angle to the wind. It ends with the sailor's feet and face pointing toward the sail and into the wind. The sailor then stands to leeward of the sail, which the wind tends to thrust toward him. He resists the windforce, using his skates to oppose sail motion.

Sailing on Other Surfaces

The owners of versatile Roller Sails or Windskate sails owe no loyalty to pavement or roller skates. These sails will propel them over ice or grass, surfaces that demand ice or all-terrain skates. Over a hard snow surface, even Sled Dogs® will serve as footgear for a skater with a Roller Sail. Sled Dogs are snow skates, not animals at all.

They resemble Alpine ski boots but their soles are molded plastic skis. The ski-sole length equals the boot length, and the soles bear sharp metal edges that prevent side-slipping and allow parallel stops.

PARAWING SAILING

To appreciate parawing sailing, which is a comparatively new sport, imagine you are flying a kite over a frozen lake and wearing ice skates. With a large enough kite and a strong enough wind, you'll soon find yourself moving, drawn by the tethering cord. Completing a circuit will be possible on snow or ice, as you tack downwind and then upwind sometimes at thrilling speeds. Therefore, you won't be dependent on a chase vehicle to collect you downwind of your starting point after a voyage slower than the wind. What makes all this feasible are the ordinary principles of sailing and the extraordinary shape of your kite (Figure 10-17). Made of fabric and inflated by the air, a parawing resembles the section of an airplane wing that lies between the fuselage and the tip.

Origin and Status

Parawing sailing originated during the mid-1980s in West Germany. The developer of the sport was Wolf Beringer, and he made parawing sailing popular in Europe, where convocations of kite flyers now include meetings of parawing sailors.

Parawings can do useful work. During a recent expedition to Antarctica they transported two explorers and their laden sleds. Moreover, the parawings set an impressive pace. With the help of skis, the polar explorers Arved Fuchs and Reinhold Messner sailed 93 miles within two days!

Advantages

Perhaps the main advantage of parawing sailing to ordinary sailors is to extend the sailing season to the year around. Unlike softwater and ice sailing, parawing sailing is not seasonal, so it is not restricted to the warm or cold months. This extension is a consequence of the versatility of the sport, which allows sailing over many different kinds of surface.

Parawing sailing also brings its enthusiasts two other bonuses, the opportunities for kite-flying and out-of-plane sailing. In a wind too weak for a parawing to move a sailor, the craft can be pleasurably flown as a kite rather than as a conveyance. With a stronger wind, sailing over snow and sand mounds is possible, as is sailing up sloped pavement and down grassy hills — provided that the sailor matches his footwear to his surface. Sailing over the greatest variety of surfaces requires ice skates, homemade sand skates, skis, in-line roller skates, or the commercial but hard-to-find turf skis used for summertime training. With a surf board or water skis, parawing sailing in water is feasible, too!

Shape

A parawing is a three-dimensional fabric sail. In flight it resembles a rectangle with the cross-sectional shape of an airfoil. The underside of a flying parawing is flat, while the top surface curves like an airplane wing. When the parawing is aloft, the wind enters the leading, long edge of the rectangle. This inflates the sail so that it adopts its characteristic airfoil shape, which comes only from wind pressure and sail design. The design calls for a strip of cloth mesh or a row of small holes to admit air to the leading edge.

No rigid framework or battens shapes a parawing, which in this respect resembles a balloon or parachute more than it resembles a kite or skate sail. Filled balloons and parachutes depend largely on inflation for their three-dimensional shapes. Kites and skate sails rely to a greater extent on solid frames and spars for their shapes.

If a flying parawing is mishandled or the wind dies, its airfoil shape is utterly lost. Then the soft nylon fabric will no longer sustain even its own flight, but will plummet abruptly to the ground as a kite will do. The parawing, like a sailing vessel, usually restricts its skipper to traveling only over the surface, although it travels in any direction through the air like a fixed-wing plane.

Size

A parawing will convey its skipper over many kinds of surface, including ice, snow, pavement, hard-packed sand, grass, and water. This astonishing freedom is due partly to different sail sizes used over different surfaces. The most resistant surfaces require the greatest parawing size. For example, sailing on grass calls for a parawing of about 105 square feet, if the sailor weighs as much as 200 pounds (Figure 10-17). The rectangular surface of such a sail would thus have dimensions of 7 by 15 feet. For sailing on ice, which offers the least resistance, the same sailor would need a parawing of about 35 square feet.

Rigging

The underside of a parawing bears narrow cords over the entire surface, and some parawings carry more than 200 such lines. Bound into groups, the lines travel about 15 feet to a control bar, and wrap around it. (For more information about this bar, read on.) One group of descending lines controls the leading edge of the parawing, another group leads to its center, and the third group affects the trailing edge. Because the cords are numerous and evenly distributed, no one of them experiences any great pull from the sailor. As a result, none of them distorts the flat undersurface of the parawing, which retains its airfoil shape.

Some parawings also bear cloth strips perpendicular to their undersides. The strips descend about seven inches from the lower surfaces, and run along the narrower dimension of the parawing rectangle between the leading and tailing edges. These strips divide the bottom side into as many as seven air-filled cells, which help the flying parawing keep its shape.

The parawing sailor holds a control bar, a tube about two feet long and 1½ inches in diameter. Fastened to it and wrapped around it are the grouped lines leading to the parawing; and from it runs a line to a harness. The bar is held perpendicular to the long axis of the rectangle that is the two-dimensional parawing shape.

Sailing a large parawing requires a wind surfer's harness, which wraps around the sailor's waist and passes between his legs. The harness supports part of the sailor's body weight when the parawing flies high. It permits the sailor's weight to counter the downwind thrust of the parawing. Also, the harness frees his arms and hands completely to control the wing, rather than partly to oppose the thrust.

Sources of Parawings

Ready-to-sail parawings are now commercially available in the United States. Entirely handmade, they can be sewn to order in a variety of sizes. A start-up New Hampshire firm, the North American Parawing Company, offers a custom-made, 105-square-foot parawing for about $850 (Table 10-1). Kits for making a parawing and a video tape showing how and where to sail the craft are available from the European developer of the sport, Wolf Beringer (Table 10-1).

Launching

To launch a parawing, the sailor begins by spreading it on the sailing surface. The side of the wing bearing the suspension lines should touch the surface, and the leading edge should lie upwind of the trailing one. Now the sailor seizes the control bar and moves upwind from the sail, paying out the suspension lines as he goes. He faces the parawing and holds the bar vertically so that those lines between it and the leading edge are uppermost. When the bar takes this position, the sailor hauls its upper half toward him, raising the leading edge and the wind inflates the parawing. As the parawing fills and rises, he continues to pull.

With the parawing aloft, the sailor is standing upwind of the sail and facing it; and in a good breeze, he will soon be drawn toward it. The leading, long edge of the sail faces the oncoming wind and the sailor, but initially turns away from the travel destination. Accelerating calls for turning into the wind.

Accelerating, Steering, and Slowing

The control bar accelerates, steers, and slows a parawing in flight. Paying out the lines favors thrust over lift, and speeds the craft forward. Rotating the bar in a plane perpendicular to the ground raises (or lowers) one short edge of the parawing more than the other, and turns the craft in the direction of the rotation. Taking in the lines creates more lift, reducing the sailor's forward motion but partly supporting his weight. Resistant surfaces like grass or sand impede upwind sailing, which is possible only on the slippery ones of ice and snow. (Why the craft will sail upwind on some surfaces, however, is an aerodynamic topic beyond the scope of this book.)

Escaping Trouble

A parawing sailor in trouble can readily extricate himself by two means. He can rotate the control bar enough to collapse the sail. Doing this immediately removes his source of propulsion, and leaves him holding the lines leading to the now-deflated parawing as he moves toward it. Alternatively, the sailor can free himself entirely by disengaging the quick-release catch, which links the harness to the control bar, and dropping to the ice. Disengaging the catch requires only one hand and can be carried out instantly.

BIBLIOGRAPHY OF ICE SKATE SAILING

Books and Brochures

Andresen, J., *Sailing on Ice*, A. S. Barnes and Company, Inc., New York, 1974.

Benson, E. F., "Blow, Blow, Thou Winter Wind," plate XLVII in *Winter Sports in Switzerland*, Dodd, Mead & Co., New York, (undated).

Berringer, W. *Faszination-Parawing*, Vth Verlag, Baden Baden, 1996.

Buck, H. A., "Ice Sailing" in *Skating*, 1st ed., Longmans, Green, and Co., London, 1892.

Burgass, E., "Spiele und sonstige Leibesübungen auf Schlittschuhen und auf dem Eise" in *Winterliche Leibesübungen in freier Luft*, Band 6 in Kleine Schritten, Drud und Verlag B. Teubner, Leipzig und Berlin, 1910.

Catton, B., *Waiting for the Morning Train: An American Boyhood*, Doubleday & Company, Inc., Garden City, 1972.

Claussen, W. Van B., *Practical Suggestions for Making and Using Skate Sails*, (distributed by the Skate-Sailing Association of America), 1926.

Dědič, J., *Světovépiruety,* Olympia, Prague, 1991.

Dier, J. C., ed., *A Book of Winter Sports*, The Macmillan Company, New York, 1912.

Fellbom, Å., "Skridskosegling" in *Långfärdsskridsko.* Sesam (en Aldus Handbok), Stockholm, 1970.

Friary, R., "Ice Skate Sailing" in the *Encyclopedia of World Sport*, ed. D. Levinson, ABC-CLIO, Denver, 1996.

Friary, R., "Icewing, Roller Skate and Ski Sailing" in the *Encyclopedia of World Sport*, ed. D. Levinson, ABC-CLIO, Denver, 1996.

Gardiner, F. H., *Wings on the Ice*, Yachting Publishing Corp., New York, 1938.

Gyger, W. J., *Winter-Sport in der Schweiz: Praktisches Handbuch*, Engadin Press Co., Samaden und St. Moritz, 1925.

Hammer, W., "Eissegelsport" in *Eissport und Eisspiele*, Verlag von Friedrich Burchard, Elberfeld-Sonnborn und Leipzig, 1911.

Heathcote, J. M., "Skating as Recreation," Chapter IV in *Skating*, 2nd ed., Longmans, Green, and Co., London, 1894.

Jefferson, R. C., *Skate Sailing*, Harrison & Smith, North Minneapolis, 1957.

Jessup, E. H., *Snow and Ice Sports: A Winter Manual*, E. P. Dutton & Co., New York, 1923.

Lieberath, E., *När isen brister*, Sveriges Scoutförbunds Bibliotek No. 21, Sveriges Scoutförbunds Förlagaktiebolag, Stockholm, 1942.

Marchaj, C. A., *Aero-Hydrodynamics of Sailing*, International Marine Publishing, Camden, 1988.

Mulier, W., "Ijszeiltjes" in *Wintersport*, De Erven Loosjes, Haarlem, 1893.

Rogers A. and Beard, D. C., *Skating, Ice Yachting, and Skate-Sailing*, Macmillan, New York, 1902.

Sahlin, A., *Skridskosegling: Teknik och Prylar*, (distributed by the Skate-Sailing Section of the Swedish Ice Sailing Association (Svenska Isseglarförbundet, Mellansundet, 725 92 Västerås, Sweden), 2nd ed., 1989.

Scheibert, J. W. und Fr., "Schlittschuhsegeln" in *Der Wintersport*, 2nd Auflage, Grethlein & Co., Leipzig, 1910.

Scholander, E., "Skridskosegling" in J. E. Cederblom and V. Balck's *Jdrottsboken*, Stockholm, 1888.

Thomas, W. W. Jr., *Sweden and the Swedes*, Rand, Mc Nally & Co., Chicago and New York, 1893.

Patents

Alexander, L. W., "Wind Powered Propulsion Device," U. S. No. 4,634,136 (Jan. 6, 1987).

Ansteensen, Eric, U. S. No. 5,448,961 (Sept. 12, 1995).

Babson, R. M., "Hand-Held Skate Sail," U. S. No. 4,978,140 (Dec. 18, 1990).

Bowman, R. R., and Dak, M. S., "Sail for Skater," U. S. No. 2,793,870 (May 28, 1957).

Brown, R. L., "Hand-Held Sail," U. S. No. 4,269,133 (May 26, 1981).

Eastman, J. J., "Sail Construction," U. S. No. 4,473,022 (Sept. 25, 1984).

Freeman, J. L., "Sail Apparatus for a Land Vehicle," U. S. No. 4,204,694 (May 27, 1980).

Fries, J. E., "Skating Sails," U. S. No. 4,311,324 (Jan. 19, 1982).

Goldberg, D. E., "Skate Sail," U. S. No. 3,768,823 (Oct. 30, 1973).

Hardt, C., "Individual Sail Device," U. S. No. 2,018,062 (Oct. 22, 1935).

Harpole, G. B., "Sail Assembly," U. S. No. 4,186,680 (Feb. 5, 1980).

Holmgren, K., "Tool for Sailing with Skates," U. S. No. 4,489,957 (Dec. 25, 1984).

Huff, P. P., "Variable and Normally Open Vented Parachute Device and Method of Using and Controlling a Parachute Device," U. S. No. 4,722,497 (Feb. 2, 1988).

Kern, F. R. and Spivack, M., "Hand-Held Sail," U. S. No. 3,924,870 (Dec. 9, 1975).

Knight, E. A., "Physical Training Accessory," U. S. No. 4,854,572 (Aug. 8, 1989).

Le Bail, R. C., "Sail Having Variable Propelling and Lifting Effects," U. S. No. 4,563,969 (Jan 14, 1986).

Longoria, L. V. and Longoria, L. P., "Parachute and Skate Apparatus," U. S. No. 5,120,081, (June 9, 1992).

Lupton Jr. , B. M., U. S. No. 1,178,165.

Lux, G., "Ski Sail Apparatus," U. S. No. 4,234,211 (Nov. 18, 1980).

Nelson, C. H., "Skating Sail," U. S. No. 302,517 (July 22, 1884).

Nimchuck, A., "Portable Sail Structures," U. S. No. 4,136,631 (Jan 30, 1979).

Pearson, M., "Sport Vehicle," U. S. No. 3,421,773 (Jan 14, 1969).

Seidel, J. C., "Wind Propulsion Apparatus," U. S. No. 4,533,159 (Aug. 6, 1985).

Sprinkle, S. A., "Folding Skate Sail," U. S. No. 1,859,178 (May 17, 1932).

Strasilla, D., "Apparatus for the Propulsion of a Person by the Force of Wind," U. S. No. 4,127,247 (Nov. 28, 1978).

Verdon, S. M., "Skate Sail," U. S. No. D266446 (Oct. 5, 1982).

Periodicals

Anon.,"Skatesailing Wing Startles Iceboaters,"*Yachting*, April, 1979, pages 192-193.

Anon., "A Good Skate: Backs to the Wind," *TWA Ambassador* **14**, 37 (January, 1981).

Anon., "Best Sailor is Husky New York Banker," *Life Magazine*, 45 (March 11, 1940).

Anon., "Lake Aquitaine for Sail," *The Mississauga Times and Star* (Wednesday, Feb. 6, 1980).

Anon., "Sailing on Skates," *National Geographic World*, No. 100, page 16 (Dec., 1983).

Anon., "Sailing on Skates," *The Illustrated London News*, 107 (Jan. 31, 1880).

Anon., "Skate Sailing," *Scientific American* **80**, 85 (Feb., 1899).

Anon., "Skate Sailing: It Looks So Graceful," *Minneapolis Sunday Tribune* (Jan. 12, 1958).

Anon., "Yachting on Skates," *The Philadelphia Inquirer Magazine*, page 12 (March 7, 1954).

Anon., "Yachting Without the Aid of a Yacht," *The New York Times*, section IV, page 1 (Sunday, Feb. 14, 1915).

Beard, D., "Skate Sailing," *Outing* **43**, 613 (Feb., 1904).

Beard, D., "How to Make and Manage All Kinds of Skate Sails," *Outing* **49**, 547 (Jan. , 1907).

Brown, S., "Skate-Sailing is Thrilling Sport," *Popular Mechanics* **49**, 137 (Jan., 1928).

Bruce, E., letter to J. Morwood in *Foils, Ice Yachts and Sails*, Publication No. 66A, Amateur Yacht Research Society (Pengelly House, Wilcove, Torpoint, Cornwall, PL11 2PG, The United Kingdom), 1968.

Burton, W. E., "Wings," *Popular Science* **136**, 172 (Jan., 1940).

Catton, B. E., "The Joy Above the Stars, the Terror Below the Ice," *Family Weekly*, 4 (Dec. 30, 1973).

Claudy, C. H., "Skate-Sailing for Life," *St. Nicholas* **XXXVII**, 298 (Feb., 1910).

Claudy, C. H., "The Girl and the Skate Sail," *Woman's Home Companion* **39**, 29 (Jan., 1912).

Claussen, W. Van B., "Sailing Soldiers," *The New York National Guardsman* **XI**, 10 (Jan., 1935).

Cole, A. E., "One Sheet to the Wind," *New York Magazine* **13**, 37 (January 14, 1980).

Darling, A. M., "Sails on Ice," *American Way*, 75 (Dec., 1983).

De Chillo, S., "Skate Sailing: One Sheet to the Wind," *The New York Times*, page 11 (Sunday, Feb. 24, 1980).

Fishman, J. A., "Skate Sailing Makes the Frozen Lakes a Speedway," *The New York Times* (Feb. 19, 1979).

Friary, R., "Lying on the Wind: Ice Skate Sailing," Part One, *Speedskating Times* **1** (5), 6 (April, 1990).

Friary, R., "Lying on the Wind: Ice Skate Sailing," Part Two, *Speedskating Times* **1** (6), 6 (May, 1990).

Friary, R., "More on Skate Sailing," *Silent Sports* **6**, 4 (Jan., 1990).

Goodwin, A. H., "The Joyous Sport of Skate-Sailing," *Country Life in America* **7**, 137 (Dec.,1904).

Gordon, W., and Raska, R., "Skate Sailors Brave Elements," *Sunday Star-Ledger* (Newark, N. J.), section 2, page 1 (Jan. 21, 1990).

Gunther, M., "The Lure of Black Ice," *Travel & Leisure* **4** (1) (Jan., 1974).

Haan, E. R., "Ride the Wind with a Skate Sail," *Popular Mechanics* **100**, 165 (Dec., 1953).

Hamilton, J. F., letter to a Mr. Lamble in *Foils, Ice Yachts and Sails*, Publication No. 66A, Amateur Yacht Research Society (Pengelly House, Wilcove, Torpoint, Cornwall, PL11 2PG, The United Kingdom), 1968.

Hanmer, T. F., "The Danish Skate Sail," *Century Magazine* **XXIII**, 726 (Feb., 1882).

Kaplan, L. F., "A Colder Cousin of Wind Surfing," *Sunday Magazine* (Westchester, N.Y.), page 68 (Feb., 1979).

Kelly, J. G., "The Blade Runners," *Outside*, **17** (Jan.-Feb., 1988).

Levy, N., "Ice Skate Sailing," *Silent Sports* **6**, 14 (Dec., 1989).

Lieghley, E. O., "Go Like the Wind," *Popular Mechanics* **69**, 114 (Jan., 1938).

Mathus, F. K., "Eisseglenein — wenig bekanntes Vergnügen," *Neues Zürcher Zeitung* (Feb. 10, 1962), see also *L'Illustration*, 23 February 1901, No. 3026, p. 119.

Morwood, J., letter to E. Bruce in *Foils, Ice Yachts and Sails*, Publication No. 66A, Amateur Yacht Research Society (Pengelly House, Wilcove, Torpoint, Cornwall, PL11 2PG, The United Kingdom), 1968.

Newkirk, A. E., "John S. Apperson and His Associates," *Adirondac* **XLVI** (mid Dec., 1982).

Nordin, K., "Skate Sailing Inexpensive Fun," *The Christian Science Monitor* (March 17, 1967).

Ollie, W. F., "Skate-Sailing Made Easy," *Outing* **45**, 424 (Jan., 1905).

Otterbein, M. E., "Caution: Low Flying Skaters," *Columbian Squires* **37**, 5 (Feb., 1965).

Plumley, L., "To Make a Skate-Sail," *St. Nicholas* **47**, 267 (Jan., 1920).

Rosenthal, H., "Skate-Sailing," *Amateur Sports*, 111 (July, 1932).

Tussing, L., "Go Skate Sailing," *Hi Way* **3**, 7 (Dec., 1961).

Vallé, A., "The Sport of Skate Sailing," *Country Life* **27**, 71 (Dec., 1914).

White, W. M., "The Lost Art of Skate-Sailing," *Adirondac* **XLVI**, 14 (mid Dec., 1982).

Zullo, A., "Sailing on Ice," *Sky*, page 116 (Nov., 1983).